California's topography is characterized by great variety. Its coastline varies from the low, sandy beaches of Southern California to the rocky headlands of Cape Mendocino and other northward protrusions. The Coast Ranges, one of the state's two great mountain systems, runs generally parallel to the coast.

Within the spurs of the Coast Ranges lie many of the state's most fertile agricultural valleys. Eastward is the Central Valley, California's richest agricultural region, which has a width of up to fifty miles. The Central Valley is walled in to the east by the Sierra Nevada rampart, which at Mount Whitney, the highest mountain in the continental United States outside Alaska, reaches an altitude of 14,496 feet.

From the summit of Mount Whitney one can see the weird sink known as Death Valley, 282 feet below sea level, the lowest spot in the United States. Stretching southward are the nation's two largest deserts, the Mojave and the Colorado. By contrast, the topography of northern California contains such large bodies of water as Lake Tahoe and Clear Lake.

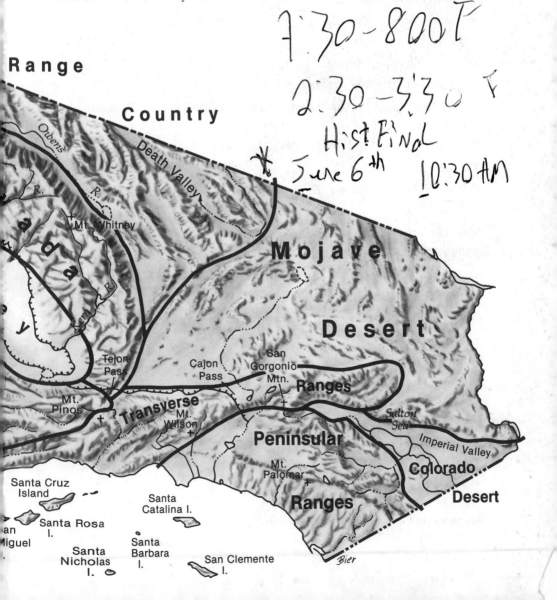

Also by Andrew Rolle

Riviera Path, 1946

An American in California: The Biography of William Heath Davis, 1956

The Road to Virginia City: The Diary of James Knox Polk Miller, 1960

Lincoln: A Contemporary Portrait (with Allan Nevins, Irving Stone, and others), 1961

Occidental: The First Seventy-Five Years, 1962

California: A Student's Guide to Localized History, 1965

Editor of *Helen Hunt Jackson, A Century of Dishonor: The Early Crusade for Indian Reform,* 1965

The Golden State: A History of California, 3rd Ed. (with John Gaines), 1965, 1979, 1990

The Lost Cause: Confederate Exiles in Mexico, 1965, 1990

Los Angeles, A Student's Guide to Localized History, 1965

The Immigrant Upraised: Italian Adventurers and Colonists in an Expanding America, 1968

Editor of *Alfred Robinson, Life in California,* 1971

The American Italians, 1973

Essays and Assays: California History Reconsidered (with George Knoles and others), 1973

Studies in Italian American Social History (with Francesco Cordasco and others), 1975

Los Angeles: The Biography of a City (with John Caughey and others), 1976

Crisis in America (with Allan Weinstein and others), 1977

Perspectives in Italian Immigration and Ethnicity (with Silvano Tomasi and others), 1977

The Italian Americans: Troubled Roots, 1981

Los Angeles: From Pueblo to City of the Future, 2nd Ed., 1981, 1995

Occidental College: A Centennial History, 1987

Henry Mayo Newhall and His Times, 1991

John Charles Frémont: Character as Destiny, 1992

California

A HISTORY

Revised and Expanded Fifth Edition

Andrew Rolle

Cleland Professor
of History Emeritus
Occidental College
Research Scholar
Huntington Library

Harlan Davidson, Inc.
Wheeling, Illinois 60090-6000

Library of Congress Cataloging-in-Publication Data

Rolle, Andrew, F.
        California: a history / Andrew F. Rolle. — 5th ed., rev., and expanded.
                p.   cm.
        Includes bibliographical references (p.   ) and index.
        ISBN 0-88295-943-3 (cloth)   ISBN 0-88295-938-7 (paper)
        1. California—History.   I. Title.
F861.R78   1998
979.4—dc21   97-21438
                                                        CIP

Cover photograph, "Blooming Coreopsis, Los Angeles, CA," by Frank Balthis. Courtesy of Ocean Stock.
Cover design by DePinto Graphic Design

Manufactured in the United States of America
01 00 99 98 2 3 4 5 MG

Contents

Maps, Tables, and Photographs

Maps and Tables

Photographs

Preface

This is the fifth edition of *California: A History*. From its inception, this book was designed for the general reader and students alike. Since its original publication the work has been enjoyed by many thousands of readers. As in prior editions, my aim in the pages that follow is to recount the state's history from its origins to the present in a format that is engaging as well as informative.

A history of California must first do justice to its initial inhabitants and then to the long years of Spanish colonialism and the Mexican era; both shaped past and present. It must also consider those dramatic changes that began after the province's American conquest. Such a volume needs to focus upon the implications of the recent population explosion, as well as give attention to the state's economy and the mesh of modern cultures. In the ten years since the last edition of this book appeared, enormous social and material changes have overcome California. Therefore, I have expanded those sections of the book devoted to women, the environment, ethnic unrest, crime, sports, and new developments in transportation.

Careful deletion of certain details has produced a more direct narrative, one better suited to today's readers. The bibliographies that follow each chapter also have been brought up to date. An avalanche of writing about California continues to appear. Thus, some older articles and books need to be supplanted by more recent scholarship helpful to those readers who wish to delve deeper into the state's history. Finally, an "Index of Authors Cited" links authors to references old and new.

My publisher, Andrew Davidson, suggested this revision. Professor Judson Genier provided excellent suggestions, based upon having used the book in his university classes. Others who have been helpful include Professors Jackson Putnam, Gordon Bakken, Martin Schiesl, and Jacqueline Braitman. Frances Squires Rolle has prepared the index to all editions.

A. R.

California's Distinctiveness

///////// CHAPTER 1

The name California brings to mind extremes and paradoxes in both geography and climate. The state's mountains are the highest in the continental United States outside Alaska, its redwoods are the oldest and tallest, its scenic shoreline vast; but its deserts are among the most forbidding in the western hemisphere, its rains, floods, and fires are often the most catastrophic in the nation, its droughts among the most severe, its earthquakes among the most damaging.

California offers virtually every climatic, geologic, and vegetational combination: the wettest weather and the driest; poor sandy soil in the desert regions and rich loam in the Central Valley; some of the hottest recorded temperatures on earth and also among the coldest; the highest peak in the United States outside Alaska (Mount Whitney, 14,496 feet) and the lowest point in the country (Bad Water in Death Valley, 282 feet below sea level). In the summertime it is possible to experience a sweltering temperature of well over 100 degrees in the Central Valley and in half an hour travel to San Francisco Bay, fogbound at less than 50 degrees. In midwinter, the few remaining orange groves of southern California lie in valleys framed by snowy peaks.

California's literature expresses a distinctive regionality which underlies the "local color" of Bret Harte, the wit of Mark Twain's tall tales, the humanity of John Steinbeck, as well as the celebration of nature in the poetry of Robinson Jeffers. In architecture, the fusion of the New England and Spanish heritages has produced the Monterey-style house, with its balconies, adobe walls, red-tiled roof, and white woodwork. Variety is at the heart of California's past and present.

Desert flora. Courtesy of Andrew Rolle.

Perhaps no other American state would, standing alone, be so truly a nation in itself. Among the states, California is third in size, but first in population. The counties that make up southern California are nearly as large as all six New England states combined, and larger than Illinois, Iowa, or Alabama.

The province's natural wealth once lay unexploited. The melting snows of the Sierra rushed down unharnessed rivers into the sea. Underground reservoirs of petroleum lay untapped. Gold, shining in the bottom of mountain streams, awaited the picks and shovels of Yankee miners. Magnificent timber stands also remained untouched. In the American period, the missions and ranchos of the Spanish and Mexican eras gave way to the demands of commerce as vineyards and orange groves surrendered space to oil derricks, aircraft factories, steel mills, residential subdivisions, and Hollywood.

These developments occurred in a state whose shoreline spans the Pacific seaboard for 1,200 miles. The length of California is 824 miles while its maximum width is 252 miles. The chief surface features are two mountain chains that traverse almost the entire length of the state. The great Central Valley lies between the mountains of the Coast Ranges and the Sierra Nevada. The combined San Joaquin and Sacramento valleys, 400 miles long and 50 miles wide, are one of the great granaries of the world. Because farmers can raise crops during three growing seasons—instead of the usual one—California remains the nation's top agricultural state.

It is more accurate to speak of California's "climates" than to refer to one single climate. For scores of specialized, micro-climates exist. What is usually thought of as "California climate" prevails south of San Francisco to the Mexican border, and between the Coast Ranges and the Pacific Ocean. In this region the seasons drift by mildly, almost unperceived. The heat of the day is fanned by prevailing westerly winds. Climatic comfort is also maintained by low clouds known as *veloes*.

California's coastline is cooled by a meteorological process called "upwelling." Warm winds swirl inward from a northwesterly direction, bringing colder ocean waters to the surface. When the warm air contacts the cold water, condensation forms fog and low clouds which sit over the ocean, creeping inland at night and retreating seaward toward dawn. During the course of the day, the heat of the landmass helps to dissipate this fog.

Although more than half the state's people live in southern California, most of the raw materials and 90 percent of the fresh water are located in northern California. Annual rainfall in the northwest corner of the state, above Eureka, reaches 110 inches, making the area a virtual rain forest. Precipitation in the Central Valley is heavier at Sacramento and Stockton than at other cities farther south, including Fresno and Bakersfield. At San Francisco, the average annual rainfall is nearly 23 inches; at San Luis Obispo it falls to 19 inches, and to less than 15 inches at Los Angeles. At San Diego, near the Mexican border, rainfall generally amounts to only 10 inches per year. Precipitation, the heaviest from November to April, averages only 6 inches at Bakersfield and as little as 1 or 2 inches in desert areas.

The coastal ranges partly control California's weather; in the winter, North Pacific storms crash down on them. The rain clouds push through the canyon gaps in these mountains into the Central Valley. Most fast-moving storms, however, break up along the Sierra crest. Below the eastern Sierra the scorching temperature sometimes rises to 130 degrees in Death Valley, where there is hardly any vegetation. In the bleak volcanic area of northeastern California, agriculture and ranching are also limited by a rocky topography.

In northern California, the danger of annual floods is severe. Since the Gold Rush era, Sacramento, Stockton, Oroville, and Marysville have repeatedly been plagued by winter inundations. Paradoxically, one of the most serious flood threats also exists in semi-arid southern California. There, the burned-out chaparral provides poor cover for unstable winter watersheds.

The wide range of climate makes possible a corresponding variety in vegetable and floral products. Almost every plant, tree, or shrub that grows in temperate zones, and many indigenous to the tropics, can be grown somewhere in California. The state also is known for unique forms of vegetation, especially its giant sequoias, which have their roots deep in the ancient past. Along with the bristle-cone pines of the White Mountains, these monarchs of the forest are probably the oldest living things on earth. Some sequoias now standing were in their prime at the time of Christ. In fact, their age may be 5,000 or more years. Most "big trees" that have perished have been the victims of human ravages or of lightning or fierce storms. Sequoias are virtually immune to diseases that afflict other trees, and their tannic bark is practically resistant to fire.

The gnarled Monterey cypress, a picturesque denizen of the seacoast, is found along a rugged section of the Monterey shoreline. These trees, clinging precariously to promontories like Cypress Point, are totally exposed to Pacific storms. Heavy winds have twisted them into fantastic forms, and yet they survive. Similar in tenacity are the rugged Torrey pines of the coastline above San Diego.

California's skies were once darkened by flocks of geese, ducks, and other migrating birds who wintered there. Although wildlife has been seriously depleted, 400 species of mammals and 600 varieties of birds still make the state their home. From the horned toad and desert tortoise to the bobcat, weasel, and blacktailed deer, California's fauna is as diversified as its other natural features. In the wilderness, coyotes, mountain lions, and wolverines still roam. Big-horn mountain sheep and wapiti, commonly known as elk, once common, are now rare, and the California grizzly bear is extinct. The condor and the sea otter have, for the time being, barely escaped extinction.

Geologically, California is still young. The 400-mile-long Sierra scarp, caused by uplifting and faulting, and the Cascade and Klamath ranges

Floor of Yosemite Valley before silting of Mirror Lake occurred. Courtesy of Andrew Rolle.

in the north are all in youthful stages of development. The California coastline, pushed up out of the Pacific's depths at Points Pinos and Lobos, as well as at Cape Mendocino, is a rocky one, with headlands jutting out to sea. This coastline, unlike the eastern shore of the United States, is one of emergence, rather than submergence; in fact, the entire Pacific shoreline is sharply uplifted. This geologic pattern has given California few navigable rivers or harbors comparable to those of Boston, New York, Philadelphia, or Baltimore. With the exception of San Diego Bay in the south, San Francisco Bay in the middle, and Bodega and Humboldt bays, both lesser estuaries, on the northwestern shore-line of the state, natural harbors are few in number.

Stupendous changes, frequently abrupt, sometimes gradual, have shaped the face of California in past geologic ages. The two principal mountain chains, the Sierra Nevada and the Coast Ranges, were titanic upheavals from beneath the earth's crust. The fiery origin of the Cascade mountains to the northeast is revealed by their lava formations and extinct cinder cones. One supposedly dead volcano, Lassen Peak, came back to life in 1914, spouting out a mass of hot mud and ash that devastated everything in its path. At intervals, Lassen floats a pennant of smoke from its summit as if to warn that its inner fires still smolder. Seething geysers and hot sulphur springs—safety valves for subterranean heat and pressure—testify that underlying fires are far from extinguished at Calistoga and Geyserville in the Napa Valley.

Glaciers, changes of weather and temperature, volcanic and chemical action, running water, successive earthquakes—all have shaped the mountains of California. The Yosemite Valley is a mythic symbol of California's vanishing wilderness. Its U-shaped chasm is lined with glacially carved perpendicular walls, out of which cascade magnificent waterfalls.

Continuous earth tremors also have altered geography. The sheer precipice of the eastern Sierra, facing Owens Valley and Nevada, drops 10,000 feet below Mount Whitney. It provides a striking example of a vertical fault caused by earthquakes. Seashells, whale bones, and beach boulders are to be found on mountain tops far above the present level of the sea, for ages ago ocean waves washed the base of the Sierra Nevada range.

Prehistoric California went through numerous transitions of climate, including both arctic cold and tropical heat. A few small glaciers still exist in the Sierra range as mementos of its last ice age; while the tropical past is locked into the asphalt beds at Rancho La Brea, now a municipal park in Los Angeles. During the tertiary age, the quaking, sticky surface of this prehistoric swamp became a death trap for animals and birds long since extinct. The blackened skeletons of creatures caught in these tar pits furnish evidence of the kinds of animal and plant life that once existed in the region. Museum dioramas can only suggest an era of huge mammoths, camels, horses, saber-toothed tigers, and ground sloths that once roamed through primeval forests. Carbon-dating has established the age of some animal and mineral remains taken from La Brea as more than 28,000 years.

California's remoteness long kept it isolated. Visitors had to cross the Pacific Ocean, only to risk a dangerous landing on the craggy shore, or traverse an unexplored continent, sometimes unfordable rivers, waterless deserts, and rugged mountain peaks covered with snowfields. When the American explorer John Charles Frémont entered the remote province in 1844, his expedition narrowly escaped death in the icy Sierra range. Two years later the Donner Party lost half of its members in these same mountains. Conversely, Death Valley acquired its name from overlanders who perished in that unforgiving inferno. California's actual "discovery" by Europeans came by sea. That event occurred relatively late in human history, partly because, as mentioned, it was not that easy to reach its shores by boats. In 1542 Spain's mariners, after repeated voyages, finally sighted that distinctive and still unexplored "terrestrial paradise at the left hand of the Indies."

We begin California's story with the native peoples the Spaniards encountered.

Selected Readings

For descriptions of the geologic and natural wonders of California see Roderick Peattie, ed., *The Pacific Coast Ranges* (1946) and Peattie's *The Sierra Nevada* (1947); Allan Schoenherr, *A Natural History of California* (1992); Alfred Runte, *Yosemite, The Embattled Wilderness* (1989); John McPhee, *Assembling California* (1993); Jeffrey F. Mount, *California Rivers and Streams* (1995); David Hornbeck and Phillip Kane, *California Patterns: A Geographical and Historical Atlas* (1983); Warren A. Beck and Ynez D. Haase, *Historical Atlas of California* (1973); David W. Lantis, Rodney Steiner, and Arthur E. Karinen, *California: Land of Contrast* (1963) and Robert Tacopi, *Earthquake Country* (1964).

General histories include Hubert Howe Bancroft, *History of California* (7 vols., 1884–90); Theodore H. Hittell, *History of California* (4 vols., 1885–97); Zoeth S. Eldredge, ed., *History of California* (5 vols., 1915); Charles E. Chapman, *A History of California: The Spanish Period* (1921); Robert G. Cleland, *A History of California: The American Period* (1922), which preceded Cleland's *From Wilderness to Empire* (1944) and *California in Our Time* (1947).

More recent histories are by John Caughey (1940), Andrew Rolle (1963–97), Walton Bean (1968), as well as Warren Beck and David Williams (1972). Kevin Starr has produced the following useful interpretive volumes: *Americans and the California Dream* (1973), *Inventing the Dream* (1985), *Material Dreams* (1990), *Endangered Dreams* (1996), and his *The Dream Endures* (1997). Two guides are: James D. Hart, *A Companion to California* (1987) and Doyce Nunis and Gloria Lothrop, eds., *A Guide to the History of California* (1989).

The Native
Americans
//////// CHAPTER 2

Some observers have professed that California's original inhabitants did not compare favorably with other tribal groups in North America. Yet, from ancient times, the local natives had arrived at a harmonious adjustment to their environment. Though their culture may today seem simple, they developed complex religions, intricate basket designs, acorn-leaching operations, and skill in flint chipping. A few tribes, among them the Hupa and Yurok, possessed sophisticated tribal rituals.

It is difficult to generalize about so many different tribal groupings. But California's natives, isolated from other North American cultures by steep mountain barriers and bleak deserts, developed a way of life well-suited to their needs. Living close to the soil, most of California's natives developed an uncomplicated and peaceful culture. Long dependent upon acorns as a basic food source and without metal tools, these people were not inclined toward organized agriculture. Similarly, their accomplished basketry work may have accounted for their neglect of pottery, except in the Owens Valley and lower Colorado River areas. In this culture, one's livelihood revolved around food-gathering as well as hunting and fishing, rather than the deliberate sowing, planting, and harvesting of crops. Therefore, instead of describing the native Californians' way of life in terms of a culture-lag, it is more accurate to speak of the native culture as realistic. After all, theirs was a social system that remained intact for thousands of years.

As to the origins of California's natives, the ancient bones of "Laguna Man" are thought to be 17,000 years old. Flint chips from another site near Calico have been dated as 20,000 to 100,000 years in age. In recent years, evidence of a link with certain Asian societies has also been discovered. More than 10,000 words and grammatical forms used by California's natives resemble those still employed in remote parts of eastern Russia. This language linkage reminds us that the first humans to reach the Pacific coast of North America were probably Mongoloids who traveled westward via the Bering Straits to Alaska and southward. An ice-bridge may well have made this approach possible. California's Penutians, who lived in the area north of Monterey, appear to have arrived only 3,000 years ago. In addition to linguistic similarities, the earliest Californians' domestic practices and religious beliefs resembled those used in far-off Siberian tribal societies.

Most California natives were sturdy and long-lived. Chief Solano of the Suisunes, for whom Solano County is named, was six feet, seven inches in height. That these natives were hardly dull-witted is shown by the speed with which they learned the Spanish language from the missionaries, who also taught them to read music and even to sing religious chorals in Latin.

California's missions were erected by the natives under the direction of the Franciscan friars. In them they were taught carpentry, weaving, and the basics of Western-style agriculture. In a short time, the natives became excellent cattle herders, although they had not previously possessed domesticated animals, including horses, before the coming of the Spaniards.

Basket-making was largely in the hands of the women, who were also expert in dressing skins and in fashioning rushes into bedding mats. California's coastal Indians built dugout canoes with no better tools than wedges of elk horn and axes fashioned from mussel-shell blades. Household utensils included stone mortars with which to grind seeds and acorns. Horn knives and flat spoons or paddles were used to stir acorn gruel. They also used looped sticks for cooking meat in baskets with red-hot stones, as well as nets of vegetable fiber to catch fish and to carry small objects. They also made wooden trays and bowls.

The first sound to be heard on approaching a native village was often the pounding of pestles in mortars. Pulverized acorns were sometimes mixed with dried salmon and nuts, becoming basic provisions during winter. But, before acorns could be consumed, they had to be hulled and parched, with the tannic acid leached out. This was done in a basket-pot, or in a sand basin. Next, the natives boiled the sweetened ground acorn meal. The Shastas roasted moistened meal, while the Pomo and other groups mixed red earth with their meal and baked it; the resultant mixture was eaten immediately or stored for later use. These original Californians also ate, after boiling, the green leaves of certain plants. Roots too were roasted. The natives distilled no intoxicating beverages, but a mild state of inebriation was induced by prolonged smoking or chewing of wild tobacco and jimson weed, their equivalent of marijuana.

Dwellings were of the simplest construction, varying in accordance with the climate. In northwest and central California, they were sometimes built half below the ground, with sides and roofs of slabs hewn from trees. These dwellings kept the natives warm in cold weather. The Klamath River tribes sometimes constructed shelters with bark and redwood planks. Among the Chumash, houses consisted of poles drawn together in a semicircle and tied at the top with reeds. Thatched with grass, foliage, or wet earth, such dwellings were well-suited to the mild climate of the Santa Barbara coastline.

Weapons were few in number—usually small bows and arrows, and flint-tipped lances. When hunting large game, the natives made up for lack of advanced weapons by employing clever strategies. Skilled in stalking game, they contrived disguises with the heads and upper parts of skinned animals. They also set out decoys to attract birds within arrowshot. Game drives were likewise organized, with the animals herded past hunters lying in ambush. Less common was the practice of running down a deer by human relays, until the animal fell to the ground from exhaustion. Pits and traps were constructed to catch larger game. Wood rats, squirrels, coyotes, crows, rabbits, lizards, field mice, and snakes were all relished foodstuffs. Cactus apples and berries too formed part of the diet.

Some tribelets ate snails, caterpillars, minnows, crickets, grubs (found in decayed trees), slugs, fly larvae (gathered from the tops of bushes in swamps), horned toads, earthworms, grasshoppers, and skunks (the latter killed and dressed with all due caution). Seafood and shellfish formed an important part of the diet of coastal inhabitants. Others fished inland along northern rivers where great schools of salmon once spawned.

Nature, in addition to furnishing the natives with food, also provided basic clothing. When weather permitted, the men went naked except for moccasins, sandals, and (in the north) snowshoes fashioned from animal products. In the coldest weather the natives utilized rabbit or deerskin cloaks and skin blankets. Some women wore skirts made of tule grass or aprons of animal skin. In cold weather they employed a cape of deerskin or rabbit fur or covered their breasts with furs, including those of the otter and wildcat. Some painted their faces and bodies in intricate patterns; others braided their hair with decorative seashells.

For ceremonial occasions both sexes donned elaborate headdresses of feathers and beads. Northern natives wore basketry hats, while those of the central region bound their heads with hairnets.

Another source of pride was watercraft, which the males handled with dexterity and skill. Small boats included tule balsas, or reed rafts, made out of woven river rushes. These were poled or paddled along inland waters, as were plank canoes, the burned- or chopped-out trunk segments of large trees. While the men engaged in hunting and fishing, the women and older children hunted small animals, gathered acorns, scraped animal skins, fashioned robes, hauled water and firewood, wove baskets, barbecued meat, and even constructed dwellings. Yet it is misleading to label the males as lazy. They simply became specialized in their roles. Among the Hupa the males made bows, arrows, nets, and pipes, dressed hides, and used dry sticks to start fires.

Dancing was not only a social amusement, but also an important part of highly structured ceremonies. There were special dances to honor the newborn child, the black bear, the new clover, the white deer, and the elk. Other dances were used for welcoming visitors. Additionally there was a dance of peace and one of war, for which young braves were painted and dressed in plumes and beads. Dancing also took place during separate puberty rites for boys and girls. The Yurok held a first-salmon dance at the mouth of the Klamath River. The Hupa, in addition to staging a first-eel ceremony, also celebrated an autumnal first-acorn feast.

Singing became spirited whenever the natives indulged in the chewing or smoking of jimson weed, whose narcotic effect is similar to that of mescaline or marijuana. Some religious rituals, such as those of the Toloache cult, used music as an adjunct to narcotics. Accompanied by the hum of the bull roarer (a slat of wood swung at the end of a thong), chanting and singing would go on late into the night.

Among other types of celebrations were those during which participants boasted about the fine huts they had built or the victories warriors had won. All such achievements were recounted by wizened elders in lengthy orations, to which onlookers listened in solemn silence. Celebrating crowds did not gorge themselves, but usually ate abstemiously.

Some tribes held a special ceremony each summer to memorialize the dead. The ritual included building a large fire into which clothing, baskets, and other possessions were thrown as offerings to the departed. Indian braves then danced in a circle around the fire, accompanied by the rattle of a melancholy chant of mourning. Organized mourning for the dead by close relatives was practiced by nearly all tribes. This often took the form of smearing of the face with a wet paste mixed from the ashes of the deceased. The natives kept this facial covering on until it wore off, for as long as a year. A few tribes buried their dead; others practiced cremation.

Today, many native customs might seem especially strange. In northwestern California, for example, a wife could be purchased for strings of shell money or deerskins. In fact, a man was disgraced if he secured his wife for little or nothing. Polygamy was practiced by males who could afford more than one wife. Some of the men were inveterate gamblers, who would risk their last possession, including their wives, in games of chance. A "strip poker" guessing-game was popular, as were other games of chance involving the use of stone pebbles under sea shells. In ball games, and in leaping, jumping, and similar contests, the contestants accepted defeat with the same good sportsmanship as they displayed in victory.

Each family was a virtual judiciary system unto itself. The bodies of young men and women were painted by shamans who acted as temporary guardians, or "spirit helpers," of adolescents during their rites of passage into adulthood. At all times obedience to elders was very important. There was no fully systematic punishment for crime. Although atonement for injuring another was expected, some offenses could be excused by recompense. A murderer might even buy himself off by paying the aggrieved family of the deceased in skins or shells.

Because approximately 135 different dialects were spoken, a strict political or tribal system was not universal. One should, therefore, avoid use of the term "tribe." Except for a minority of well-defined tribes or tribelets, including the Yumas and some of the Indians of California's northwest coast, the basic political unit was the village community settlement. The Spanish called these village units *rancherías*. They were loosely-knit groups of several hundred persons within each of which were clans identified by individual totems. A ranchería had a patrilinear leader, who received deference. One can apply the term "chief" only loosely. The children of a male or female chieftain inherited a family's power, but only if they demonstrated similar talents.

California's natives were not generally nomadic. A clan's boundaries were usually well-defined. If one passed beyond a local boundary line, this could mean death to the offender. Mothers, therefore, were careful to teach their children the specific landmarks of their family or tribal areas. These lessons were often imparted via a singsong enumeration of certain stones, boulders, mountains, trees, and other objects on the landscape beyond which it was dangerous for a child to wander. Controversies between families, sometimes over the abduction of women, or concerning access to food sources, were occasionally severe. Rock fights

Major Native Linguistic Groups in California

Adapted from A. L. Kroeber, *Handbook of the Indians of California*, (Bureau of American Ethnology Bulletin 78, Washington, D.C., 1925), Plate I.

might break out about who had the right to use acorn groves or salmon streams. One of California's northern counties, Calaveras (or "skulls"), was named after a river where the Spanish Lieutenant, Gabriel Moraga, found whitened skulls scattered along its banks.

The first Californians revered the "medicine man," and had faith in his ability to cure illnesses. One treatment administered by these holy men consisted mainly of reciting incantations, after which the medicine man placed the end of a hollowed-out wooden tube against the body of the patient. He then pretended to suck out the cause of the disease, which might be a sliver of bone, a sharp-edged flint flake, or a dead lizard or other small animal, which he had previously secreted in his mouth. His success, in fact, depended partly upon his ability to fabricate

Members of the Diegueño tribe, Mesa Grande, 1906. Courtesy Museum of the American Indian.

entertaining (sometimes almost unbelievable) stories. Notwithstanding the pretenses of these practitioners, they did have some sort of working knowledge of the medicinal properties of herbs, roots, and other natural remedies, which they used to the benefit of their patients.

Even the Spanish consulted medicine men, or shamans, when other means failed to cure them of afflictions such as dysentery. Until the coming of the Spaniards the natives seem not to have suffered from such white man's diseases as smallpox, influenza, and measles. Tuberculosis was unknown to them, the common cold rare, and venereal disease did not yet exist among them. Constant scratching from lice and fleas, however, bloodied their bodies, and they were kept awake many a night by the vermin living in the animal skins they used as bed covers.

In colder areas one of the favorite treatments of illness was a visit to the local *temescal*, or sweathouse; this was a mound-like structure, usually made of timbers hermetically covered with earth, with only one small opening. A large fire was built inside the sweathouse. There, among steaming hot stones, the patient remained until dripping with perspiration. Then he rushed out of the sweathouse and leaped into the nearest lake or stream, sometimes into ice-cold water. This was a sort of "kill or cure" remedy similar to the Finnish sauna.

Natives also sought freedom from pain with the aid of a medicine man who sometimes engaged in a "doctors' dance"; there were rain, rattlesnake, and bear doctors as well who possessed clairvoyant and curative powers. Various tribal groups practiced a well-defined shamanism, not only to cure disease, but also to serve religious needs. Part of such healing rituals involved dream-interpretation similar to that practiced in ancient Greece.

There were also religious cults that explained the creation of the world and its first devastating flood. One tradition held that at a remote time in the past a billowing sea rolled up onto the plains to fill the valleys until water covered the mountains. All living beings were destroyed in this deluge, except for a few protected ones on high peaks who had been chosen by a supreme being. In eternity, worthy persons would go to a happy land beyond the water. When the coming of the new moon was celebrated, an old man would dance in a circle, saying, "As the moon dieth and cometh to life again, so we also, having to die, will live again."

What of California's native languages? No less than 22 linguistic families, with, as mentioned, 135 regional dialects, have been identified. All but one of these (Yukian) extended beyond the state's present borders. This confusion of tongues was one of the principal difficulties with which the missionaries had to contend. Because of so many dialects, good interpreters were hard to find. Some native groups, though separated by only the width of a stream, could not understand one another's speech. Among the better known linguistic classifications are the Hupa or Hoopa, Pomo, Modoc, Maidu, Mono, Yurok, and Yuma. Some smaller language groups have become extinct, their local dialects lost forever.

The names of nine California counties—Colusa, Modoc, Mono, Napa, Shasta, Tehama, Tuolumne, Yolo, and Yuba—come from native tribal groups. Two more county names—Inyo and Siskiyou—are also of probable native origin. These place names remain an enduring monument to the first lords of California's remote past.

The native population was once quite dense, partly because of the mild climate and once ample food supplies. One estimate places the original number of Native Americans in California at 100,000 to 150,000; others at 300,000. After devastating diseases to which the native peoples had no natural immunity were introduced by white invaders, these numbers were drastically reduced. It has also been alleged that when the

Native Population Table[1]

Pre–1542	300,000[2]
1769–1822	100,000
1870	30,000
1880	16,277
1890	16,624
1900	15,377
1910	16,371
1920	17,360
1930	19,212
1940	18,675
1950	19,947
1960	39,014
1970	91,018
1980	198,275
1990	236,078[3]

1. Population census statistics are muddled by changing criteria. Indians were not included in census data before 1890. Early data are approximate. Later figures include in-migration from other areas.

2. Only 133,000 to 150,000 according to A. L. Kroeber. The larger figure is based upon Sherburne F. Cook's estimate of 310,000.

3. Includes some Yumas, who also live in Arizona. The figure is also confused by Chicanos being numbered as Indians.

natives entered the confinement of the missions, they gave up the old practice of periodically burning down their dwellings, as well as use of the sweathouse. This supposedly removed a major protection against vermin, decreasing sanitation and making natives even more susceptible to the white man's diseases.

Shortly after the beginning of California's American period, mining operations destroyed the natives' vital food sources. Salmon no longer swam up northern streams to spawn, and many acorn groves had been levelled by miners in need of firewood. By the year 1900 the native population had decreased to an estimated 16,000 persons. The record of this tragic decimation is examined in a later chapter. Only in recent decades has the Native-American population been restored.

Selected Readings

Basic to an understanding of California's aborigines is Alfred L. Kroeber, *Handbook of the Indians of California* (Bureau of American Ethnology, Bulletin

78, 1925); and Frederick W. Hodge, *Handbook of the American Indians North of Mexico* (2 vols., 1959). Also useful are Kroeber's monographs in the University of California's Publications in Archaeology and Ethnology, especially his "California Culture Provinces," in volume 17 (1920). See also *Aboriginal California: Three Studies in Culture History* (1963), the combined work of A. L. Kroeber, James T. Davis, Robert F. Heizer, and Albert B. Elsasser. Consult Sherburne F. Cook, *The Conflict Between the California Indian and White Civilization* (1943), and his *The Population of the California Indians, 1769–1970* (1976); C. Hart Merriam, *Studies of California Indians* (1955); C. Alan Hutchinson, "The Mexican Government and the Mission Indians of Upper California, 1821–1835," *The Americas* 21 (April 1965), 335–62; Daniel Garr, "Planning, Politics, and Plunder: The Missions and Indian Pueblos of Hispanic California," *Southern California Quarterly* 54 (Winter 1972), 291–312.

A modern summary is Lowell J. Bean, "Indians of California: Diverse and Complex Peoples," *California History* 71 (Fall, 1992), 302–23. Consult also Robert H. Jackson, *Indian Population Decline: The Missions of Northwestern New Spain* (1994); Robert F. Heizer, "The California Indians, Archaeology, Varieties of Culture, Arts of Life," *California Historical Society Quarterly* 41 (March 1962), 1–28, and Heizer's *Languages, Territories and Names of California Indian Tribes* (1966).

Other sources include Galen Clark, *Indians of the Yosemite Valley and Vicinity* (1904); R. F. Heizer and M. A. Whipple, *The California Indians: A Source Book* (1951), R. F. Heizer, *California Indians* (1978); R. F. Heizer and J. E. Mills, *The Four Ages of Tsurai* (1952) as well as C. D. Forde, *Ethnography of the Yuma Indians* (University of California Publications in Archaeology and Ethnology 31, 1928) and, in the same series, P. E. Goddard, *Life and Culture of the Hupa* (1903).

Religion is discussed in James R. Moriarty, "A Reconstruction of the Development of Primitive Religion in California," *Southern California Quarterly* 52 (December 1970), 313–34. See also Edward W. Gifford and Gwendoline H. Block, *California Indian Nights Entertainment* (1959); Theodora Kroeber, *The Inland Whale* (1959) and her *Ishi in Two Worlds: A Biography of the Last Wild Indian in North America* (1961).

For the origin of place names consult Erwin G. Gudde, *California Place Names* (1960); Phil Townsend Hanna, *The Dictionary of California Land Names* (1951); Barbara and Rudy Marinacci, *California's Spanish Place Names* (1980) and A. L. Kroeber, *California's Place Names of Indian Origin* (1916).

More recent scholarship includes: George H. Phillips, *The Enduring Struggle: Indians in California History* (1981); James J. Rawls, *Indians of California: Their Changing Image* (1984); Robert H. Jackson and Edward Castillo, *Indians, Franciscans and Spanish Colonization* (1995); William McCawley, *The First Angelinos, The Gabrielino Indians of Los Angeles* (1996) and Diana Bahr, *From Mission to Metropolis: Cupeño Indian Women in Los Angeles* (1993) and Albert L. Hurtado, *Indian Survival on the California Frontier* (1988).

Exploring Baja and
Alta California

California's name was derived from a sixteenth-century Spanish novel, *Las Sergas de Esplandían* (The Exploits of Esplandían) by García Ordóñez de Montalvo. This volume was one of those impossible romances of chivalry that grew out of the crusades of the eleventh century. Las Sergas centers around Esplandían, a knight bound to vows of courage and chastity, and sworn to follow in his father's footsteps as *conquistador* of all his enemies. The word "California" appears as the name of a wonderful island of tall, bronze-colored Amazons ruled by a powerful queen, Calafía, who leaves the island to go to the assistance of forces besieging Constantinople. These women, who also repelled male suitors, excited the imagination of Spanish soldiers who read the book.

The *Las Sergas* saga was at its height of popularity when Hernando Cortés arrived in New Spain. Following his conquest of Mexico in 1519–1521, Cortés wrote to the Spanish King about a rumored island of Amazon women "abounding in pearls and gold." The Spaniards then still believed the peninsula of Baja California to be an island.

By the mid-1530s, mariners sent by Cortés had landed in Baja, or Lower, California. Most historians, however, give credit for the first official use of the name "California" to Francisco de Bolaños, who in 1541 also explored the Baja peninsula. Whoever first named the province probably did so in anticipation of finding pearls, gold, and other riches mentioned in Montalvo's romance about the mythical island of Queen Calafía.

There might also have been Asian contact with Alta, or Upper, California before 1542, when the first Spanish navigator, Juan Rodríguez

Cabrillo, arrived there. Junks sailing from Asia via the north Pacific Ocean could utilize the Japanese current to drive them as much as 100 miles per day. The longest distance between the Commander and Aleutian islands is about 150 miles. Some sinologists maintain that early mariners traveled eastward to a mysterious land known as "Fusang," possibly the Pacific Coast of North America.

In 1972 a huge doughnut-shaped stone, supposedly of Chinese origin, turned up off Point Conception. In ancient times such stones were used to clear seaweed from anchor chains. Other artifacts found over the years in California include a Chinese bronze fan and some ancient Chinese coins. Glass Japanese globes, used to hold up fishing nets, have also regularly washed ashore in California. As late as 1697, Francesco Giovanni Gemelli-Careri, an Italian merchant who traveled in a Manila galleon along its coastline, believed that California "bordered upon Great Tartary," an extension of the Far East. All such conjectures do not alter the fact that the first *effective* discovery of Alta California was made in 1542 by Cabrillo.

For a long time, rumors continued to circulate that rich cities lay on the banks of a northern strait that led to distant Cathay. These legends included tales of the Seven Cities of Cibola, the Kingdom of La Gran Quivira, and of a gold hoard called El Dorado. During the 1530s dramatic reports led the Spaniards into a futile search for interior villages of the Zuñi Indians, said to be the fabled Seven Cities. At La Gran Quivira, according to Spanish lore, even kitchen utensils were made of gold

After Cortés completed his conquest of Mexico, he was commissioned by King Charles V to search for the Strait of Anián. The Spaniards became obsessed with the legend that such a body of water directly connected North America with the Far East. From the west coast of Mexico, Cortés in 1532 sent an exploring expedition to Baja California that ended in mutiny. The mutineers who went ashore at La Paz in order to get fresh water were killed by fierce natives. Two sailors who had remained offshore on their ship brought back news of some pearl beds off the Lower California cape, which stimulated further exploration. In May of 1535 Cortés personally entered the bay where the massacre had occurred.

Although discouraged by the aridity of the land surrounding the bay, in 1539 he ordered Francisco de Ulloa to make a further voyage northward. In command of three small vessels, Ulloa turned toward the Sea of Cortés, or Vermillion Sea, as the Gulf of California had come to be called. Following the mainland shore, he then made his way to the head of the gulf, expecting to find a passage around the "island" to the open sea. After vain efforts to find such a passage, he returned southward, hugging the eastern shore of Baja California. While attempting to round the peninsula, Ulloa met a violent tempest on the open sea. For eight days his ships beat up and down the coast. Finally they reached the tip of Lower California and turned northward into the Pacific.

On January 5, 1539, Ulloa's expedition sighted Cedros Island, with tall cedars on its summit. After landing, they encountered natives who attacked with sticks and stones. Later, while battling opposing winds, Ulloa, at 30 degrees north latitude, was compelled by lack of provisions to turn about, thereby missing the chance to be the first white man to land in Upper California. As a result, the misrepresentation of California as an island continued to appear on maps made as late as 1784.

Obviously, these earliest expeditions in and around Baja California extended only slightly Spain's knowledge of North America's Pacific shore. The Viceroy of New Spain, Antonio de Mendoza, in a further attempt to discover the Strait of Anián, decided to send one more exploratory party north by sea. This one had orders to explore the coast beyond the latitude reached by Ulloa. Its leader was Juan Rodríguez Cabrillo, the real discoverer of California.

Cabrillo's two small ships unfurled their sails on June 27, 1542, out of the port of Navidad on the west coast of Mexico. These vessels were poorly built and badly outfitted; their anchors and ironwork had been carried overland across Mexico to the Pacific. Their emaciated crews, made up of scarcely provisioned conscripts, were soon decimated by scurvy—that deadly peril of all seamen.

This voyage took seven and one-half months, during which Cabrillo explored the coast as far as 41 degrees and 30 minutes north latitude. Cabrillo's tiny fleet, beaten back by northwest winds, and at other times becalmed, rocked idly on the waves for days, unable to make a northing. The captain, the documents say, paced the deck, peering anxiously into the dense fogs ahead. He did not realize that he was about to make a great discovery, and to lay down his life in so doing.

On Thursday, September 28, 1542, after three months at sea, Cabrillo's ships entered the future harbor of San Diego. This formally marked the discovery of Alta (or Upper) California. When the party landed, they learned from the natives that people like themselves, bearded and wearing clothing, had apparently been seen toward the interior. The local aborigines made gestures to show how the white men they had seen threw their lances. And, by galloping along the ground, they further suggested that the strangers had been on horseback. We shall never know if the Ulloa maritime expedition of 1539, or the Coronado land party of 1540, possibly could have met these natives.

When Cabrillo's ships reached what was later called Santa Catalina Island, he encountered other astonished natives. Along the shoreline opposite present-day Santa Monica, he noted an indentation on the mainland that he called "the Bay of Smokes." Even in those days long before smog, Indian campfires covered the bay near today's Los Angeles with spirals of smoke. Further northward, the shoreline of the Santa Barbara Channel seemed to be teeming with a dense Indian population.

Above today's Santa Barbara, heavy winds forced Cabrillo's ships to land at today's Cuyler Cove on San Miguel island. It too was populated by Indians, their long hair intertwined with cords into which they had thrust daggers of flint, bone, and wood. These natives wore no clothing and painted their faces in squares, like a checkerboard.

As Cabrillo beat his way northward, he skirted Monterey Bay and the narrow opening that Frémont later called the Golden Gate without seeing San Francisco Bay. From offshore, the Berkeley Hills blend in with the coastline, obscuring the entry to that vast body of water. Cabrillo next drifted northward, and on November 16 sighted Drake's Bay. Because of heavy seas, he set sail to the south once more, again missing the Golden Gate. Unable to make a landing on the rocky coast north of Point Conception, and buffeted by high winds over the next two months, the expedition was compelled to winter at San Miguel Island.

On January 3, 1543, its commander died, probably as the result of a violent fall during which he broke his arm. After his men laid Cabrillo to rest they renamed the island La Isla de Juan Rodríguez in their captain's honor. Drifting sand and falling cliffs later obliterated his last resting place. Not even the name of the island commemorates the true discoverer of Alta California.

As he lay dying, Cabrillo had charged his men to explore the coast as far northward as possible. His pilot, Bartolomé Ferrer (or Ferrelo), took command, and the expedition again set sail to the north. Scudding before a storm, Ferrer possibly reached the Rogue River area on the Oregon coast. At this point the crews, crazed from scurvy, forced Ferrer to turn back southward.

This first voyage to Alta California had, of course, failed to find the fabled Straits of Anián. Furthermore, Cabrillo had seen no cities with gold and silver walls—indeed no civilization nearly so rich as the Aztec or Inca empires. Yet he and his men had opened the sea route to a remote province at least vaguely familiar to all the world.

In 1564, King Philip II, in order to protect Spain's claims to California against other nations, ordered a fleet sent from today's Mexico to the Spanish-held Philippine Islands. Finding a new route across the

Pacific could be entrusted only to New Spain's most skilled navigator. This was Andrés Urdaneta, chief cartographer and sailing master of the king's fleet. On November 24, 1564, Urdaneta left the port of Acapulco for the Philippines. He returned after a voyage of only 129 days, having established a landfall in Alta California at about the latitude of Cape Mendocino.

Henceforth, Spain's Manila Galleons, for two and a half centuries, would carry silver bullion from Acapulco to be exchanged for Oriental goods at Manila. These lumbering vessels would return via California loaded with silks and spices as well as precious stones, musk, aromatic resin, amber, porcelain, carved and inlaid chests, and exotic birds that talked and played tricks. The Asian rarities brought to New Spain were snapped up by local buyers, enriched from mining Mexican and Peruvian silver. Some luxuries were then reshipped to Spain and sold all over Europe.

Mariners in the Philippine trade risked their lives on the cumbersome and insecure galleons. Ordinarily the outward trip from Acapulco required only 60 to 90 days. But the return voyage took from 7 to 9 miserable months, during which a ship's foodstuffs usually became rancid, the water supply often failing altogether. This compelled the crew to gather rainwater, which they caught with both sails and barrels. When scurvy, a vitamin deficiency, set in, body after body was thrown into the sea. On the way back from Manila, crews many times became so decimated that, by the time they sighted the California coastline, there were usually not enough able-bodied men onboard to go ashore for fresh water, or even to raise anchor once dropped. Some ships, therefore, limped on, in sight of the California coast, without stopping. Despite leaky hulls, spoiled provisions, and putrid water, somehow, occasional sick and dying crews reached Acapulco. Many did not.

Spain's viceroy in New Spain eventually realized the need to find a safe landing place for battered returning galleon crews in need of wood, water, meat, and repairs. This haven, he ascertained, lay somewhere along the coast of California. Meanwhile, in the late sixteenth century, the intrusion into Pacific waters of the English privateers Francis Drake and Thomas Cavendish rudely shocked the Spaniards. Little more than licensed pirates, these English buccaneers braved passage through the dangerous Strait of Magellan in order to reach the west coast of the Americas, where they could lie in wait for Spain's overloaded galleons returning from Manila. Though armed with small cannon, muskets, and catapults for hurling stones, the unmaneuverable galleons were virtually helpless against raids by the fast and graceful English corsairs.

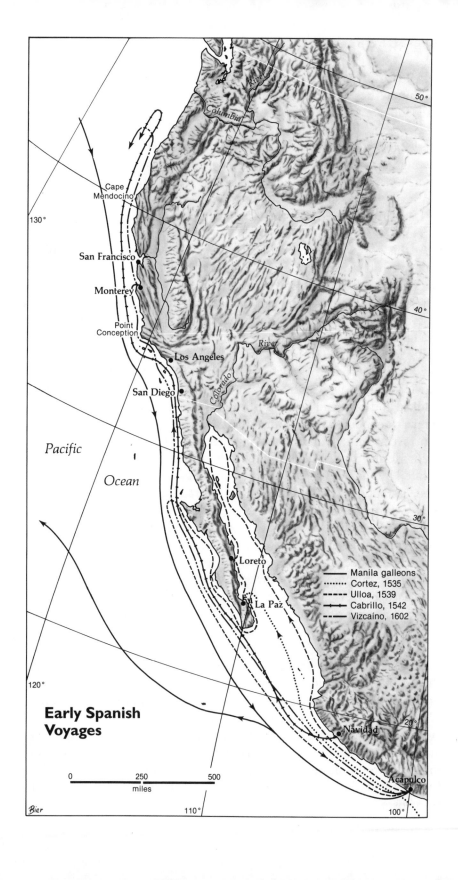

Early Spanish Voyages

50°

Columbia *River*

130°

Cape
Mendocino

San Francisco

Monterey

Point
Conception

40°

Pacific

Ocean

• Los Angeles

San Diego •

River

Colorado

30°

Loreto •

La Paz •

120°

	Manila galleons
	Cortez, 1535
	Ulloa, 1539
	Cabrillo, 1542
	Vizcaíno, 1602

0   250   500
miles

110°

20°

Navidad •

Acapulco

Bier

100°

In 1577 Drake, bearing a secret commission from Queen Elizabeth I to "annoy the King of Spain in his Indies," set sail from Plymouth in England on a voyage that would last several years. In his vessel, the *Golden Hind*, he made his way through the Magellan passage and proceeded to swoop down upon unsuspecting Spanish outposts like a hawk among barnyard fowl. On the high seas Drake likewise attacked ship after ship, sending them to run before the wind with all sails flying after looting gold and silver from their cargoes. He also stopped in the ports of Lima in present-day Peru and at Guatulco in today's Mexican province of Oaxaca, sacking both towns.

At this point Drake's *Golden Hind* was loaded almost to the sinking point with treasure. Fearing that Spanish ships would be lying in wait back at the Strait of Magellan, he sought a northward passage back to England. We do not know exactly how far north Drake sailed. Most historians have placed him somewhere along the Alta California coast. On June 17, 1579, his lookout sighted a "convenient and fit harborough," at 38 degrees and 30 minutes north latitude. There he entered a sandy bay for the purpose of repairing his ship. Drake remained there until July 23, during which time his men tipped the vessel onto her side, caulked and careened her, and mended a bad leak. The exact location of Drake's anchorage in California has long been a matter of historical controversy. Strong arguments have been advanced for the bight under Point Reyes, today called Drake's Bay, a white-cliffed harbor then inhabited by the Miwok Indians. Others believe that Drake anchored at Bodega Bay. One historian maintains that Drake did not even land in Alta California.

As to San Francisco's spacious bay, no evidence has been produced that Drake or his men ever laid eyes upon it. Books and articles on the subject of Drake's anchorage still debate its whereabouts. Only in 1775 did the Spanish ship *San Carlos* become the first vessel to enter San Francisco Bay. As the *Golden Hind* was seriously damaged by having battered against rocks, it is probable that Drake's expedition entered a bay that was more sandy than San Francisco's.

The exact location of his landing notwithstanding, he seemed to have established friendly relations with local Indians, exchanging gifts with them and undergoing ceremonials that the English later chose to regard as acceptance by the natives of England's sovereignty over the area. These symbolic acts probably corresponded to the smoking of a "peace pipe." After completing repairs on their ship, Drake's party held religious services, during which the natives made incantations led by their medicine men. Before he departed, Drake claimed title to the country for his Queen by leaving behind "a plate of brasse, fast nailed to a great and firm poste."

In 1934 a metal plate was reportedly found near the Laguna Ranch on Drake's Bay; after being thrown away it was supposedly "rediscovered" in 1936 under circumstances that led skeptics to question its authenticity. For more than forty years, however, most historians considered this artifact genuine. Professor Herbert Bolton of the University of California, Berkeley, fatuously pronounced it "one of the world's long lost historical treasures." Only in 1977 did metallurgists reexamine the plate, pronouncing it a modern forgery. It contained too much zinc and too little copper or lead to be genuine sixteenth-century brass. Other historians had been suspicious about the quality of the lettering, believing that Drake's gunsmiths could have done a far more elegant job; the plate in question obviously had been cut by modern machine tools.

The first English chroniclers who described Drake's contacts with the California Indians also possessed a vivid imagination. Their accounts made a princely personage out of an Indian chieftain, who would actually have been attired in rabbit skins; his rude basketwork hat was transformed into a royal crown, and his every gesture into a courtly mannerism. Accounts of the Drake voyage were set down by writers who embroidered descriptions of California's geography and primitive inhabitants. Drake's own account was never printed; in all probability it was suppressed lest it cause England diplomatic complications with Spain. Drake gave the name "New Albion" to the place where he had landed, before continuing on a westward course around the world. The chief result of his anchorage was to make the Spaniards wary of the occupation of California by another nation.

By 1584, Spain's viceroy at Mexico City, aroused by the continued threat of foreign interlopers, ordered Francisco de Gali to sail along the Upper California coast on his return from the Philippines. Gali, who was to look for a new port in California waters, reported observing a "very fair land, wholly without snow and with many rivers, bays, and havens." Presumably he landed somewhere along the California coastline.

Ten years later a Portuguese navigator, Sebastián Rodríguez Cermenho (sometimes Cermeno), explored and marked out Gali's course, beginning where the galleon bound from the Philippines reached the California coast. On November 4, 1595, Cermenho's ship, the *San Agustín*, out of Cavite in the Philippines, supposedly entered the same bay in which Drake had anchored sixteen years before. At this shallow roadstead, Cermenho's *San Agustín* was driven ashore by a squall and wrecked, scattering her cargo along the beach. Fortunately the crew was able to free a launch into which seventy men crowded, their principle provision being acorns obtained from the local natives. On their remarkable return southward, Cermenho noted the entrance to Monterey Bay, thereby qualifying as its real discoverer. On January 7, 1596, Cermenho finally arrived at his home port of Navidad; almost his entire crew, meanwhile, had died at sea.

Cermenho's disastrous voyage awakened New Spain's viceroy to the folly of exploration with unwieldy galleons. These undertakings risked the loss of too many precious cargoes and the lives of crewmen. Future expeditions to California would be made on ships of lighter draught. In 1602, Viceroy Monterey sent out such an exploratory party. On May 5, under the protection of Our Lady of Carmel, Sebastián Vizcaíno, at the head of a fleet of three tiny vessels, passed out of the harbor of Acapulco. The group reached and renamed many of the points visited in 1542 by Cabrillo. To the Vizcaíno expedition we owe now familiar place names— San Diego, Santa Catalina Island, Santa Barbara, Point Conception, Monterey, and Carmel.

On December 16, 1602, Vizcaíno sailed into Monterey Bay. As he looked about him at the ring of hills, dark with the growth of pines, he became enamored of the place. His fulsome description of the area in his report to the viceroy was so misleading that the next Spaniards to see Monterey, in 1769, failed to recognize it as such. On their way back down the coast, forty-five members of Vizcaíno's crew died, mostly from scurvy. Because of sorely ulcerated mouths and the loss of their teeth, they could not eat the coarse food they had onboard.

After Vizcaíno returned to Acapulco, a new viceroy, the Marques de Montesclaros, became lukewarm about sending future expeditions toward Alta California. In the years from 1602 to 1769 no ship entered California waters from the south, while the crews of the Manila galleons that passed by Alta California during that time left few records of what they saw. By 1815, voyages by the galleons were discontinued. For more than a century and a half, thus, there was little addition to the knowledge of California produced by Vizcaíno's voyage. Colonization of New Spain's distant province lay in the future.

Selected Readings

About the origin of the name California, see Herbert D. Austin, "New Light on the Name California," *Historical Society of Southern California, Publications* 12 (1923); Ruth Putnam, *California, The Name* (1917); Irving Berdine Richman, *California Under Spain and Mexico, 1535–1847* (1911), especially pp. 362–66; and George Davidson, *The Origin and Meaning of the Name California* (1910). See also Donald C. Cutter, "Sources of the Name 'California,'" *Arizona and the West* 3 (Autumn 1961), 233–43 and Dora Polk, *The Island of California: A History of the Myth* (1991).

Discussion of Asian contact with California is in Charles E. Chapman, *A History of California* (1921); Edward Payson Vining, *An Inglorious Columbus; or Evidence that Hwui Shan and a Party of Buddhist Monks from Afghanistan Discovered America* (1885); Naojiro Murakami, "Japan's Early Attempts to Establish Commercial Relations with Mexico," in *The Pacific Ocean and History* (1917) and Zelia Nuttall, "The Earliest Historical Relations Between Mexico and Japan," *University of California Publications in Archaeology and Ethnology* 4 (1904). See also Douglas S. Watson, "Did the Chinese Discover America?" *California Historical Society Quarterly* 14 (March 1935), 47–57; Charles G. Leland, *Fusang, or the Discovery of America by Chinese Buddhist Priests in the Fifth Century* (1875); C. W. Brooks, "Report of Japanese Vessels Wrecked in the North Pacific Ocean From the Earliest Records to the Present Time," *Proceedings, California Academy of Sciences* 6 (1876).

On the exploration of California see Henry R. Wagner, *Spanish Voyages to the Northwest Coast of America in the Sixteenth Century* (1929), as well as Wagner, *Juan Rodríguez Cabrillo, Discoverer of the Coast of California* (1941) and his *Cartography of the Northwest Coast of America to the Year 1800* (2 vols., 1937); Robert R. Miller, "Cortés and the First Attempt to Colonize California," *California Historical Quarterly* 53 (Spring 1974), 5–16 and Juan Paez, "Relation of the Voyage of Juan Rodríguez Cabrillo," trans. and ed. by Herbert E. Bolton in *Spanish Exploration in the Southwest* (1916).

Other references regarding exploration are: Maurice G. Holmes, *From New Spain by Sea to the Californias, 1519–1668* (1963); Jack D. Forbes, "Melchior Díaz and the Discovery of Alta California," *Pacific Historical Review* 27 (November 1958), 351–57; Harry Kelsey, *Juan Rodríguez Cabrillo* (1985), and Kelsey's "Mapping the California Coast: The Voyages of Discovery, 1533–1543," *Arizona and the West* 26 (Winter, 1984), 307–26. See also R. V. Tooley, *California as an Island: A Geographical Misconception Illustrated by 100 Examples from 1625 to 1770* (1964).

On the Spanish advance by land see Herbert E. Bolton, *The Spanish Borderlands* (1921) and Philip W. Powell, *Soldiers, Indians and Silver: The Northward Advance of New Spain, 1550–1600* (1952).

On the Manila galleon trade see William L. Schurz, *The Manila Galleon* (1939). Regarding Drake consult Norman Thrower, ed., *Sir Frances Drake and the Famous Voyage, 1577–80* (1984); Henry R. Wagner, *Sir Francis Drake's Voyage Round the World: Its Aims and Achievements* (1926) and Wagner, *Drake on the Pacific Coast* (1970); C. G. Fink and E. P. Polushkin, "Drake's Plate of Brass Authenticated," *California Historical Society,* Publication No. 14 (1937); R. B. Haselden, "Is the Drake Plate of Brass Genuine?" *California Historical Society Quarterly* 16 (September 1937), 271-74; Robert F. Heizer, *Francis Drake and the California Indians* (1947) and Heizer's *Elizabethan California* (1974).

An entire issue of the *California Historical Quarterly,* 53 (Fall 1974), was devoted to Drake. Also see Robert H. Power, "Drake's Landing in California: A Case for San Francisco Bay," *California Historical Quarterly*

52 (Summer 1973), 100–30; Frank M. Stanger and Alan K. Brown, *Who Discovered The Golden Gate?* (1969). Francis P. Farquhar and Walter A. Starr, "Drake in California: A Review of the Evidence and the Testimony of the Plate of Brass," appears in the *California Historical Quarterly* 36 (March 1957), 21–34. Walter A. Starr, "Drake Landed in San Francisco Bay in 1579, the Testimony of the Plate of Brass," *California Historical Society Quarterly* 41 (September 1962), 1–29, reopens the hotly contested controversy, but unconvincingly. See also Adolph S. Oko, "Francis Drake and Nova Albion," *California Historical Society Quarterly* 43 (June 1964), 135–58. Warren L. Hanna, *Lost Harbor: The Controversy Over Drake's California Anchorage* (1979); Edward Von der Porten, *Drake and Cermenho in California: Sixteenth Century Chinese Ceramics* (1973) and his *Porcelains and Terra Cottas of Drake's Bay* (1968). Most important are several Bancroft Library publications: *The Plate of Brass Reexamined* (1977) and *Supplementary Report* (1979), both of which find the Drake plate a fake. See also N. B. Martin, "Portus Novus Albionis: Site of Drake's California Sojourn," *Pacific Historical Review* 48 (August 1979) 319–34; *Early California: Perception and Reality* by Henry J. Bruman and Clement W. Meighan (1981) as well as Harry Kelsey, "Did Francis Drake Really Visit California," *Western Historical Quarterly* 21 (November 1990), 445–62.

On Cermenho see Henry R. Wagner, "The Voyage to California of Sebastián Rodríguez Cermenho in 1595," *California Historical Society Quarterly* 3 (April 1924), 3–24. In the same journal, Robert F. Heizer's "Archeological Evidence of Sebastián Rodríguez Cermenho's California Visit," 20 (December 1941), 315–28, identifies artifacts left by Cermenho at Drake's Bay. On Vizcaíno, see W. Michael Mathes, *Vizcaíno and Spanish Exploration in the Pacific Ocean, 1580–1630* (1968).

For buccaneering in Pacific waters see Peter Gerhard, *Pirates on the West Coast of New Spain, 1575–1742* (1960).

Colonizers of the Frontier

////////// CHAPTER 4

New Spain's northern border eventually extended, in an arc, from garrisons in present-day Louisiana to a remote chain of Jesuit missions spread throughout northern Mexico and both Californias. Along this vast frontier were located missions, mining camps, cattle ranches, and crude adobe *presidios,* or forts.

Three Jesuit clerics contributed to colonization of the approaches to California. Foremost of these was Eusebio Francesco Kino, a native of Trento in today's Italy. Father Kino was responsible, in the years 1678–1712, for the founding of missions on New Spain's northern frontiers. By his explorations, Kino proved in 1702 that California was not an island. Aiding him was another Italian Jesuit, the square-jawed, flinty Juan Maria de Salvatierra, who in 1697 founded the first of a chain of missions in Lower California. A third major "blackrobe," a term used by Native Americans to refer to the missionaries, was Father Juan de Ugarte who labored for years among newly converted Indians.

In 1763, after the defeat in North America of France by the British during the Seven Years' War, Spain feared more than ever that England might attempt to extend its New England colonization further west, possibly into Spanish territory. To prepare for such incursions, in 1765 Charles III, one of Europe's enlightened monarchs, appointed José de Gálvez *visitador-general,* or inspector general, of New Spain. In 1768 Gálvez, commissioned to reform colonization procedures, sailed to Lower California on an inspection tour of the peninsula's scraggly frontier missions.

While Gálvez, an avid expansionist, was in Baja California, he was ordered by King Charles to expel the Jesuits from the Spanish colonies.

All over Europe there was then distrust of that order's political power. Fearing the Jesuits would eventually control Spain's colonial settlements, the King ordered the Jesuits replaced in distant Baja California. Gray-robed Franciscan friars arrived at La Paz to continue the work begun earlier by Father Kino and his fellow Jesuits. These Franciscan priests would become the key colonizers for Gálvez in Alta California.

Russian encroachments on New Spain from the north—particularly the voyages to the American Northwest by Vitus Bering and Alexei Chirikof in 1741—also disturbed the Spaniards. Furthermore, Russian sea otter–hunting ships were extending their cruises farther southward each year. Gálvez, therefore, felt a pressing need for Spaniards to occupy Alta California, although he personally would never see an outpost in the province.

As Spain's inspector general, Gálvez next arranged a vital four-pronged expedition into Alta California. Two divisions were to go by sea and two by land; if one party should fail, another might succeed. If all went well, the four groups would convene at San Diego before pressing onward to Monterey, so highly praised by Vizcaíno. Religious supervision of the expedition was entrusted to the Franciscan missionaries. The peninsular (Baja) missions contributed to the exploring parties all the horses, mules, dried meat, grain, cornmeal, and dry biscuits they could spare.

Gálvez took great care to select the right cleric to lead the Franciscans into the new land. His choice was Fray Junípero Serra, a fifty-five-year-old priest of great endurance. Selection of Gaspar de Portolá to head the military branch of the expedition was equally shrewd. Serra, a kind of zealot, and Portolá, the dutiful soldier, were to become the first colonizers of Alta California. Serra, a native of the Mediterranean island of Majorca, had first come to America in 1749 to labor among the Indians of the New World. Before he was called to take charge of the missions of both Californias, he served for nine years among the Pamé Indians in the Sierra Gorda mountains of Mexico.

Father Serra repeatedly brushed aside obstacles that would have stopped lesser men, including a lame leg, from which he suffered nearly all his life. When he set out on the 1769 expedition to Upper California, he was in such poor health that two men had to lift him onto the saddle of his mule; but when his friend Fray Francisco Palóu, discouraged by the sight, bade him a regretful farewell, Serra insisted that, with the aid of God, he would successfully reach Alta California.

Serra's military companion, Portolá, had served the king as a captain of dragoons, becoming Baja California's first governor. In addition to occupying San Diego and Monterey, Portolá and Serra hoped to establish five missions. Church ornaments and sacred vessels did not constitute all of Serra's cargo, however; he brought along seeds and implements with which to plant future mission gardens. The two land parties also herded along 200 head of cattle, the descendants of whom would roam the hills and valleys of Alta California, becoming the chief source of the province's pastoral wealth for several generations.

Two tiny vessels, the *San Carlos* and the *San Antonio*, were to form the sea expedition. On January 9, 1769, the *San Carlos* was ready to start at La Paz in Lower California. Added to her crew were 25 Catalan military volunteers, needed, it was felt, to overcome any native resistance encountered after landing. Five weeks later the *San Antonio* left the same port and shook out her billowing sails, likewise moving northward toward San Diego.

By the latter part of March, Captain Fernando Rivera y Moncada, in command of the first land division—his force strengthened by 25 seasoned leather-jacketed soldiers and 42 Christianized natives—was ready to start northward. Rivera was accompanied by Fray Juan Crespi. On March 22, 1769, their small army began to march up the spiny Baja peninsula. They would become the first overland party to reach Alta California. The other land contingent, commanded by Portolá, bronzed and bearded, riding at its head, set out for San Diego on May 15, 1769.

The *San Antonio*, though she had set sail a month later than her sister ship, was the first to arrive at the rendezvous in San Diego, on April 11. When she sailed into port, the natives at first mistook the *San Antonio* for a great whale. On April 29, to the joy of those on the *San Antonio*, the *San Carlos* nosed alongside her and dropped anchor. The 110-day voyage of the *San Carlos* had resulted in such severe scurvy on board that there were no men able to lower a shore boat when it finally arrived. A third ship, the *San José*, had also been dispatched by Gálvez but was lost at sea.

Ashore, tents of sails sheltered the crewmen, many of whom suffered from dysentery. Pedro Prat, who came on the *San Carlos* as surgeon, scoured the shore in search of green herbs with which to heal the sick. Because so many of the men had died, the further voyage to Monterey had to be postponed. All available men were busy caring for the sick. The dead were buried at a place that has since borne the name *La Punta de los Muertos*, or Dead Men's Point.

On May 14, 1769, the gloom was lightened by the appearance of Captain Rivera's land party from Baja California. To assure a better water supply, Rivera moved the entire camp nearer a stream at the foot of today's Presidio Hill. At the end of June his camp was joined by the arrival at San Diego of Portolá's and Serra's second land party.

More than a third of the 300 men who had set out for Alta California, by land and sea, had failed to survive the trip. Half of those still alive were physically weakened by hunger, dysentery, and scurvy. After the founding of Mission San Diego de Alcalá, Portolá left behind a small garrison of soldiers to care for those who were still too ill to travel.

Then, with the least-emaciated soldiers, he pressed on further northward. The 64 members of his expedition included those with surnames later prominent in California history—such as Ortega, Amador, Alvarado, Carrillo, Yorba, and Soberanes. These troops wore leather jackets of thick deerskin and carried bull-hide shields. Lances and broadswords were among their weapons, as well as short muskets.

Portolá made frequent stops to rest his men and animals. Their route may be traced by the place names which Father Crespi carefully recorded in his daily journal—Santa Margarita, Santa Ana, Carpintería, Gaviota, Cañada de los Osos, Pajaro, and San Lorenzo. Portolá pressed on until he reached the shallow Salinas River.

Nearing Monterey Bay, he stood upon a hill and saw an open *ensenada*, or gulf. But the place he beheld did not seem to fit Vizcaíno's enthusiastic description of "a fine harbor sheltered from all winds". Indeed, Monterey can hardly be described as a well-protected port. Instead, the little company gazed at a long, curving beach. Where was the grand landlocked harbor Vizcaíno had described? Great swells from the ocean rolled in upon sandy beaches without obstruction, and there was no refuge from the wind except in a small shoreline indentation. Thus, for good reason, Portolá failed to recognize the bay of Monterey.

He now concluded that his only hope of finding Monterey or Point Reyes and other Vizcaíno landmarks, was by continuing further northward. Portolá's party, therefore, moved up the coast past today's Santa Cruz. By this point, eleven of his men were so ill that they had to be carried in litters swung between mules. Near Soquel they had their first sight of the "big trees," which Portolá named *palos colorados*, or redwoods, because of the color of their wood. At one stopping place they saw a giant tree of this species, which they called *palo alto* (high tree); the town located there still bears that name.

As Portolá's advance party moved northward, their path was hindered by *arroyos*, or gulches, which had to be bridged. Eventually an advance party reported seeing a "great arm of the sea." This was San Francisco Bay, which the whole group viewed for the first time on November 2, 1769. Astonished by the sight of so magnificent a body of water, the explorers now concluded that Monterey Bay must actually be behind them, for this splendid sight they now beheld must be a different large estuary. For decades ships had bypassed San Francisco Bay. Ironically, it remained for a land expedition to discover the greatest harbor on the Pacific coast.

Around this grand estuary, waterfowl were so abundant and gentle that they could be knocked down with long sticks. After his men had feasted on geese, ducks, and mussels, Portolá decided to return southward to Point Pinos. When his party reached Carmel Bay, they erected a large cross near the seashore, with a letter buried at its base; this missive informed any passing ships that Portolá's expedition had been there first. His men then crossed Cypress Point, and near the area which they still did not recognize as Monterey Bay, they erected another wooden cross. On its arms they carved these words: "The land expedition is returning to San Diego for lack of provisions, today, December 9, 1769."

On January 23, 1770, Portolá and his party returned to their base at San Diego. When they arrived, those who had stayed behind rushed out to greet them. In the years to come, Serra and his fellow Franciscans would develop missions near Portolá's camp sites. At the moment, survival was as stake. As provisions grew short, Portolá sent the *San Antonio* back to San Blas on the Mexican west coast for supplies. As the ship had not yet returned, on February 10, 1770, he ordered Captain Rivera and a small party of the strongest men back into Baja California to seek supplies from its missionaries. As for hunting wild game, scarce ammunition had to be saved for defense against possible native attacks.

Each day the missionaries knelt in prayer for the coming of a supply ship. Finally, on March 19, 1770, the San Diego encampment briefly spotted a sail. But then it disappeared. Four days after being sighted, the *San Antonio* reappeared and finally dropped her anchor. She carried the badly needed supplies.

With the San Diego base more secure, Portolá made a further trip northward by land. This time he finally recognized Monterey Bay, where he established a presidio. On June 3, 1770, Father Serra conducted mass there amid the ringing of bells and salvos of gunfire. Here was founded the second mission in Alta California, dedicated to San Carlos Borroméo. For convenience in obtaining wood and water, the mission was later removed to Carmel, four miles from Monterey. From Carmel, which became Serra's new mission site, he wrote his friend Father Palóu, "If you will come I shall be content to live and die in this spot."

On July 9, 1770, Portolá turned his governorship over to Pedro Fages and sailed away on the *San Antonio,* later becoming governor of Puebla in New Spain. Portolá deserves to be remembered not only as the first governor of both Californias (1767–1770), but also as leader of the expedition over the thousand-mile trail from the peninsula that discovered San Francisco Bay. Father Serra, Portolá's trail companion, remained behind to begin a chain of mission establishments in the far-off province.

Selected Readings

The best portrayal of Kino is still Herbert Eugene Bolton's *Rim of Christendom* (1936). See also Rufus Kay Wyllys, *Pioneer Padre: The Life and Times of Eusebio Kino* (1935) and Bolton's *The Padre on Horseback* (1932), as well as Frank C. Lockwood, *With Padre Kino on the Trail* (1934). Kino's astronomical activities are discussed in Ellen Shaffer, "The Comet of 1680–1681," *Historical Society of Southern California Quarterly* 34 (March 1952), 57–70. Finally, on Kino, consult Ernest J. Burrus, trans. and ed., *Kino Reports to Headquarters* (1954).

On Salvatierra see Miguel Venegas, *Juan María de Salvatierra*, translated and edited by Margaret Eyer Wilbur (1929). For other early Jesuit activity in the Southwest, see J. J. Baegert, *Observations in Lower California*, translated and edited by M. M. Brandenburg and Carl L. Baumann (1952); also Peter M. Dunne, *Pioneer Black Robes on the West Coast* (1940) and Dunne's *Pioneer Jesuits in Northern Mexico* (1944), *Early Jesuit Missions of the Tarahumara* (1948), and *Black Robes in Lower California* (1952). See also Theodore E. Treutlein, ed., *Pfefferkorn's Description of Sonora* (1949).

On Gálvez see Herbert I. Priestley, *José de Gálvez, Visitador-General of New Spain* (1916). See also the translation of Father Javier Clavigero's *Storia della California* (1789) in Sara E. Lake and A. A. Gray, *The History of Lower California* (1937).

Regarding the Russian threat to California see Frank A. Golder, *Russian Expansion on the Pacific, 1641–1858* (1914), and Golder's *Bering's Voyages* (2 vols., 1922–25). Good accounts of the first colonization of California are Charles E. Chapman, *The Founding of Spanish California* (1916); Irving Berdine Richman, *California Under Spain and Mexico, 1535–1847* (1911); Douglas S. Watson, *The Spanish Occupation of California* (1934).

Missionary activity has been widely chronicled. *The diario of Fray Francisco Palóu* appears, in translation, in Herbert E. Bolton, ed., *Historical Memoirs of New California* (5 vols., 1926). See also Herbert I. Priestley, ed., *A Historical, Political and Natural Description of California by Pedro Fages* (1937). Lives of Serra include Abigail H. Fitch, *Junípero Serra* (1914); Agnes Repplier, *Junípero Serra: Pioneer Colonist of California* (1933) and Father Zephyrin Engelhardt, *The Missions and Missionaries of California* (4 vols., 1908–15).

The best work on Serra is Maynard J. Geiger's *The Life and Times of Fray Junípero Serra* (2 vols., 1959); see also Geiger, trans. and ed., *Palóu's Life of Fray Junípero Serra* (1955) and Geiger, "Fray Junípero Serra: Organizer and Administrator of the Upper California Missions, 1769–1784," *California Historical Society Quarterly* 42 (September 1963) 195–220, as well as Geiger, *Franciscan Missionaries in Hispanic California, 1769–1848: A Biographical Dictionary* (1969). For Serra's successor see Francis Guest, *Fermin Francisco de Lasuén (1736–1803): A Biography* (1973).

Regarding Portolá, see Robert Selden Rose, ed., *The Portolá Expedition of 1769–1770: Diary of Vicente Vila* (1911); also Costansó, *The Narrative of the Portolá Expedition of 1769–1770,* Frederick J. Teggart ed., (1910); Theodore E. Treutlein, "The Portolá Expedition of 1769–1770," *California Historical Society Quarterly* 47 (December 1968), 291–313; Janet R. Fireman and Manuel P. Servín, "Miguel Costansó: California's Forgotten Founder," *California Historical Society Quarterly* 49 (March 1970), 3–19; and *The Costansó Narrative of the Portolá Expedition* ... trans. by Ray Brandes (1970).

Spanish claims are in Henry Raup Wagner, "Creation of Rights of Sovereignty Through Symbolic Acts," *Pacific Historical Review* 7 (December 1938), 297–326; Manuel P. Servín, "Symbolic Acts of Sovereignty in Spanish California," *Southern California Quarterly* 45 (June 1963), 109–21; and Servín's "The Instructions of Viceroy Bucareli to Ensign Juan Pérez," *California Historical Society Quarterly* 40 (September 1961), 243–46.

Missions, Presidios, and Pueblos

//////// **CHAPTER 5**

Among the three institutions used by the Spanish crown to colonize California—the mission, the presidio, and the pueblo—the mission must take first place; the other two agencies served mainly to support and defend this primary establishment. Spain's ostensible purpose in the operation of its missions was the saving of the souls of pagan aborigines, but actually the crown sought to transform the converted natives into a reliable labor force. In this way, future missionization would be economically viable and serve Spain's main goal, the expansion of the empire.

By 1776, Father Serra hoped for an increase in the population of the province of Alta California, expansion of its agricultural possibilities, and further missionary establishments along its northern coast. Twenty-one missions were ultimately built, forming a chain from San Diego to Sonoma. These were separated by about a day's travel on horseback—some thirty miles apart. The King's Highway, or *El Camino Real* of the tourist literature, the only road from mission to mission and from presidio to presidio, was then scarcely more than a dusty path.

Three requisites determined the choice of a mission site—arable soil for crops, water supply, and a large local native population. By the time the twenty-one missions were established, the friars had in their possession much of the choicest land in the province. Later this would lead to resentment by civilian leaders and settlers.

The first mission buildings were mere huts of thatch and sticks, plastered with mud or clay, and roofed with tule—not the adobe-brick or cut-stone buildings of today. The stone walls at Mission San Carlos

Mission San Luis Rey, from Robinson's "Life in California before the Conquest," 1846. C. C. Pierce Collection; courtesy of The Huntington Library, San Marino, California.

Borroméo were never seen by Serra, who is buried there. The California padres, in their isolation, modified Moorish and Roman architectural styles to render structures appropriate to the environment. Thus "California mission architecture" is characterized by open courts, long colonnades, arches, and corridors. The typical red-tiled mission roofs were one way to avoid fires in wooden structures. Destruction of earlier buildings by earthquakes led to the use of thick adobe walls reinforced with occasional buttresses.

At the missions the padres assumed a paternal attitude toward the Indians, treating them as wards. There were usually two friars at each establishment, the elder of whom had charge of interior matters and religious instruction, while the younger attended to agricultural and outside work. Each mission was subject to the authority of a father-president for all of California. He in turn bowed to the orders of the College of San Fernando, headquarters of the Franciscans in Mexico. Except in the punishment of capital crimes, the friars had control of their native charges. Floggings and other corporal punishments were administered for unacceptable offenses. The missionaries defended their discipline on the ground that it was the only effective means of controlling unruly natives, the souls of whom they were trying to "save."

Modern clerical scholars have countered accusations of harshness by the Franciscans toward California's aborigines. Flagellation, or use of rope *disciplina*, as well as use of whips and hairshirts, formed part of the clerical mortification of the flesh. Although delinquent natives were whipped, sometimes excessively, and some lost their lives due to poor sanitation conditions in and around the missions, one needs to place both the punishment and high mortality rates of those at the missions within the context of eighteenth-century medical standards on a distant frontier. Yet, most historians continue to consider treatment of the natives by the Spanish clergy and military as harsh. Those who were missionized did, indeed, suffer high casualty rates from a variety of causes.

The missions were not devoted entirely to religious instruction. Each was also a school in which natives did daily work and were taught trades. Guided by the missionaries, the native peoples proved to be remarkably good students. The friars were also musicians, weavers, carpenters, masons, architects, and physicians.

Putting their own hands to the plow, they raised enough food for mission use, and occasionally a surplus of meal, wine, oil, hemp, hides, or tallow. These extra products were then exchanged in New Spain for scarce clothing, furniture, and tools. The missionaries also transplanted traditional Spanish crops to California. Orange, lemon, fig, date, and olive trees flourished in mission gardens, as did grape vineyards. Even cotton was grown at several of the missions alongside livestock.

Among those who helped assure progress at the missions was the new viceroy, Antonio María Bucareli. He placed great faith in the leadership of Father Serra as well as Fathers Francisco Palóu and Fermín de Lasuén. Palóu had been among the last of the Franciscans to turn over their Lower California missions to the Dominican order, and in 1773 he joined Serra in Upper California. Palóu was also the author of the first book ever written in California, *Noticias de la Nueva California*; this and his *Vida de Junípero Serra* are basic works about California's history. At Serra's death, in 1784, he and his fellow Franciscans had been in California nearly sixteen years. By then their missions could claim a total of 5,800 native converts. Lasuén, also a cleric of talent and character, filled the post of president with distinction after Serra died.

These priests desired that California's presidios, or frontier fortresses, be built to protect their missions from native uprisings and to guard Spain's claims to the area against foreign interlopers. Each presidio was located at a strategic position, generally at the entrance of the best ports. Small dwellings, inhabited principally by settlers, traders, and the families of garrisoned soldiers, grew up around the presidios.

These presidial pueblos came to include San Diego, founded July 16, 1769; Monterey, June 3, 1770; San Francisco, September 17, 1776; and Santa Barbara, April 21, 1782. At first they were under military rule. The presidios themselves consisted of a square enclosure, surrounded by a ditch and rampart of earth or brick, within which were located a

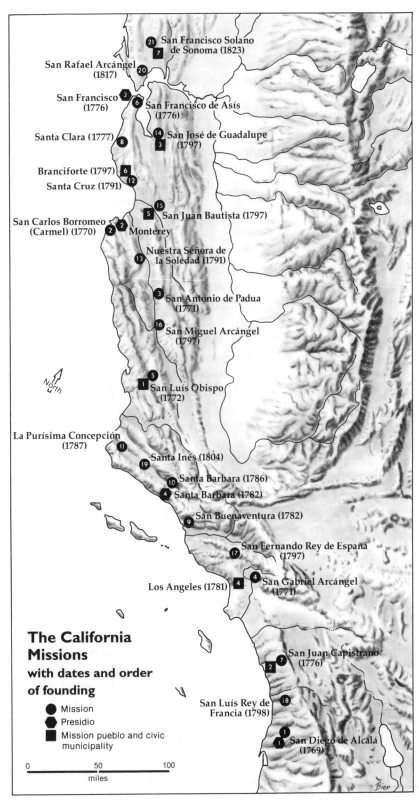

San Francisco Solano
de Sonoma (1823)

San Rafael Arcángel
(1817)

San Francisco
(1776)

San Francisco de Asís
(1776)

Santa Clara (1777)

San José de Guadalupe
(1797)

Branciforte (1797)

Santa Cruz (1791)

San Juan Bautista (1797)

San Carlos Borromeo
(Carmel) (1770)

Monterey

Nuestra Señora de
la Soledad (1791)

San Antonio de Padua
(1771)

San Miguel Arcángel
(1797)

North

San Luís Obispo
(1772)

La Purísima Concepción
(1787)

Santa Inés (1804)

Santa Barbara (1786)

Santa Barbara (1782)

San Buenaventura (1782)

San Fernando Rey de España
(1797)

Los Angeles (1781)

San Gabriel Arcángel
(1771)

**The California
Missions**

**with dates and order
of founding**

● Mission

⬟ Presidio

■ Mission pueblo and civic
municipality

San Juan Capistrano
(1776)

San Luís Rey de
Francia (1798)

San Diego de Alcalá
(1769)

0   50   100
miles

Bier

small church, quarters for officers and soldiers, civilian housing, store-houses, workshops, and cisterns.

With only a few bronze cannons mounted on ramparts, and often without sufficient powder to discharge the weapons, not one of the coastal presidios could have stood up against an attack by a well-equipped ship of war. Indeed, they were maintained more as a symbolic warning against possible enemies, with little expectation of their serving well in a fight. In time the cannon rusted and the presidios took on an air of dilapidation.

The duties of soldiers who manned the presidios included the care of outlying herds and flocks. They also cultivated the soil of nearby fields, utilizing native laborers, who for their hard work received such occasional rewards as a string of beads, an extra dish of porridge, a pair of shoes, or a piece of cloth.

San Francisco's presidio was established largely through the efforts of Juan Bautista de Anza. He was one of the significant trailbreakers and toughest Indian fighters of the West. Anza had long planned to explore and establish a route northwestward from Sonora to the northern California coast. Such a land passage would reduce the delay and perils of sea voyages, on which California still relied for contact with the outside world.

Viceroy Bucareli, wishing to strengthen California's settlements, saw in Anza's proposal an opportunity not only to open a new land route, but also to send colonists north under the protection of a capable leader. Women settlers, as well as provisions, and domestic animals remained in great demand in the new province. Anza, in January of 1774, with the trails-priest Francisco Garcés as his guide, and a band of thirty-four men, set out westward from Tubac in northern Mexico. Theirs was the first sizable crossing by Caucasians into California from the Colorado basin through the San Jacinto Mountains.

A key to the success of this party was Father Garcés, who three years before had penetrated into California beyond the junction of the Colorado and Gila rivers, to the walls of the southern Sierra range. Utilizing his expertise, Anza's party, on March 22, 1774, reached Mission San Gabriel in the Los Angeles basin, which had been founded three years before.

Anza had opened up a new overland route some 2,200 miles long. In 1775, Viceroy Bucareli sent Anza with another party to Alta California. This group consisted of colonists recruited throughout Sinaloa and Sonora. On October 23, Anza left Tubac leading a group of 240 men, women, and children, along with a herd of 200 cattle, beyond the Colorado River to Mission San Gabriel, and then on to Monterey.

A few colonists then accompanied him farther to the site of the future San Francisco. On September 17, 1776, Anza formally dedicated the

Presidio of San Francisco de Asís. On October 9 Mission Dolores was founded by Father Palóu, the year the American Declaration of Independence was signed.

The viceroy had also sent Captain Juan Manuel Ayala, in command of the vessel *San Carlos,* to explore the area's vast bay, which still had no name. No ship had yet passed through the Golden Gate, and Ayala feared danger along its narrow, rocky shoreline. At nightfall on August 5, 1775, the *San Carlos* moved into the bay, cautiously dropping her lead line until she reached today's North Beach. Ayala named San Francisco Bay's two islands—*Nuestra Señora de los Angeles* (Our Lady of the Angels) shortened later to Angel Island, and *Alcatraz* or "Pelican," because of the large number of those birds flying over it.

At the local Presidio of San Francisco, even its officers lived under primitive conditions. Virtual exiles in a strange land, they waited for the day when they might return to more comfortable quarters. The Englishman George Vancouver, visiting in 1792, described the house of the *comandante* at Yerba Buena, or San Francisco, as consisting of only two rooms with earth floors;the windows had no glass, and furniture was almost completely lacking.

In addition to presidial and mission pueblos, there was a third category of early settlements—the civic pueblos. These were established by then Governor Felipe de Neve who granted each pueblo four square leagues of land. Facing upon a plaza were the council house, church, and

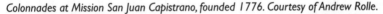

Colonnades at Mission San Juan Capistrano, founded 1776. Courtesy of Andrew Rolle.

jail. The life of the community revolved around these central squares, in which bullfights sometimes were held.

Each pueblo settler was entitled to a house lot, livestock and implements, an allowance in clothing and supplies, and use of public land as common pasture. He was required to sell any surplus agricultural products to the presidios, and to hold himself, his horse, and musket in readiness for military service. He was also to build a house, dig irrigating ditches, cultivate the land, and maintain his own animals. After five years of exemption from taxes, pueblo residents were to receive title to their land. Taxes were levied by the governor at Monterey from settlers in the province in which they had been granted land.

In the California settlements, municipal officers consisted of an *alcalde* (similar to a mayor) and *regidores,* or councilmen, members of a local governing body, the *ayuntamiento.* The alcalde decided cases of minor importance, while those charged with high crimes were brought before the governor at Monterey. Anyone had the right to demand trial by "good men" (*hombres buenos*), a jury of three to five members. The powers of an alcalde were respected, for these officials were generally honest administrators. The alcalde was, in effect, the *patrón,* or "little father," of a town, to whom citizens carried their troubles.

The Los Angeles ayuntamiento had jurisdiction over territory as large as the state of Massachusetts. It was a dignified body whose members were attired in black. The ayuntamiento received petitions and complaints from dissatisfied ranchers as well as townsmen. As a badge of office, alcaldes carried a silver-headed cane. They and the regidores were the arbiters of pueblo justice.

The first civic pueblo was San José de Guadalupe (now San José), founded on November 29, 1777. Originally it consisted of a few mud huts on the banks of the Guadalupe River. Further southward, the second civic pueblo, *Nuestra Señora la Reina de los Angeles de Porciuncula,* today's Los Angeles, was founded on September 4, 1781, by eleven couples and their twenty-two children—a total of forty-four *pobladores,* or settlers. Its first citizens were of Indian and African blood, with a moderate admixture of Spanish. Not one of Los Angeles's first settlers could write his or her name.

California's third civic community, Branciforte, named after a prominent viceroy, was established in 1797 near the present Santa Cruz. Its founders were mostly convicts banished to the far north by Mexican legal officials, but Branciforte soon passed out of existence. Along with San José and Los Angeles, these new settlements would eventually form the basis of California's provincial life.

Selected Readings

Basic to understanding the missions is Herbert E. Bolton, "The Mission as a Frontier Institution in the Spanish American Colonies," *American Historical Review* 23 (October 1917), 42–61. See also Harry W. Crosby, *Antigua California: Mission and Colony on the Peninsular Frontier* (1994); Theodore Maynard, *The Long Road of Father Serra* (1954) and Omer Englebert, *The Last of the Conquistadores: Junípero Serra, 1713–1784* (1956). Also consult Maynard Geiger, ed., *Palóu's Life of Fray Junípero Serra* (1955).

On Anza see Herbert E. Bolton, ed., *Anza's California Expeditions* (5 vols., 1930); also Frederick J. Teggart, ed., *The Anza Expedition of 1775–1776* (1913); Douglas D. Martin, *Yuma Crossing* (1954).

About Los Angeles and other pueblos and presidios see John Langellier and Daniel Rosen, *El Presidio de San Francisco . . . 1776–1846* (1997); Edwin Beilharz, *Felipe de Neve, First Governor of California* (1972); W. W. Robinson, *Ranchos Become Cities* (1939); Andrew Rolle, *Los Angeles: From Pueblo to City of the Future* (1995); Francis Guest, "The Establishment of the Villa of Branciforte," *California Historical Society Quarterly* 41 (March 1962), 29–50; Theodore Grivas, "Alcalde Rule: The Nature of Local Government in Spanish and Mexican California," *California Historical Society Quarterly* 40 (March 1961), 11–32.

About native relations see Harry Kelsey, "European Impact on the California Indians," *The Americas* 61 (April 1985), 494–511; James Sandos, "Levantamiento: The 1824 Chumash Uprising Reconsidered," *Southern California Quarterly* 57 (Summer 1985), 109–33; William McCawley, *The First Angelinos: The Gabrielino Indians of Los Angeles* (1996).

California and Its Spanish Governors

//////// **CHAPTER 6**

Portolá was followed by several interim governors. Probably the best of Spain's governors in Alta California was Felipe de Neve (1775–1782). Like Portolá, Neve was both military commander and governor. Though a soldier, he had a statesman's mind. He soon drew up regulations to guide local civic and military affairs. As we have noted, Neve also founded California's new pueblos.

As these settlements badly needed colonists, in 1781 Captain Rivera y Moncada received orders to conduct a motley party bound for Los Angeles and San José. Tragedy resulted. At the Colorado River, having moved northward from Sonora and Sinaloa, Rivera sent the colonists ahead, while he and his soldiers, accompanied by the trails-priest, Father Garcés, stopped to rest. On July 17, 1781, the Yuma Indians attacked two missions—Purisma Concepcion and San Pedro y San Pablo—that had been established as way stations near the river crossing. All the friars in the mission, the male settlers in the area, and the men in Rivera's command, including himself and Father Garcés, were shot or clubbed to death while the women and children were herded off into slavery. The Yumas had been promised supplies and good treatment by the Spanish. But, when they saw the expedition marching through their cornfields and pumpkin patches, their resentment swelled to the bursting point. The Yuma Massacre led to abandonment of this dangerous route to California, which had originally been opened by Anza, and neither pueblos nor missions were reestablished on the Colorado River. As a further result, the province of Alta California continued in its isolation from Spain, the mother country.

From 1782 to 1791 Pedro Fages served as governor. Fages, a sturdy officer, had also been an Indian fighter and an explorer who, in 1770 and 1772, led expeditions to San Francisco Bay. He had helped keep the California colony alive, during a period when supply ships were delayed, by providing bear meat from Cañada de los Osos (Bear Canyon), near San Luis Obispo. His rather brusque manner soon involved him in disagreements between California's missionaries and Fages' young wife, Doña Eulalia Fages, all of which the missionaries recorded in entertaining detail in the mission archives. As she so hated frontier life, the padres eventually asked for the couple's removal from Monterey where they disturbed mission life.

In 1794 another governor arrived. He was a Basque named Diego de Borica. Like Fages, Borica was a good soldier and administrator. The new governor, however, established a more harmonious relationship with the friars, authorizing Father Lasuén to search for new mission sites.

Together they decided that five more such establishments could be founded. Borica believed that conversion of more natives would make it possible to reduce the necessary number of provincial guards. The missions had been isolated units; Borica now proposed to link them into one chain, nearer together so that they served the area from San Diego northward to San Francisco and between the Coast Ranges and the ocean. Eventually one could travel safely over a distance of 500 miles and enjoy the hospitality of the missions each night without having to carry along provisions.

Governor Borica also instituted new irrigation works and guarded the provincial revenues. He proved to be a steadfast friend of the local natives. Doing what he could to see that they were not despoiled of their lands, he believed that capital punishment should not be inflicted upon them, even for the crime of murder.

Upon Borica's retirement in 1800, José Joaquín de Arrillaga served a second term as governor and continued the cordiality between the military and religious officials that had been missing in Father Serra's days. Meanwhile, the viceroy in Mexico City was losing interest in the missions and sending little money to support them. The presidios and civil establishments too fell into a deplorable state; buildings were half ruined by wind and rain; cannon rusted from exposure to the weather and by disuse. Spiritless frontier troops remained badly equipped and went without pay for long periods of time. Mission expansion came to a temporary halt with the death of Father Lasuén in 1803.

One of Governor Arrillaga's principal worries concerned the founding of a Russian settlement in California. The Russians had arrived in 1806 to examine fur-trading opportunities. But after they established

Fort Ross, north of Bodega Bay, the Russian threat to California had become real.

California's last Spanish governor was Pablo Vincente Solá. His arrival at Monterey in 1815 was marked by days of feasting and dancing, exhibitions of expert horsemanship, and gory bull and bear fights in the capital's muddy plaza. The vain royalist governor wrongly considered this welcome as an expression of California's loyalty to Spain. Actually, local allegiance was growing weaker.

Solá, proud of his Spanish birth and inclined to look with contempt upon colonials as incompetent whelps, was soon angered by the smuggling that had grown up between the Californians and foreigners. Each year increasing numbers of foreign ships arrived in California ports. The appearance of vessels sailing under the flag of the new American Union particularly alarmed the governor. When these ships casually landed in California to take on wood and water, he learned how poor his shore fortifications were. Yet, when he himself faced scarcities of clothing, furniture, and household necessities, the governor managed to ignore the widespread smuggling.

But Solá's stormy tenure in office would soon be immaterial, for Spain's empire was about to crumble throughout Latin America. California, though a mere appendage of a far-flung empire, also could not escape the magnetic lure of revolution.

Selected Readings

The Spanish governors are examined in Donald A. Nuttall, "The Gobernantes of Spanish Upper California," *California Historical Society Quarterly* 51 (Fall 1972), 253–80; also Herbert E. Bolton, *Outpost of Empire* (1931); Herbert Priestley, trans., *Pedro Fages, A Historical, Political and Natural Description of California* (1937), and Henry R. Wagner, trans., *Letters of Captain Don Pedro Fages and the Reverend President Fr. Junípero Serra at San Diego . . .* (1936).

For the Yuma Massacre see Douglas D. Martin, *Yuma Crossing* (1954); Herbert Priestley, trans., Pedro Fages, *The Colorado River Campaign 1781–1782* (1913); Elliot Coues, *On the Trail of a Spanish Pioneer* (2 vols., 1900); John Galvin, ed., *A Record of Travels in Arizona and California, 1775–1776* by Fr. Francisco Garcés (1965).

For mission architecture see Kurt Baer, *Architecture of the California Missions* (1958), and Baer, *Paintings and Sculpture at Mission Santa Barbara* (1955), as well as Baer, "Spanish Colonial Art in the California Missions," *The Americas* 17 (July 1961), 33–54; also Norman Neuerburg, *The Decoration of the California Missions* (1987).

See also Herbert Priestley, *Franciscan Explorations in California* (1946); Henry R. Wagner, "Early Franciscan Activity on the West Coast," *His-*

torical Society of Southern California Quarterly 23 (September 1941), 115–26; John A. Berger, *The Franciscan Missions of California* (1948): Maynard Geiger, *Mission Santa Barbara, 1782–1965* (1965); Clement Meighan, "Indians and the California Missions," *Southern California Quarterly* 69 (Fall 1987), 187–201; Robert H. Jackson, "The Changing Economic Structure of the Alta California Missions, A Reinterpretation," *Pacific Historical Review* 61 (August 1992), 387–415; James A. Sandos, "Junípero Serra's Canonization and the Historical Record," *American Historical Review* 93 (December 1988), 1253–69; Francis Guest, "An Inquiry Into the Role of Discipline in California's Mission Life," *Southern California Quarterly* 71 (Spring 1989), 1–68.

Exploration and
Foreign Interference

During the long period when Alta California was being settled by priests, soldiers, and colonists, the Spanish crown continued to press forward with its program of exploration. From Mexico City, New Spain's Viceroy, Antonio Bucareli, asked his mariners to find out what lay beyond the northernmost reaches of California's coastline. In March 1775 he commissioned two explorers, Captains Bruno de Heceta and Juan Francisco de la Bodega, to sail northward from San Blas. At latitude 41 degrees north, their ships headed into a fine bay. Its shores, covered with wild roses, iris, manzanita, and tall pines, were so inviting that the Spaniards landed and took possession in the name of the king. Since this event took place on the day of the Holy Trinity, they called the bay Trinidad, by which name it is still known.

Captain Heceta also deserves credit for the discovery of the Columbia River, on July 27, 1775, although the achievement is sometimes ascribed to the American sea captain Robert Gray who arrived on the site in 1792. When Heceta reached Nootka, on the west coast of Vancouver Island, the miserable condition of his crew forced him to sail back down the coast to California.

As for Bodega, though short of food and water and with a crew crippled by scurvy, when the cold autumn rains set in, his men suffered so severely from insufficient clothing that he was also compelled to return southward. The trip was a stormy one and great seas rolled over Bodega's ship, carrying away everything movable and filling the hold with water. On October 3, 1775, his vessel drifted into a bay four leagues north of Point Reyes, on whose banks he saw bear and deer feeding. His navigator named the bay Bodega after the captain. The area, however, would remain remote for many years.

Geographic isolation from Spain forced its colonists to lead calm but rather dull lives. Generally, the *Californios* knew the name of their king and that of the pope but little more about events abroad. In time, only ships flying the flags of other nations could bring them needed goods, which the decrepit Spanish supply system failed to provide. California would have remained a virtual island had not foreign visitors called attention to its future possibilities.

The growing fur trade on the northwest coast attracted European and American ships to ports further south in California.In August 1785, the French scientist and navigator Jean François de Galaup de la Pérouse arrived from Brest, heading a geographic, scientific, and commercial expedition. His two vessels anchored in Monterey Bay. During La Pérouse's ten-day stay his geologists and botanists collected specimens and made careful drawings of what they observed. The Californians supplied the visiting ships with cattle, vegetables, milk, poultry, and grain. The visitors reciprocated with cloth, blankets, beads, tools, and seed potatoes from Chile.

The La Pérouse expedition departed after a farewell that turned out to be final. Nothing more was ever heard of the party until 1825, when the wreckage of two French ships was found on the reefs of an island north of New Hebrides. Had it not been for the forethought of La Pérouse in forwarding installments of his California journal to France, the records of his voyage would have been lost to posterity.

In September of 1791 the Californios hosted yet another scientific expedition, this one from Spain but led by an Italian mariner, Alejandro (Alessandro) Malaspina. He was on a round-the-world mission with instructions to search for the long-sought Strait of Anián. Malaspina's account, while valuable, is not as complete as that of La Pérouse or, later, of the Englishman George Vancouver. But Malaspina did bring to California the body of the first American to land on its shores. This was John Green, a sailor from Boston who had shipped as a gunner's mate and who had recently died.

English interest in California remained high during the remainder of the eighteenth century. In 1792 Vancouver received orders to examine the extent of Spanish possessions, and to seize any unclaimed territory. On November 14, he entered San Francisco Bay in the sloop-of-war *Discovery*. Despite strained relations between Spain and England, Vancouver was given a cordial reception by the local padres and military officials.

Vancouver's party also visited Mission Santa Clara, the first foreigners to penetrate so far into the interior. From there they returned to San

Francisco, where they gave the Spaniards some English table utensils, bar iron, and ornaments for the local church. At Carmel Mission the fathers entertained their foreign guests. Upon a return visit, Vancouver was offended not to receive the same cordial welcome as he had enjoyed the year before. In the interim, Governor Arrillaga had objected to allowing any more foreign visitors to penetrate into the province's interior, for they were an increasing threat to Spanish authority.

In 1796, the first U.S. vessel to anchor in a California port, the *Otter* out of Boston, arrived. Its master secretly landed ten men and a woman on the Carmel beach at night, forcing them from a rowboat with a pistol. These were convicts from Botany Bay, the English penal colony in the South Pacific, who had boarded the *Otter* to escape. Governor Borica, though offended by their presence, put the escapees to work as carpenters and blacksmiths, paying them nineteen cents per day.

Although not really welcome, American masters in search of sea otters kept putting into California ports. Spain's local officials were almost powerless to prevent contraband trade with visiting "Boston ships." During 1799 the *Eliza,* another Yankee vessel, anchored at San Francisco and obtained supplies on the condition that it would not touch at any other port in the province.

The arrival of increasing numbers of such poachers and traders roused the viceroy at Mexico City to issue stricter orders against trading with foreign vessels. Since, however, he had no means of carrying out such *pronunciamientos,* the Yankee traders continued to defy local regulations. On March 22, 1803, shots were exchanged between the American vessel *Lelia Byrd* and a shore battery at San Diego after part of the ship's crew had been captured while ashore trading. Although several shots struck the sails, rigging, and hull of the ship, no one was hurt. The captain, William Shaler, got his men safely away to the Hawaiian Islands and then to China. The next year the *Lelia Byrd* was back in California doing a flourishing fur business. This time, Captain Shaler and his leaky ship carefully avoided the refortified ports of San Diego and Monterey.

Although American traders ultimately broke down the restrictions imposed by the Spanish Crown, they sometimes suffered severe consequences. In 1813, Captain George Washington Eayrs of the ship *Mercury* ran into a Spanish longboat. Eayrs and his men were captured and taken to Santa Barbara, where they were interned for two long years.

Illegal coastal trafficking, by which New England wares or Chinese luxuries were exchanged for sea otter furs, steer hides, tallow, and cow horns (to be made into buttons), continued to be dangerous. Yet the rewards were great. In a single season 18,000 prime otter pelts were delivered to the China market from California.

Hardy New England whalers, battered by the gales of the North Pacific, were grateful to find protected West Coast ports in which they could repair both their ships and spirits. Richardson's Bay, near today's San Francisco, was an early rendezvous for whaling vessels. There they took aboard longed-for fresh meat, fruit, grains, and other provisions for the long homeward voyage around the Horn. These ships carried manufactured goods to exchange either for coins or local products. Out of their sea chests came needles, stockings, thread, and bolts of cloth. At Monterey, whalers from Nantucket and New Bedford left behind a permanent souvenir of their stay—a whalebone sidewalk—as a token of appreciation for the shelter the town had afforded them. They, furthermore, carried home to chilly New England repeated glowing accounts of pastoral California. These further popularized the province.

The Russians also continued to arrive in California, not with sword in hand, but, like their American competitors, as traders. In the 1740s, Vitus Bering had prepared groundwork for the Russian-American Fur Company in Alaska. Since then that company had accumulated valuable caches of furs at their trading station in Sitka. But the harsh Alaskan climate and barrenness of the country made agriculture in the vicinity virtually impossible. And the abundance of sea otters in California waters proved profitable enough to risk confrontation with Spanish local officials.

In 1805, Nikolai Petrovich Rezanov, a chamberlain of the czar, was sent out to inspect the Russian colonies in the North Pacific. At Sitka he found emaciated settlers reduced to eating crows. As Russian supply ships had faltered in caring for the colony, Rezanov decided to go to California in search of supplies. His party was courteously received at San Francisco, but a novel element was injected into the negotiations between the Russians and the Spaniards: the Russian envoy fell in love with Concepción Argüello, the beautiful and willing fifteen-year-old daughter of the comandante of the port. Rezanov, suddenly a prospective family member, had little trouble persuading Comandante Argüello to furnish supplies for the starving Sitka colony.

Rezanov's ship, the *Juno*, was also loaded up with wheat, barley, peas, beans, tallow, and dried meat. On May 8, 1806, he sailed away, ostensibly to gain permission to marry, promising to return to San Francisco to claim his bride. Rezanov, however, never came back to California. Only in 1850, after endless years of waiting, did Señorita Argüello, who had become a nun, finally learn of Rezanov's death in Siberia.

Meanwhile, in 1809, another officer of the Russian-American Fur Company, Ivan Kuskov, arrived in California from Alaska. He had been ordered to select a site for a southern outpost. In 1812 Kuskov returned, this time with equipment to set up a trading station and with Aleut natives who had been contracted to fish and hunt for the community. The Aleuts were paid with a part of this catch. Meanwhile Kuskov made no pretense of consulting California officials; he simply chose a strategic shoreline site, eighteen miles north of Bodega Bay. There he built a sturdy rectangular fort, surrounded by a palisade with its corners pierced for artillery. Inside the stockade a wooden house of six or eight rooms, furnished with carpets, a piano, and boasting glass windows, was constructed for the officers. Granaries, workshops, and huts for the Aleuts were located outside the stockade. The Russians also erected a wharf, a tannery, and a bath house. They named this place "Ross," a derivation from the word "Russia." Because of its fortifications, it became known as Fort Ross.

During 1812–1813, while Kuskov was building Fort Ross, the Spanish officer Gabriel Moraga arrived there to investigate Russian activities. Moraga reported that the Russians seriously needed food. In January of 1813 he returned with three horses, twenty head of cattle, several *fanegas* (a Spanish unit of measure) of wheat, and with permission from Governor Arrillaga to trade with Fort Ross.

Although New Spain's viceroy at Mexico City later ordered Kuskov to remove his settlement, Arrillaga's weak garrisons were in no position to enforce the viceroy's order. The Russians, therefore, continued to tan hides, fire bricks and tiles, to construct barrels and kegs, and to make rope from hemp. They also built and launched four small wooden vessels and even managed to raise delicate plants in a glass hothouse. Indeed, the flowers they planted around the outpost gave the place a false look of permanence.

The population of foggy Fort Ross was never larger than one hundred to four hundred persons, including Aleuts and their wives. Before long the Russians cleared most of the sea otters out of the coastal waters between Trinidad and San Francisco bays. From 1812 to 1840 they also maintained a hunting and fishing post at the Farallones Islands.

The Russians were also active explorers. During the years between 1808 and 1821, with Spain's colonies in rebellion, Otto von Kotzebue, a Russian sailor-scientist, made two visits to Alta California. On his maps the interior area between the Coast Ranges and the Sierra Nevada, was termed *tierra incognita*, or unknown and hardly inviting land.

Except for Anza, who had crossed the desert diagonally from southeast to northwest, few had even seen California's great Central Valley. Only Father Garcés had ventured into the southern Sierra, near Lake Tulare in today's Kern county. Furthermore, the exposed interior was inhabited by Indians who were far more aggressive than the missionized natives.

After 1806, Lieutenant Gabriel Moraga took part in forty-six inland campaigns against hostile natives. His *entradas* into the interior can be traced by the names he bestowed upon several rivers. The Kings River was named by Moraga, as were the Merced River and Mariposa Creek. He called the Feather River *El Río de las Plumas* (the river of the feathers) because of the multitude of wildfowl feathers that he observed floating on its waters. The county through which the river flows retained the name Plumas, while that of the stream itself has been translated into the English word, Feather.

After the departure of Governor Solá, Spanish officials like Moraga would no longer control either the interior or the settled portions of California. The remote province would, instead, be governed by the officials of Spain's rebellious colony, Mexico.

Selected Readings

Regarding Spanish exploration see Donald Cutter and Iris Engstrand, *Quest for Empire: Spanish Settlement in the Southwest* (1996); also Theodore Treutlein, *San Francisco Bay, Discovery and Colonization, 1769–1776* (1968); Francisco Antonio Maurelle, *Journal of a Voyage in 1775 . . .* (1781); *Journal of José Longinos Martínez . . . 1791–92,* Lesley Byrd Simpson, trans. and ed., (1961); *Henry R. Wagner, The Last Spanish Exploration of the Northwest Coast* (1931).

English explorations are in George Vancouver, *A Voyage of Discovery to the North Pacific Ocean and Round the World* (3 vols., 1798); Marguerite Eyer Wilbur, ed., *Vancouver in California, 1792–1794* (1953); George Godwin, *Vancouver: A Life, 1757–1798* (1930) and G. H. Anderson, *Vancouver and His Great Voyage* (1923).

Regarding the La Pérouse expedition of 1786 see Gilbert Chinard, ed., *Le Voyage de Lapérouse sur les Côtes de L'Alaska et de la Californie* (1937). The Malaspina expedition is in an article by Edith C. Galbraith, *California Historical Society Quarterly* 3 (October 1924), 215–37 and Donald Cutter, *Malaspina in California* (1960).

The *Lelia Byrd* episode is in Lindley Bynum, ed., *Journal of a Voyage Between China and the North-western coast of America made in 1804 by William Shaler* (1935); Roy F. Nichols, *Advance Agents of American Destiny* (1956); Andrew Rolle, "The Eagle Is Seized," *Westways* 46 (December 1954), 16–17.

Regarding the sea otter commerce see Adele Ogden, *The California Sea Otter Trade, 1784–1848* (repr. 1975) and Ogden's "New England Traders in Spanish and Mexican California," *Greater America: Essays in Honor of*

Herbert Eugene Bolton (1945), 395–415. Consult also William Henry Ellison, ed., *Life and Adventures of George Nidever* (1937) and Magdalen Coughlin, "Boston Smugglers on the Coast (1797-1821)," *California Historical Society Quarterly* 46 (June 1967), 99–120.

Russian contact with California is in Raymond H. Fisher, *Bering's Voyages* (1977); T. C. Russell, ed., *The Rezanov Voyage to Nueva California in 1806* (1926), and Russell's *Langsdorff's Narrative of the Rezanov Voyage to Nueva California in 1806* (1927); Hector Chevigny, *Lost Empire: The Life and Adventures of Nicolai Petrovich Rezanov* (1937); Otto von Kotzebue, *A Voyage of Discovery in the South Sea* (3 vols., 1821); S. B. Okun, *The Russian-American Company* (1951).

Regarding Moraga and interior exploration see Donald Cutter, ed., *Diary of Ensign Gabriel Moraga's Expedition of Discovery in the Sacramento Valley* (1957); S. F. Cook, *Colonial Expeditions to the Interior of California's Central Valley* (1960), and *Cook's Expedition to the Interior of California's Central Valley, 1820–1840* (1962).

Arcadia

//////////CHAPTER 8

That distant province which the ancient Greeks called Arcadia was a land isolated from the rest of the world. Its inhabitants led a proverbially happy and natural life. Was California such a place?

Spain's paternal government tried to send supply ships until the Californians could become self-supporting. But her empire's lines of communication were stretched too thin. As a result, its colonials became increasingly self-reliant.

Fortunately for the Californios, they enjoyed abundant pastureland and fresh water in addition to a ready supply of native labor. Ranching conditions were almost perfect. The climate was mild enough to permit animals to live throughout the year with little shelter, and *rancheros* did not generally fence in their stock. Neighbors were trusted amid a pastoral way of life that had been inherited from the Spanish homeland.

The small band of 200 cattle brought to California by Gaspar de Portolá's expedition, and the few that survived the overland trek with Anza's party, provided the original stock from which local herds developed. These eventually yielded hides and tallow in abundance for export.

No phase of California's history had more far-reaching consequences than the large land grants made during the Spanish and Mexican eras. Today's land titles are grounded upon these grants, once regarded as the very origin of local wealth. Many grants are still known by their original names, for example, *El Toro* (the bull), *Los Laureles* (the laurels), and *La Sagrada Familia* (the Holy Family).

In 1784 Governor Fages was empowered to make individual grants not to exceed three square leagues. He and his successors ceded less than thirty of these during the Spanish period. But, after the establishment of the Mexican Republic in 1821, the number of land grants increased. By 1830 there were some fifty private ranchos in California. Any Mexican of good character, or any foreigner willing to become naturalized and to accept the Catholic faith, might petition for as much as eleven square leagues, or nearly 50,000 acres. A square league comprised a little more than 4,438 acres. In modern California this would constitute a large ranch. A rancho of four or five leagues was, however, then considered small.

The blossoming of the rancho era occurred during the thirteen years between secularization of the California missions by the Mexican government in 1833 and occupation of the province by the Americans. As late as 1848, the entire white population of the province was estimated at only 14,000, divided nearly equally between Californios and foreigners.

Rancho boundaries were loosely defined by such landmarks as a hilltop, a clump of cacti, a stream bed, or the whitened skull of a steer. Beginning at a point marked by a pile of stones, called a *mojonera,* a horseman measured a tract with a fifty-foot-long *reata* (or lariat) trailing behind him. The actual quantity of land comprising many estates was, therefore, rather vague, with a phrase used in Latino cultures, *poco mas ó menos* (a little more or less), appearing in many land title documents. This would cause protracted litigation in the American era.

Family fortunes were founded on huge ranchos. For example, Francisco Pacheco owned the Ranchos San Felipe, San Luís Gonzaga, and other properties totaling 125,740 acres. The two ranchos alone contained 14,000 head of cattle, 500 horses, and 15,000 sheep. David Spence, a Scot who married into the Estrada family, counted 25,000 acres in the Buena Esperanza rancho, with 4,000 head of cattle. Henry Delano Fitch of Massachusetts held the Rancho Sotoyome of eleven leagues, with 14,000 cattle, 1,000 stallions and mares, and 10,000 sheep. Another American, Abel Stearns, owned thousands of acres on which grazed 30,000 cattle, 2,000 horses and mules, and 10,000 sheep. The Swiss settler Johann Augustus Sutter eventually operated eleven leagues of land, extending sixty miles in length. The sites now occupied by Oakland, Alameda, and Berkeley form only a part of what was once the Rancho San Antonio, the property of Don Luís Peralta; his lands furnished pasture for 8,000 head of cattle and 2,000 horses. More than a thousand ranchos were stocked with an average of 1,500 head of cattle during the Mexican era.

Cattle were the mainstay of the economy. Leather hides provided harnesses, saddles, shoes, even door hinges; cattle horns were used for protection atop adobe walls as well as to make shoe buttons. Tallow went into molding candles, a vital undertaking in an age before kerosene lamps or electric lights. Hides and tallow became the main items of exchange. Little cash was exchanged. The Californios obtained much of their clothing and other necessities by bartering hides with foreign vessels. The term "California bank note," a dried steer hide, had a value of approximately one dollar.

Native herders, despite previous lack of experience with stock animals, seemed to take naturally to handling horses and cattle. And *vaqueros,* or "cowboys," were required in large numbers. Some ranches employed over a hundred native laborers, under the direction of a *mayordomo* who himself might be an Indian. In the absence of fences, stock became so wild that it was unsafe to venture among herds on foot or unarmed; also any rider of the range might need to defend himself against ferocious grizzlies, then found near the mountains. Also indispensable in herding cattle were the rancho's horses. A horse could usually be bought for three dollars—less than the cost of a saddle and bridle.

During drought years, ranch hands had to "cut out" less desirable stock. Like cattle, horses too sometimes ran wild. When they overmultiplied to the point that local pasture could not support them, some were driven over precipices into the sea. The *rodéo* (or roundup) was the principal means of separating and branding stock. The rodéo was conducted under a *juez de campo,* or field judge, who settled disputes over the ownership of individual animals. Rancheros also held bloody *matanzas,* or cattle slaughterings. Riding at full speed through the herds, the skillful vaqueros killed the animals with one cut of a knife directed at a vital part of the neck. Next, skinners stripped off the hides and cut the meat into strips for drying. The tallow was melted and poured into bags made of hides, to be delivered to trading ships by floating them out to the offshore vessels.

The artist Titian Ramsay Peale, who traveled to California in 1841, noted that the hills and valleys of the province were dotted with carcasses. So many bleached and brittle bones lay underfoot that Peale was struck by the constant crushing of bones under the hoofs of his horse.

No widespread planting of crops occurred on the ranchos. But at the missions, where oranges and grapevines were first raised in the province, agriculture was well organized. At Mission San José the padres harvested a tract of wheat a mile square. Nonetheless, their farming implements were crude. The natives scratched the ground with a wooden plow, perhaps fashioned from the crooked limb of a tree. Grain was cut with hand sickles and bound in sheaves.

For threshing, a circular piece of ground was fenced in and its surface watered and pounded until, after drying, the soil became very hard. The wheat was then thrown into the enclosure and mules were driven around and around until the grain was trampled out. Next came winnowing by tossing the wheat in baskets against the wind. At first grinding was performed by hand with stone mortars and pestles, but eventually the padres constructed water-driven grist mills. In time the most common method of grinding was by the *arrastra*, two circular millstones, one on top of the other. The lower stone remained stationary, while the upper stone rotated when the cross beam attached to it was dragged in a circle by a mule. The grain between the stones was crushed, a process used in Spain for centuries.

The Californios never held sheep in the same esteem as they did cattle; nevertheless, each mission and most ranchos raised small flocks for mutton and wool. The wool was coarse and wiry, but strong, and was woven into cloth and blankets. Hogs were raised mainly for their lard, which was mixed with ashes in soap making.

Life on the ranchos was carried on within a simple, patriarchal system. The rancho family was a self-sustained unit. The ranchero was the unquestioned master, obeyed by his family and native retainers. Arising long before dawn to partake of a breakfast of bread and chocolate, the ranchero then mounted his horse and was off on the daily round of his herds.

A strong bond linked parents and children on the frontier, although the family observed strict discipline. A father could administer corporal punishment to sons as old as sixty, and no son dared smoke in his father's presence. Dances were begun by elders, while young people stood by and awaited their turn.

Rancho life was a blend of abundance and barrenness. Supplies of clothing and other manufactured articles were always insufficient. But the ranchero and his family had inherited austerity from their Spanish ancestors. When women could not get shoes, silk stockings, and other articles of clothing, including *rebozos* or *mantillas*, they learned to do without.

The hunting of grizzly bears, elk, and other game was popular. There were also *meriendas*, or picnics, to which rancheros rode their best horses, while the women and children might arrive in two-wheeled *carretas* pulled by oxen. The meriendas featured *carne asada* (roasted beef), barbecued on spits over a bed of glistening coals, as well as roasted chickens, turkeys, *enchiladas*, or *tamales*. The native women pounded corn in *metates*, or stone mortars, to make *tortillas*.

It was a rare evening when there were no guests to join a ranching family in dancing the *jarabe* or *fandango*. The hospitality of the ranchero was often a point of pride and dispensed generously. For example, a host might leave coins in a dish on a table in order to save an indigent visitor the embarrassment of asking for money before departing. A traveler who arrived with an exhausted horse often found a fresh one ready in the morning, saddled up for his use.

Schooling in the province was limited. Among the teachers were discharged soldiers whose only qualification was some knowledge of reading, writing, and "figuring." During the Mexican period the best-known teacher was William E. P. Hartnell, an English trader with a knowledge of half a dozen languages who had settled near Salinas.

Theft, murder, and other crimes were rare in provincial California. Visiting sea captains would sometimes sell goods to rancheros along the coast on credit and return months later to receive their promised pay in hides and tallow. Banditry, however, grew after the beginning of the American era in 1846. The noted bandit Joaquín Murieta ascribed his criminal career to the brutal treatment he had received at the hands of American miners.

The padres did much to stabilize provincial life. Baptisms, confirmations, marriages, and other vital ceremonies were, of course, performed at the missions. The missions also served as a hospice for wayfarers, who could always count on a night's lodging. Mission accommodations were of the barest sort—usually consisting of a bed of rawhide, scratchy flaxen sheets, and simple meals. But on a stormy night, as the wind whipped across the mission's tile roofs, the weary traveler was thankful for the fragrant pine logs burning in their fireplace grates.

Modern California retains many cultural reminders of its pastoral era. Rivers, mountains, and towns are still known by names that originated with the founding Spaniards. In addition to rancho and rodéo, other words that grew out of the state's Spanish heritage include *adobe,* or sun-dried brick; *arroyo,* a creek or its dry bed; *cañada,* a deep valley; *cañón,* a narrow passage between high banks; *chaparral,* a thicket of brambly bushes; *corral,* an enclosure for livestock; *embarcadero,* a landing place; *fiesta,* a celebration; *placer,* where gold is found in the loose earth; *plaza,* an open square in a town; *pueblo,* a chartered town; *sierra,* literally a saw, but applied to a saw-tooth mountains; *tule,* a water reed, and *vaquero,* or cowboy.

The prefixes San and Santa, the masculine and feminine forms of the word "Saint," were used to name missions which, in turn, bestowed their names on counties, including San Diego, San Luis Obispo, and Santa Clara. Other counties, like Merced and Sacramento, took the names of their principal streams. Among these is Kings County (from *El Río de los Santos Reyes,* or river of the Holy Kings). The Merced River was first called *El Río de Nuestra Señora de la Merced* (the river of Our

Lady of Mercy) by Gabriel Moraga's exploring party of 1806, after an exhausting march through inhospitable country. Moraga also named Mariposa Creek after the butterflies found on its banks and the Sacramento River after the Holy Sacrament.

Fresno (ash) County was named after the abundance of ash trees in the region, and Madera (timber) County after the forests that covered its valleys. The bay of Monterey was named to honor Viceroy Gaspar de Zúñiga y Acevedo, Count of Monterey. Mendocino was named after Antonio de Mendoza, first viceroy of New Spain. Some towns and cities bear the names of such prominent early Californians as the Martinez's. Vacaville commemorates the Vaca family. Alviso bears the name of one of Anza's colonists; Benicia that of the wife of General Mariano Vallejo while the town of Vallejo honors the general himself.

An Alvarado Street, named after a Mexican governor, can be found in both Monterey and Los Angeles. One of the main streets of the latter city, Figueroa, honors yet another governor, and dozens of Los Angeles street names commemorate the past—among them Pico, San Pedro, Aliso, and Sepulveda. In San Francisco, there is a Junípero Serra Boulevard, as well as streets named Noriega, Pacheco, Ortega, Rivera, Taraval, Ulloa, Guerrero, Valencia, and Palou. Oakland has two main avenues with Spanish names—Alcatraz (pelican) and San Pablo (Saint Paul).

Place names and architecture, however, are not the only reminders of California's Hispanic past. The Anglo cowboy inherited his know-how, horse, outfit (including reata, spurs, and chaps), lasso, and lingo largely from the Spanish. California's legal system retains Spanish provisions concerning mining, water rights, trespass regulations, tribunals of conciliation, and the property rights of women.

Pageants and plays that commemorate the Spanish past include the Mission Play of San Gabriel, the Portolá Festival of San Francisco, the "De Anza Days" celebration at Riverside, and a yearly "Spanish" fiesta at Santa Barbara. Finally, there has been persistent exploitation (often inaccurate) of California's Hispanic past by genealogists, artists, architects, promoters of tourism, and even historical societies.

Selected Readings

Sources regarding Hispanic folkways include William Heath Davis, *Seventy-Five Years in California* (1929); Andrew Rolle, *An American in California: The Biography of William Heath Davis* (1956); Richard Henry Dana, *Two Years Before the Mast* (1840); Richard J. Cleveland, *Narrative of Voyages and Commercial Enterprises* (2 vols., 1842); Samuel Shapiro, *Richard Henry Dana Jr., 1815–1882* (1961). Later romanticized accounts include Nellie

Van de Grift Sánchez, *Spanish Arcadia* (1929); Gertrude Atherton, *Before the Gringo Came* (1894) and Charles F. Lummis, *The Spanish Pioneers* (1893).

Other appraisals include Hubert Howe Bancroft's *California Pastoral* (1888); Alberta J. Denis, *Spanish Alta California* (1927); Susanna Bryant Dakin, *A Scotch Paisano: Hugo Reid's Life in California* (1939) and Dakin, *The Lives of William Hartnell* (1949); George D. Lyman, *The Scalpel Under Three Flags in California* (1925); *The Blond Ranchero: Memories of Juan Francisco Dana*, as told to Rocky and Marie Harrington (1960).

For more on place names see Raymund F. Wood, "Anglo Influence on Spanish Place Names in California," *Southern California Quarterly* 58 (Winter 1981), 392–413.

Mexican California

//////// CHAPTER 9

After three centuries of dominance by the homeland, the Spanish colonies in the New World grew restive. Discontent kindled the flame of revolution, which spread from province to province between 1808 and the mid-1820s. Almost to the last, California remained loyal. This was partly because little news reached provincial California of revolutionary activities in Mexico and elsewhere in Latin America. An aristocrat, Governor Solá, looked upon revolutionary activities south of his capital at Monterey as the work of misguided fanatics. Although opposed to independence, Solá was interested in the welfare of California and skillful in managing its affairs.

The first significant manifestation of discontent in California occurred when, after 1808, ships from San Blas failed to arrive in sufficient number to supply the populace. Revolutionary attacks against Spanish ships aggravated the situation, so that fewer and fewer relief vessels were able to visit California ports. Along with the American trading ships that helped fill the gap, a number of privateers began to appear in the Pacific, some fitted out in the United States; these roamed the high seas, threatening the shoreline of Spain's colonies. Also, news of the blockade of the South American Pacific colonial ports of Valparaíso, Callao, and Guayaquil by revolutionists and privateers so worried Solá that he ordered a stricter watch along the shore for suspicious vessels. Although Californians made complaints against the viceroy in Mexico City for his failure to send supplies to the settlers and back pay to the soldiers, they had no initial thought of resisting his authority or that of Governor Solá. They were more concerned with pirates, still a menace to Spain's shipping lanes.

In November 1818, two mysterious ships were sighted by a sentinel at Point Pinos, near Monterey. The larger of the two vessels, the *Argentina*, was commanded by a Frenchman, Hippolyte de Bouchard, who had served in the patriot navy of the new "Republic of Buenos Aires." He was a big and brutal captain of fiery temper, who exercised an iron rule over his men. The other vessel, smaller in size, was the *Santa Rosa*, under the command of an English soldier of fortune named Peter Corney, who had fallen in with Bouchard in Hawaii where Bouchard was trading gold chalices and silver crucifixes he had looted from churches throughout Latin America. Bouchard's crews were a motley lot of some 350 cutthroats, thieves, and revolutionists; among them were Malays, Portuguese, Spaniards, Englishmen, and Australians—all aiming to profit from the unraveling of the Spanish empire.

The *Santa Rosa* dropped anchor in front of the presidio of Monterey and opened fire. Captain Corney and his crew, expecting little resistance from the dilapidated fort, were surprised at the brisk return of cannon balls from a battery hastily established on the beach by the presidio's forty soldiers. At this point Bouchard moved in with the *Argentina* and sent ashore, under a flag of truce, a demand for the immediate surrender of Monterey.

Bouchard received a defiant reply from Governor Solá, although the Californians had little means of resisting. The pirate landed several hundred men and a number of field pieces near Point Pinos. Greatly outnumbered, Solá retreated, with a supply of munitions and the provincial archives, to the Rancho del Rey, near the present site of Salinas. At Monterey many townspeople fled. Some took refuge at Missions San Antonio and San Juan Bautista. In the meantime, the invaders sacked and burned both the presidio and town of Monterey. Few buildings escaped. Even mission orchards and gardens were destroyed.

Concerning the conduct of his crew during this pillage, Corney later wrote, "The Sandwich Islanders, who were quite naked when they landed, were soon dressed in the Spanish fashion; and all the sailors were employed in searching the houses for money and breaking and ruining everything." Something over a week was spent by the attackers in burying their dead, caring for their wounded, and repairing the *Santa Rosa*. They also made efforts to win over to their cause those of the inhabitants who had the courage to remain in the pueblo; but such propaganda, ostensibly promoting the cause of liberty, failed to impress the Californians whose homes had been despoiled.

After replenishing their larders, the *Argentina* and the *Santa Rosa* set sail, and Governor Solá returned to Monterey. The privateers next moved down the coast, stopping at points on the way to burn and pillage. Rancho del Refugio was burned in revenge for the loss of three pirates who were lassoed and ignominiously dragged off by a party of local vaqueros. San Juan Capistrano was one of the places sacked and robbed of its store of wines and spirits, much of which immediately went down the throats of the pillagers. After taking two native girls aboard, the pirates sailed south from that mission, and California was finally relieved of their presence.

This attack by Bouchard constitutes California's only contact with outside revolutionists during the wars of independence. Once Bouchard left the province, life in California resumed its calmness; not long afterwards, events of great importance to the New World occurred in Mexico. In February 1821, Agustin Iturbide, a colonel in the royal army in Mexico City, suddenly defected to the insurgent cause, raised a revolutionary flag, and made New Spain, thereafter always to be called Mexico, independent.

When news reached California of the seizure of political control in Mexico, it was at first received with disbelief. In April 1822, however, Governor Solá convened a *junta,* or caucus, consisting of officers from the presidios and padres from the missions and swore allegiance to the new government. Former royal officials and some of the padres took an oath to Iturbide without hesitation, although the friars sensed that a nonroyal government in Mexico would lead to the decline of the mission system. The Californians had to face the fact that a new government was in actual control at Mexico City.

The California junta chose Solá as its delegate to the new Mexican *Cortés,* or congress. Before the governor could even leave for Mexico City, however, an official arrived at Monterey from that capital to preside over the transfer of authority from Spain to Mexico. Aware of some Californian's royalist sympathies, this agent of the new regime arrived in a ship that flew a green, white, and red flag from its masthead. The eagle in the flag's center, the symbol of Mexico, indicated to those residents who lined the Monterey docks to receive the agent that Governor Solá's control over California had clearly ended.

Succeeding Governor Solá was Luís Antonio Argüello, a native Californian who had served as comandante at San Francisco. Argüello announced that the decrees of the Mexican government would be accepted and the title "nacional" would be substituted for "imperial" in all documents; public and private letters were thereafter to be signed with the words "God and Liberty," and the old title "Don" was to give way to "Ciudadano," or Citizen.

California, far from the vortex of the revolutionary struggle, luckily received independence from Spain without blood-letting. Yet the province did not escape personal rivalries. Scarcely a governor during the Mexican period would serve his term without local outbreaks against him.

Governor Argüello, who came from northern California, had been favored by northerners over a prominent southerner, José de la Guerra. This began a rift between northern and southern California which has continued into the present. Argüello established his own *diputación*, or junta. Because of a severe money problem, local crops as well as branded cattle were to be taxed as never before. The padres protested that crops raised by the missions were untaxable, but these establishments encountered increased surveillance. While no direct steps toward mission secularization occurred under Argüello, missionary power was nearing its end.

During Argüello's governorship, still more foreign traders and settlers arrived. He had been personally friendly with the Russians since the days when Rezanov had courted his daughter, Concepción. The Russians had long desired to enter into a partnership for sea otter hunting and trading with the Californians. Now Governor Argüello signed a contract with Fort Ross that furnished him with his own contingent of Aleut hunters, who in return were to be fed and supplied by the Californians.

As the governor also was forced increasingly to condone foreign trading, the padres signed an agreement with McCulloch and Hartnell, a subsidiary of the English firm of John Begg and Company, today purveyors of Scotch whiskey. Its representatives, Hugh McCulloch and William E. P. Hartnell, arrived from Lima in 1822. They were allowed to bring one cargo a year to the province and take out all the hides the missions had to offer at the price of one dollar apiece, as well as suet, lard, tallow, wheat, wine, furs, and pickled beef.

Soon dozens of "warm-water Yankee" traders reaped rewards from the marketing of their all-year stock of goods. Some roving traders became local residents—including Nathan Spear, William Heath Davis, Jr., John R. Cooper and Alfred Robinson—who distributed their merchandise on land as well as from aboard ships. Ship captains eventually were allowed to load and unload their vessels at designated collecting points, rather than engaging in smuggling at secret landfalls.

One Boston firm, Bryant, Sturgis & Company, maintained a chain of ships plying the sea lanes between California, Hawaii, and China. They imported hundreds of thousands of hides for New England's shoe industry. Other Boston shippers included Marshall & Wildes as well as William Appleton & Company. Their vessels carried hundreds of commodities, from silk stockings to tobacco. The crews of these floating commissaries processed great quantities of hides purchased from interior ranchos. First the skins were soaked in sea water, then stretched on the ground and pegged fast with wooden stakes. When they were dry the hides were sprinkled with salt and scraped. Floated out to ships beyond the surf, these hides were accompanied by large cowhide bags filled with tallow.

Some foreign traders married "daughters of the country," and founded families in California. One of them, John R. Cooper, arrived in 1823 as captain of the American ship *Rover* and settled at Monterey. With Cooper came Daniel Hill and Thomas Robbins of Massachusetts, who decided to make their homes at Santa Barbara. At Yerba Buena, William A. Richardson married the daughter of the comandante, was baptized in the Catholic Church, and became a developer of San Francisco. A generation of these pre-pioneer foreigners, thus, established close relations with the Californios long before the first overland parties of Anglos crossed the Great Plains.

Mexican California was generally a safe place in which to live. Eventually, however, its native inhabitants learned how to use forbidden firearms. In February of 1824, revolts started among the neophytes of Missions Purísima Concepción, Santa Inés, and Santa Barbara. Soldiers at Santa Inés, who were attacked without warning, faced well-armed assailants who set fire to mission buildings. At La Purísima, after seven natives and four whites had been killed in an Indian uprising, its guards were compelled to surrender. The natives kept possession of the mission for nearly a month, erecting fortifications, cutting loopholes in the church walls, mounting two rusty cannon, and warding off attackers with guns as well as bows and arrows. But inexperience in handling both guns and powder quickly brought about their defeat when they were attacked by Lieutenant José Mariano Estrada and a force of 100 men. At Santa Barbara, unfriendly Indians also entrenched themselves in the mission buildings. Comandante de la Guerra attacked them there, and after a fight of several hours the natives fled to the hills, taking with them all the property they could carry. Succeeding expeditions were required to quell the revolt. In mid-1825, Governor Argüello reported to the Mexican government regarding the miserable state of the Indians, calling attention to the injustice of keeping them any longer in virtual slavery.

Under Argüello the change to Mexican rule had been quietly accepted by the Californians, and a beginning was made at representative government. Sleepy California had, somehow, managed to substitute the paternalistic and conservative regime of Spain for the unsettled sovereignty of Mexico. As a result, subsequent governmental instability would lead to further factional fights.

José María Echeandía, Argüello's successor, was a tall, thin, juiceless man, possessing seemingly little force of character. But he was much concerned about the effect of the California climate upon his not too robust health. At first Echeandía so feared the foggy weather at Monterey that he came no farther into California than San Diego. Echeandía claimed that Alta California's most southern town was more centrally located for transacting the business of the two provinces. Nothing in his instructions required this hypochondriac to live at Monterey, so he was acting within his rights in conducting California affairs from the city of his choice. Though no formal transfer of the capital was made, southerners were delighted by Echeandía's residence at San Diego. As the jealousy between north and south gained momentum, however, the new governor started out handicapped by unpopularity in northern California. A rivalry between Echeandía, who was a bachelor, and a young American sea captain, Henry Delano Fitch, for the hand of Señorita Josefa Carrillo of San Diego suggests that a romantic motive as well as reasons of health had something to do with the new governor's decision to stay in the south.

A more pressing question facing Echeandía concerned providing supplies for the unpaid soldiers and their families. The new governor also faced two northern rivals. Expressing the discontent of the frustrated soldiers and the suspicious padres, Joaquín Solís and José María Herrera issued a *pronunciamiento* accusing the governor of tyrannical behavior toward the populace. In 1828, Solís and Herrera led a local revolt against him that began at Monterey and which extended as far south as Santa Barbara. But both men were arrested and shipped off to San Blas. So ended the first abortive uprising against Mexico's authority in the province.

The Mexican government's sending of over one hundred convicts to California had much to do with local antagonism against the unlucky Governor Echeandía. Then, in 1829, he faced another Indian revolt, this one under Chief Estanislao, a former alcalde of San José. Estanislao and a band of angry renegades fortified themselves in a camp in the dense woods, from which they sent out defiant challenges. That summer, forty of Echeandía's soldiers, armed with muskets and a swivel gun, engaged these native rebels. The Indians killed two of the soldiers and wounded eight others. The rest were forced to abandon the siege when their ammunition ran out and the heat became insufferable. Because he feared that the uprising might become widespread, Echeandía then sent in cavalry and artillery under Mariano Vallejo. After the soldiers burnt down the Rebels' cover, Estanislao took refuge with Father Narciso Durán, president of the missions, who concealed him until a pardon could be obtained.

But Echeandía's troubles were far from over. During his governorship other foreign expeditions arrived. On November 6, 1826, the British ship *Blossom* sailed into San Francisco Bay under the command of Captain F. W. Beechey. He, like Vancouver, was struck by the contrast between the natural beauty of the country and Mexico's neglect of its residents.

In January 1827 another visitor arrived in California waters: Auguste Bernard du Haut-Cilly, in command of the French ship *Le Héros*. A close observer and entertaining writer, this Frenchman was accompanied by Dr. Paolo Emilio Botta, a prominent Italian archaeologist. Like almost all of such foreign visitors to California, Du Haut-Cilly was critical of the both the government and the powerful missionaries.

At this point the new nation of Mexico desired to convert the missions into civic pueblos, but secularization had to be approached cautiously. The friars were the only ones who could induce the neophytes to work. If these padres should ever leave, California would suddenly be at a loss for labor and exposed to even more raids by increasingly hostile natives. The "missionized" Indians were not generally a threat, however. Knowing this, on January 6, 1831, Governor Echeandía partially secularized some of the missions, which were to become pueblos. As the friars were henceforth reduced to the role of curates, their power suffered a major dilution. Church and state no longer ruled California together. From now on civic leaders would dominate political affairs in the province.

Selected Readings

On the Bouchard raid see Peter Corney, *Voyages in the Northern Pacific* (1896); Lewis W. Bealer, "Bouchard in the Islands of the Pacific," *Pacific Historical Review* 4 (August 1935), 328–42.

For the transition from Spanish to Mexican control, consult George P. Hammond, ed., *The Larkin Papers* (10 vols., 1951–66); George L. Harding, *Don Agustín V. Zamorano: Statesman, Soldier, Craftsman, and California's First Printer* (1934); Terry E. Stephenson, *Don Bernardo Yorba* (1941) and Robert G. Cleland, *The Place Called Sespe* (repr. 1957).

Regarding early Americans see Robert Ryal Miller, *Captain Richardson: Mariner, Ranchero, and Founder of San Francisco* (1995); Reuben L. Underhill, *From Cowhides to Golden Fleece* (repr. 1946); Harlan Hague and David Langum, *Thomas Oliver Larkin: A Life of Patriotism and Profit* (1990); Adele Ogden, "Alfred Robinson, New England Merchant in Mexican California," *California Historical Society Quarterly* 23 (September 1944), 193–218 and Ogden's "Hides and Tallow: McCulloch, Hartnell and Company, 1822–1828," *California Historical Society Quarterly* 6 (September 1927), 254–64.

See also David J. Langum, *Law and Community on the Mexican California Frontier* (1987); Antonio Ríos Bustamante and Pedro Castillo, *An Illustrated History of Mexican Los Angeles, 1781–1985* (1986); Marion L. Lathrop,

"The Indian Campaigns of General M. G. Vallejo," *Society of California Pioneers Quarterly* 9 (September 1932), 161–205 and Albert Hurtado, *Indian Survival on the California Frontier* (1988).

Regarding Beechey and Du Haut-Cilly see Frederick W. Beechey, *Narrative of a Voyage to the Pacific and Bering's Strait* (2 vols., 1831); *Auguste Bernard du Haut-Cilly, Voyage autour du Monde . . .* (2 vols., 1934); Charles F. Carter, ed., "Duhaut-Chilly's [sic] Account of California in the Years 1827–28," *California Historical Society Quarterly* 8 (June–September 1929), 131–66, 306–36.

Family life is the subject of Gloria Miranda, "Hispano-Mexican Childrearing Practices in Pre-American Santa Barbara," *Southern California Quarterly* 65 (Winter 1983), 307–20 and Miranda, "Racial and Cultural Dimensions in Gente de Razón Status in Spanish and Mexican California," *Southern California Quarterly* 70 (Fall 1988), 265–78.

Infiltration
and Revolt

//////// **CHAPTER 10**

Among California's foreign visitors were a hardy band of American fur trappers—"mountain men"—unafraid of forbidding deserts, wild animals, rugged mountains, and swollen streams.

During Echeandía's governorship Jedediah Strong Smith, one of these young trappers, blazed the initial overland trail into southern California. Smith, at the head of a small group, was in search of beaver and river otter pelts. The southwestward trek of this "Knight in Buckskin" has kindled the imagination of historians because of the courage Smith displayed in withstanding Indian attacks, severe shortages of food and water, and many other wilderness dangers. On one occasion a ferocious grizzly bear attacked him, taking Smith's head between its jaws and leaving an ear and part of the scalp hanging from his bleeding skull. After one of Smith's men stitched up the lacerated trapper with needle and thread, he was on his way again.

On August 22, 1826, Smith, who had initially gone west from St. Louis, led a trapping expedition of fifteen to twenty men and fifty horses out of Bear River Valley, in today's Utah. This departure signaled the beginning of an extensive penetration of the region between the Great Salt Lake and the Pacific shoreline by way of unexplored deserts. The party moved along the banks of the Sevier River southwestward toward the Virgin River, continued onward to the Colorado River, and then to the desolate Mohave villages. Venturing across alkali wastes, Smith, at the age of twenty-eight, became the first Caucasian to reach California overland from the eastern United States.

On November 27, 1826, he and his bedraggled men reached luxuriant Mission San Gabriel. In exchange for food, wine, and lodging, the trappers provided the friars, astonished to behold such strange-looking visitors, with bear traps with which to catch Indians who poached oranges from mission groves.While his men stayed behind with the padres, Smith rode to San Diego to seek Governor Echeandía's permission to trap in the province.

When Smith failed to convince the suspicious governor that—lost and hungry—he had simply stumbled into the province, Echeandía seized his weapons and placed him under arrest. Smith protested that he was "no Spy," producing a passport and diary that listed the members of his party in order to prove that they were bona fide trappers. Nonetheless, Escheandía considered Smith and his men interlopers and, unable to decide whether or not to let Smith go, sent to Mexico for instructions.

While languishing in a dirty San Diego *calabozo,* or jail cell, Smith scrawled a letter in brown ink to the U.S. minister at Mexico City, Joel R. Poinsett, complaining: "I am destitute of almost everything with the exception of my Traps (guns which I can not now call mine), Ammunition, etc." Smith was finally freed from imprisonment upon condition that he and his men leave California, never to return.

Instead, Smith moved northward through the province, trapping along the Stanislaus and Kings rivers. On May 20, 1827, he next left most of his men behind and set forth through the High Sierra toward the Great Basin of Utah. Although having failed in an earlier attempt, Smith's was the first white party ever to cross the perilous Sierra crest. He reached the Salt Lake area after about a month of arduous travel.

California, however, had not seen the last of Jedediah Smith. On July 13, 1827, further disregarding the warnings of Governor Echeandía, he began the trek back to rejoin the men he had left in the Central Valley. Near the Mohave villages, as Smith and his men approached the Colorado River, some Mojaves attacked and killed ten of the Americans and wounded another.

Despite the loss of more than half his group, Smith eventually reached Mission San José. While attempting to garner supplies there, he was once more detained, this time by Father Narcisco Durán who accused him of enticing neophytes to desert from the mission. Stripped of his guns and under heavy guard, Smith again appeared before Governor Echeandía, who was then in the north. After much argument, Smith was released for a second time. In December 1827 he departed from California promising once more not to return.

He took more than six months to traverse northwestern California on his way out of the province. He moved first up the Sacramento Valley, then paralleling the coastline toward today's Oregon border. On July 5, 1828, while trapping near the Umpqua River of southern Oregon, Smith's group suffered an Indian massacre which only he and two other men survived. They then proceeded as far northward as the Hudson Bay Company's post at Fort Vancouver, where they received welcome relief supplies.

Jedediah Smith was not only a fur trapper but also a unique pathfinder. Other hunters and traders would follow his trails into the farthest West.

Meanwhile, in California resentment toward the central government was increasing not only because of its indifference and neglect, but also because of its overbearing and mediocre governors. Californians felt contempt for these invading officials. They also yearned for local freedom. Successive revolts following the Solás debacle were halfhearted, bloodless affairs; but they might have become precursors of a movement for independence had not California's dissatisfaction been interrupted by American conquest.

Political changes in Mexico were repeatedly reflected in California. Echeandía was supplanted by Lieutenant Colonel Manuel Victoria, a militaristic conservative and an opponent of secularization. Echeandía had already issued his decree of secularization of January 6, 1831, with the purpose of rushing the measure into effect before turning over the government to his successor.

When Governor Manuel Victoria arrived in Monterey in 1831, his reception was a particularly unfriendly one. Victoria, however, made no attempt to conceal his contempt for unruly Californios. He even ordered the death penalty put into effect, boasting that he was determined to make it safe for any man to leave even his handkerchief or watch lying in Monterey's plaza. He also ran roughshod over his political rivals; several residents—including the American Abel Stearns as well as José Antonio Carrillo and José María Padres—were exiled to Mexico, without trial.

Active opposition to the governor mounted. Over fifty rebels, after taking possession of the presidio at San Diego, marched to Los Angeles, seizing control of that pueblo. There they found prominent local leaders in jail, by order of Victoria, and these bolstered their antigovernment forces. Victoria marched southward from Monterey with a detachment of soldiers. A few miles from Los Angeles, near Cahuenga Pass, he was surprised to meet some of his own forces, accompanied by 150 resurgent recruits, arrayed against him. Victoria called upon the soldiers to come over to his side. When they refused he directed his men to fire a volley over the heads of all "enemies," to frighten rather than to harm them. The southerners replied with a few shots; then, their courage failing, they turned to run away, but Victoria was due for another surprise.

Among the Angeleños was a popular daredevil, José María Ávila, noted especially for his skillful horsemanship. Ávila suddenly rode out alone toward Victoria and his subaltern, Captain Romualdo Pacheco, and rushed at them with his lance leveled, as if in chivalric personal combat. Ávila drew an ancient pistol and shot Pacheco through the heart. In the ensuing battle Ávila was unhorsed and killed, some say by Victoria himself, who received a deep lance wound in the face.

Due to popular demand, Victoria was forced to give up the governorship after only one year. Echeandía again took over the reins of government, concluding a truce with Captain Agustín Vicente Zamorano—Victoria's loyal secretary whom the governor had left in command in his absence due to the Los Angeles revolt—at Monterey, and with Pío Pico, a civic leader of Los Angeles, both of whom claimed the governorship. This understanding, however, lasted only until the arrival in 1833 of a newly appointed Mexican governor.

This was José Figueroa, comandante-general of the Mexican states of Sonora and Sinaloa. So amiable and conscientious was the new governor that he helped overcome the prejudice against imported governors. Figueroa's first act was to issue a proclamation granting amnesty to all who had taken part in recent political disturbances.

Although Figueroa, like Governor Victoria, believed that the missions were not quite ready for full secularization, a sweeping decree of August 1833 came out of Mexico City. The missions were to become parish churches immediately. Figueroa then ordered that half of the mission lands and livestock be distributed among the neophytes. But some of these natives hung about the missions, reluctant to leave the only homes they had known, in some cases for sixty years. Other, less acculturated, mission dwellers joined tribelets in the interior. Now, with the padres no longer overseeing the coastal Indians, the Californios feared further outbreaks of violence by the increasingly restive natives.

During 1834 Governor Figueroa experienced still more trouble when a party of 200 colonists arrived from Mexico under the leadership of José María Padrés and José María Hijar. These men planned to establish a new colony that included doctors, lawyers, teachers, and artisans, a group hardly outfitted to survive a harsh winter in the Sonoma Valley. Figueroa, on May 8, 1834, arrested the plans of Padrés and Hijar and sent them both packing for San Blas, Mexico. Some of their colonists were, however, allowed to remain behind. Most settled in northern California.

As the process of secularization continued, a worn-out Figueroa died on September 29, 1835. He had probably been the best of California's Mexican governors. Had he lived longer, he might have softened the effects of Mexican-ordered secularization. As it turned out, the mission lands intended for the natives ultimately passed into the hands of local government administrators and their relatives. Repeatedly, looters stocked their ranchos with animals filched from mission herds. As mission buildings began to crumble into dust, an important bulwark of California life had all but disappeared. The ranchos had already replaced the missions as the dominant economic and social institutions in pre-American California.

Selected Readings

Regarding Jedediah Smith consult Maurice S. Sullivan, *The Travels of Jedediah Smith* (1934), and Sullivan's *Jedediah Smith, Trader and Trail Breaker* (1936); Dale L. Morgan, *Jedediah Smith . . .* (1953); Robert Glass Cleland, *This Reckless Breed of Men* (1950); Harrison C. Dale, *The Ashley-Smith Explorations . . .* (repr. 1941); Donald McKay Frost, "Notes on General Ashley, the Overland Trail and South Pass," *Proceedings of the American Antiquarian Society* 54 (October 1944), 161–312; A. M. Woodbury, "The Route of Jedediah S. Smith," *Utah Historical Quarterly* 4 (April 1931), 35–46; Andrew Rolle, "Jedediah Strong Smith: New Documentation," *Mississippi Valley Historical Review* 40 (September 1953), 305–8, and Rolle, "The Riddle of Jedediah Smith's First Visit to California," *Historical Society of Southern California Quarterly* 36 (September 1954), 179–84; George R. Brooks, ed., *The Southwest Expedition of Jedediah S. Smith* (1977); David J. Weber, *The Californios Versus Jedediah Smith* (1990).

Consult also Gerald J. Geary, *The Secularization of the California Missions* (1934); John B. McGloin, *California's First Archbishop* (1966); Madie Brown Emparan, *The Vallejos of California* (1968); Alan Rosenus, *General M. G. Vallejo and the Advent of the Americans* (1995) and C. Alan Hutchinson, *The Hijar-Padrés Colony and its Origins, 1769–1835* (1969).

On the Eve of American Rule

////// CHAPTER 11

Governor Figueroa had managed to retain the allegiance of the province more by personal charm than by the authority of his office. After his death, Californians again grew restless. Local tensions were aggravated, as usual, by constant changes of governmental policies in Mexico. Nicolás Gutiérrez, who succeeded Figueroa as governor *ad interim,* filled the office for four months until the next appointee arrived.

California's next regular governor, the Mexican-born Mariano Chico, was a political reactionary unpopular with the majority of Californians. Public resentment rose to the boiling point, and Chico was expelled from California after only three months in office. The ouster was clandestinely accomplished, with the insurgent Californians managing to avoid open conflict with the national government. Chico threatened to return with troops to take vengeance, but his was an empty boast.

Mexican governors were not really welcome in California; one after another found the place hostile. Indeed, most provincials no longer called themselves Mexicanos, but Californios.

Upon the expulsion of Chico the civil and military commands again temporarily fell to Gutiérrez. This time he experienced a stormier tenure. Though easygoing and inoffensive, he was a Spaniard by birth, and regarded as a foreigner. A petty quarrel between him and Juan Bautista Alvarado provided an excuse for his overthrow. The Californians were determined to secure home rule for the territory. Why should a Vallejo, an Alvarado, a Carrillo, or any other California leader be in a position of inferiority to an outsider whom he considered his inferior? Contact with foreigners had emphasized the backwardness of Mexico and awakened local ambitions. The ease with which the Californians had expelled Victoria and Chico emboldened them to act independently. But they did not yet feel strong enough to walk alone. Hence their struggle was to secure autonomy in internal affairs.

The Californios grew increasingly determined to secure home rule for their province. As a result, by 1836, Juan Bautista Alvarado, considered a local patriot, or *hijo del país,* suddenly decided to seize the governorship. At Monterey, Alvarado and an ally, José Castro, assembled a force of seventy-five men, armed with antiquated muskets. Among those recruited was Isaac Graham, an American fur trapper and hunter who ran a whiskey distillery. A backwoods ruffian from Tennessee, Graham was induced to join the revolutionists by promises of land and other favors. Alvarado would regret the day he sought Graham's allegiance.

Graham headed up a band of some 50 riflemen—Indians, Americans, and renegade Mexicans. Alongside Alvarado and Castro's force of 100 Californios, Graham's men took possession of Monterey on November 3, 1836, without bloodshed. One cannon ball struck Governor Nicolas Gutiérrez's house and he surrendered immediately. After he was expelled, a *diputación* named Alvarado governor.

However, soon thereafter sectional jealousies arose. In the extreme south, San Diegans had long wanted the provincial customhouse to be moved there from Monterey. This and other local disagreements resulted in another armed encounter near Ventura, with Castro heading up the northerners and Carlos Carrillo commanding the southerners. Only one man was killed. After another skirmish at Las Flores, in which the two factions met in "a battle for the most part of tongue and pen," Alvarado persuaded Carrillo to disband his forces and formally requested the Mexican government to accept him as governor.

A few years of respite followed the abortive 1836 uprising. Because the missions continued to deteriorate severely, Governor Alvarado appointed the honest and hardworking businessman William E. P. Hartnell as his inspector of the missions. A Scot, Hartnell reported that some non-Christianized Indians of the interior were conducting raids on the most exposed missions, running off horses and mules and killing unguarded cattle.

Governor Alvarado also faced the threat of renewed insurrection from Carlos Carillo. Another foe, Pío Pico of Los Angeles, sulked over the refusal of Monterey's junta to move the capital southward to his settlement. Furthermore, the number of foreigners in and around the capital continued to increase, a few of them troublemakers who refused to settle down. These included Isaac Graham who made his Monterey cabin a center for dissident American fur trappers and sailors.

In April 1840, Alvarado arrested 120 of these malcontents. He sent Graham and 45 accomplices in irons to San Blas. But Mexican officials later released Graham, giving him and his followers free ship-passage back to Monterey! This was a clear rebuke to Alvarado, whose governorship was barely sanctioned by his superiors in Mexico.

Interest in California from abroad was also clearly mounting. In 1837, the French naval frigate *Venus,* under the command of Captain Abel du Petit-Thouars, remained at Monterey for a month. His official report included descriptions of the "Alvarado Revolution" and of California's turbulent political climate. In 1840 Alavarado greeted yet another French expedition led by the explorer Eugéne Duflot de Mofras.

Foreign governments were eager to obtain information about the province. In 1841 the United States sent a naval expedition to the Pacific Coast. Its leader, Commodore Charles Wilkes, though dour and pessimistic in his report to Washington, praised what he called the greatest natural harbor in the world, San Francisco.

California, meanwhile remained a dumping ground for unemployed Mexican officials. Late in 1842 Alvarado had to give way to another Mexican-appointed Governor, Manuel Micheltorena, who entered San Diego with a company of 300 tough *cholos*. Most of these toughs were actually ex-convicts and bullies who could not resist the temptation to steal kettles, pots, chickens, jewelry, even clothing. Also called *rateros,* or low-lifes, they proceeded to molest the señoritas of San Diego, where they were billeted.

Even before Governor Micheltorena left that pueblo for the capital, Monterey, he received some startling news. An American Commodore, Thomas Ap Catesby Jones, while in Peruvian waters, had mistakenly heard that war had been declared between the United States and Mexico. Commodore Jones proceeded to Monterey, where he landed marines and raised the American flag. Convinced of his error within only a few hours, he restored the Mexican flag and, though embarrassed, sought to make amends.

Micheltorena grudgingly excused the confused commodore and turned to more threatening internal matters. By November 22, 1844, Micheltorena, like the governors before him, faced another revolt under the leadership of Alvarado and José Castro. Foreign residents were on both sides in the quarrel with Governor Micheltorena. Abel Stearns and Isaac Graham ultimately took sides with Alvarado. Johann Augustus Sutter, the Swiss adventurer who had built a fort on the Sacramento River, also opposed Micheltorena and his unpopular jailbird cholos. Sutter would eventually buy out the moveable objects the Russians left behind after they abandoned Fort Ross.

On February 20, 1845, the opposing forces met at Cahuenga Pass, outside Los Angeles, and engaged in a two-day artillery duel, at such long range, however, that there was little danger of anyone being hit. Ultimately, Micheltorena, with his foreign support vanished, agreed to be deported from California and to take his cholos with him. His departure amounted to the province's virtual independence from Mexico. There was now no stopping local control.

The Californios proclaimed Pío Pico their next governor. José Castro, another native son, as powerful at Monterey as Pico was in Los Angeles, became military comandante. But, after Pico moved the capital to Los Angeles, California remained a house divided. Governor Pico controlled all legislation. Castro, however, remained in possession of provincial revenues. This tension between comandante and governor, north versus south, dragged on during 1845–1846.

It was this intense regional factionalism, which constantly threatened to erupt, that slowly reconciled the Californios to eventual U.S. rule. Although the Americans were not natives, they came from a more stable society than these locals had ever known.

Selected Readings

Regarding foreign visitors see Richard Batman, *The Outer Coast* (1985); Charles N. Rudkin, trans., *Voyage of the Venus: Sojourn in California* (1956); Marguerite Eyer Wilbur, trans. and ed., *Duflot de Mofras' Travels on the Pacific Coast . . .* (2 vols., 1937); Charles Wilkes, *Narrative of the United States Exploring Expedition . . .* (5 vols., 1844); Daniel M. MacIntyre, *The Hidden Coasts* (1953); David B. Tyler, *The Wilkes Expedition* (1968).

On Americanization see Doris Wright, *A Yankee in Mexican California: Abel Stearns, 1798–1848* (1977); Robert Glass Cleland, *The Cattle on a Thousand Hills* (repr., 1951); Judson Grenier, *California Legacy . . . The Watson Family* (1987) and Ronald C. Woolsey, *Migrants West: Toward the Southern California Frontier* (1996).

Trappers, Traders, and Homeseekers

//////// CHAPTER 12

In the midst of California's continuing political turmoil, still more Americans arrived. They were a mixed lot whom the Californians found difficult to understand.

Among these was James Ohio Pattie, who in 1824 set out with his father, Sylvester, on a fur-trapping expedition that would last for several years. After their party crossed the Missouri River frontier, the Patties trapped for beaver along muddy streams which no white men had ever seen before. Prospects for the party seemed excellent until Indians stole their pack animals. By September 1827, the Patties, with about thirty companions, continued westward from Santa Fe to trap along the Gila and Colorado rivers. At one campsite a band of Yuma Indians stampeded their horses. This left the Patties no choice but to build canoes from cottonwoods. Floating down the Colorado to its mouth, they set beaver traps along its banks.

Proceeding overland to San Diego, the Patties found Governor Echeandía in residence there. Like Jedediah Smith, they were harshly treated by the governor as unwanted interlopers. After he threw the party into a dank jail, Sylvester Pattie died. Fortunately for the young Pattie, the governor needed an interpreter to deal with the increasing number of American intruders. James Pattie, years later, put together a tall-tale about a smallpox epidemic that allegedly was sweeping through California. Supposedly, when the governor learned that the Patties had brought along some scarce vaccine, he promised James his freedom if he would agree to vaccinate California's population. This may well be an utter fabrication, but parts of Pattie's narrative are reasonably verifiable.

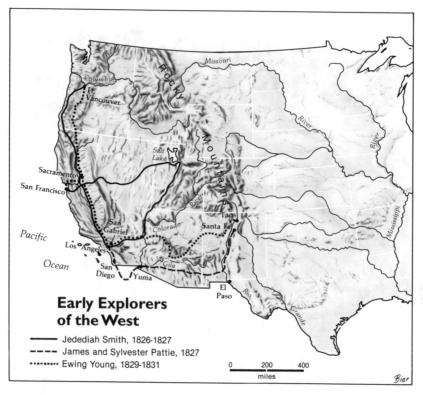

Early Explorers
of the West

——— Jedediah Smith, 1826-1827
- - - - James and Sylvester Pattie, 1827
••••••••• Ewing Young, 1829-1831

0   200   400
miles

Bier

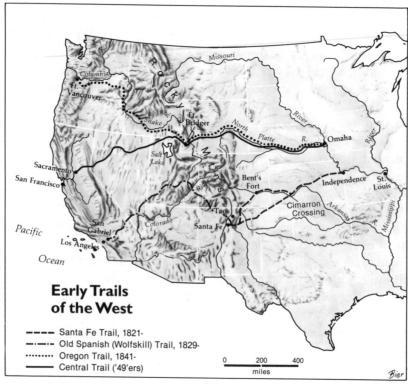

Early Trails
of the West

- - - - Santa Fe Trail, 1821-
-·-·- Old Spanish (Wolfskill) Trail, 1829-
••••••••• Oregon Trail, 1841-
——— Central Trail ('49'ers)

0   200   400
miles

Bier

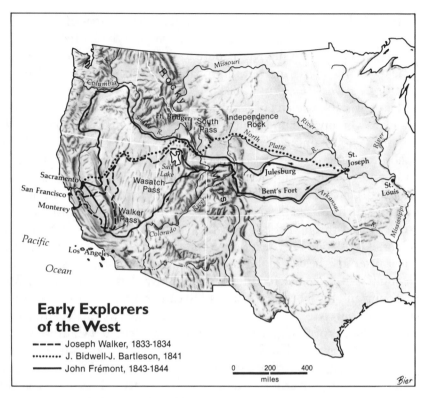

Early Explorers of the West

- - - - Joseph Walker, 1833-1834
- ·········· J. Bidwell-J. Bartleson, 1841
- —— John Frémont, 1843-1844

0   200   400
miles

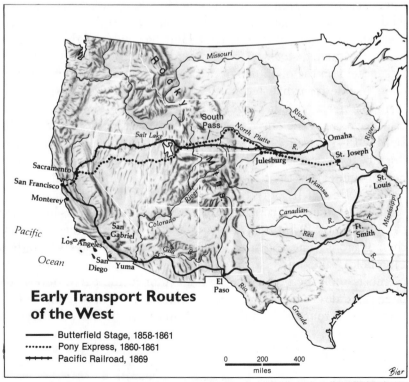

Early Transport Routes of the West

- —— Butterfield Stage, 1858-1861
- ·········· Pony Express, 1860-1861
- +++++ Pacific Railroad, 1869

0   200   400
miles

In 1830 James Ohio Pattie disappeared from the pages of history. His narrative retained some significance only because the Patties had seemingly pioneered the Gila River route to California. He also left behind one of the most exciting, yet improbable, records of western adventure entitled *Personal Narrative* (1831).

Pattie was followed by other trappers, among them Joseph Reddeford Walker, who opened up a trail across the Sierra ridge. In August 1829, another "mountain man," Ewing Young, headed a party westward from Taos, traveling down the Gila and the Colorado rivers. In this group was a protégé of Young, Kit Carson, who eventually became a famous frontier scout. The Young party traveled over parts of the "Old Spanish Trail," which crossed the Mohave Desert into southern California. They then moved through the Cajon Pass and, early in 1830, reached San Gabriel Mission. The next year Young returned to California to trap river otter and beaver along the Kings River and stretches of the San Joaquin. He also collected furs as far northward as the Umpqua River.

Young and his fellow trappers had to carry on their activities clandestinely, for only Mexican citizens possessed licenses to trap legally. Nonetheless dozens of foreign trappers subsequently entered California. One of these, the Swiss Johann Augustus Sutter, would play a unique role in Americanizing the province. In 1839 this "dreamer with a gifted tongue" obtained from Governor Alvarado a 50,000-acre (11 square leagues) tract near the junction of the Sacramento and American rivers. In this wilderness Sutter began construction of an outpost that he named New Helvetia, in honor of his homeland. Here he combined the occupations of trapper, trader, stock raiser, and feudal ruler.Because New Helvetia was located on the main line of overland immigration, it offered a welcome respite for exhausted parties winding their way down the trails from the Sierra Nevada range.

Sutter was not the only foreigner to settle in the interior at this time. In May 1841 a twenty-year-old school teacher named John Bidwell had organized an overland party to California. His motley caravan, which became known as "the first emigrant train to California," started from Sapling Grove, Missouri. Staggering through the alkali flats near the Great Salt Lake, with constant mirages ahead, the travelers had to jettison their heavy furniture, washpans, butter churns, baggage, and even their wagons. The footsore group wandered for days through the Humboldt Valley and Carson Sink, most of their provisions gone. Some members took the best horses and abandoned the party. Several days later these deserters shamefacedly returned to camp, having failed to find a better route toward the Sierra's snowy crest. Early in November

1841, almost six months after their departure, Bidwell's party finally reached California's Sacramento Valley.

That same year the Workman-Rowland overland party managed to avoid winter's hardships by taking a southern route into California. Along the Santa Fe trail they drove flocks of sheep, and party members were in good physical shape when they arrived at Mission San Gabriel.

Beginning in 1846, increasing numbers of Americans also reached California by water. Among these was a group of several hundred Mormons headed by Samuel Brannan who arrived at the Golden Gate. They originally intended to move on to Salt Lake City, where Brigham Young awaited them. Brannan urged his followers, however, to stay on in California.

A new American era of exploration by government survey parties was about to begin. The year 1843–44 saw the arrival of John Charles Frémont, a young naturalist and explorer, on his second expedition to the Far West. After a dangerous crossing of the Sierra, Frémont reached Sutter's Fort in March of 1844. He then moved southward along the San Joaquin Valley to the Kings River, crossing the Tehachapi Pass on his way back to Saint Louis. The explorer's official report, thousands of copies of which were printed, made Frémont a national figure. From what he had observed he produced a series of accurate maps that induced still more overland groups to move toward California.

In the spring of 1846 one such party was doomed to play a tragic role in the history of the American West. This was the Donner party, which started its journey in Springfield, Illinois. Bad luck as well as poor judgment plagued them, although some of the participants would display notable heroism in the midst of disaster.

At Fort Bridger in Wyoming, the Donners decided to follow the foolish advice of Lansford W. Hastings's *Emigrant's Guide to Oregon and California* (1845), which described a new route to California, allegedly 200 miles shorter than by way of Fort Hall at today's Idaho. This route, called "Hastings Cut-off" (which Hastings had never seen), terminated eight miles west of modern Elko, Nevada. It ran south of the Great Salt Lake via Fort Bridger and joined the California Trail on the Humboldt River. The illusory cutoff turned out to be a nightmare for the Donner party.

On July 20, the Donners broke camp and plunged into an unknown wilderness. Along an almost impassable route, they fought their way through the Wasatch Mountains. At times the party was compelled to use ten yoke of oxen to draw a single wagon up the side of a steep gulch. The emigrants were a month—instead of a week, as they had planned—in reaching the shores of the Great Salt Lake. The loss of time proved costly. West of Salt Lake it became apparent that the supplies would give out before the group could reach California. Two members of the party volunteered to proceed on horseback to procure food from Sutter's Fort. Because of lack of water the party left thirty-six head of cattle on the desert. A mirage, revealing the waters of a lake, turned disappointment into anguish. Return to Fort Bridger was impossible; there was no alternative but to continue onward.

The tension increased when John Snyder inadvertently struck the wife of James F. Reed with a bull whip. Reed, enraged, stabbed Snyder to death; he then used the boards from his wagon to make a coffin for the dead man. The Donner party passed a severe judgment on the murderer, who cried out that he had acted in self-defense. There on the remote desert floor of western America, miles from the nearest habitation, Reed's companions forced him to leave the train. With his gun and a few provisions he set out alone for California. Each day thereafter Reed's wife and children looked for traces of him along the way—the feathers of a bird killed, or an occasional note pinned onto a bush. They wondered whether he might be scalped by Indians, or whether he would ever make it alone to some frontier outpost. The Donner party had banished one of its most needed members.

In the Sierra Nevada winter was coming on fast. Instead of pressing forward, the party tarried four days for a badly needed rest. Truckee Meadows, near the present city of Reno, Nevada, was covered with grasses and clover of good quality. It was difficult to leave such security behind and proceed toward the unknown. On October 19, one volunteer bravely returned from Sutter's Fort with two Indian guides, seven mules, and limited amounts of beef and flour. Three days later the Donners crossed the winding Truckee River "for the forty-ninth and last time in eighty miles." The party moved northward through barely passable canyons. Clouds high on the mountain crest gave a clear indication of approaching winter, and there was a nip in the air. As they moved into higher elevations their wagons could not be dragged through the early snows that fell in the Sierra that year. One wagon broke its axle and tipped over onto little Eliza Donner, three years old, and Georgia, age four; the children were almost crushed by the avalanche of household goods that fell upon them. There was further delay as the party repacked provisions onto cumbersome oxen.

A stormy winter descended upon upper Alder Creek almost a month early. One part of their train bogged down in the snow near today's Donner Lake. Another small remnant holed up under brush and canvas sheets about six miles away. There they waited four months until early spring, sheltered only by snow-covered pines on one of the Sierra's windiest passes. The snow that winter reached a depth of twenty-two feet. Scattered into small clusters, the Donners made repeated efforts to get out of the mountains. They improvised snowshoes from oxbows and strips of rawhide. In mid-December 1846, a party known as "The Fifteen" left the rest behind. After weeks of severe suffering, dazed and stumbling about in the snow, seven survivors emerged via Emigrant Gap.

On the nineteenth of February, 1847, those left behind on the Sierra crest were startled by shouts. The strongest of them, climbing to the top of a huge snow bank, witnessed the "most welcome sight of their lives"— a reconnaissance party of seven men, reprovisioned by Sutter, composed of formerly snowed-in survivors. Each bore a pack. Even Reed, banished earlier, arrived with a second relief group to save some of the very men who had cast him out. He was overjoyed to find his wife and four children still alive. Suddenly a third contingent appeared. By then George Donner was too weak and sick to travel. His wife refused to leave her husband, allowing her little daughters to be taken from her to safety. When the fourth and last relief party arrived in the spring they found that Mrs. Donner too had died. Only forty-five of the seventy-nine persons in the original Donner party survived. Some lived on in California for years, becoming virtual culture heroes.

The Donners became symbolic of the hardy westering pioneers. Theirs was a mixture of frontier individualism and religious conviction, a nationalism encapsulated in the phrase "manifest destiny." Despite adversity and suffering, such Americans vowed to build a new world beyond the mountains in distant California.

Selected Readings

Regarding the fur trade see Paul C. Phillips, *The Fur Trade* (2 vols., 1961) and Cleland, *This Reckless Breed of Men;* also Charles L. Camp, ed., *James Clyman: American Frontiersman* (1928); Alpheus H. Favour, *Old Bill Williams, Mountain Man* (1936); Richard Batman, *American Ecclesiastes: The Stories of James Pattie* (1985); Stanton A. Coblentz, *The Swallowing Wilderness* (1961); Clifton B. Kroeber, ed., "The Route of James Ohio Pattie on the Colorado in 1826: A Reappraisal by A. L. Kroeber," *Arizona and The West* 6 (Summer 1964), 119–36; Rosemary K. Valle, "James Ohio Pattie and the Alta California Measles Epidemic," *California Historical Quarterly* 52 (Spring 1973), 28–36; Iris Wilson, *William Wolfskill, 1798–1866: Frontier Trapper to California Ranchero* (1965) and LeRoy Hafen, ed., *The Mountain Men and the Fur Trade of the Far West* (6 vols., 1965–68).

Regarding Sutter consult Kenneth Owens, ed., *John Sutter and a Wider West* (1994); Erwin G. Gudde, *Sutter's Own Story* (1936); James Peter Zollinger, *Sutter: The Man and His Empire* (1939) and Marguerite Eyer Wilbur, *John Sutter: Rascal and Adventurer* (1949).

About overland travelers see Rockwell D. Hunt, *John Bidwell: Prince of California Pioneers* (1942) and Bidwell, *California Before the Gold Rush* (repr. 1948). Regarding the Donners consult C. F. McGlashan, *History of the Donner Party: A Tragedy of the Sierra* (repr. 1947); George R. Stewart, *Ordeal by Hunger: The Story of the Donner Party* (1936, 1960); Walter M. Stookey, *Fatal Decision: The Tragic Story of the Donner Party* (1950); Eliza P. Donner Houghton, *The Expedition of the Donner Party* (1920); David E. Miller, "The Donner Road through the Great Salt Lake Desert," *Pacific Historical Review* 27 (February 1958), 30–44.

Overland trail materials include J. Gregg Layne, *Western Wayfaring: Routes of Exploration and Trade in the American Southwest* (1954); Arthur Peters, *Seven Trails West* (1996) and George R. Stewart, *The California Trail* (1962).

American Conquest

////////CHAPTER 13

A merican sentiment for the acquisition of California had deep roots. As early as 1829 President Andrew Jackson had sent Anthony Butler as his envoy into Mexico to negotiate for the purchase of territory in the American Southwest. Butler's suggestion of a bribe that would lead to acquiring California, Texas, and New Mexico offended the Mexicans, and he returned home in disgrace. The idea of adding California to U.S. territory, however, was never abandoned by Jackson, nor by his successors, Presidents Van Buren, Tyler, and Polk. Furthermore, the laxity of Mexican control over California made it obvious that the province might well fall into the hands of some outside power. The strategic location of San Francisco Bay alone, with its matchless harbor and rich surrounding countryside, greatly increased American sentiment for California's annexation.

In 1842 two flags flew over the province. The Stars and Stripes had already momentarily supplanted the Mexican Eagle when Commodore Jones had mistakenly raised the American flag over Monterey. Furthermore, James K. Polk, elected president of the United States in 1844, committed himself to a popular expansionist policy. Polk relied upon an alert consul at Monterey, Thomas Oliver Larkin, to prepare the groundwork for peaceful American penetration of California. On April 15, 1846, following a questionable dispute with Mexico over its border with Texas, Polk's administration requested a declaration of war from the U.S. Congress.

Frémont, already aware that conflict with Mexico was possible, had left St. Louis in May of 1845 on his third exploring expedition. With a party of sixty-two soldiers, scouts, topographers, and six Delaware Indians, he again crossed the Sierra, reaching Sutter's Fort on December 9, 1845. This time he traveled on to Monterey, where he met with Consul Larkin. José Castro, commander of its garrison, though suspicious of the explorer's motives, gave Frémont permission to winter in California.

In early March 1846, Frémont withdrew toward a nearby bluff named Gavilan, or Hawk's Peak, where he built a log fortification overlooking the Salinas Valley and defiantly raised the American flag. A warning letter from Consul Larkin, and the realization that Castro seemed to be preparing to dislodge him, persuaded Frémont to move his men northward toward Oregon. Frémont's rashness had embarrassed Larkin and other American residents who still hoped for annexation of California by quiet, behind-the-scenes contacts.

On the way north Frémont and his group were overtaken by Lieutenant Archibald H. Gillespie, a U.S. Marine Corps officer who had crossed Mexico in disguise. He produced secret messages from officials in Washington, including Secretary of State James Buchanan, as well as from Frémont's wife, Jessie Benton, and her father, Thomas Hart Benton, the expansionist chairman of the U.S. Senate Committee on Territories. Gillespie's dispatches probably warned Frémont that war with Mexico was likely and directed him to cooperate with land and naval forces of the United States should a conflict break out.

As Frémont approached the Marysville Buttes, north of Sutter's Fort, dissident Americans flocked into his camp. They too had heard the rumors of approaching war between the United States and Mexico. Though the young explorer had no actual instructions to support a revolt among Americans in California, his very presence encouraged some of the men in his company to plot the capture of General Vallejo at Sonoma. Although Vallejo was a supporter of Americans in California, at dawn on June 14, 1846, a group of these frontiersmen burst into his home and routed the general from his bed. They placed Vallejo under arrest and took him to Sutter's Fort.

Frémont's role was an ambivalent one. He stayed on the sidelines as William B. Ide became the leader of this American revolt. His followers fashioned a flag with a grizzly bear on it to identify their movement. On the day the Bear Flaggers captured Sonoma, they proudly raised their new standard over its central plaza. They then pronounced a "California Republic." The Bear Flag movement, however, came to a sudden halt when the American flag was raised in California. U.S. naval forces captured Monterey on July 7, 1846, and that act set aside the Bear Flag Revolt. As a result, Vallejo was released from imprisonment at Sutter's Fort.

Provincial pride and historical romanticism has created the legend that the Bear Flag Revolt produced an independent California, which then became part of the United States. Actually, this tiny uprising was of limited significance in the acquisition of California; its American conquest would have occurred anyway.

A week after Commodore John Drake Sloat, commander of U.S. naval forces in Pacific waters, landed some 250 marines and seamen at Monterey, the flag of the United States was flying at Yerba Buena, Sutter's Fort, Bodega Bay, and at Sonoma. On July 15, Commodore Robert F. Stockton arrived at Monterey on the USS *Congress* to replace Sloat. Stockton issued a new proclamation, organizing Frémont's volunteers into a unit called the California Battalion of Mounted Riflemen.

On August 13, 1846, Commodore Stockton's forces entered Los Angeles. Captain Gillespie, the courier who had met Frémont with messages from Washington, was left in command there with a garrison of fifty men. In enforcing a curfew, the captain angered many Angeleños who, on September 23, surrounded his small garrison on a hilltop in the middle of Los Angeles. Besieged and short of water, Gillespie, under cover of darkness, secretly sent a messenger to Stockton for aid. The dispatch he carried was written on cigarette papers and concealed in his long hair. The message received, Stockton replied by sending 350 sailors and marines to Gillespie's aid.

The reinforcements arrived aboard the USS *Vandalia*, which dropped anchor at San Pedro, outside Los Angeles, on October 7, 1846. By then Gillespie's hilltop position had become untenable. He had virtually surrendered to the Californios but had been allowed to retreat with his men to San Pedro and to depart by sea when they reached that port.

After the U.S. forces landed at San Pedro, there followed "The Battle of the Old Woman's Gun," on the Dominguez Rancho. In this conflict the *locales* were mounted on horses and armed with sharp willow lances and smooth-bore carbines. Their most damaging weapon, however, was a four-pound cannon. This antique firearm, which had been hidden by an old woman during the first American assault on Los Angeles, was tied with leather reatas, or thongs, to the tongue and wheels of a mud wagon. The Californios whipped the cannon up and down a hillock, firing it effectively and forcing the Americans to retreat to their ships. Though Lieutenant Gillespie had seemingly been rescued, for a time the territory south of Santa Barbara was again in the hands of Castro's Californio forces.

At San Diego, as Stockton planned to retake Los Angeles, an important message arrived that modified the military situation in California. This was a desperate dispatch from General Stephen Watts Kearny. The

Los Angeles, 1857. From a contemporary print.

War Department had ordered Kearny to proceed overland with an "Army of the West" from Fort Leavenworth, Kansas, to pacify New Mexico and to proceed to California to set up a government there. As Kearny moved westward from Santa Fe, he ran into Kit Carson. Now a celebrated scout, Carson was taking dispatches from Commodore Stockton eastward to Washington. Carson told the general that the American flag was already flying throughout California. Not knowing that renewed fighting had broken out near Los Angeles, Kearny sent most of his force back to Santa Fe, while he continued onward with only 100 dragoons. This was a mistake.

On December 5, 1846, General Kearny ran into a hornet's nest. More than 150 armed Californios, under Andrés Pico, were encamped at San Pascual (near present-day Escondido). During a cold rain storm, the Californios charged Kearny's forces. The Americans, their ammunition wet, tried to beat off the onslaught by hand-to-hand combat during which 22 Americans died.

Kearny's tired and bony army mules were no match for the quick California ponies, and his short sabres had offered little defense against the long lances of mounted opponents. Soon the general was surrounded by hostile forces, his powder damp, and his supplies dangerously low. Kearny's tired dragoons were forced to subsist for four days on mule flesh and a scanty water supply. But their spirits were heartened when Commodore Stockton sent 200 rescuing sailors and marines from San Diego.

General Kearny had suffered a significant defeat at what became known as the Battle of San Pascual. He was grateful that Stockton had relieved his tattered forces. After Pico's men finally withdrew, Kearny resumed his march into California.

After resting at San Diego, the general joined Commodore Stockton's forces. With 600 army dragoons, marines, and sailors, they left San Diego to retake Los Angeles. At the same time, Frémont was also about to approach that pueblo (from the north) with 400 volunteers. On January 10, 1847, Kearny and Stockton entered the City of the Angels and marched to its plaza, where Captain Gillespie hoisted the flag he had been compelled to haul down the previous September. Andrés Pico, however, preferred to surrender to Frémont, which he did on January 13, 1847, on the outskirts of Los Angeles. His brother, Pío Pico, the last Mexican governor of California, had fled to Sonora. Although Frémont was acting over the head of Kearny, a brevet brigadier general, he pardoned Andrés Pico and other local leaders. The generous peace treaty that Frémont concluded became known as the Cahuenga Capitulation.

A conflict in orders from the Navy and War departments now led to a three-way quarrel over which of California's conquerors commanded the thousand or more U.S. servicemen under them at Los Angeles. Kearny rightly considered himself the ranking U.S. commander in California. But Stockton now personally decided to relinquish his authority in favor of Frémont and traveled to the East Coast, leaving General Kearny and Frémont to fight it out over who would govern California. Ultimately the general prepared court-martial charges against the unbending Frémont. This led to one of the great military trials of the nineteenth century.

As to the war between the United States and Mexico, it came to an end with the signing of the Treaty of Guadalupe Hidalgo on February 2, 1848. A new southwestern boundary now gave the United States all of Upper California as well as New Mexico and a greatly enlarged Texas. Nevertheless, the immediate political future of California still remained unsettled. But its control was no longer in the hands of Latino leaders.

Selected Readings

Regarding the last days of Mexican rule see George Tays, "Pio Pico's Correspondence with the Mexican Government, 1846–1848," *California Historical Society Quarterly* 13 (March 1934), 99–149.

Concerning the acquisition of California, see Paul Bergeron, *The Presidency of James K. Polk* (1987); Charles Seller, *James K. Polk* (2 vols., 1957–66) also Allan Nevins, ed., *Polk: The Diary, of a President* (1929).

On Frémont in California see Allan Nevins, ed., *Narratives of Exploration and Adventure* (1956) and his *Frémont: Pathmarker of the West* (1939); Cardinal L. Goodwin, *John Charles Frémont: An Exploration of His Career*

(1930); Andrew Rolle, *John Charles Frémont: Character as Destiny* (1991); also *Proceedings of the Court Martial in the Trial of (J. C.) Frémont* (1848).

The Bear Flag revolt is in Fred B. Rogers, *Bear Flag Lieutenant: The Life Story of Henry L. Ford* (1951); also see the reprint of Simeon Ide, *A Biographical Sketch of William B. Ide* (1967).

Kearny's march west is in Dwight L. Clarke, *Stephen Watts Kearny, Soldier of the West* (1961); William H. Emory, *Notes of a Military Reconnaissance* (1848); Joseph Warren Revere, *A Tour of Duty in California* (1849); Arthur Woodward, *Lances at San Pascual* (1948); Philip St. George Cooke, *The Conquest of New Mexico and California* (1878).

On the Mexican War in California see Neal Harlow, *California Conquered: War and Peace in the Pacific, 1846–1850* (1982); Justin H. Smith, *The War with Mexico* (2 vols., 1919); Glenn W. Price, *Origins of the War with Mexico: The Polk-Stockton Intrigue* (1967); Edwin A. Sherman, *The Life of the Late Rear Admiral John Drake Sloat* (1902); Samuel Bayard, *A Sketch of the Life of Com. Robert F. Stockton* (1856); Harlan Hague and David J. Langum, *Thomas O. Larkin: A Life of Patriotism and Profit* (1990); Fred B. Rogers, *Montgomery and the Portsmouth* (1959); Werner H. Marti, *Messenger of Destiny: The California Adventures . . . of Archibald H. Gillespie* (1960).

Regarding postconquest military regimes see Theodore Grivas, *Military Governments in California* (1963).

Gold

////// CHAPTER 14

Following the American conquest of California, a world-class event would shape the future development of the state. On January 24, 1848, James Wilson Marshall, a native of New Jersey who worked for Sutter, saw some gold flakes in the tailrace of a sawmill he was building on the south fork of the American River. There, at a place that the Indians called Coloma, Marshall hardly realized that he had discovered a new El Dorado, far beyond that for which the Spaniards had once searched in vain.

Marshall's was not the first discovery of California gold. Minor finds had been made before 1848, principally by mission Indians who brought the metal to the padres; but the friars reputedly cautioned the natives not to divulge the location of the gold, lest the province be inundated by money-mad foreigners.

Equipped with a modest education, a flintlock rifle, and some skills in his father's trade as a coach and wagon builder, Marshall had come to California by emigrant train in 1844. Buying land on nearby Little Butte Creek, he built and repaired spinning wheels, plows, ox yokes, and carts. In 1846 after participating in a campaign against the Mokelumne Indians, he joined the Bear Flag group and then enlisted in Frémont's California Battalion, continuing in military service until after the American conquest. Marshall had then returned to Sutter's Fort, "barefooted and in a very sorry plight," to find that nearly all his livestock had strayed from his ranch or had been stolen. Like many another California combatant, Marshall had received no compensation for his volunteer war services.

Sutter, desiring to expand his operations, now sent Marshall to search for new stands of timber and a suitable location for a new saw and flour mill. There Marshall saw gold, and he rushed back to tell Sutter. Once they realized the enormity of the their find, both men hoped to keep it a secret while they plotted their best course of action.

But, several months after the discovery, the Mormon Sam Brannan, who since his arrival in California had become a merchant at Sutter's Fort, galloped into San Francisco with dust and nuggets from the gold fields. As he rode along its streets he shouted "Gold! Gold! Gold from the American River!" swinging his hat wildly with one hand and in the other waving a medicine bottle full of bright dust.

Immediately a great human tide surged toward the icy streams of the Sierra in quest of riches. Locally, labor costs near the coast soared. Almost all businesses, except for the most urgent stopped. Seamen deserted ships in San Francisco Bay, and soldiers left behind their barracks and accumulated wages in a frenzy of excitement. A few gold seekers even hobbled on crutches toward the Sierra. Amidst the hysteria, San Francisco's newspaper, the *Californian,* suspended publication on May 29, 1848, announcing that most of its subscribers had left town. At Monterey, Consul Thomas Oliver Larkin bitterly lamented his town's depopulation as well. Within a few months news of the California gold find reached every part of the globe. Exaggeration of the riches was so prevalent that one writer remarked, "A grain of gold taken from the mine became a pennyweight at Panama, an ounce in New York and Boston, and a pound nugget at London."

After President Polk learned of the gold discovery in newly conquered California, he could not resist inserting the news in a presidential message of December 5, 1848. This proclamation caused a virtual rush to San Francisco by land and by sea. As a result, California's population quickly ballooned. At the beginning of 1849 there were, exclusive of Indians, only some 26,000 persons in the newly conquered province. By the end of that year the number had reached 115,000. Approximately half of the adult residents were engaged in some branch of mining, including some 20,000 foreign immigrants from Mexico, Great Britain, Germany, France, Spain, Chile, Peru, China, and the Hawaiian Islands.

Most Americans who reached California during those hectic days did so by way of one or another of three main routes—"around the Horn," "by way of the Isthmus," or "across the plains." The route around Cape Horn required up to nine months of travel aboard vessels of light tonnage, not all of which were seaworthy. Actual passage around Cape Horn was hazardous. It might take a vessel weeks to break through the choppy and often fogbound Strait of Magellan. Yet thousands made it to California via what became known as the "whitecollar route," because lack of exercise softened up seasick passengers who were often merchants, lawyers, or doctors, not workingmen.

Others arrived by crossing the Isthmus of Panama or Nicaragua. The isthmus route was the quickest of the principal routes. The voyage from

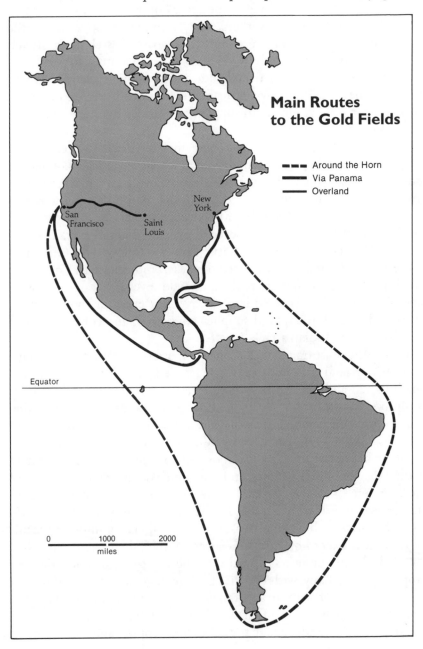

Main Routes to the Gold Fields

- – – – Around the Horn
- ▬▬▬ Via Panama
- ▬▬▬ Overland

New York

San Francisco

Saint Louis

Equator

0   1000   2000
miles

New York to the Panama Coast was 2,500 miles, and the trip across the Isthmus 60 miles more; from Panama to San Francisco it was 3,500 miles. But travel conditions on this route were hardly pleasant. Malarial fever was prevalent in all parts of Central America, as was cholera, dysentery, and yellow fever. Part of the isthmus crossing entailed travel through swampy water in long canoes poled or paddled by native boatmen. Then one had to go overland, usually on muleback, to the Pacific side of the isthmus. Once there, a shortage of coastal vessels might stretch the traveler's stay into months. On a second ocean journey to San Francisco, most vessels offered wretched accommodations, their food and water supplies vile. Pacific Mail Steamship Company ships, powered by steam, began only gradually to supplement service by the worm-eaten and leaky sailing vessels.

Even more than the clipper ship or steamer, it was the covered wagon, or "prairie schooner," that symbolized the vast American population movement during the Gold Rush. The favorite overland trail was a northern route leading west from St. Louis through South Pass in the Rocky Mountains. This was taken by 30,000 gold seekers in the year 1849 alone. A southern approach proceeded over the Santa Fe Trail, which ran from Westport (later Kansas City). This trail followed the Gila River to the Colorado, and finally crossed the desert into southern California.

With luck, the 2,000 miles to the gold fields over either of these overland routes could be covered in 100 days. But even for the fortunate, rivers had to be forded, food supplies conserved, and covered wagons guarded against Indian attack.

Among the most tragic of all pioneer experiences were those encountered by overland gold hunters whose fate led them into Death Valley, one hundred and ten feet below sea level, a "seventy-five mile strip of perdition." Constant hot winds blew across its sands, and the blinding glare of the sun parched the skin and induced a feverish, half-crazed state. In 1848–1849, a party led by William Lewis Manly encountered innumerable delays, making it impossible for them to reach the Sierra in time to avoid the fall snows, and the group was aware of the plight of the Donners. Near Salt Lake, Manly's little band joined forces with another party headed by Asabel Bennett, an acquaintance of Manly's. Nonetheless, the whole group was soon lost, wandering through a seemingly endless sea of hot sand. One after another, their oxen were killed for food. As the pioneers dipped into the last sacks of flour, Bennett proposed that Manly, with the strongest men, go ahead on foot to seek help. The main party was to await their return from the California settlements with supplies. After fourteen days Manly's party luckily reached Mission San Fernando, where they obtained supplies and pack animals.

Floor of Death Valley. Courtesy of Andrew Rolle.

When they finally returned to their camp, they found only a few survivors huddled under their wagons. After the bedraggled survivors in the Manly group finally reached southern California, they had spent an entire year on their journey west, yet they were still more than 500 miles from the mines. The story of the Bennett-Manly party, as told by Manly in his book, *Death Valley in '49*, remains a classic account of western history.

California's placer camps, however, hardly resembled the paradise envisioned by gold seekers. Mining was tiring work, and conveniences were practically nonexistent. Most "claims" lay along the banks of streams, where thousands of persons tried to strike "pay dirt." Miners worked both "dry diggings" in flats and gullies as well as "wet diggings" along swift stream beds.

For washing gold ore, panning was the simplest method. The sifting pan was made of tin or sheet iron, with a flat bottom and sides at an angle of forty-five degrees. The lonely prospector, gold pan in hand, his meager supplies loaded on the back of a donkey, became the symbol of the Gold Rush. But really effective mining involved the use of elaborate sluice and waterwheel systems, including "flumes," or open ditches constructed of boards, and later of iron pipe. Lighter gravel running through the chutes was washed away by the action of the water. With luck, the heavier gold remained.

California's principal ore-bearing region was divided into the Northern and the Southern Mines. The northern mining area included the American River, and its various tributaries. Sacramento was the chief depot for provisions. The Southern Mines, whose headquarters was Stockton, included camps lying below the Mokelumne River.

A number of picturesque place names came to be applied to the towns that mushroomed in the mining regions. These included Git-up-and-Git, Lazy Man's Canyon, Wildcat Bar, Skunk Gulch, Gospel Swamp,

"Sundry Amusements in the Mines," 1848–1849. Contemporary print, courtesy of The Huntington Library, San Marino, California.

Whisky Bar, Shinbone Peak, Humpback Slide, Bogus Thunder, Hell's Delight, Poker Flat, Ground Hog Glory, Delirium Tremens, Murderers Bar, Hangtown (later Placerville), and Agua Fria ("cold water"). Hangtown was so named because of a lynching there in 1849.

Most prospectors were law-abiding. But while miners awaited the arrival of a regular legal system, they judged criminal offenses before local courts and meted out such penalties as ear cropping, whipping, and even branding and hanging. This extralegal justice involved some abuses, but it discouraged crime. This was the beginning of vigilantism. The ratio of men to women in the gold fields was approximately twenty to one. Within six months after arrival, one-fifth of the men were dead. Some perished because of deplorable sanitary conditions in the mining camps and shanty towns. Others were killed as the result of too much liquor or the occasional homicidal dispute. In this predominantly male society, prostitutes were in great demand, which is why they flocked there.

Despite the rowdy environment, miners practiced fellowship and hospitality in their tents and dugouts. Sundays were both a day of rest and when one did the week's washing, baking, or mending. Those with wives and children back home wrote letters. Sunday afternoons and evenings were enlivened by swapping yarns, drinking, or gambling.

The bleak days that prospectors spent grubbing for wealth made them especially appreciative of traveling performers who stopped in many a mining town. Prominent among them were Lotta Crabtree, Edwin Booth, and the flaming international celebrity Lola Montez. A more frequent means of entertainment for lonesome men was singing in groups from a booklet entitled *Put's California Songster*. The lyrics of mining-camp songs were usually set to such well-known airs as "Pop Goes the Weasel," or "Ben Bolt." No song quite equaled "The California Emigrant" in popularity, the chorus set to the tune of "Oh! Susannah!". Pioneer women were also acclaimed in the song "Sweet Betsy From Pike."

Sarah Royce was one of these frontier women. The mother of future Harvard philosopher Josiah Royce, hers was a hard and scarcely rewarding life, as were those of other frontier women. Mary Bennett Ritter, one of California's first physicians and reputedly the first American woman to come to California (1849) via Panama, recalled that "there were from ten to forty men to be cooked for, beside the general housework, the washing and ironing, the churning, bread making and sewing for four children—plus making my father's shirts and underwear." Ritter and her mother heated the water for Saturday night baths and made their own soap and candles.

A woman's view of the gold rush was often different from that of males. Sarah Haight, seeing the damage wrought by mining, wrote in

Broadside advertisement of the Mormon Island Emporium, in the California Mines, 1848–1849. Such stores also served as mail, express, and banking centers. Courtesy of The Huntington Library, San Marino, California.

her diary: "How unsightly it makes the country appear. How few flowers and how little vegetation there is where there is gold."

Like the land's resources, the savings of the miners were all too quickly used up. Due to the boom, prices in California were fantastically high, in this age when money in the eastern United States had many times today's purchasing power. Copies of eastern newspapers were grabbed up at $1 apiece. A loaf of bread, which cost 4 or 5 cents on the Atlantic seaboard, sold for 50 or 75 cents at San Francisco. Kentucky bourbon whiskey leaped to $30 a quart; apples sold for $1 to $5 apiece, eggs for $50 a dozen (one boiled egg in a restaurant cost as much as $5), and coffee for $5 a pound. Sacramento merchants sold butcher knives for $30 each, blankets for $40, boots for $100 a pair, and tacks to nail flapping canvas tents for as much as $192 a pound. Medicine cost $10 a pill, or $1 a drop.

By the early 1850s much of the loose ore had been panned out of California's stream beds. No longer could miners hope to wrest fortunes from California's rocks and cliffs with primitive tools and by the sweat of their brow. Henceforth, technological innovations for more complex mining operations required heavy capital. The technique known as hydraulicking involved the use of canvas hoses and nozzles to wash away top soil, making gold particles more accessible. Whole rivers were thereby diverted and canyons stripped bare. Hundreds of miles of canals and flumes carried water through iron pipes to devices that could extract gold. Stamp mills then reduced tons of rock to powder ore. The days of pick, shovel, pan, and burro were clearly over. Now it was mining companies, rather than individual miners, who tunneled their way through bedrock.

Once the "easy pickings" drew to a close by the middle of the 1850s, discouraged prospectors left makeshift ghost towns behind and flocked into the cities, anxious to find any sort of work. Traveling theater troupes that had been able to charge as much as $55 for stall seats now played to almost empty houses. Merchants found it difficult to sell the expensive "Long Nine" Havana cigars that had commanded high prices in boom days. Shopkeepers threw sacks of spoiled flour into the streets of Sacramento and San Francisco to help fill muddy holes; unsalable cast-iron cookstoves were dismantled, their plates used as sidewalks. No longer did miners send laundry as far as Hawaii and even China to be washed.

Although California's first bonanza was seemingly over, the gold rush of '49 had further altered its future forever.

Selected Readings

On mining see Rodman Paul, *California Gold* (1947); John Caughey, ed., *Gold Is the Cornerstone* (1948); Erwin Gudde, *Bigler's Chronicle of the West: The Conquest of California, Discovery of Gold, and Mormon Settlement* (1962); Kenneth N. Owens, ed., *John Sutter and the Wider West* (1994); Alonzo Delano, *Life On the Plains and Among the Diggings* (1854); William Lewis Manly, *Death Valley in '49* (1924); Elza Edwards, *The Valley Whose Name is Death* (1940); Roy and Jean Johnson, eds., *Escape From Death Valley* (1987).

Ocean routes to the gold fields are in James P. Delgado, *To California By Sea: A Maritime History of the California Gold Rush* (1990); Raymond Rydell, *Cape Horn to the Pacific* (1952); John H. Kemble, *The Panama Route* (1943) and Oscar Lewis, *Sea Routes to the Gold Fields* (1949).

Regarding overland trail conditions and legality in the diggings see John P. Reid, *Policing the Elephant* (1996); Charles H. Shinn, *Mining Camps: A Study of American Frontier Government* (1885); Bayard Taylor, *Eldorado, or Adventures in the Path of Empire* (2 vols., repr. 1949); Edwin Beilharz and Carlos Lopez, eds., *We Were '49ers: Chilean Accounts of the California Gold Rush* (1976); and Jo Ann Levy, *They Saw the Elephant: Women and the California Gold Rush* (1990).

Under the pseudonym "Dame Shirley," Louise Amelia Knapp Smith Clappe wrote *The Shirley Letters from the California Mines,* Carl I. Wheat, ed., (1949). Other accounts include E. Gould Buffum, *Six Months in the Gold Mines* (1850) Franklin A. Buck, *Yankee Trader in the Gold Rush* (1930); David M. Potter, ed., *Trail to California: The Overland Journal of Vincent Geiger and Wakeman Bryarly* (1945); Irene D. Paden, *In the Wake of the Prairie Schooner* (1943).

See also Ralph P. Bieber, *Southern Trails to California in 1848* (1937) and his "California Gold Mania," *Mississippi Valley Historical Review* 35 (June 1948), 3–28; F. P. Wierzbicki, *California . . . A Guide to the Gold Region* (1933); George W. Groh, *Gold Fever* (1966) and James S. Holliday, *The World Rushed In* (1982).

Approaches
to Statehood

//////// **CHAPTER 15**

During the Mexican War, California had been treated as conquered territory, subject to military rule. Under international law, it retained its civil municipal institutions, while the American conquerors issued temporary laws and regulations.

The alcalde, a remnant of Mexican bureaucracy, temporarily remained the major judicial officer of California. His traditional functions were maintained, but his authority became variable. Walter Colton, an American who acted as alcalde of Monterey, referred to his position as embracing the responsibilities of "guardian of the public peace." Nearly all California alcaldes were succeeded by Americans, who superimposed upon that Mexican institution the common law they had brought west with them. That law, then, began gradually to supplant the procedures of the past, providing, with the sanction of the military governor, such legal safeguards as trial by jury.

In 1847 American rule was confused by the controversy between Commodore Stockton and General Kearny over their respective authority. Stockton had continued as military governor until, following the Cahuenga Capitulations, he resigned in favor of Frémont, who acted as California's governor for some fifty days. But instructions from Washington designated Kearny as the senior officer in the newly conquered area. The Frémont-Kearny controversy ultimately led to Frémont's court-martial, conviction, and resignation from the army.

American residents now complained about Mexican law, which continued to be enforced without benefit of constitutional courts. Frequent murmurings were heard over infringements upon the right of self-government. Kearny was eventually succeeded as governor by Colonel Richard B. Mason. Mason recognized the popular discontent over government, but ruled under military restrictions. Nevertheless, a few days before he received news of a peace treaty with Mexico, he prepared for a new code of laws for California. This code unfortunately was not immediately issued, and, as American immigration into California increased, discontent among the settlers grew. The Treaty of Guadalupe Hidalgo, ratified on May 20, 1848, concluded the Mexican War and resulted in the final cession of California to the United States. Mason hoped that Congress would soon confer upon Californians their constitutional rights as U.S. citizens. Unfortunately the political machinery for a civil territorial government was slow to be authorized. Mason, in turn, was succeeded as military governor by General Persifor F. Smith.

California clearly needed permanent self-government. General Bennett Riley, the next military governor, issued a proclamation that called for selection of delegates to a convention in order to form a state constitution and plan a territorial government. To support that process, President Zachary Taylor sent a congressional leader, Thomas Butler King, as his personal agent. King was to measure popular sentiment for the territory's admission into the Union. He stayed on as collector of the port of San Francisco and later became a senatorial candidate.

On September 3, 1849, the state's first constitutional convention opened at Colton Hall, a newly constructed white building overlooking the town of Monterey. As its delegates met to write a state constitution, California would seek admission into the Union without yet being officially an American territory.

Forty-eight men were sworn in as delegates to the constitutional convention. They included former Californios as well as early American settlers and "forty-niners," reflecting divergent backgrounds. But the delegates were mostly young and flexible. Their average age was only thirty-six; the oldest delegate, José Antonio Carrillo, was only fifty-three years old. There were few libraries to which the members of the convention could refer for precedent; probably not more than fifty volumes of law and history were to be found in the locality of Monterey. These books, however, included copies of other state constitutions already enacted.

The Californios, who numbered seven out of the forty-eight delegates, were shown special courtesies. General Vallejo, dignified and popular, was to render valuable services as a member of the first California senate. Another Californio convention member, Pablo de la Guerra of Santa Barbara, had much in common with Vallejo. Both were tolerant, well-educated men. The Swiss immigrant Johann Sutter had come to be regarded almost as an American. The most influential delegate was William M. Gwin, a southern politician who would later be elected to represent California in the U.S. Senate. Thomas O. Larkin, "first and last American consul to California," also lent his authority to solving complicated problems as the diverse group grappled to write the new document.

Because miners had not wanted slaves working beside them, they favored admission as a free state. In addition to Gwin, other southerners had migrated to California. Many of these settled near Los Angeles, hoping that, somehow, slaves could be brought into a new American state. Most delegates to the constitutional convention, however, were determined to make California a free state. Ultimately that viewpoint prevailed.

Another debate concerned California's boundaries. The point in greatest dispute was its future eastern border. Some thought the future state should embrace the great desert area east of the Sierra Nevada, and even perhaps the Salt Lake basin inhabited by the Mormons. The convention finally agreed upon a line of demarcation just east of the Sierra crest. This decision to restrict the size of California helped to make its new constitution more acceptable to the U.S. Congress, which was soon to debate future statehood.

As the delegates affixed their signatures to the constitution, a salute of thirty-one guns was fired at the Monterey presidio over the hill from Colton Hall, in honor of the states then in the Union. After the cannonade ended, the crowd assembled outside Colton Hall cheered and tossed their hats in the air as California's newly adopted Great Seal was publicly displayed.

This seal bears thirty-one stars, representing the states then in the Union. Minerva, sprung from the brow of Jupiter, is the foreground figure, symbolic of California's admission to the Union without passing through territorial probation. A grizzly bear crouches at her feet; a miner, with rocker and bowl, depicts "the golden wealth of the Sacramento"; and beyond the river, whose shipping typifies commercial greatness, rise the Sierra Nevada Mountains. At the top of the seal is the legend EUREKA, still the state's motto.

The Constitution of 1849, ratified by popular vote on November 13, 1849, endured for thirty years as the fundamental law of a growing state. After Peter H. Burnett was elected the first civilian governor, General Riley resigned his post. California was now in almost every respect a state, though not yet admitted to the Union.

The legislature named two senators to be sent to Washington. One of these was Frémont, who had returned to California after his court-martial. The other senator was Gwin. When the two laid copies of the new state constitution before Congress and requested admission of California into the Union, southern members of Congress were concerned by the prospect of creating so large a free state. Northern abolitionist congressmen, on the other hand, wanted to exclude slavery from all the lands acquired from Mexico as a result of the war. The process by which California sought admission to the Union soon triggered a violent controversy between North and South.

Only after weeks of deadlock did the U.S. Congress enact its famous "Compromise of 1850." Finally, on September 9, 1850, this agreement authorized California to enter the Union as a free state. New Mexico and Utah territories, incidentally, were at the same time made official territories, with no mention of slavery. Although this compromise temporarily assuaged southern hard feelings, it did not put an end to tensions between North and South, nor within California. In a little more than a decade this rancor would lead to a great Civil War.

California's north-south conflict even affected the choice of its future capital. Several towns vied for selection. In addition to the claims of Monterey and San Francisco, support arose for San Luis Obispo, Benicia, Stockton, and Santa Barbara. San Jose was the site of the first session of the legislature, dubbed the "Legislature of a Thousand Drinks" due to the late-night carousing of its members. A proposal by General Vallejo to lay out a new capital city along the Carquinez Straits received northern support, and, in June 1851, the government archives were moved from San Jose to a bleak site named Vallejo.

In February 1853 another resolution adopted by the legislature established Benicia as the third state capital. That town, which offered only a two-story brick building in the middle of some mud flats, was hardly more suitable than San Jose or Vallejo. Next Sacramento made such a strong bid for the capital that the legislature convened there in 1854. That city, though originally isolated, and plagued by hot weather each summer, remains California's permanent seat of government.

Selected Readings

The Frémont-Kearny-Stockton controversy is in *Proceedings of the Court Martial in the Trial of (J. C.) Frémont* (repr. 1973).

Statehood issues are in David A. Johnson, *Founding the Far West: California, Oregon, and Nevada* (1992) See also William H. Ellison, *A Self-Governing Dominion: California, 1849–1860* (1950); Cardinal L. Goodwin, *The Establishment of State Government in California, 1846–1850* (1914) and Joseph Ellison, *California and the Nation, 1850–1869* (1927); J. Ross Browne,

Report of the Debates in the Convention of California (1850); Rockwell D. Hunt, *The Genesis of California's First Constitution* (1895); Samuel H. Willey, *The Transition Period of California* (1901); James A. B. Scherer, *Thirty-first Star* (1942); Peter H. Burnett, *Recollections and Opinions of an Old Pioneer* (1880); and Donna C. Schuele, "Community Property Law and the Politics of Married Women's Rights in Nineteenth-Century California," *Western Legal History* 7 (Summer/Fall, 1994), 245–281.

Social Ferment

////////// **CHAPTER 16**

Although California had finally entered the American Union, it faced serious social problems. The sheer number of persons who had arrived during and after the gold rush created a formidable challenge of assimilation.

By 1850 the state's population had reached 100,000. It grew to more than 300,000 by 1860. Nearly one-fourth of these persons had migrated from foreign countries. Among whites, men outnumbered women by a ratio of twelve to one. There were fewer than 1,000 blacks. An uncounted number of natives, confused and divided by the American conquest, were everywhere to be seen. With so divergent a population, California faced great social unrest.

At San Francisco, because law enforcement was so weak, a number of "respectable citizens" took it upon themselves to stamp out crime. Because municipal corruption had also become entrenched, they enforced their own morality. Soon mob justice was to be condoned as the answer to repeated frustrations over the failings of law and order. Local vigilantes, not constitutional legal authorities, devised their own punishments against lawbreaking drifters who had filtered back into the city from abandoned mining camps. New white vigilance committees, already established in several mining communities, considered themselves to be "popular tribunals" as well as "champions of justice and of right."

After the discovery of gold, hundreds of potential criminals paralyzed the infant municipal organization of San Francisco. In 1849 a band of toughs, who called themselves the "Hounds," or "Regulators," terrorized the city. The members of a similar group of hoodlums, known as the "Sydney Ducks," had arrived from Great Britain's prison colony in Australia. They greatly confused law and order at the Golden Gate.

Nativism, a form of racial hatred, became entwined with the sordid activities of antiforeign gangs. On Sunday, July 15, 1849, a rowdy crowd of "Regulators" held a "patriotic" parade. After touring various saloons, where they demanded liquor and smashed windows, they began to assault Chilean families who lived in makeshift tents on San Francisco's sand dunes. Although a citizens' court ultimately disciplined the Regulators, murderers and thieves continued to roam about the city's streets.

In 1851, however, two-hundred members of a "Committee of Vigilance of San Francisco" organized themselves to eradicate public disorder. At the head of the committee to purge the city of vice was William T. Coleman, a successful young merchant. He came to be called the "Lion of the Vigilantes." This new-found status made him one of San Francisco's future nabobs. The city's fire bell rang out, beckoning its members to the Monumental Fire Engine House to consider the case of John Jenkins, a convict from Sydney, Australia, who had burglarized a shipping office, making off with its strongbox. Jenkins boldly defied anyone to stop him. When several vigilantes sought to do so, he contemptuously threw the box into San Francisco Bay. Within a few hours the vigilantes took Jenkins to Portsmouth Square where a scaffold was hastily readied, a noose draped round his neck, and he was hanged until his eyes bulged out. San Francisco's "best citizens" heartily approved the guilty sentence.

On the morning of July 11, 1851, the bell on the firehouse again summoned the vigilance committee to judge another Sydney Duck, "English Jim" Stuart, a self-confessed criminal. Through mistaken identity, the committee prepared to execute an innocent man. After they realized their mistake and found Stuart guilty instead, he was led to the Market Street Wharf where he was hanged aboard the deck of a ship.

Apologists for such "do-it-yourself justice" cite the remoteness or corruption of the police and courts. But the distinction between vigilance activity and lynching was often lost sight of and grave abuses continued to be committed. Presumption of guilt sometimes resulted in the execution, ear cropping, or whipping of the accused. Yet, Professor Gordon Bakken has shown, contrary to accepted opinion, that some vigilance committees did act responsibly, freeing suspects they found not guilty.

Nonetheless, whenever a mob got out of hand, foreigners were likely to bear the brunt of its fury, as in the lynching of Juanita, an "evil" Mexican woman. On the evening of July 4, 1851, at Downieville, a town on the Yuba River, a group of American Independence Day celebrants smashed in the door of Juanita's shack. After she knifed one of her assailants, a vigilante jury speedily sentenced her to be "strung up" from a wooden bridge that spanned the river. It did not help Juanita's cause to be a Latina.

Some of the persecution of foreigners, however, had an economic motivation. Immigrant miners, among them Chileans, Frenchmen, and Hawaiian Kanakas, were frequently chased out of select diggings. Yet these foreigners were too valuable a source of cheap labor to exclude permanently. After 1850 Mexican laborers could be obtained in the mines for as little as $1 per day. Thus, when restrictions got so severe as to drive foreigners permanently out of California, some employers tried to shield their foreign laborers against mobs. A few landowners went so far as to advocate repeal of a foreign-miners tax that had been enacted by 1850. This unfair state legislation failed to produce anything like an estimated $2,400,000 in potential revenue. The law was eventually repealed in favor of a small head-tax levied on foreign workers entering California.

In April of 1850, California's governor signed into law "An Act For Better Regulation of Foreign Miners." It came to be known as the Foreign Miners' Tax and imposed a charge of $20 per month on all non-U.S. citizens at work in the diggings. French and Chilean miners flew flags and unfurled banners protesting the regulation. Local merchants too supported the protestors, fearing that it would drive away foreign workers who had become valuable customers. By 1852, Chinese immigrants poured into the Sierra in large numbers. Although Americans fired bullets into foreign flags, the state legislature next levied a lesser foreign miners' tax. It was designed to add money to the state treasury without driving foreigners away.

In the 1850s, some self-imposed guardians of respectability also turned their wrath upon suspected prostitutes, thieves, or drifters. At Sacramento, 215 citizens formed themselves into a committee to police that city. At Marysville, after 17 homicides occurred within one week, another vigilance committee took "prompt steps" to punish suspects. Some hangings were actually popular. At Mokelumne Hill, an alleged thief was executed in the presence of nearly 1,000 witnesses.

Only five years after San Franciscans dissolved their first vigilance brigades, another group came into being there. This became the most reputable and orderly of all such California vigilantes. It regularized its proceedings, having regrouped only because crime had again increased. Indeed, the hangman's noose had faded from memory; approximately 1,000 unpunished murders had occurred in San Francisco from 1849 to 1856 alone.

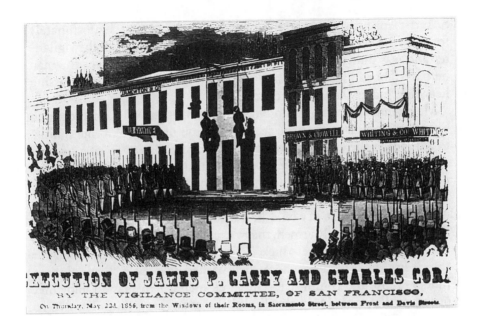

The execution of Casey and Cora, 1856. Contemporary print, H.G. Hills Collection, courtesy of the Bancroft Library, University of California, Berkeley.

By stuffing ballot boxes and using toughs at polling places, corrupt officials had also become entrenched in San Francisco's municipal posts. Political lawlessness was related to the murder of James King of William, the gadfly editor of the *Daily Evening Bulletin*. In his editorials, King had openly attacked prominent politicians, including James P. Casey, an unsavory and opportunistic local office holder. When Casey demanded an apology, he was ordered out of the newspaper's editorial room. He then vowed he would kill King, who scoffed at this threat in his column of May 14, 1856. That evening, Casey approached the newspaperman on the street, drew a revolver and pulled the trigger. As King breathed his last, Casey was locked up in the city jail. Three days later several thousand vigilantes, enraged over this latest homicide, seized Casey and another accused murderer, Charles Cora, from the city jail and sentenced them to death before a tribunal. As King's funeral cortege moved through the city streets, the vigilantes executed both Casey and Cora.

Within a fortnight almost 10,000 men had rejoined the vigilantes. This San Francisco Vigilance Committee of 1856 appointed its own chief of police and 25 policemen to supplement local law enforcement.

A new state Law and Order party objected to the harsh verdicts of this latest vigilance committee. California's Supreme Court Justice David

S. Terry lent his support to the Law and Order faction. Unfortunately for Terry, he became involved in a knifing fracas with one of the vigilantes and was indicted by the vigilance committee. Fortunately, the man he had stabbed did not die, and after almost a month of embarrassing hearings, Judge Terry was acquitted.

Meanwhile, Governor John Neely Johnson asked William Tecumseh Sherman, commander of the second division of the California militia, to aid him in the enforcement of state law. Sherman, who later became a prominent Civil War general, could hardly cope with the forces he now faced. Some 6,000 of the vigilantes had personally taken up arms. Their headquarters, which came to be called "Fort Gunnybags," was so heavily fortified that it would be futile to attack the vigilantes inside that building. Strongly armed, they were protected by bags of sand piled ten feet high and six feet thick. The vigilance committee produced a "black list" of offenders whom they wished to deport. Beginning on June 5, 1856, the committee sent three men off to Hawaii and three others to Panama. Only slowly did the avenging group dissolve itself, then forming a local political party that continued to control San Francisco.

Both vigilante activities and filibustering were typical of mid-nineteenth-century life on an unpoliced frontier. The term "filibuster," which is today applied to prolonged speech-making to delay legislative procedures, once had a different connotation. In the late nineteenth century, citizen filibusterers took it upon themselves to go abroad to "free" unprotected territory from foreign control.

Filibustering was a phenomenon of a restless, youthful America, convinced of its Manifest Destiny to expand toward the country's "natural frontiers." Southerners were particularly attracted to filibustering as a way of spreading their cherished institution of slavery beyond the American South. Apologists for filibustering professed admiration for the courage of adventurers willing to shoulder rifles in foreign fields, seeing them as patriotic soldiers of fortune.

Unsettled conditions in California in the 1850s stimulated filibustering as disillusioned gold seekers looked covetously beyond American territory for adventure. However, the filibustering expeditions that originated from California after its admission to statehood were uniformly unsuccessful. The first one, in 1851 under the leadership of Alexander Bell, was foolishly undertaken to reinstate a deposed president of Ecuador. That same year Sam Brannan, the apostate from Mormonism who had become a prominent Californian, led a party of adventurers to Hawaii. In his foolish attempt to capture those islands, Brannan was lucky to escape incensed Hawaiian pikemen who threatened to run their spears through him. Other adventurers used San Francisco as a base to raise small groups of filibusters who mostly feuded among themselves. In 1851 Joseph Morehead's plan to take the spiny peninsula of Lower California proved equally futile.

California's growing foreign population included other footloose adventurers. Among these were various Frenchmen who had fled their country as a result of the revolutionary movements of 1848. These failed aristocrats were captivated by plans to colonize Mexico. Three independent freebooters left their mark upon the history of both California and northern Mexico: the Marquis Charles de Pindray, Lepine de Sigondis, and Count Gaston de Raousset-Boulbon. During the 1850s all three men led hopeless expeditions from California into Mexico.

The best known of all California filibusters, however, was William Walker. A restless native of Tennessee, Walker arrived at San Francisco in June 1850. Following a short venture into journalism, during which his caustic pen landed him in jail, he entered into law practice at Marysville. Called "the gray-eyed man of destiny," Walker wanted to bring about the independence of the Mexican states of Sonora and Lower California, where he also hoped to extend slavery.

In 1854, Walker left the Golden Gate by ship with 48 followers and landed at La Paz, where he was reinforced by 200 seemingly sympathetic Mexicans. He then proclaimed the independent "Republic of Lower California." This short-lived "government" he quickly abolished, however, in order to launch the "Republic of Sonora," with himself as president. But once in Sonora, native Mexicans began to resent Walker's harsh punishment of deserters from his group. He had been reduced to 35 adherents by May of 1854 when they finally returned to the United States via Tijuana. At San Diego they surrendered to American authorities. Although tried at San Francisco on a charge of violating the U.S. neutrality laws, Walker was somehow acquitted by a sympathetic jury.

On May 3, 1855, Walker again set sail, this time for Nicaragua with a force of 60 men. After landing there, he declared himself to be its president. Two years later, following a series of revolts, he again fled back to the United States. Amazingly still undaunted, Walker launched one last enterprise which involved a landing in Honduras, where he was finally killed in 1860.

By then filibustering had become an outmoded stepchild of Manifest Destiny. But the problem of public disorder had hardly been brought under control in California.

Selected Readings

Vigilante activities are in Hubert Howe Bancroft, *Popular Tribunals* (2 vols., 1887); Mary Floyd Williams, ed., *History of the San Francisco Committee of Vigilance of 1851* (1921); William T. Coleman, "San Francisco Vigilance Committees," *Century Magazine* 43 (November 1891), 133–50; Stanton A. Coblentz, *Villains and Vigilantes* (1936); George R. Stewart, *Committee of Vigilance: Revolution in San Francisco* (1964); Robert Senkewicz, *Vigilantes in Gold Rush San Francisco* (1985) and Alan Valentine, *Vigilante Justice* (1956).

Condemnations of vigilantism appear in Walter Van Tilburg Clark's novel, *The Ox Bow Incident* (1942); see also John W. Caughey, *Their Majesties the Mob* (1960) and Leonard Pitt, "The Beginnings of Nativism in California," *Pacific Historical Review* 30 (February 1961), 23–38.

Legal matters are in Gordon Bakken, *Practicing Law in Frontier California* (1991); John Boessenecker, *Badge and Buckshot: Lawlessness in Old California* (1988); Gordon Bakken and Christian Fritz, "California Legal History: A Bibliographical Essay," *Southern California Quarterly* 70 (Summer 1988), 203–22; Kevin Mullen, *Let Justice Be Done: Crime and Politics in Early San Francisco* (1989); Ronald C. Woolsey, "Crime and Punishment: Los Angeles County, 1850–1856," *Southern California Quarterly* 61 (Spring 1979), 79–98 and Woolsey, "Rites of Passage? Anglo and Mexican-American Contrasts . . . 1860–1870," *Southern California Quarterly* 69 (Summer 1987), 81–95; Robert Blew, "Vigilantism in Los Angeles, 1835–74," *Southern California Quarterly* 54 (Spring 1972), 11–27; Lawrence E. Guillow, "Pandemonium in the Plaza: The First Los Angeles Riot, July 22, 1856," *Southern California Quarterly* 77 (Fall 1995), 183–97; Jacqueline Barnhart, *The Fair But Frail: Prostitution in San Francisco, 1849–1900* (1986).

Regarding filibustering see William O. Scroggs, *Filibusters and Financiers* (New York, 1931); Laurence Greene, *The Filibuster* (1937); Andrew Rolle, "California Filibustering and the Hawaiian Kingdom," *Pacific Historical Review* 19 (August 1950), 251–63 and Rolle, "Futile Filibustering in Baja California, 1888–1890," *Pacific Historical Review* 20 (May 1951), 159–66.

A New Culture at the Golden Gate

////////// **CHAPTER 17**

California's great gold rush had been a defining American epic. From many parts of the world fortune-hunters flooded into the newly conquered province. In 1849 alone, more than 36,000 immigrants arrived in San Francisco by sea. In the next twenty years it became California's first real city. But, before it could exchange its cultural primitiveness for cosmopolitan tastes and ideas, pressing civic problems still demanded action.

The fire hazard in San Francisco continued to grow because of a large number of flimsy wooden structures. The need for more permanent dwellings increased drastically. After the gold rush an enclave called "Happy Valley" still contained about a thousand tents. Six conflagrations swept over San Francisco in a period of eighteen months. The first great fire took place in December 1849. A second occurred in May 1850. After an interval of scarcely a month came a third fire. Most damaging of all of them was the disaster of May 4, 1851, which destroyed a large part of the town. Only later would San Francisco rebuild itself in brick and stone.

The air of uncertainty was also reflected in the city's commercial market, where, after the gold rush, prices dropped sharply. Pickled beef and pork went from $60 to $10 per barrel; flour decreased from $800 to $20 per barrel. Quite suddenly, unwanted imports piled up at the wharfs and few items remained difficult to obtain.

The gold rush boom had coaxed bankers, traders, and merchants into speculations that were to prove their undoing. From 1849 to 1855 the steadily declining yield of gold from the placers decreased the influx of population, causing a reversal in property values. Housing sites that had cost $15 before the rush reached $8,000 during its height, only to plummet to less than $100 later.

More profitable were the city's saloons and gambling parlors, decorated with plush furniture, chandeliers, and mirrors. The "El Dorado," with its eight gaming tables, velvet-upholstered chairs, and spacious bar, attracted great crowds. Upstairs there were convenient prostitution cribs. Customers were expected to keep their derringers out of sight, unless attacked. A few of the wealthiest citizens got their start as faro dealers or card men.

San Francisco was still predominantly a city of young men, far away from home and removed from family restraints. Gambling, dueling, theatrical performances, and ostentatious living, held more appeal than churchgoing. This, however, was not the whole story. In 1849 the Reverend Albert Williams organized the First Presbyterian Church of San Francisco. Mission Dolores served as a place of worship for Catholics until 1849, when the first secular church, named for St. Francis, was organized.

Regardless of unsteady economic and social conditions, education became a major concern at San Francisco. In 1849 John C. Pelton arrived from Boston to open a municipal school on Portsmouth Square, based upon New England traditions of instruction. By 1853 the first Academy of Science in the West was begun.

California's first English-language newspaper, the *Californian*, had appeared at Monterey on August 15, 1846. This weekly was printed in two columns, English on one side and Spanish on the other. It had to be printed on any stock available, even on wrapping or tissue paper, because newsprint was in short supply. Only a few months after this paper appeared, Sam Brannan founded the *California Star*. In 1849 the two papers merged as the *Alta California*. Eventually, the paper's use of the Spanish language was dropped.

Midcentury California, with San Francisco as its cultural center, also welcomed reminiscences written by pioneers who had come to California by sea. Richard Henry Dana's *Two Years Before the Mast* (1840) was one of the first books to introduce pastoral California of hide and tallow days to a wide reading public. A less well-known pioneer chronicle by a Yankee sea trader was Richard J. Cleveland's *A Narrative of Voyages and Commercial Enterprises* (1842).

Lonely readers clamored for every sort of literary fare. San Francisco's *The Golden Era*, founded in 1852, was California's first weekly of any literary pretension. It was followed by the *Pioneer* (1854), *Hutchings' California Magazine* (1856), and *The Hesperian* (1858). *The Golden Era*, longest-lived of these early journals, continued to be published until 1893.

The strongest magazine was the *Overland Monthly,* which began publication in 1868. Bret Harte, its editor, encouraged other authors to write for the *Overland* and gained a national audience for them. In 1868 Harte attracted attention to the *Overland* by the publication of his story, "The Luck of Roaring Camp." This was followed by "The Outcasts of Poker Flat," in which he created a stereotype of the western miner as a bearded, red-shirted romantic figure. Harte also helped to introduce a national school of "local color" writers.

A crude literature of burlesque was then fashionable. One of the exponents of this jokester style was an army officer, Lieutenant George Horatio Derby, known under two pen names, "The Veritable Squibob," and "John Phoenix." In 1856 he wrote a salty book, *Phoenixiana,* which became immensely popular. Readers roared at such Derby remarks as "Absinthe makes the heart grow fonder," and "They came to cough and remain to spray." Coarse humor also characterized the writing of Alonzo "Old Block" Delano. His *Pen Knife Sketches* (1853), *Life on the Plains And Among the Diggings* (1854), and melodramatic play, *A Live Woman in the Mines* (1857), were a favorite of miners. Educated and uneducated alike reveled in the literary horseplay brought into lonely and obscure camps. Local colorists and frontier satirists boasted about the achievements of a proud generation of hardy pioneers and were prone to high-flown exaggeration. Nonetheless, their writings help the historian to understand the otherwise bleak environment of primitive mining camps.

A then obscure writer, Samuel Langhorne Clemens, better known later as Mark Twain, went into mining in Nevada. When bad weather kept him from work in the diggings, he amused himself by writing burlesque sketches. These he signed "Josh" and sent to the *Territorial Enterprise,* a newspaper at Virginia City in today's Nevada. In 1862 Twain walked 130 miles from a lonely mining site to take a job on the *Enterprise* for $25 per week. Two years later Twain drifted into San Francisco, where he became a reporter for its *Morning Call.* In California, in a cabin near Angel's Camp, Twain wrote "The Celebrated Jumping Frog of Calaveras County." The piece made him famous almost overnight, and he went on to write a book of mining tales, *Roughing It.*

San Francisco also nourished a notable artistic colony. Among its foreign-born craftsmen was the German etcher and printmaker Edward Vischer. Vischer traveled throughout California making sketches of ruined missions. Another foreign artist was the Scottish painter William Keith. Keith also painted the missions; but his water colors of the Yosemite Valley made him one of the most appreciated artists in the West.

John W. Audubon, son of the noted naturalist, toured the California diggings making hundreds of pencil and watercolor sketches, which he

North Beach, San Francisco, ca. 1860. H. G. Hills Collection, courtesy of The Bancroft Library, University of California, Berkeley.

decided to ship to the East Coast. Because his portfolios were too bulky to go overland, he entrusted them to a friend traveling eastward in 1857 on the ship *Central America*. Unfortunately, both Audubon's friend and most of his work went down with that ship.

At the time San Francisco's Bohemian quarter stretched from North Beach across Telegraph Hill. There Albert Bierstadt, like Vischer a German artist, first set up a studio in 1858. His canvases idealized natural wonders. Some of his best oils, like those of Keith, were unfortunately destroyed in the great fire of 1906.

Descriptions of the city of the "golden fifties and champagne sixties" stress its opulence as revealed in architecture. The same Italian artists who painted the interiors of future railroad-magnate Mark Hopkins's baroque castle on Nob Hill also decorated theaters, saloons, and brothels along the city's Barbary Coast. Gilt-edged Victorian residences, like that of Hopkins's associate Charles Crocker, overlooked hilly lawns sprinkled with cast-iron animals. Popular legend has it that in the vicinity of the Hopkins mansion there were so many brass fences that one man was employed the year-round polishing them.

In an atmosphere of opulence, entertainment flourished. At the Jenny Lind Theater, Lola Montez's fans flocked to see her perform her exotic "Tarantula Dance." Lola was known as a notorious woman with many lovers, including King Ludwig of Bavaria. But it was her exquisite fig-

Residences of Mrs. Mark Hopkins and Governor Stanford, San Francisco. H. G. Hills Collection, courtesy of The Bancroft Library, University of California, Berkeley.

Colton and Crocker Mansions, San Francisco. H. G. Hills Collection, courtesy of The Bancroft Library, University of California, Berkeley.

ure, flashing eyes, and raven-black hair that captivated male audiences. At the mining camp of Grass Valley she charged $100 per admission. Brandishing a whip on stage, Lola shivered and trembled, driving lonely miners into a frenzy. A flaming redhead companion of Montez's, Adah

Menken, clad in flesh-colored tights, was showered with gold nuggets and diamond brooches thrown onto the stage by admirers who had struck it rich. Lotta Crabtree, a home-grown chanteuse and dancer who had charmed lonesome miners during the gold rush, remained popular in San Francisco through its midcentury.

From 1850 to 1859, over one thousand dramatic productions were also staged in San Francisco. Especially popular were the great Shakespearean troopers Junius Brutus Booth and his son Edwin. It would take years before other California cities could begin to match the cultural activity swirling about the Golden Gate. Literature, art, and drama had made San Francisco the cultural mecca of the American West.

Selected Readings

Social turbulence is treated in William B. Secrest, *Lawmen and Desperadoes . . . 1850–1900* (1997). See also Bayard Taylor, *Eldorado, or Adventures in the Path of Empire* (repr. 1949); T. A. Barry and B. A. Patten, *Men and Memories of San Francisco* (1873); Robert E. Cowan, *Forgotten Characters of Old San Francisco* (1938); William Drury, *Norton I: Emperor of the United States* (1986); John H. Kemble, ed., *San Francisco Bay* (1957). Julia Altrocchi, *The Spectacular San Franciscans* (1949); William M. Camp, *San Francisco, Port of Gold* (1947); Julian Dana, *The Man Who Built San Francisco* (1936); George D. Lyman, *Ralston's Ring* (1937); Robert W. Lotchin, *San Francisco, 1846–1856: From Hamlet to City* (1974); Gunther Barth, *Instant Cities: Urbanization and the Rise of San Francisco* (1975) and Peter Decker, *Fortunes and Failures: White Collar Mobility in Nineteenth Century San Francisco* (1978).

Education is discussed in Nicholas C. Polos, *John Swett: California's Frontier Schoolmaster* (1978). For literature see Franklin Walker, *San Francisco's Literary Frontier* (1939). The theater is in G. R. MacMinn, *The Theater of the Golden Era* (1941). Biographies include Ivan Benson, *Mark Twain's Western Years* (1938); Edgar M. Branch, *The Literary Apprenticeship of Mark Twain* (1950); George R. Stewart, *Bret Harte: Argonaut and Exile* (1931) and Stewart, *John Phoenix, Esq.: The Veritable Squibob* (1937).

An entire issue of *California History*, 71 (Spring 1992), concerns California artists in the nineteenth century. See also Eugen Neuhaus, *William Keith: The Man and the Artist* (1938); Brother Cornelius, *Keith, Old Master of California* (1942). Sketches of John W. Audubon, Albert Bierstadt, William Keith, Charles C. Nahl, and Victor Prevost are in *California Centennials Exhibition of Art* (1949); also Carl Dentzel, ed., *The Drawings of John Woodhouse Audubon* (1957).

Post–Gold Rush Commerce

////// CHAPTER 18

As California's gold deposits were quickly "played out," and its richest ores grew scarcer, numerous gold diggers settled down to running hardware stores, livery stables, and saloons. As pan and cradle gave way to quartz-crushing and ore-pounding machinery, the chemist became a partner of the miner. The pulverizing of quartz, treated with mercury to form an amalgam, was a new technological development that accompanied the discovery of big silver deposits.

By 1853, prospectors had poked about the brush-strewn slopes of the Washoe area east of the Sierra. This region, not then officially part of Nevada, was an extension of California, financially and technologically. There miners unearthed a bluish-tinged ore that, at first, was cast aside. In 1859 an assayer found that this "blasted blue stuff" was actually sulfide containing high percentages of silver and gold.

For more than fifteen years the region around today's Carson City, Reno, and Virginia City, Nevada, was gripped by speculation. By the 1860s thirty mills were in operation. William C. Ralston and his Bank of California invested heavily in what came to be called the Comstock Lode. Thousands of feet of timber as well as machinery came over the Sierra from California to shore up tunnels amid rich veins of silver. The San Francisco financiers who made up "Ralston's Ring" turned the Comstock into a honeycomb of conduits and shafts propped up by wooden beams, the lode coming to be called the tomb of the Sierra forests.

In 1873 Adolph Sutro began to build a tunnel into the heart of the potentially dangerous Comstock. This engineering feat provided the "hot sumps" below the ground with ventilation and drainage. But completion of Sutro's tunnel in 1878 came many years too late, and his stockholders failed to reap its promised benefits. Other millionaires, however, got their start in the Comstock. The pooled investments of George Hearst, E. J. ("Lucky") Baldwin, John W. Mackay, James Fair, James C. Flood, William S. O'Brien, John P. Jones, and Alvinza Hayward all financed the uncovering of huge hidden ore bodies. Half the mansions in their San Francisco were eventually constructed with silver and gold earnings from the Washoe area.

"The King of the Comstock," William Sharon—who controlled vital lumber and rail interests from California—had coaxed Ralston into sinking millions into the "Washoe Madness." But, during the national panic of 1873 the failure of Ralston's Bank of California set off a string of financial bankruptcies. In 1875 Ralston, distraught at the prospect of ruin, met his death—either by suicide or accident—in the icy waters of San Francisco Bay.

Possibly as much capital was put into the Comstock Lode as was ever taken out. Once the "blue stuff" gave out, speculators returned to San Francisco. Sutro became its mayor and founded a noted library. Mackay lent his energies and capital to a cable and telegraphic system. James Fair's family name is perpetuated in today's renowned Fairmont Hotel on Nob Hill.

California's two great mining rushes also stimulated staging and freighting operations. As early as 1849, James E. Birch established the California Stage Line Company, which connected Sacramento and Coloma. Miners paid Birch a fare each way of two ounces of gold, or $32. In 1850 John Whistman inaugurated stage service between San Jose and San Francisco. The 45-mile run took 9 hours to make.

So poor was delivery service that for six weeks during the winter of 1852–1853 Los Angeles received no mail. Eventually two eastern staging firms, Adams and Company Express and Wells, Fargo and Company, absorbed much local mail service. Wells Fargo, a firm with national connections, transported $58 million worth of gold into San Francisco alone in a five-year period. In time both companies also took on banking functions.

It was no easy job to drive the large teams of mixed mustangs hitched to heavily loaded stages over the steep grades of the Sierra. A good driver communicated with his mules or horses through gentle movements of the reins. Tough as saddle leather, and inured to the dust and heat of the trail, these drivers, or "whips," raised stage driving to an art.

Nonetheless, most stage coach travelers endured bone-jarring rides. Although the introduction of lighter, faster stages was shrinking travel

Placer miner on the Colorado River, ca. 1890. C. C. Pierce collection, courtesy of The Huntington Library, San Marino, California.

time, a week of travel through clouds of dust and in the rain and snow so upset some passengers that they stopped the stages to duel with one another. At outlying stage stations drivers obtained fresh horses and passengers had the opportunity to rest from their journey.

The best stage lines used light Concord carriages, manufactured by Abbott, Downing and Company in New Hampshire. The coaches rode on a leather cradle of "thorough braces" that cushioned passengers against the buffetings of the road. Strongly constructed of New England ash wood and select Norwegian iron, the Concord coaches were sometimes ornately paneled. Though considered "light," the 2,500-pound carriages required three spans of good horses to pull them. Most stage lines, however, merely modified old mud wagons such as were to be seen on almost every California ranch. These heavier, springless vehicles, fitted out to carry only twelve passengers, were slow and hardly comfortable vehicles.

In 1858, with a federal financial subsidy, John Butterfield began to carry the mails cross-country. By using relays of horses exchanged at ten-mile intervals, his coaches could cover the 2,800 miles between Missouri and San Francisco in twenty-four days, eighteen hours, and twenty-six minutes. The schedule called for an average speed of five miles an hour, day and night. Fresh horses greeted the Butterfield carriages at a series of wayside stops. Eventually he employed more than 1,000 men across the country.

As the Civil War approached, Butterfield began to transfer equipment northward. In 1861 his Overland Mail service offered passengers a connection from St. Louis to California via Salt Lake City. Sectional tension kept the nation from settling upon a future transcontinental railroad route.

In 1855 a picturesque episode in the story of southwestern transportation had also begun. This was the appearance of the army's "Camel Corps." The short-lived "lightning dromedary express" made a first trip from Arizona into California in fifteen days, the camels swimming the Colorado River en route. Three years later, in January of 1858, the population of Los Angeles turned out to witness the appearance of the first camel caravan to reach their city. The camels were on their way to Fort Tejon, where Lieutenant Edward Fitzgerald Beale supervised subsequent trips between that fort and Albuquerque, New Mexico. These freight-carrying "ships of the desert" developed sore legs from cacti, prickly pear, and sagebrush, leading the army to give up their use.

Still another innovation in western transportation involved young single riders using relays of fresh horses to carry mail more quickly between distant points. The Pony Express had first begun to function on April 3, 1860, with the departure of a rider from St. Joseph, Missouri, for California. The westward route of the Pony Express was much the same as that taken by overland wagons. After reaching Sacramento, both rider and horse went from the capital by steamboat down the Sacramento River and across the bay to San Francisco. The run of 1,966 miles was completed in nine days and twenty-three hours, less than half the time required by the best stages to California from Missouri.

The Pony Express consisted of 80 riders, 190 relay stations, 400 stationmen, and 400 fast horses. Young, light riders were selected, armed only with a six-shooter and a knife. Each man changed horses every ten miles, but "Buffalo Bill" (William F. Cody) is credited with one continuous ride of 384 miles. Letters, transported in leather pouches, were written on the thinnest of paper in order to keep the loads light; with the Express in place, the rate of postage fell from $5 per half ounce to $1. Completion of a transcontinental telegraph line in 1861 ended the Pony Express. Though operated for only sixteen months, and failing to make a financial profit, it had demonstrated the practicality of a central transcontinental route, the forerunner of the route of the Central Pacific Railroad.

Another pre-railroad entrepreneur was Ben Holladay, a boisterous and coarse buccaneer. He moved from Kentucky to Missouri, where he operated a general store and saloon. During the Mexican War he also freighted supplies westward for the army. At the war's end, he purchased wagons and oxen from the government at bargain prices. Holladay's trans-Missouri state line earned him the titles "King of Hurry," as well

Going into the Southern California mines by stagecoach, 1904. Diggings are in the canyon in the background. C. C. Pierce collection, courtesy of The Huntington Library, San Marino, California.

as "Napoleon of the Plains." In addition to operating 3,300 miles of stage routes as far west as Placerville, California, he eventually financed steamboat and rail services throughout America's middle west. Holladay sold his staging operation to Wells Fargo.

Few stages traveled at night, for fear of Indians, dangerous potholes, and bandits who could suddenly appear at a coach door. Bandits, masked and armed, quickly relieved passengers of valuables and the stagecoach of its strong box. Resistance meant instant shooting. Among local banditti was Joaquín Murieta, whose name struck terror from one end of the state to the other. He has been called the super bandit of California's past. He became such a problem that the legislature took extraordinary measures and offered a $1000 reward for his capture. Texas Ranger Harry S. Love was hired to track Murieta down. In 1853, Captain Love finally captured and killed a man alleged to be Murieta, whose head was later exhibited at freak shows in a jar of alcohol. The grizzly remains disappeared in the rubble of San Francisco's 1906 earthquake and fire.

Equally feared was the bandit Tiburcio Vásquez, captured in 1874 after evading the law for years. A sheriff's posse blasted him out of a hideout in the Cahuenga hills and hanged him. In northern California "Black Bart," yet another road agent, wore a flour sack over his head. He achieved renown because of the doggerel verses, which he mockingly left at the scene of his robberies, and the terse four-word phrase he uttered upon stopping a stage: "Throw down the box!" From 1875 to 1883, twenty-eight different drivers readily complied and threw down their express boxes to "Black Bart." But he inadvertently dropped a handkerchief at one robbery; its laundry mark led detectives to San Francisco, where he turned out to be Charles E. Bolton, a mining engineer. He was sent to San Quentin Penitentiary, served his sentence and then disappeared forever.

In 1853, accompanying transportation developments, were the beginnings of telegraph service via a connection between the lighthouse at Point Lobos and San Francisco. By 1860, Los Angeles was also linked telegraphically with the Bay area. The next year the first telegraphic message arrived on the East Coast from California, addressed to President Lincoln.

Banking was yet another enterprise related to communication. Some frontier bankers began as saloon keepers or stage coach operators who had strong safes on their premises. On their visits to town, miners entrusted their hard-earned treasure to these men for safekeeping. Merchants charged interest for storing money, in contrast with modern banks which pay interest to their depositors. Early western banks considered keeping a miner's doeskin bag of nuggets or "poke" of gold dust to be a

L. Lichtenberger's carriage factory, 147–149 Main Street, Los Angeles, 1883. C. C. Pierce Collection, courtesy of The Hungtington Library, San Marino, California.

risky venture. Only the large national express companies possessed the facilities for the safe transportation of money.

By the mid-1850s travel by water had entered a new era. Upon finally arriving at the Golden Gate, river boats took passengers to interior ports. These included Marysville, Sacramento, and Stockton. The fastest steamboats, among them the *Senator, Cornelia,* and *New World,* sometimes engaged in dangerous racing. On several occasions passengers on riverboats moving under high steam felt the explosion of iron boilers as decks literally buckled beneath them.

Steamboats and barges along California's inland rivers irregularly serviced outlying ranches. The smaller vessels continued up the Sacramento and San Joaquin rivers, trading supplies en route. The smaller vessels were able to reach shallow bodies of water, including the Mokelumne River and Lake Tulare, which was once linked to the turbulent lower Kern River and the nearby new town of Bakersfield.

After the Civil War, San Francisco remained California's major port. By 1870, an increasing number of ships entered its waterfront, sometimes in ballast, to load grain, lumber, wool, quicksilver, and flour. In and around the city, nearly 100 flour mills were in operation, as were scores of lumber and textile mills, foundries such as the Risdon and Pacific Iron Works, the San Francisco chocolate factory of Domenico Ghirardelli, the sugar-beet refineries of the Oxnard Brothers and Claus Spreckels, several cigar and boot factories, tanneries, ship repair yards, and gun powder works. San Jose, Stockton, Sacramento, Marysville, and Merced each possessed woolen mills.

California suddenly also needed more blacksmiths, harness and saddle makers, wheelwrights, and carpenters. Almost every sizable town also acquired a brewery or distillery and a metal or iron shop; soon canneries would make their appearance. John Studebaker at Placerville and Phineas Banning at Wilmington began to build excellent wagons and carriages. After 1867 Banning also operated a stage line into Los Angeles and eventually a railroad that reached San Pedro's harbor.

As the state's population grew, fishing and whaling also became more important. In 1855 alone, 500 whaling vessels visited the California coast. That year a number of firms as far north as Sacramento were smoking and salting salmon. As canned salmon production increased, Monterey emerged as a terminus for anchovy and sardine fleets while San Pedro became a tuna-packing center. In time San Diego was processing tons of mackerel, sole, sand dabs, skipjack, albacore, rockfish, and barracuda. In order to meet the demand for shellfish, clams, crabs, and abalone also were increasingly harvested all along California's coast.

The building of a transcontinental railroad would expand local fish and produce marketing, making California's products available for national consumption.

Selected Readings

Regarding the Comstock Lode see George D. Lyman, *The Saga of the Comstock* (1934) and his *Ralston's Ring: California Plunders the Comstock Lode* (1937). Also see Lucius Beebe and Charles Clegg, *Legends of the Comstock Lode* (1950); Oscar Lewis, *The Silver Kings* (1947); Grant H. Smith, *The History of the Comstock Lode* (1943); Robert E. Stewart and Mary Stewart, *Adolph Sutro: A Biography* (1962) and Rodman W. Paul, *Mining Frontiers of the Far West* (1963).

For staging and freighting see Oscar O. Winther, *Express and Stagecoach Days in California* (1936); Le Roy R. Hafen, *The Overland Mail, 1849–1869* (1926); Frank A. Root and William Elsey Connelley, *The Overland Stage to California* (1901); William Tallack, *The California Overland Express: The Longest Stage Ride in the World* (1935), William and George H. Banning, *Six Horses* (1930); Ernest A. Wiltsee, *The Pioneer Miner and Pack*

Mule Express (1931); Roscoe P. and Margaret B. Conkling, *The Butterfield Overland Mail, 1857–1869* (3 vols., 1947); Walter Lang, ed., *The First Overland Mail* (2 vols., 1940–45); M. H. B. Boggs, *My Playhouse Was a Concord Coach* (1942); Noel Loomis, *Wells Fargo* (1969); Ellis Lucia, *The Saga of Ben Holladay, Giant of the Old West* (1959); J. V. Frederick, *Ben Holladay the Stagecoach King* (1940) and Edward Hungerford, *Wells Fargo: Advancing the American Frontier* (1949).

See also Martin Ridge, "Reflections on the Pony Express," *Montana, The Magazine of Western History* 46 (Autumn 1996), 2–13; Samuel H. Adams, *The Pony Express* (1950); William Lightfoot Visscher, *A Thrilling and Truthful History of the Pony Express* (1908); Raymond W. Settle and Mary Lund Settle, *Empire on Wheels* (1949) and their *Saddles and Spurs* (1955) as well as his *War Drums and Wagon Wheels: The Story of Russell, Majors and Waddell* (1966). The camel experiment is in Lewis B. Lesley, *Uncle Sam's Camels* (1929) and Harlan Fowler in his *Camels to California* (Palo Alto, 1950).

Descriptions of travel include William H. Brewer, *Up and Down California in 1860–1864* (1930); W. Turrentine Jackson, *Wagon Roads West* (1952). The telegraph is in Robert L. Thompson, *Wiring a Continent* (1947).

California's most notorious courtesan is the subject of James F. Varley, *Lola Montez* (1997). Regarding outlaws see William B. Secrest, *Lawmen and Desperadoes . . . 1850–1900* (1997); Joseph Henry Jackson, *Tintypes in Gold: Four Studies in Robbery* (1939) and Jackson, *Bad Company* (1949); Ben C. Truman, *Life, Adventures and Capture of Tiburcio Vásquez* (1874) and Walter Noble Burns, *The Robin Hood of El Dorado* (1932).

Early banking is in Ira B. Cross, *Financing an Empire* (4 vols., 1937); Robert G. Cleland and Frank B. Putnam, *Isaias W. Hellman and the Farmers and Merchants Bank* (1965); Robert G. Cleland and Osgood Hardy, *The March of Industry* (1929); Harris Newmark, *Sixty Years in Southern California* (repr. 1930) and J. A. Graves, *My Seventy Years in California* (1929).

The Land
Problem

By the time of the American conquest, almost 14 million acres had been granted to rancheros by Spanish and Mexican officials. A few of these claims were gargantuan; one covered 1,775,000 acres. In 1846, the last year of the Mexican era, eighty-seven grants had been made by Governor Pico alone, mostly to personal friends. American land seekers were appalled at the size of such grants. Two different legal traditions—the Spanish and the American—were now about to collide, at a time when old-time Californios came under extreme pressure.

Rancheros, stuck with herds of stunted cattle on overgrazed pastures, were caught in a net of rising costs and fierce competition. Land-hungry American squatters also challenged their right to hold huge grants intact. These avaricious newcomers, oblivious to personal property rights, roamed about the countryside, living in wagons, using up water and grazing areas, even claiming ownership of unbranded calves and loose cattle. Squatters asked what right had the Vallejos, the Argüellos, or the Swiss Captain Sutter to estates of eleven or more leagues? This despite the fact that both Commodore Sloat's Proclamation and the subsequent Treaty of Guadalupe Hidalgo guaranteed existing grantee rights in California.

A congressional act of March 1851 created a Land Commission to pass upon the validity of California's Mexican titles. Land claimants who failed to appear before the commission in San Francisco to present claims within two years would forfeit rights to their lands. These then would be considered "a part of the public domain of the United States." The Land Commission subjected native landowners to complicated legalities—especially after some fraudulent claims were uncovered.

One of the most astounding frauds was perpetuated by José Limantour, who asserted that he owned 600,000 acres, including several islands and four square leagues within and adjoining San Francisco Bay. Arrested and awaiting trial for embezzlement, Limantour deposited a $30,000 bond. This he suddenly forfeited, fleeing the country. He was never again seen in California.

Meanwhile, nothing but superior force could dislodge other San Francisco squatters. Some seized vacant lots in the middle of the night, erecting flimsy shanties. During the city's fire of 1851 nervy squatters even fenced in disputed lots while the ashes were still hot, to prevent their claims from being "jumped" by newcomers.

Accurate surveys of grants did not yet exist. Most original boundary marks had disappeared or become unrecognizable. Sometimes an owner's cattle brand was burned into a tree, only to be obliterated by whims of nature. Further confusion arose because of duplications and vagueness in the boundaries of grants. The Californios had almost never quarreled among themselves over boundaries; land was abundant and shared by all rancheros.

The Land Commission stayed in session at San Francisco until 1856. During that period, land owners diligently searched their adobes for original grants issued by past Mexican governors. The burden of legal proof remained on the rancheros though none of the land commissioners spoke or read the Spanish language. Eventually rancheros were forced to mortgage their lands, usually at high interest rates, to pay for legal fees and expensive trips to Washington in order to appeal to federal officials.

American attorneys charged the rancheros large retainers for unraveling complicated land-title snarls that involved vaguely defined or overlapping boundaries. Supposedly "final" decisions of the Land Commission were, furthermore, repeatedly contested in both lower and upper courts, sometimes culminating in appeals to the United States Supreme Court. In one case a claimant had to wait thirty-five years before he could officially call his land his own. From 1865 to 1880, the owners of Rancho Palos Verdes underwent seventy-eight law suits, six partition suits, a dozen suits over the ejection of squatters, and three condemnation proceedings. Landowners also experienced repeated angry squatter confrontations, including knifings and shootings, outside the courts.

Confusion reigned over all land titles. Eventually litigation over pueblo land claims retarded municipal settlement of both San Francisco and Los Angeles. San Francisco, under Spanish legal tradition, was, like every pueblo, entitled to four square leagues of land. At Los Angeles, however, its city fathers voraciously staked out claims to four leagues square (an area considerably larger than four square leagues).

John Charles Frémont, when still a senator, lobbied for speedy confirmation of land grants, even those of a questionable nature So did his brother-in-law, William Carey Jones, who acted as an official examiner of land titles. Both had bought former rancho lands. Indeed, confirmation of Frémont's claim to a huge Mariposa mining and logging property raised questions as to the commission's neutrality even when dealing with claimants who were Americans.

The U.S. government also continued to foist rigid land-title examinations upon befuddled Latino residents who had only recently become citizens. Without knowledge of either American law or language, intimidated rancheros, when threatened by squatter violence, generally yielded. Land law was often interpreted by squatter judges, squatter juries, and squatter sheriffs. For many years no genuine title to land could be firmly established, which eventually led to the founding of state title-insurance businesses. By then most Latino rancheros were hopelessly in debt.

Obviously the 1860s were difficult years on California's ranchos and farms. Insolvent landowners received only temporary relief through the forced sale of land parcels. To make matters worse, a grasshopper invasion was followed by floods, and then, in the middle of the decade, bone-dry aridity. Five thousand head of cattle were marketed at Santa Barbara in these years for only 37 cents each. The annual income of land baron Abel Stearns fell to only $300. Desperate rancheros tried to sell out corrals of horses, to rent animals for plowing, to cut up cordwood for sale in nearby towns—anything to recoup their losses. As if all this misfortune were not enough, livestock in the state began to suffer from a new cattle disease—anthrax.

California's original rancho tradition, the "Arcadia" of yore, could not withstand the all-consuming process of Americanization. As a result, new and more efficient agricultural developments would take its place.

Selected Readings

Regarding the land problem see W. W. Robinson, *Land in California* (1948) and Robinson, *Ranchos Become Cities* (1939). Paul W. Gates has written the following articles: "Adjudication of Spanish-Mexican Land Claims in California," *Huntington Library Quarterly* 21 (May 1958), 213–36; "Pre-Henry George Land Warfare in California," *California Historical Society Quarterly* 46 (June 1967), 121–48; "The Fremont-Jones Scramble For California Land Claims," *Southern California Quarterly* 56 (Spring 1974), 13–44; and "Carpetbaggers Join the Rush for California Land," *California Historical Quarterly* 56 (Summer 1977), 98–127. See also Henry George, *Our Land and Land Policy: National and State* (1871). Though dated, George remains an important contemporary source.

California
and the Union
////////CHAPTER 20

California was one of the few states that skipped the interim territorial stage of political organization. Its rapid growth was partly responsible for movement directly into statehood, and its population continued to increase at a prodigious rate—310 percent by the end of its first decade as a state. In 1860 California had a population of 380,000, of which residents born outside the state outnumbered the native-born by two to one.

With General Zachary Taylor's election to the presidency in 1848 the Whig party took over many eastern governmental positions, releasing a flood of unemployed Democrats. Among them was New York's Irish Tammany regular David C. Broderick, who sought to transfer that city's ward system to San Francisco. Other shrewd politicians, with years of political experience, helped tie the new state more closely to the Union, although full "economic statehood" was not achieved until the railroad finally linked California with the rest of the nation.

Another new leader was William M. Gwin of Tennessee, who became one of California's first two senators. Gwin and Broderick soon developed loyal followings. In an age of political simplicity these politicos attained power partly because of general disinterest in state politics. In frontier areas, settlers were absorbed in the process of daily life, mending leaks in their cabin roofs, lining wells with bricks, and fencing property boundaries.

After California's constitution was ratified, the first legislature met at San Jose in December 1849, and Peter H. Burnett was sworn in as governor. A pioneer from Oregon, Burnett, a Democrat, remained in office until January 1851. He was succeeded by another Democrat, John McDougal. These early governors performed their duties for the most part ably but did not generally demonstrate unusual capacities.

Among the first tasks to which California's early politicians turned their attention was the organization of new counties. The former military governor, General Bennett Riley, had divided the state into ten districts to be represented at the constitutional convention of 1849. These were subdivided by the first legislature into twenty-seven counties. By 1907 the number of counties would grow to fifty-eight.

Equally important were the beginnings of party organization in California. The functioning of the Democratic party in the state dates from a meeting of its stalwarts at the temporary capital of San Jose during March 1851. Later that year a Democratic convention at Benicia nominated a new candidate for governor, John Bigler, who had worked at Sutter's Fort before the discovery of gold. Bigler received the backing of his fellow Democrat, Senator Gwin, won the election, and was inaugurated governor on January 8, 1852.

The legislative practices of the time were actually quite venal. Corruption went unquestioned. Individuals rather than parties dominated the political scene. For more than a decade there was but slight change in the relative strength of California's political parties, the state usually continuing Democratic.

In 1851 the legislature failed, after 142 ballots, to elect a successor to Senator Frémont, leaving Gwin for the better part of a year the only accredited representative at Washington. The proslavery southern viewpoint that Gwin represented stood in contrast to California's "free state" admission into the Union back in 1850. Under Gwin's tutelage the next session of the state legislature was marked by persistent efforts to promote sentiment in favor of slavery. The passage both of a notorious fugitive slave act and of discriminatory laws against blacks were out of harmony with the antislavery record of California. Gwin's proslavery forces were bound to be challenged, and soon.

The campaign of 1853–1854 brought on a serious split in California's Democratic party. Broderick faced Gwin's prosouthern cohorts head-on. In Sacramento, at the state Democratic convention of 1854, the tension was high enough that delegates of both groups toted concealed pistols and bowie knives. When the factions failed to settle their differences, the party split, and two separate conventions convened, each wing selecting its own candidates.

In the middle 1850s the nativist espousals of the upstart Know-Nothing party spread to almost every town and mining camp. The Know-Nothings, who were anti-Catholic as well as antiforeign, earned their sobriquet in earlier times when many of them had belonged to a secret fraternal order that admonished them to reply "I know nothing" when asked about the order's activities. This little-understood party, which used secret handclasps and passwords, also pushed for Asian exclusion in California. By 1856 a tide of "Americanism" swept a Know-Nothing, J. Neely Johnson, into the governor's mansion.

But the real center of controversy remained the contest for California's senatorial posts between Gwin and the volatile Broderick. The two Democrats clashed not only politically, but personally. A stately Gwin was the picture of the courtly southern gentleman. His enthusiastic followers, who held strong proslavery views, were known as the Chivalry Wing of the Democratic Party, or "Chivs." In sharp contrast, Broderick, a bold and bitter fighter and a northerner, was unequivocally opposed to slavery and its extension. In those years the legislature chose congressional representatives, voting to award Broderick and Gwin California's two senatorial seats. After Senator Gwin denounced him on the floor of the Senate, Broderick charged Gwin with misappropriation of government money.

In the summer of 1859, Judge David S. Terry, a close friend of Gwin and a southern sympathizer, became irritated by Broderick's abusive public statements toward Gwin. When the Irishman sharply attacked Terry as well, the judge demanded a retraction. When Broderick refused, a duel was all but inevitable: this in an age when "affairs of honor" were in vogue. On September 13 the principals met outside San Francisco. Terry's shot lodged in his adversary's chest and Broderick fell to the ground. Suddenly Broderick's faults were forgotten, and the duel in which he lost his life caused genuine public remorse.

After the Terry-Broderick duel, Gwin's prosouthern views became a political liability to the Democrats, especially during the election of 1860, in which Abraham Lincoln rode a Republican ticket to the White House. The next year, following the outbreak of the Civil War, Gwin was arrested as disloyal to the Union cause. In the last year of that conflict, both he and Terry went into exile in Mexico with other disgruntled Confederates.

As California had entered the Union as a free state, relatively few slaves had been brought there from the South. There were, however, blacks in the original pueblos and, later, on the frontier as well. Among the latter were Jacob Dodson, who walked with Frémont on his 1842 expedition, James P. Beckwourth, a scout and trapper who came west in 1844 naming Beckwourth Pass, and William A. Leidesdorff, vice consul to Mexico at Yerba Buena, who was of African-American and Danish parentage.

Increasingly, blacks were appearing in California. During the Gold Rush, Fritz Vosburg, Abraham Holland, Gabriel Simms, and other black miners operated the Sweet Vengeance mine profitably. Another black man, Alvin Coffey, used gold dust mined in the High Sierra to purchase his freedom for $1,000; subsequently he paid equal amounts for the manumission of his family members. But, after accepting his money, Coffey's unscrupulous master took him back to St. Louis and sold him to a new owner. In 1854 Coffey, duped and reenslaved, returned to the California mines; after several more years of hard labor, he earned $7,000, with which he purchased his freedom for a second time.

The census of 1850 listed about 1,000 black residents of California. By 1852 their number had grown to 2,200. Legally, none of these people were slaves. The terms of California's admission to the Union prohibited slavery within its borders. But the California Fugitive Slave Act of 1851, passed at Senator Gwin's behest, had provided that slaves brought into California before the advent of statehood might legally be forcibly returned to slave states. This law was pronounced constitutional by the state Supreme Court. In numerous instances, however, slaves brought into California before its ban against slavery became effective were freed by masters who wished to remain in the state.

Darius Stokes, a black pastor who by September 1856 had founded fourteen churches in California, claimed that the assessed valuation of property owned by the black population of San Francisco that year was $150,000. Three-quarters of a million dollars had been sent to the South by California blacks to purchase freedom for members of their families. Stokes remarked that "men had paid as high as $2,000 each for their companions who were enslaved, to gain their freedom, and bring them to this State." Among those who purchased the freedom of others were mining engineer Moses Rodger and mine owners Gabriel Simms, Freeman Holland, and James Cousins. One man purchased eight of his own children for a price of $9,000, having earned the money by washing clothes. Another, Mifflin Wistar Gibbs, helped his people with money earned as a merchant. Mary Ellen Pleasant, known as "Mammy" Pleasant, in addition to running a house of prostitution, donated $30,000 to buy rifles for the John Brown raid at Harpers Ferry, Virginia, and to help other blacks escape slavery.

In 1855 the "Convention of Colored Citizens of California" in San Francisco formulated plans for improving the status of blacks in their community. This organization pushed for repeal of local restrictive ordinances. A militant newspaper owned and edited by blacks, *The Elevator*, became the voice of the "Colored Convention."

Leland Stanford, ca. 1875. Courtesy of the Bancroft Library, Univesity of California, Berkeley.

As national disagreement between North and South grew, a majority of Californians remained loyal to the Union. An antislavery group within the state included Collis P. Huntington, Cornelius Cole, Mark Hopkins, Charles and Edwin B. Crocker, and Leland Stanford, while pro-South sympathizers tried to kindle the fires of secession.

Among southern residents of California was Kentucky-born General Albert Sidney Johnston, Army commandant at the presidio of San Francisco. To him the "coercion" of California into a state of war by the North was flagrantly unconstitutional. When General Johnston's loyalty came into question, he gave up his California command to join the Confederate Army. Various southern officers from California's Sixth Army Regiment followed him into the Confederacy.

There was other opposition to the Union. Before Lincoln's inauguration there was talk of a "Pacific Republic" by Representative John C. Burch. This fiery legislator urged Californians, in case of a fratricidal war, to "call upon the enlightened nations of the earth to acknowledge our independence, and to protect us. . . ." John B. Weller, who became governor in 1858, also advocated that California, instead of siding with North or South, should establish on the shores of the Pacific "a mighty republic, which may in the end prove the greatest of all." In January 1861, a resident of Stockton hoisted a flag to represent a Pacific Republic. This touched off the raising of the Stars and Stripes throughout the city. It was clear that Union feeling remained strong. The dream of a Pacific Republic had finally died.

In 1861, when hostilities began, California's legislature debated whether it would support President Lincoln. On May 17 of that year, its lawmakers resolved that "the people of California are devoted to the Constitution and the Union now in the hour of trial and peril." They allocated funds to train volunteers at Drum Barracks in San Pedro.

Paradoxically, nearby Los Angeles became a hotbed for secessionists. The Los Angeles *Star* was banned from the mails for its seditious editorials. The Bella Union Hotel on Main Street was out of bounds for Union troops because its bar was a gathering place for southern sympathizers, who toasted Robert F. Lee with tumblers of bourbon and referred to Abraham Lincoln as "that baboon in the White House." The Los Angeles *News,* a pro-Union newspaper, editorialized: "Los Angeles County is disloyal, double-eyed in treason, and the inhabitants break out in broad grins upon hearing the news of a Confederate victory. . . ."

Secret supporters of the Confederacy included the Knights of the Golden Circle, Knights of the Columbian Star, and the Committee of Thirty. The members of these organizations avoided large meetings. Advocacy of secession sometimes also broke out in public speeches, in sermons and prayers from the pulpit, and at covert celebrations of Confederate victories. During the war, newspapers that went so far as to urge independence for California included the San Francisco *Herald,* Sacramento *Standard,* Alameda *Country Gazette,* Marysville *Gazette,* and Sonora *Democrat.* The Tulare *Post,* which changed its name to the Visalia *Equal Rights Expositor* printed such inflammatory editorials that the paper and its printing plant were destroyed by the state militia. Five "disloyal" papers were wrecked by mob violence.

To counteract secessionist sentiment, the California legislature enacted severe emergency measures. A new law made it a misdemeanor "to display rebel flags or devices." Illegal behavior also came to include "adherence to the enemy" by "endorsing, defending, or cheering" the subversion of United States authority. Other state laws were enacted "to exclude traitors and alien enemies from the courts of justice in civil cases." Secessionist dissension at El Monte, Visalia, San Luis Obispo, Santa Barbara, San Bernardino, and Los Angeles was discouraged by federal troops.

Californians were spared actual warfare at home. Pro-Union demonstrations took place in all parts of the state, with resolutions of loyalty adopted at mass meetings in various towns and counties. San Francisco Home Guards promoted enlistments in the Union Army, kept an eye out for conspiracy, and worked vigorously for the election of a pro-Union war governor. Californians, having cast their vote for Lincoln in 1860, chose Leland Stanford, one of the builders of the Central Pacific Railroad, as their wartime governor. Lincoln's popularity remained so great that in 1864 he would again receive the state's vote for the presidency.

During the Civil War, California's gold provided indispensable financial strength for the Union cause. As a "hard-money" state it did not at first gracefully accept national laws making paper greenbacks legal tender. Californians, accustomed to gold and silver, did not trust greenbacks as a stable currency. California gold flowed into the federal treasury, bolstering the nation's economy during the stressful wartime period. The state also helped to supply the Union armies with wool, wheat, and other raw materials.

The war hastened California's integration into national life in other ways also. Passage of the Pacific Railroad Bill of 1862 by Congress was facilitated by the absence of Southern legislators who had blocked adoption of a Northern railroad route. During 1863, work on the Central Pacific Railroad began at Sacramento. As that project's principal advocate, Governor Stanford joined national party leaders in temporarily abandoning the name "Republican." They sought the support of all citizens under a Union party label. Anyone who deviated from expressions of northern loyalty was apt to feel the whip of public censure.

During the war years, Californians were moved to new heights of sentiment for the Union cause by Thomas Starr King, a popular Unitarian preacher. As many as 40,000 persons came to hear him at mass meetings. Although King lived in California less than four years, he was an extraordinary figure in the history of the state. After his arrival from Boston in 1860, King became a major spokesman for the Union cause and raised funds for the Sanitary Commission, forerunner of the Red Cross. Over one-fourth of the money donated throughout the country came from California. King's eloquence was so great that his supporters said of him, "King saved California for the Union."

Relatively few Californians saw active service. Conscription was never enforced. A total of about 15,000 of its men enlisted in the Union army. A number of California volunteers spent the war years pacifying Indians in Arizona and New Mexico. The "California Column," volunteers under the command of Colonel James H. Carleton, marched to Yuma, then into New Mexico, but too late to forestall a Confederate invasion there. There they fought "the battle of the fleas."

Because Masachusetts paid large bounties for volunteers out of a special fund earmarked for recruiting, a company, consisting mainly of native-born Californians, was organized at San Jose. They were equipped with lassoes, in the use of which they were expert. Another unit, the "California Hundred," sailed through the Golden Gate on December 11, 1862, leaving cheering crowds behind at dockside. Five weeks later, after a trip around Cape Horn, these troops reached Boston for service in the Union Army. Finally, during 1865, Californians rode with General Philip H. Sheridan in the defeat of Robert E. Lee's Army of Northern Virginia. Some were even present for Lee's surrender to Ulysses S. Grant at Appomattox Court House.

Once the war ended, Governor Stanford went on to serve in the U.S. Senate from 1885 to 1893. Railroad builder and skillful politician, Stanford created one of the largest fortunes in the West. Also repeatedly reelected to the Senate was George Hearst, father of the well-known publisher. One other senator was a geriatric wonder. Cornelius Cole, during his 102 years from 1822 to 1924, lived within the life spans of every United States president from John Adams through John F. Kennedy—already born when Cole died.

In the years after the Civil War, both of the major political parties remained relatively conservative. Except for the anti-Chinese movements, most public concerns in California were shared by the nation as a whole. Among prevalent issues were the call for "free-silver," the debate over the import tariff, and the widespread distrust of labor unionism. Not until the Progressive era would Californians be moved by the champions of reform.

Selected Readings

Regarding state politics see A. R. Buchanan, *David S. Terry of California: Dueling Judge* (1956); David Williams, *David C. Broderick: A Political Portrait* (1969); Jeremiah Lynch, *A Senator of the Fifties: David C. Broderick of California* (1911); William H. Ellison, ed., "Memoirs of Hon. William M. Gwin," *California Historical Society Quarterly* 19 (1940), 1–367; Earl Pomeroy, "California, 1846–1860: Politics of a Representative Frontier State," *California Historical Society Quarterly* 32 (December 1953), 291–302; H. Brett Melendy, "Who Was John McDougal?" *Pacific Historical Review* 29 (August 1960), 231–43.

Civil War California is in Percival J. Cooney, "Southern California in Civil War Days," *Historical Society of Southern California Annual* 13 (1924), 54–68; Helen B. Walter, "Confederates in Southern California," *Historical Society of Southern California Quarterly* 35 (March 1953), 41–55; Benjamin F. Gilbert, "The Confederate Minority in California," *California Historical Society Quarterly* 40 (June 1941), 154–70; Jay Monaghan, *Civil War on the Western Border* (1955); Oscar Lewis, *The War in the Far West, 1861–1865* (1961); Aurora Hunt, *The Army of the Pacific* (1951); Gerald Stanley, "Civil War Politics in California," *Southern California Quarterly* 54 (Summer 1982), 115–32, and Stanley, "Slavery and the Origins of the Republican Party in California," *Southern California Quarterly* 50 (Spring

1978), 1–16; John W. Robinson, *Los Angeles in the Civil War* (1977); Leo P. Kibby, "Some Aspects of California's Military Problems During the Civil War," *Civil War History* 5 (September 1959), 251–62; Milton H. Shutes, *Lincoln and California* (1943); Edward A. Dickson, "Lincoln and Baker: The Story of a Great Friendship," *Historical Society of Southern California Quarterly* 34 (September 1952), 229–42.

For Civil War politics see Richard H. Peterson, "Thomas Starr King in California, 1860–64," *California History* (Spring 1990), 12–21; Ronald C. Woolsey, "Disunion or Dissent? . . . Southern California Attitudes Toward the Civil War," *Southern California Quarterly* 66 (Fall 1984), 185–205; George T. Clark, *Leland Stanford* (1931); Ann Casey, "Thomas Starr King and the Secession Movement," *Historical Society of Southern California Quarterly* 43 (September 1961), 245–75; Russell M. Posner, "Thomas Starr King and the Mercy Million," *California Historical Society Quarterly* 43 (December 1964), 291–307; George Upshur, *As I Recall Them: Memories of Crowded Years* (1936); Carl B. Swisher, *Stephen J. Field, Craftsman of the Law* (1930, 1969) and John Higham, "The American Party, 1886–1891," *Pacific Historical Review* 19 (February 1950), 37–46.

Regarding early blacks in California, see Douglas Henry Daniels, *Pioneer Urbanites: A Social and Cultural History of Black San Francisco* (1990); Eugene H. Berwanger, *The Frontier Against Slavery* (1967); J. Max Bond, *The Negro in Los Angeles* (1972); Delilah Beasley, *Negro Trail Blazers of California* (1919); Rudolph M. Lapp, *Blacks in Gold Rush California* (1977); Sue Bailey Thurman, *Pioneers of Negro Origin in California* (1952); Lionel U. Ridout, "The Church, the Chinese and the Negroes in California, 1849–1893," *Historical Magazine of the Protestant Episcopal Church* 28 (June 1959), 115–38; William E. Franklin, "The Archy Case," *Pacific Historical Review* 32 (May 1963), 137–54; Mifflin Wistar Gibbs, *Shadows and Light: An Autobiography* (1902) and Charlotta Bass, *Forty Years: Memoirs From the Pages of a Newspaper* (1960). Shirley Ann Wilson Moore, "African Americans in California: A Brief Historiography," *California History* 75 (Fall 1996), 194–8. In the same issue of this journal are articles about early blacks in California by Clarence Caesar, Susan Bragg, and Rick Moss.

A useful bibliography covering this period is Richard Quebedeaux, *Prime Sources of California and Nevada Local History . . . 1850–1906* (1992).

Ships and Rails

////////// CHAPTER 21

As more reliable transportation to California became an urgent necessity, the building of a transcontinental railroad was imperative. Meanwhile, maritime transportation continued to flourish.

By the mid-1850s, the California Steam Navigation Company virtually controlled traffic in and around San Francisco Bay and along the inland rivers. Some smaller competitors found "California Steam" so powerful in setting freight and passenger rates that they eventually welcomed the monopoly-breaking transcontinental railroad.

The expense of getting to California by sea averaged $400, and the trip sometimes took as long as 120 days. Advocates of a transcontinental railroad pointed out that such a trip might be made by rail for as little as $150. Critics maintained that the cost of construction of the railroad would be prohibitive unless huge government land grants and loans compensated the builders. Otherwise the financial risks involved were too stiff.

Nevertheless, the idea of a railroad to the Pacific gradually gained acceptance. The deeply rutted wagon trails westward were clearly inadequate. The country was straining to expand: moving mail, passengers, and freight more quickly was essential. There was no disagreement that a cross-country railroad should traverse the shortest possible distance. But the exact route was debated for years.

Washington legislators had no experience with the colossal problems involved: Should construction and operation of a transcontinental railroad be administered by the government? Or should the railroad be built and operated privately? How far should federal and state governments go toward financial encouragement of and direct subsidies to the railroad construction companies?

As early as 1852, a route that swung southward from the Midwest through Texas and then proceeded by way of Arizona's Gila Valley to Yuma, and on westward to San Diego, was advocated by numerous southern senators and congressmen. Finally, in 1853, the U.S. Congress appropriated funds to sponsor four western survey parties. These were instructed to lay out prospective overland railroad routes. But when specific recommendations emerged, congressmen, north and south, clashed as tensions mounted over where future government-financed rail routes should go. The outbreak of the Civil War eventually brought to an end all prospects of a southern route.

On June 28, 1861, the Central Pacific Railroad Company was founded in Sacramento by three California merchants: Leland Stanford acted as president, Collis P. Huntington as vice-president, and Mark Hopkins as treasurer. These three and Charles Crocker came to be called the "Big Four." Originally, their enterprise relied less on their own efforts than on the determination of a young civil engineer, Theodore D. Judah.

Judah had laid out the rails of the Sacramento Valley Railroad to serve the mining regions along the slopes of the Sierra Nevada mountain range. His railway consisted of only twenty-three miles of track. In an age of widespread skepticism, some called him "Crazy Judah." Others accused him of promoting the construction of railroads purely for personal gain. Judah, however, had considerable construction experience. In Washington he pressured Congress for passage of a transcontinental railroad bill. Ultimately Judah became chief engineer of the Central Pacific Railway Company.

On July 1, 1862, Congress did pass the long-awaited Pacific Railroad Bill. This legislation authorized two construction companies to begin laying track that would eventually link both coasts of North America. The Union Pacific Company would build 1,006 miles of track westward from Omaha, Nebraska, while the Central Pacific's crews moved eastward out of California. In addition to a 400-foot right of way, each construction company was to receive huge sections of terrain, which stretched off in checkerboard fashion on either side of the track, for the length of their lines. The two construction companies were also entitled to 1,280,000 acres of public land for every hundred miles of track they laid, plus $3 million in credit. Both the Central Pacific and the Union Pacific companies were supported by government bonds.

Judah had induced Congress to subsidize a loan to the Central Pacific of $16,000 per mile of track laid across level land, $32,000 a mile in the foothills, and $48,000 per mile across mountainous areas. As if the deal were not generous enough, the "Big Four" connived to collect twice the prescribed subsidy on some hundred miles of track they laid. This they did by convincing Congress that the foothills of the Sierra Nevada began farther west than government maps specified. This reasoning, written into the bill, "moved" the Sierra range within only ten miles of Sacramento—near the center of the great valley of California.

Who were the "Big Four?" Originally Stanford was a grocer; Crocker owned a dry-goods store. Huntington and Hopkins operated a hardware business. In 1863 Judah, the key originator of the enterprise, went eastward via Panama to seek a loan with which to buy out his avaricious partners. En route he was stricken with yellow fever and died.

The generous provisions of the Pacific Railroad Act were further increased in 1864, when an amendatory act doubled the land grants and other financial inducements to the two railroad companies. The original intention of Judah's partners was to amass the lucrative federal subsidies by laying down the roadbed and track as quickly as possible. Crocker, who supplanted Judah as the Central Pacific's construction manager, not only wanted to build cheaply, he wished to get out quickly by selling the company to other investors, who would take over actual operation of the road.

Building eastward from Sacramento, the Central Pacific had to ship machinery and building supplies around Cape Horn, or via Panama, at great expense. Also, the Sierra Nevada presented a more formidable obstacle to the engineers of the Central Pacific than the Rocky Mountains were to offer the builders of the Union Pacific. The Sierra, however, did supply timber for ties, trestles, and the long snow sheds required to move heavy items in midwinter—a resource lacking to the Union Pacific as it worked its way across the treeless Great Plains.

In the Sierra, Central Pacific crews used picks, blasting powder, axes, and dumpcarts. Some 15,000 recently arrived Chinese workers made up the C.P.'s poorly paid track crews. In general, they were not well-treated and assigned dangerous tasks. These "Celestials," a name taken from "the Celestial Empire" of China, were tied by ropes around their middles as they chipped away at the sides of cliffs. After they had chiseled out a footing along canyon walls, other Chinese made use of this toehold to blast out a roadway for the track. Despite repeated delays, the Central Pacific crossed the Sierra summit in December of 1867. Beyond lay less rugged terrain.

As the rail lines stretched toward one another, a lively rivalry between the two railway companies developed, one which became intense when Crocker announced a schedule of a mile of track for every working day. His Chinese labor force—referred to as "Crocker's Pets"—amazingly responded to every new demand made upon them. By June 1868 they had reached Reno. After the Union Pacific reported laying 6 miles of track in one day, Crocker's Chinese countered with 7 miles, ultimately

Chinese construction workers on the Central Pacific Railroad at "Cape Horn," a strategic point in the crossing of the Sierra crest. From a contemporary print.

setting a record with 10 miles and 56 feet of track laid in under twelve hours. Crocker took personal pride in their more than successful competition with the U.P.'s Irish track-layers.

Because the government's payments were based upon mileage of track laid, each railroad company was eager to cover as much ground as possible. Therefore, as the distance between the rival construction crews lessened, their competition became more keen. For a time grading crews of the respective railroads worked within a few hundred yards of each other along parallel lines, since they could not agree as to where the tracks should join. Early in 1869, federal railroad commissioners ruled that the two lines must meet in northern Utah Territory, 56 miles west of Ogden, 1,086 miles from Omaha, and 689 miles from Sacramento. There the construction gap between the railroads closed.

Eventually, it remained only to drive the ceremonial last spike. On the tenth day of May, 1869, near Utah Territory's desolate Promontory Point, the ceremony was performed, uniting Atlantic and Pacific with bands of steel. Two bonnet-stacked, wood-burning locomotives faced each other on the shining new tracks, one headed east, the other west. Several hundred witnesses were present, including the Twenty-first Infantry Regiment of the U.S. Army, officials of both railroads, a photographer, and nearby settlers. Following the symbolic driving of Arizona's spike of gold, silver, and iron, and Nevada's spike of silver, the final tie, crafted of California's laurel, was put in place and the last spike, of California gold, was readied. Each blow of the silver sledge that drove the final spike was announced via telegraph to eastern cities.

San Francisco gave itself up to three days of celebration after the telegraph announced: "The last rail is laid! The last spike is driven! The Pacific Railroad is completed!" At Sacramento the bells and whistles of thirty different locomotives joined in a chorus with the bells of the city's churches and fire houses. Completion of the largest engineering job yet undertaken in North America was, indeed, a decisive event. Exactly one-hundred years after California's settlement by the Portolá-Serra expedition, its frontier isolation had come to a close.

After completion of the Central Pacific line, the "Big Four" obtained a charter for a second railroad to be called the Southern Pacific. This new line extended their north-south routes through California's Central Valley and along the coast from Oregon to southern California. The S.P., as it came to be called, also reached out from Los Angeles to Yuma on the Arizona border, then on to Tucson, Arizona, and into New Mexico Territory. By 1882, the S.P. met the Texas and Pacific Railroad in Texas. The next year the Southern Pacific's "Sunset Route" reached New Orleans.

Not only did Palace Sleeping Cars carry thousands of excursionists and new settlers westward, long lines of boxcars also transported wheat, gold, silver, and lumber, which brought the "Big Four" wealth undreamed of by their late engineer, Judah. Their Southern Pacific Railroad Company ultimately serviced thousands of miles, with steamship connections that linked California with New York and Havana.

The Southern Pacific was granted over 11 million acres of government land within California alone. The railroad also demanded possession of a great deal of county and city lands; the extent of a city's favors helped the "Big Four" decide what places they would service. The governments of California towns large and small soon realized that enticement of the railroad required money, with which a community would buy construction bonds. When the S.P. was repeatedly accused of extorting funds from towns along prospective routes, the "Big Four" retorted that it needed this money for building bridges, overpasses, and for grading track beds. Among the interior towns that mushroomed because the railroad ran through them were Fresno, Merced, Tulare, Modesto, and Bakersfield. Some communities which the railroad by-passed were left to slumber and ultimately died.

Not until the 1880s was the S.P.'s blatant monopoly challenged. By building westward, the Atchison, Topeka and Santa Fe Railroad reached El Paso in 1881. It then crossed New Mexico and Arizona, sending its woodburning locomotives into California at Needles, where it bridged the Colorado River. Next the Santa Fe purchased and rented a series of short lines, entering Los Angeles in 1887. With a new track northward from Bakersfield to Stockton, the Santa Fe also bought or negotiated its way into San Francisco. Though the Southern Pacific economics and political power would still reign supreme in California for many years, there was no denying that a new railroad age had arrived.

Selected Readings

Inland water transportation is in Jerry MacMullen, *Paddle Wheel Days in California* (1944) and in Andrew Rolle, "Turbulent Waters: Navigation and Central California's Southern Central Valley," *California History* 75 (Summer 1996), 128–37.

Regarding railroads see George Albright, *Official Explorations for Pacific Railroads* (1921); Creed Haymond, *The Central Pacific Railroad Company: Its Relation to the Government* (1888); John Moody, *The Railroad Builders* (1921); Robert E. Riegel, *The Story of the Western Railroads* (1926); Wesley S. Griswold, *A Work of Giants* (1962); Carl Wheat, "A Sketch of the Life of Theodore D. Judah," *California Historical Society Quarterly* 4 (September 1925), 219–71; John H. Kemble, "The Big Four at Sea: The History of the Occidental and Oriental Steamship Company," *Huntington Library Quarterly* 3 (April 1940), 330–58; John D. Galloway, *The First Transcontinental Railroad* (1950); Neill C. Wilson and Frank J. Taylor, *Southern Pacific: The Roaring Story of a Fighting Railroad* (1952). Glenn C. Quiett, *They Built the West: An Epic of Rails and Cities* (1934); Gilbert H. Kneiss, *Bonanza Railroads* (1941); Glenn D. Bradley, *Story of the Santa Fe* (1920); James Marshall, *Santa Fe: The Railroad That Built an Empire* (1949); L. L. Waters, *Steel Trails to Santa Fe* (1950).

Recent scholarship includes William Deverell, *Railroad Crossing: Californians and the Railroad* (1994); Donovan Hofsommer, *The Southern Pacific* (1986); David Lavender, *The Great Persuader* [Collis P. Huntington] (1970); Ward McAfee, *California's Railroad Era, 1850–1911* (1973) and Keith Bryant, *History of the Atchison, Topeka, and Santa Fe Railway* (repr. 1982). The absorption of only one of many small railroads is in Andrew Rolle, *Henry Mayo Newhall and His Times* (1991).

Agricultural and Urban Growth
//////// CHAPTER 22

Most agricultural states are limited to a few crops, such as corn, tobacco, or cotton. California produces more than two hundred farm commodities. It became the nation's leading agricultural state long before urbanization further shaped the state's future.

By the early 1860s, more than 3 million cattle roamed the hills and the valleys of California and several hundred thousand sheep grazed on the state's ranges. When sheepmen erected sheds and fences, and their lambs overcropped the ranges, trouble was bound to flare up between them and cattlemen. In this conflict, which occasionally reached the stage of violence, individual sheepherders seldom emerged victorious. The cattlemen were more powerful and better organized. Two German-born butchers, Henry Miller and his partner Charles Lux, established a ranching empire that covered more than 800 thousand acres. Their lands stretched from the Mexican border northward into Oregon and eastward to Nevada. Miller and Lux, by controlling water rights, became the largest ranchers on the Pacific Coast. In addition to raising more than 1 million head of cattle, they also herded sheep and grew crops on 500 thousand acres of land. Such cattle and land barons drove small ranchers and farmers out of business, particularly in drought periods. Some monopolists were backed by Eastern, English, and Scottish capital.

During the devastating drought of 1863–1864 the dust on the ranges was so dense that it clogged the nostrils of the dying animals. The bleached skeletons of thousands of cattle, sheep, and horses dotted the hillsides. By the late 1860s, range land sold for as little as ten cents per acre.

As the situation for the small rancher worsened, powerful land barons took over choice pasture lands, which they guarded from encroachment. Improved methods of range management not only rescued the cattle industry, they were also applied to sheepherding.

Neither butter nor milk had been marketed aggressively during the Mexican period, the chief value of cattle being their hides and tallow. In the new era the production of dairy products grew steadily. The breeding of fine Holstein and Jersey cattle (breeds known for the quality of their milk) transformed Stanislaus and San Joaquin counties into important dairy centers. Dairies close to large centers of population eventually helped to make Los Angeles County first in the nation in dairy production.

Before and after the Civil War a mechanical revolution in agriculture provided iron and steel plows, as well as mowers, reapers, and threshers. Wheat and corn were increasing in demand on international markets, and California's climate and soil were splendidly suited to growing these and other grains. Whereas the state had previously imported most of its grain, vast new ranches in the Central Valley made that region a major exporter of oats, barley, and corn. The state produced a hard, dry wheat that was popular with British millers. In fact, much of the trade to Liverpool's Corn Exchange was controlled by Isaac Friedlander, California's "Grain King." Friedlander skillfully managed his own production, shipping terminals, and global marketing, shipping durum wheat in burlap bags to Australia and China as well as to Mediterranean countries.

By 1890, annual wheat production reached 40 million bushels and California ranked second among all states in its growth. As the profits on wheat rose, fierce competition developed between large growers and small farmers. The big landowners, however, could make more favorable deals with middlemen, railroad agents, and steamship owners, eventually buying out those farmers who could not stay solvent.

Among the new crops with expanded production during and after the Civil War was cotton. But not until the second decade of the twentieth century did cotton production boom, when irrigation projects in the Imperial and San Joaquin valleys increased markedly. The quality of California cotton was superior even to some grown in the American South, and the yield per acre frequently higher. No such success story can be told concerning efforts to produce silk in the state. In 1862, although the legislature had offered a bounty for silkworm cocoons, sericulture never became more than a passing fad.

Far more important was the development of citriculture. From the days when the padres first introduced fruit trees into mission gardens, horticulture expanded but slowly. Until the development of the refrigerated railroad car, California fruit growers, remote from large markets, could not market their perishable crops in the East. After its advent, however, some growers prospered by raising and marketing one unique crop—citrus fruit.

California's citrus fruits include lemons, tangerines, and grapefruit. But the real symbol, and source of strength, of the citrus industry is the orange. In the mission period orange groves were small and undeveloped, the trees producing a pithy, thick-skinned, and sour fruit. One of the earliest groves was planted at San Gabriel Mission. In 1834 a Frenchman, Luís (or Louis) Vignes, transplanted 35 of these trees to his residence in Los Angeles, near the present Union Station. In 1841 another Angeleño, William Wolfskill, expanded his orange grove to 70 acres. His son sent the first trainload of oranges eastward to St. Louis in 1877.

The most substantial experimentation in the cultivation of oranges occurred at Riverside. There, in 1870, Judge John Wesley North bought 4,000 acres of barren land on credit. In cooperation with the transcontinental railroads, North was successful in introducing new growers to California from Michigan and Iowa. Among the settlers in North's agricultural colony were Luther Calvin Tibbets and his wife Eliza, who in 1873 introduced the Washington Navel variety of oranges to California. Two tiny cuttings that they brought to California grew to maturity and produced a juicy, flavorful, and seedless orange. California's climate and soil was especially well-suited to the Washington Navel. The two Tibbets trees became the parent stock for planting throughout the 1880s.

In the early days of the orange industry there was no crop-inspection or fruit-quarantine system. Trouble came when destructive insects were introduced in California through imported nursery stock. The cottony cushion scale came from Australia in 1868. So injurious was this pest that, for a time, the fledgling orange industry was threatened with extinction. Then a small lady bug (also from Australia) that attacked the scale was purposely introduced in the state; eventually this species checked the spread of the scale. The black scale also seriously damaged the citrus industry, as did a sooty mold which caused decay among individual trees. To fight the mold and the black scale, growers had to wash tree trunks thoroughly. Fumigation too offered protection against diseases affecting orange trees.

Another hazard to the orange industry was frost. To protect their crops from frost citrus growers used oil heaters that burned a cheap crude. Nearby city dwellers whose house furnishings, draperies, and rugs were covered with soot from oil burners, complained bitterly. Eventually, the

Harvesting in the San Fernando Valley, ca. 1900. C.C. Pierce Collection; courtesy of The Huntington Library, San Marino, California.

Orange groves in the 1920s. Courtesy of Andrew Rolle.

orchards were protected against cold damage by wind machines, which today keep air currents in motion to prevent frost from settling on the fruit.

Growers who marketed their own fruit remained easy prey to speculative commission agents who bought citrus in large quantities, securing rebates from railroad companies. Paradoxically, the larger the individual grower's crop, the more indebted he became to middlemen and packers. As a result, in 1893 growers formed a cooperative marketing organization which became the California Fruit Growers Exchange. Its trade name, "Sunkist," inaugurated a vigorous nationwide advertising campaign.

The California citrus industry, in fact, now set about to change the American breakfast diet. Decorated trains, which dispensed oranges at whistlestops in the Midwest, gaudy advertising billboards, free orange wrappers and spoons, and essay and poetry contests all helped carry the message of California's "golden fruit" eastward. As a result of this campaign, orange juice, or sliced oranges and grapefruits, became substitutes for such staples as buckwheat cakes, bacon, ham, porridge, and waffles. A new slogan read "Oranges for health and California for wealth." Chambers of commerce and other boosters joined the advertising campaign begun by the citrus industry.

Introduction of the Eureka and Lisbon varieties of lemons rounded out the development of California citriculture. The Eureka lemon from Sicily is an early-bearing variety. The heavy foliage of the Lisbon lemon protects its fruit from sunburn. California has long produced almost 100 percent of the lemons grown in the United States.

Among those attracted to California citrus groves were retired businesspeople from the East and Midwest, some of whom had lost their health. A new life in California's sunshine and dry air often proved restorative and rewarding. Often these older immigrants brought needed capital to the state, and some built fine residences amid their groves.

Other unique crops are associated with various parts of the state. The Santa Clara Valley became the world's chief producer of Italian prunes, while Sylmar developed into an olive-growing area. In 1867, at Santa Barbara, the softshell walnut was planted commercially, and at Los Angeles, in 1873, Wolfskill and Vignes replanted the English walnut. Today that variety, once called the Madeira or Persian walnut, accounts for almost 100 percent of the nation's walnut production. California also produces virtually all the almonds grown in the United States.

The pioneer botanist Luther Burbank, from 1875 until his death in 1926, carried on experiments with garden crops at Santa Rosa. Burbank's efforts made possible increased competitive production of tomatoes, lettuce, cauliflower, carrots, alfalfa, sugar beets, celery, and potatoes. Accompanying California's burgeoning agricultural productivity was the development of a canning industry; such trade names as Del Monte, Iris, and (in the case of sugar packaging) Spreckels became familiar in thousands of American households.

A fortunate combination of climate and soil, particularly in northern California, gave viticulture a propitious start. Today, some 90 percent of the U.S. grape crop, and most of its wine, comes from California. Vines of the European *vitis vinifera* stock were originally planted at the missions, where they bore grapes for over a hundred years. Woefully neglected has been the record of European settlers upon California agriculture.

For example, in 1857 a group of Germans formed the Los Angeles Vineyard Society on lands located thirty miles southeast of Los Angeles. They gave their tract the name Anaheim, from its site in the Santa Ana Valley and the German word for home, *"heim."* Around their property they built a fence that was five and a half miles long, consisting of forty thousand willow poles. The poles took root, forming a living wall around the colony. Such "fortifications" were constructed mainly to keep out roving herds of cattle. Using water from the Santa Ana River, the colonists planted more than 400,000 vines.

Among other European wine makers was Agoston Haraszthy, a Hungarian credited with the introduction, in 1851, of zinfandel grapes at his Sonoma vineyard. Other vintners included Etienne Thée and Charles Lefranc, two Frenchmen who founded the Almaden Vineyards at Los Gatos. In 1860, Charles Krug, after planting twenty acres of vines in the Sonoma Valley, moved to the Napa Valley and founded the winery that still bears his name.

By the 1880s no organization planted quite so many grapes as did the Italian-Swiss Agricultural Colony at Asti. It was founded principally by northern Italians who had settled in the Napa and Sonoma valleys. The colony's 1897 vintage was so large that there was insufficient cooperage in all California to hold the wine.

New wineries appeared, not only in the Sonoma Valley but at Napa, in the Livermore Valley, and in the San Joaquin–Sacramento Valley. At Cucamonga, in southern California, the Secondo Guasti family owned the largest vineyard in the world; they specialized in the production of such fortified dessert wines as ports, sherries, and muscatels. At Fresno, Modesto, Madera, and other interior towns, Italian and French immigrants established even more vineyards. The Inglenook Cellars at Rutherford, the Paul Masson winery at Saratoga, and the Beaulieu vineyards of Georges de Latour, also at Rutherford, became internationally important. Both were founded by Frenchmen.

Although America's Prohibition era of the 1920s would temporarily put an end to wine making, the industry flourished again as soon as Prohibition was repealed. During this period the Louis M. Martini and

Mondavi families began to produce quality table wines near St. Helena in the Napa Valley.

Extensive land reclamation led to the opening up of other areas for the planting of such new commercial crops as artichokes and watermelons. One of the first regions to undergo reclamation was the triangle of land formed by the Sacramento and San Joaquin rivers. On this half million acres, originally consisting of a group of islands and swampy plains, were built dykes, canals, conduits, and check dams to protect new farms from floods. The delta has since become known for its output of rice, sugar beets, asparagus, spinach, celery, and other vegetables.

Eventually irrigation projects had to be devised to insure California's agricultural future. The Imperial Valley is a notable example. Sometimes called the "American Nile," this fertile valley is located in the hot southeastern part of the state. Much of the soil is sandy and alluvial. George Chaffey, a Canadian who in the mid-1880s had founded an irrigation colony at Ontario, also planned to transform the Imperial Valley. By diverting the waters of the Colorado River, which ran unchecked into the Gulf of California, Chaffey made it possible for the

Vicente Lugo ranch house and some of its landlords and neighbors, 1892. C.C. Pierce Collection; courtesy of The Huntington Library, San Marino, California.

Imperial Land Company to bring a large number of settlers into the valley by 1900. However, in 1905 a flood began that lasted almost two years, and created the Salton Sea. This torrent could not be stopped until the breach in the banks of the Colorado was sealed.

With flood damage repaired, by 1913 the Imperial Valley's canal system covered more than half a million acres, extending below the border into Mexico. This operation was then the largest irrigation project in the United States. The number of acres planted in barley, alfalfa, and other crops expanded rapidly, and the Imperial Valley, equally famous for its cantaloupes and other melons, became known as the "Winter Garden of the World." Farther northward, the arid Coachella Valley was also transformed by artificial irrigation.

As rancho holdings were broken up by controversies over legal titles, the lands fell into the hands of urban promoters, and the communities that sprang up on these sites took the names of the former ranchos. William Heath Davis converted part of Rancho San Leandro (acquired by marriage from the Estudillo family) into the central California community of San Leandro. He urged a neighboring native family, the Peraltas, to do likewise. Their claims, however, which covered part of the present sites of Berkeley, Oakland, and Alameda along San Francisco Bay, were disputed in the courts for years, and the Peraltas profited little from development of their terrain.

At first towns were little more than country crossroads, which became farm supply centers. In the 1850s, long before railroad connections with the outer world had been provided, Davis and other town founders strained their financial resources to the breaking point. They built houses, paved streets, constructed wharfs for visiting steamers, provided hotels for dusty overland travelers—in short, tried to transform a community of crumbling adobes into a city. At San Diego, Davis, however, was doomed to failure. Later, in the 1860s, the real estate promoter Alonzo Erastus Horton constructed a "New San Diego," only to lose his fortune also. But some town developers succeeded from the start. Among these was Phineas Banning, founder of Wilmington. This community was on an estuary providing maritime access to the expanding pueblo of Los Angeles. Banning's Wilmington wharf and warehouses, built between 1851 and 1858, were sheltered by a rock jetty between Terminal and Dead Man's islands, near what was to become "New San Pedro." The harbor's channel was dug deep enough to float barges and steam tugs carrying freight and passengers from ocean vessels anchored offshore. During the Civil War the U.S. Army established Camp Drum and Drum Barracks near Banning's home at Wilmington. This government installation helped to assure the future of a new port for Los Angeles.

San Diego, California.

San Diego, ca. 1852. Possibly sketched by John Russell Bartlett. Reproduced from his Personal Narrative ... *[1856].*

Later in the nineteenth century, former ranchos became almost instant towns once litigation over land titles was clarified. For example, Pasadena mushroomed out of the Rancho San Pasqual. Benjamin D. Wilson, who had come to California with the Workman-Rowland party, enticed a group of colonists from Indiana to emigrate to the area. By 1874 the group had laid out a community complete with irrigation conduits leading into new orchards and grain fields. This town, once dotted with small stands of oak and fields of poppies, became a winter playground of Eastern millionaires.

Various factors contributed to the rapid growth of towns such as Pasadena: the low cost of land; increasing population pressures caused by the railroads; and the energy of speculators in providing water as well as transportational facilities for the new sites. These speculators turned an arid countryside into prosperous cities, but in the development of the "rancho towns," it was the native Californians—the former owners of the land—who gained the least, if anything.

A flood of population descended on the state from 1870 to 1890. Flocking into southern California were unemployed cowboys and fruit pickers, farmers, engineers, health seekers, and real estate promoters.

On March 7, 1886, the Los Angeles *Times* reported that cross-country passenger fares, which had formerly been as high as $125 from the Midwest, reached as low as $1. The next year 200,000 persons arrived by railroad. New towns sprang up, accompanied by new colleges, banks, and business institutions. Within less than two years, 100 communities had been "platted" inside the Los Angeles County, which experienced prodigious growth—the result of effective advertising, the lure of the climate, and railroad competition.

Promoters familiar with Italy exploited the similarities between California and ancient Tuscany or Campania. The San Diego and Riverside chambers of commerce issued brochures that advertised "their" Italy of America. California soon had its own Hesperia, Rialto, Tarragona, Terracina, and Verona. At one such namesake, Venice, the real estate boom of the 1880s saw the building of imitation lagoons and piazzas along an open beach. Real estate speculators stopped at nothing as the state moved from agriculture to urbanization.

In northern California, at Senator James D. Phelan's Villa Montalvo, near Saratoga, Italianate rococo porticoes, cypress hedges, stone gryphons, and classical statues sustained the mood. The facade of Stanford University's chapel framed a mosaic similar to that of a church in Rome called St. Paul Outside the Walls. These architectural achievements were among the permanent results of California's real estate boom.

Selected Readings

On agriculture's interaction with mechanization see Richard Orsi, "The Octopus Reconsidered: The Southern Pacific and Agricultural Modernization in California, 1865–1915," *California Historical Quarterly* 54 (Fall 1975), 197–220. Regarding the orange industry see Richard Sawyer, *To Make a Spotless Orange: Biological Control in California* (1996); Minnie Tibbets Mills, "Luther Calvin Tibbets, Founder of the Navel Orange Industry of California," *Historical Society of Southern California Quarterly* 25 (December 1943), 127–61.

On cattle see Edward F. Treadwell, *The Cattle King* (repr. 1950); L. T. Burcham, *California Range Land* (1957); James M. Jensen, "Cattle Drives From the Ranchos to the Gold Fields of California," *Arizona and the West* 2 (Winter 1960), 341–52; Dane Coolidge, *Old California Cowboys* (1939).

On agriculture and Indians see Dennis Alward and Andrew Rolle, "The Surveyor General: Edward Fitzgerald Beale's Administration of California Lands," *Southern California Quarterly* 53 (June 1971), 113–22; Sally Miller, "Changing Faces of the Central Valley: The Ethnic Presence," *California History* 74 (Summer, 1995), 175–89; Joan Marie Donohoe, "Agostin Haraszthy: A Study in Creativity," *California Historical Society Quarterly* 47 (June 1969),

153–63; Mildred Yorba MacArthur, *Anaheim: The Mother Colony* (1959). Iris Wilson, "Early Southern California Viticulture, 1830–1865," *Historical Society of Southern California Quarterly* 39 (September 1957), 242–50; Vincent Carosso, *The California Wine Industry, 1830–1895* (1951).

For grain production see Rodman W. Paul, "The Great California Grain War: The Granger Challenges the Wheat King," *Pacific Historical Review* 27 (November 1958), 331–49, and Paul, "The Wheat Trade Between California and the United Kingdom," *Mississippi Valley Historical Review* 45 (December 1958), 391–412; Robert L. Kelley, *Gold vs. Grain: The Hydraulic Mining Controversy in California's Sacramento Valley* (1960). Irrigation is in Frederick D. Kershner, Jr., "George Chaffey and the Irrigation Frontier," *Agricultural History* 27 (October 1953), 115–22; also J. A. Alexander, *The Life of George Chaffey: The Story of Irrigation Beginnings in California and Australia* (1928). On growing silk see Nelson Klose, "California's Experimentation in Sericulture," *Pacific Historical Review* 30 (August 1961), 213–27.

Local histories include Gordon S. Eberly, *Arcadia: City of the Santa Anita* (1953); William Martin Camp, *San Francisco: Port of Gold* (1947); Works Progress Administration, *Berkeley: The First Seventy-Five Years* (1941); Chester G. Murphy, *The People of the Pueblo: or The Story of Sonoma* (repr. 1948); Clara H. Hisken, *Tehama: Little City of the Big Trees* (1948); Hallock F. Raup, *San Bernardino, California: Settlement and Growth of a Pass-Site City* (1940); Donald H. Pflueger, *Glendora* (1951) and Pflueger, *Covina: Sunflowers, Citrus, Subdivisions* (1964); L. J. Rose, Jr., *L. J. Rose of Sunny Slope, 1827–1899* (1958) and Andrew Rolle, *William Heath Davis and the Founding of American San Diego* (1953); Joseph J. Hill, *The History of Warner's Ranch and Its Environment* (1927); Robert G. Cleland, *The Irvine Ranch of Orange County, 1810–1950* (1952); W. W. Robinson, *Ranchos Become Cities* (1939); R. Louis Gentilcore, "Ontario, California and the Agricultural Boom of the 1880's," *Agricultural History* 34 (April 1960), 77–87.

On the migration after 1887 consult Glenn S. Dumke, *The Boom of the 'Eighties in Southern California* (1944); Richard W. Barsness, "Iron Horses and an Inner Harbor at San Pedro Bay, 1867–1890," *Pacific Historical Review* 34 (August 1965), 289–304; Robert C. Post, "America's Electric Railway Beginnings . . . at Los Angeles," *Southern California Quarterly* 69 (Fall 1987), 203–19; Joseph S. O'Flaherty, *An End and a Beginning* (1972) and O'Flaherty, *Those Powerful Years* (1978).

Discrimination and Accommodation

///////CHAPTER 23

Just as the transcontinental railroad was built largely with Chinese and Irish labor, California's growth was furthered by the toil of foreign immigrants: by Japanese farmers in the Central Valley; by Italian and French wine growers in the north; by Swiss and German dairymen along the Coast Ranges.

California's history, however, includes a record of violence toward specific minority groups. During the nineteenth century, Asians faced especially tough battles for acceptance in mainstream society. Their mistreatment is summed up in the phrase of the day, "He doesn't have a Chinaman's chance." Paradoxically, the first Chinese immigrants to the state were treated with consideration, in part due to a dire need for dependable labor; also, Chinese workers seemed content with meager wages.

But in 1850, after some Chinese miners managed to accumulate more gold than did whites, jealous Californians enacted the Foreign Miners' License Law, which imposed a monthly tax of $20 on immigrant miners. This law had the desired effect of driving a horde of penniless foreigners away from the mines. That law was followed in 1855 by a head tax of $50 to be paid by each foreigner upon entry into the state. When the Chinese got in the way of aggressive whites, some diggings were closed to the Chinese and other foreigners altogether. At other times, Chinese miners became the victims of groundless accusations and unprovoked violence.

"California for the Americans!" was a cry voiced in cities as well as in mining camps. Influenced by heightening public antipathy, Governor

Bigler, who in 1852 succeeded McDougal, stigmatized the Chinese as scum "coolie" laborers. He called upon the legislature to prohibit contract immigration, becoming the first important official to display anti-Chinese prejudice. When the financial panic of 1854 brought prices down with a crash, ruining some businessmen and causing public unrest, feeling against the Chinese reached new heights. Miners by the thousands drifted back to San Francisco, only to find the labor market glutted. Large numbers of Chinese in "the City" were held responsible for its distressing unemployment. White workers complained that "Orientals," by undercutting wages, deprived them of work—that they were, in fact, human leeches "sucking the very lifeblood of this country."

Governor Bigler, capitalizing on the prevailing public temper, rebuked the legislature in 1854 for its negligence in not voting for Asian exclusion and deportation laws. Prejudice among whites now extended even to little children, who were encouraged by bigoted elders to practice disrespect and insult against the Chinese. Mistreatment of the "pigtail," or "almond-eyed Celestial," had become an almost daily occurrence by the late 1850s. The Chinese, sharply set apart by their physiognomy, dress, religion, mores, and exotic food habits, were in no position to retaliate. The nadir of indignity was reached in San Francisco's notorious 1855 "Pig-Tail Ordinance." This regulation required Chinese men to cut off their queues one inch from the head. The Chinese fiercely protected the wearing of long hair, which contributed to the belief that they were unassimilable.

In spite of prejudice and persecution, from 1850 to 1900 a "Little China" was steadily growing in San Francisco on upper Sacramento Street and along Dupont Street. The mysteries of Chinatown held a great attraction for tourists. Smoke-filled gambling dens flourished, and back-room saloons, secret passages, deep basements, and hidden recesses teemed with hivelike activity, day and night. Opium smoking in filthy dens both fascinated and revolted Americans. The Chinese were also accused of importing prostitutes for the use of whites and of keeping these women in bondage.

When the Central Pacific railroad was being built, Mark Hopkins had founded his "Six Companies" to recruit, transport, and utilize Chinese labor on a large scale. This enterprise, operated by Hopkins's agents, was responsible for much of the Asian immigration in the early 1860s—about 9,000 Chinese in all. Included among "Crocker's Pets" were undernourished, sometimes sickly, laborers bound to the "Six Companies" by contract. These came chiefly from southern China, where devastating poverty existed. They were in no sense free laborers; rather, they were the tools of speculators who paid them a few pennies per hour.

Chinese butcher shop in San Francisco, ca. 1890. Wyland Stanley Collection, photography by I.W. Taber; courtesy of The Bancroft Library, University of California, Berkeley.

Shrewd brokers cooperated with railroad and steamship agents to exploit the Asians. Conversely, Governor Stanford called the Chinese "peaceable, industrious and economical, apt to learn and quite as efficient as white laborers." Since their labors made a vast fortune for him, he probably could not have had said anything less.

When the Chinese came into economic competition with other laborers in various trades, resentment exploded into violence. In 1859 Governor Weller sent a company of state militia into Shasta County to put down riots by northern miners. By 1867 "anti-coolie clubs" had grown strong enough to dictate punishment for the misbehavior of Asians. Sheriffs, courts, and juries were generally passive in the face of such action. In December 1867, various Chinese were driven out of French Corral, a settlement in Nevada County, and their cabins were destroyed. Out of a total of twenty-seven Caucasians arrested for this mob violence, one was tried and the rest set free. The guilty man was fined $100. On October 23, 1871, nearly a score of Chinese were massacred in a Los Angeles race riot that originated in a quarrel between two competing Chinese factions. This bloody episode was ignored by the law. Los Angeles earned a notoriety based on lawlessness both in its Chinatown and what came to be called "Nigger Alley."

Such racial hostility involved economic, social, and religious considerations. The press charged the Chinese with intolerable competition in mining, construction work, cigar making, and in the lesser trades. Moreover, critics accused the Chinese of draining the state of substantial sums of money, which they allegedly sent to China. They were called the "yellow peril," living on inferior food in crowded, unsanitary dwellings, a threat to "Christian values and Republican government." They were said to be pagan, depraved, and vicious. It was believed that the Chinese practiced a mysterious quasi-government among themselves that encouraged internecine wars. Their accusers found the Chinese lack of assimilation inexcusable. Although numerous Californians favored their exclusion, a treaty negotiated in 1868 by Anson Burlingame eased the passage of Asians into the state. One clause encouraged further Chinese immigration. Burlingame, formerly U.S. Minister to China, was so tactful that the Chinese emperor hired him to visit foreign countries with which he signed similar amicable treaties. Regardless of America's prejudices, cheap labor remained in much demand, especially in California where its railroad kings continued to expand their extensive network.

Still, public sentiment flowed in the opposite direction. Agitation against the Chinese continued at both local and state levels. In 1871, Governor Newton Booth was elected to office on an anti-Chinese platform. Almost every time the state legislature convened, nativists proposed an "immigrant tax." Eventually strong feeling arose for repeal of the Burlingame Treaty, which had guaranteed free immigration. Such pressures were bound to affect legislation at the national level. In 1878 Congress passed the "Fifteen Passenger Bill," restricting the immigration of Asians to fifteen passengers on any ship entering the United States. Although President Rutherford Hayes vetoed this law, an inflamed press in California pushed for a Chinese treaty with even stronger exclusionist provisions. In 1882 the Democratic state convention passed a sweeping resolution against all further Asian immigration. Both major parties were, in fact, anti-Chinese—on a national as well as a state level.

By the mid-1890s, the country was moving toward absolute exclusion. On April 30, 1902, despite stiff complaint from Chinese Minister

Wu Ting Fang to Secretary of State John Hay, Congress pushed a new federal bill, "to prohibit . . . and to regulate the residence within the United States of persons of Chinese descent." It was approved by President Theodore Roosevelt.

California can take little pride in its history of exclusion. Its bigotry, race prejudice, and chauvinism were prime factors in national agitation against Asians. On the other hand, the United States, unlike leading European powers, refrained from carving up the Chinese Empire after the Boxer Uprising of 1900, and returned an indemnity fund levied against China so that it might be used to educate young Chinese in America. But such a tardy manifestation of good will could not immediately eradicate American guilt for the treatment of the Chinese.

California still has sizable Chinese colonies at San Francisco and Los Angeles. At the turn of the century, Fresno's Chinatown boasted 5,000 inhabitants and had its own Chinese opera house. Except for celebration of the Chinese New Year and the annual moon festival, Chinese activity in California's interior towns is not to be compared with that of earlier times. Yet, a former joss house in Weaverville functions not only as a state historical monument but also as a bona fide Taoist temple. Its altar, imported from China during the gold rush, is ancient. Chinese tongs, or welfare and fraternal organizations, continue strong at both Los Angeles and San Francisco. Chinese in these large centers have remained a relatively homogeneous group as a result of the success of their restaurants and shops, in artificially created "Chinatowns" rigged for tourists.

Significant numbers of Japanese also began to enter California in the late nineteenth century. Like the Chinese, they experienced reasonable treatment at first. But after the Civil War, renewed hostility surfaced toward foreigners. "The front door has been off its hinges long enough," one California xenophobe of the 1870s declared. In this atmosphere, the Japanese posed a new cheap labor threat, and Californians also applied the term "yellow peril" to them. In the 1880s a second nativist "American Party" was formed, in the tradition of the Know-Nothings, partly for the purpose of attacking Asians.

Not until 1891 did Japanese immigration into the United States for a single year exceed one thousand, but from that time on it increased markedly. Acquisition of Hawaii by the United States in 1898 was followed by a heavy two-year influx of Japanese and Chinese from these islands, and public opinion was aroused anew against all "Orientals." Nevertheless, they still came. In 1900 alone, 12,626 Japanese entered the United States. By 1910 the number of Japanese had swelled to more than 40,000.

The first anti-Japanese exclusion meeting was held in May 1905 at San Francisco, resulting in the organization of an Asiatic Exclusion League. The next year the San Francisco Board of Education recommended establishment of special schools for Chinese and Japanese, separate from those for Caucasians. Before action on this proposal could be taken, the city experienced the great earthquake of 1906, which disrupted all civic activities except those devoted to recovery. Then the school board issued a "separate school order," which required the transfer of a majority of San Francisco's ninety-three Japanese pupils to an existing Asian school. This aroused indignation in Japan, from which diplomatic protests were promptly lodged with the U.S. government. The Japanese objected as much to the forced inclusion of their children in a school with the Chinese as to discrimination against them by whites. President Roosevelt subsequently insisted that the national government become a party to the controversy.

In accord with the president's view, the San Francisco school board's order was rescinded. But, following a recommendation by a newly organized Japanese and Korean Exclusion League, the board passed a second resolution, on October 11, 1906, which again announced that Japanese children would be received only at an "Oriental" public school, along with the Chinese. This time the federal government's view was expressed by Secretary of State Elihu Root. Exasperated, he stated that the U.S. government "would not allow any treatment of the Japanese people other than that accorded the people of other nations." The attorney general of the United States then brought legal action in California to enforce immigration agreements with Japan. However, since a legal decision (*Plessy* v. *Ferguson*) had become the law of the land, the federal suit could affect only alien Japanese children, who had treaty rights, but not the native-born, who did not. Meanwhile, the mayor of San Francisco and members of the school board journeyed to Washington to confer with President Roosevelt. As a result, the suits were dismissed, but only after the local board of education rescinded the objectionable order.

The arrival of Japanese laborers in large numbers, however, led to continued agitation against them. In 1908 demonstrations were such as to cause Ambassador Aoki to protest once more to the president, who telegraphed Governor James N. Gillett that restrictive measures then before the California legislature would strain relations with Japan at a time when the Roosevelt administration was already negotiating for the exclusion of immigrant laborers. Accordingly, the bills were withdrawn.

Obviously the major way to cut down further Japanese immigration was by diplomatic means. In order to avert an international crisis with

Japan, Roosevelt called for further negotiations, which resulted in the well-known "Gentlemen's Agreement," part of the Root-Takahira accords, which became effective in 1908. Under these new provisions Japanese and Korean laborers who surreptitiously entered the United States from Mexico, Canada, and Hawaii were deportable. Furthermore, the Japanese government agreed to restrict issuance of passports. California officials hoped this agreement would prevent the smuggling of Japanese into the United States. It did not. Immigrants subsequently entered the country illicitly in large numbers.

By 1910, California's Japanese population had reached more than 40,000. Three years later, because of anti-Japanese agitation, the state legislature passed an Alien Land Law. Popularly known as the Webb Act, this legislation prevented aliens ineligible for citizenship from holding land. Property acquired by them would be returned to the state, and agricultural lands could not be leased to aliens beyond a three year period. One way to evade the Webb Act, however, was to register land in the name of a citizen. By leasing and subleasing land in this manner, the Japanese came to control large truck-farm acreages. Californians continued to fear the efficiency of the Japanese and the possibility that they might shrewdly dominate the state's economic life. Further resentment was caused because some Japanese refused to work for whites who offered daily wages, preferring to bargain for a share of the crops they grew.

By 1920 the Japanese population in California had reached 72,000, partly because of loopholes in the "Gentlemen's Agreement" and the Webb Act. An Anti-Alien Initiative Measure of 1920 now prohibited the Issei, or first-generation immigrants, even to hold an interest in any company owning land. After World War I, as thousands of young Japanese women came to the United States, the Native Sons of the Golden West, the California State Grange, and other labor and exclusionist organizations demanded ever tighter federal immigration laws. This eventually led to the Immigration Act of 1924, which sought to put an end to Asian immigration to the United States.

Meanwhile, the French, Germans, Italians, and Irish immigrants to California encountered far fewer barriers to social and economic acceptance. In the West, these foreigners were apt to cast off the traces of their immigrant origins more quickly than their counterparts in the large cities of the East. In rural environments especially, the folkways and customs of Basque sheepherders, Swiss dairymen, and Armenian fig growers merged with those of their neighbors. Europeans who came to California to pick crops frequently became owners of the very land they once were hired to work.

Many Italians and French entered the restaurant trades or, along with the Portuguese, the fishing industry. At San Francisco's North Beach, the Italians formed the majority of the population after 1890. One of their leaders was Amadeo Pietro Giannini, founder of the modern Bank of America. Earlier called the Bank of Italy, loans from this organization contributed much to the rebuilding of the city after the fire of 1906.

Irish and German tradesmen, merchants, and farmers too became known for their thrift and industry. Among California's Germans were Adolph Sutro and Henry Teschemacher, both mayors of San Francisco. Theodore Cordua and Charles Weber became founders of Marysville and Stockton, respectively, just as the German-Swiss Sutter had earlier settled in what became Sacramento. Claus Spreckels became the "sugar king" of California, and Edward Vischer and Charles Christian Nahl, among the state's highly acclaimed artists.

Too much of California's immigrant past has been obliterated. Few issues of local foreign-language newspapers have been preserved. Little remains of the French utopian colony of Icaria Speranza, organized in 1881 near Cloverdale, or of the original German colony at Anaheim. The Danes at Solvang, above Santa Barbara, turned their community into a prosperous tourist center, which imported most of the European merchandise sold there.

But the immigrant contribution was a lasting one. As we shall see, California would one day become America's leading multi-ethnic state.

Selected Readings

Regarding the Chinese see Elmer C. Sandmeyer, *The Anti-Chinese Movement in California* (1939); Gunther Barth, *Bitter Strength: A History of the Chinese in the United States 1850–1870* (1964); Ping Chiu, *Chinese Labor in California, 1850–1880: An Economic Study* (1963); Kwang Ching Liu, *Americans and Chinese* (1963); and Thomas W. Chinn, ed., *A History of the Chinese in California* (1969); Luther W. Spoehr, "Sambo and the Heathen Chinese: California's Racial Stereotypes in the Late 1870's," *Pacific Historical Review* 42 (May 1973), 185–204, also Sucheng Chan, *Asians in California* (1991) and her *The Bittersweet Soil: The Chinese in California Agriculture* (1986).

Regarding other immigrant groups consult Roger Daniels and Spencer Olin, eds., *Racism in California* (1972); Charles Wollenberg, "Race and Class in Rural California: The El Monte Berry Strike of 1933," *California Historical Quarterly* 51 (Summer 1971), 155–64; D. S. Thomas and R. S. Nishimoto, *The Spoilage* (1946); D. S. Thomas, *The Salvage* (1952); Jacobus ten Broek, Edward N. Barnhart, and Floyd W. Matson, *Prejudice, War, and the Constitution* (1954); Roger Daniels, *The Politics of Prejudice: The Anti-Japanese Movement in California . . .* (1962) and Yuji Ichioka, *The Issei: The World of the First Generation of Japanese Immigrants, 1885–1924* (1989).

Regarding Italians see Andrew Rolle, *The Immigrant Upraised: Italian Adventurers and Colonists in an Expanding America* (1968); Dino Cinel, *From Italy to San Francisco* (1982) and Felice Bonadio, *A. P. Giannini: Banker of America* (1995). On the Germans see Erwin G. Gudde, *German Pioneers in Early California* (1927); Charles G. Loomis, *The German Theater in San Francisco, 1861–1864* (1952). About the French see Gilbert Chinard, ed. and trans., *When the French Came to California* (1944); Abraham P. Nasatir, *French Activities in California* (1945). On the Irish consult Hugh Quigley, *The Irish Race in California and the Pacific Coast* (1878); Thomas F. Prendergast, *Forgotten Pioneers: Irish Leaders in Early California* (1942) and R. A. Burchell, *The San Francisco Irish, 1848–1880* (1980).

Regarding California's Jews, see I. Harold Sharfman, *Nothing Left to Commemorate* (1969); Robert Levinson, *The Jews in the California Gold Rush* (1978); Max Vorspan and Lloyd P. Gartner, *History of the Jews of Los Angeles* (1970).

Crushing the
Natives

As California became more Americanized, assaults on its Indian population by ranchers, miners, merchants, and the military increased in number and gravity. Native lands were overrun and tribal ways were challenged by invading Caucasians who demanded that the Indians change their way of life to suit them, or get out of their way altogether.

In the last half of the nineteenth century, the U.S. War Department ordered infantry and cavalry units to patrol pressure-points and to deal sternly with all native outbreaks. The result of stepped-up white infiltration was decimation of the Indians: starvation, disease, and liquor conspired with bullet and knife against the Native Americans. Pulmonary and venereal infections, smallpox, and other Caucasian imports wiped out even the marginal well-being that the original population had known under Mexican rule.

Most American settlers cared little about the rights of the natives. These newcomers, some of whom had been shot at by Indians while crossing the Great Plains, were scarcely in a conciliatory mood upon their arrival on the West Coast. Although California's natives were hardly as fierce as the Plains warriors, some northern warriors occasionally attacked the property and livestock of white settlers. After the gold rush, raids on outlying ranches led some angry ranchers to wipe out entire tribal villages. In the pre-reservation era, natives in the towns and cities fared perhaps worst of all. Their wages and working conditions were miserable. Even worse were the disastrous effects of the new-found addiction of some to gambling and "firewater."

The management record of California's Indian reservations is hardly a matter of pride. In 1850 a federal Indian Commission, with a meager appropriation of $50,000, was charged with setting up California's reservation system. Contrary to the designs of the commission, most natives did not want to move off of their mountain homesites, where miners complained they interfered with mining operations, onto the flat lands of the Central Valley. But sheer hunger eventually forced them to negotiate with the commissioners.

In the 1850s, 18 treaties were concluded with 139 native bands, which agreed to recognize the sovereignty of the United States and to refrain from acts of retaliation. They also accepted 18 reservations, aggregating 7,500,000 acres, in compensation for vast land rights seized by the government. The commissioners, in addition, agreed to supply the reservation-bound Indians with agricultural implements and other goods, to retain the new reservations for their use in perpetuity, and to provide instruction in and supervision of farming, blacksmithing, and woodwork.

But the U.S. Senate, responding to repeated complaints of California residents, considered these agreements too costly. Although the natives justly claimed that they had promptly complied with the terms imposed by the commission, the compensatory acreages promised them were, for the most part, not forthcoming. Herded instead onto marginal plots of land in an environment of shacks and shanties, the Indians were shoehorned into a life that was neither native nor white. For years only half a reservation system existed, and a mismanaged half at that.

Some officials in charge of reservations were clearly unfit for their posts. Too often, whenever valuable land was at stake, Indian agents stood by as avaricious whites swooped in, driving the natives onto rocky or sandy terrain. Frustrated and sometimes desperate, Indians thus left their reservations to become unskilled laborers on ranches or farms. To make their plight worse, municipal ordinances encouraged a system of peonage under which a rancher or a farmer, by paying the fine of an Indian arrested for a minor offense such as public drunkenness, could pick up a laborer who was required by law to work off the amount of his fine.

Natives seldom understood the white man's regulations, which suited most whites just fine. In general, the federal policy of administering the natives was as unsuccessful in California as elsewhere—with one exception. In 1853 Edward Fitzgerald Beale became the first superintendent of Indian affairs within the state. At Fort Tejón, in the Tehachapi Mountains, Beale began to convert a wild region into a model Indian preserve that could become a self-sufficient community. Beale gave his wards a voice in their own affairs, meeting with their chiefs to discuss daily operations. He never hesitated to criticize whites, or to take disciplinary action against subordinates who treated natives unjustly. This policy resulted in complaints to Washington about Beale's administration. Charges of malfeasance forced him, in 1855, to relinquish his superintendency. Finally, in 1863, the project at Tejón was abandoned.

Herded into California's other reservations, most tribelets eventually deteriorated. Mismanagement of Indian affairs occurred partly because the War Department and the Department of the Interior quarreled over how to manage the reservations. "Pacification by feeding," which forced too many Indians into shameful dependency, and closely regulated "supervision" was the basic policy of the Interior Department. When, however, natives escaped from inhospitable reservations, the War Department ordered out the army to herd them back onto approved sites where they could be controlled.

In southern California there had been only one significant uprising, near Warner's Ranch in 1851, under a subchief named Antonio Garrá. But skirmishing took place with some frequency in northern California along the Humboldt, Eel, and Rogue rivers. Fearful whites (civilian and military) repeatedly sought to drive Indians into remote locales where

Mohave Indian family on the Colorado River, north of Needles. The unclothed man is the chief. Courtesy of The Huntington Library, San Marino, California.

they would be rendered harmless to white settlements. They relied upon the army to do this for them.

One particular expedition against retreating Indians led to a remarkable geographical discovery. In 1833 the Yosemite Valley may have been seen by Joseph Reddeford Walker's trapping expedition. But the first recorded discovery of the Yosemite chasm occurred in 1851 when Major James D. Savage was deputized to pursue marauding Yosemite and Chowchilla Indians. Savage's posse chased about 350 Yosemites into their Sierra hiding place, above the Merced River. There Savage stumbled upon one of the world's most beautiful valleys, eventually accepting the surrender of proud Chief Tenieya whose followers were forced to leave their native grounds.

The last and most dramatic of California's Indian conflicts was the Modoc War. Bloodshed first occurred in 1852, when some warriors attacked a small party of whites enroute to California, killing nearly half of them. Throwing the Modocs off guard by proposing a "peaceful" settlement, local armed Americans then retaliated bloodily against the Indians. The Modocs never forgot what they considered an infamous butchery, and for the next ten years hostilities continued intermittently.

In 1864 most of the Modoc tribe—seriously reduced in number by ongoing pressures against them—were persuaded by U.S. Indian agents to go to the Klamath Reservation in southern Oregon. But this northward migration forced the Modocs onto the hunting lands of the Klamaths. Because the Klamaths then threatened to repulse the unwanted Modoc invaders, Chief Kientepoos (Captain Jack) of the Modocs reluctantly led his flock back southward to their ancestral preserves.

In its shortsightedness the U.S. government crowded the two autonomous tribes into the same area. The Klamaths saw this as a violation of their ancient territorial rights and clearly would not permit it. Nonetheless, late in 1869 the Superintendent of Indian Affairs for Oregon persuaded Captain Jack to return to the Klamath Reservation with two hundred Modocs. When, however, the outraged Klamaths resisted the Modocs for a second time, the chief and his band again returned to their old camping grounds in present-day Modoc County.

But by coming back into northern California, the Modocs defied U.S. authority. Disturbed settlers now spoke of organizing a force to protect themselves. By the winter of 1872 an unfortunate clash occurred and eleven settlers were killed by marauding native bands. When the American cavalry closed in on the Modocs, Captain Jack retreated toward some lava beds. There he sought the safety of caves, the entrances of which were protected by jagged rocks and ledges. Though cut off from supplies, the Modocs managed to subsist by eating field mice and bats found in the caves, and by drinking water from underground springs. Nonetheless, the army was determined to force the Modocs back onto the reservation. Confusion reigned on all sides of this needless controversy.

On January 17, 1873, the army advanced on the Modocs, firing cannon volleys into their lava beds. Concealed behind rock breastworks, the natives returned fire. The army's losses in the exchange compelled retreat. At this point General E. R. S. Canby, commander of the Modoc operation, and several commissioners decided to meet with Captain Jack. With one thousand men surrounding the Modoc's position, General Canby moved his camp to the edge of the lava beds and pitched a council tent between the opposing camps. During that peace conference of April 11, 1873, the chief was goaded by some young tribesmen into a fatal act. Both he and the white emissaries had agreed to negotiate unarmed, but not only did the Modocs wear concealed weapons to the talks, several young warriors lay hidden in nearby bushes, armed with rifles. After Captain Jack gave a signal for attack, he personally killed General Canby, also stabbing and shooting one of the peace commissioners.

After a further prolonged struggle, Canby's troops finally captured Captain Jack and two of his accomplices; they were tried and hanged at Fort Klamath. All told the Modoc War had cost the U.S. government half a million dollars, plus the lives of a general and about seventy-five men. All this might have been avoided if the Modocs had been allowed to occupy their remote lava beds and the nearby marginal grazing lands.

The virtual disappearance of California's native population is a tragic story. As the eighteenth century waned, the condition of the former missionized natives was especially pitiable. Cut off both from land use and their cultural foundations, some were virtually auctioned off as private laborers. This semistate of enslavement that many Indians endured was complicated by addiction to grape-based alcohol. Scattered about in small rancherias, without support, many of these dispossessed peoples simply faced elimination. Between the beginning of the American period and the opening of the twentieth century the number of American Indians in California declined from 100,000 to 15,500.

After General U. S. Grant became president in 1869, he replaced all of California's Indian agents with army officers. Still later, various churches were allotted native agencies to supervise. That policy, too, gave way, as had the military superintendencies, to appointees of the Commissioner of Indian Affairs. Responding to the pleas of the Native Americans, President Grant in 1875 authorized nine small reservations in San Diego County and created additional reserves by executive order.

These lands were, however, mostly brush-strewn acreage that whites did not want.

Thereafter, the novelist Helen Hunt Jackson was appointed a commissioner to investigate the conditions under which the remaining Indians lived. Her two influential books, *A Century of Dishonor* (1881) and *Ramona* (1884) called attention to the mistreatment of these people. Charles Fletcher Lummis, the southwestern author, joined Jackson's public-awareness campaign, soliciting funds to relocate several tribelets onto more fertile land.

Under the 1887 Dawes Act, each Native-American family was given the right to own 160 acres of land, to be held in trust for twenty-five years—in which time, in theory, Indian landowners would learn to become self-sufficient farmers on the Anglo model. After that, the holders were to receive ownership and full American citizenship. Allotments, mostly of from five to ten acres, were made under separate acts which Congress passed from 1890 to 1910. All remaining nonallocated tracts were held in a tribal trust. But the decline of tribal autonomy came long before the allotment process began. Those natives who remained on reservations relied heavily upon the government food ration system.

Even when the natives were lucky enough to be awarded good land, they were so inexperienced with the American principles and concepts of land ownership that some were tricked by unscrupulous whites into selling their best holdings. With little experience in managing land, they often made a poor adjustment to American society. The Dawes Act had come too late to benefit a people who needed charity as much as a governmental definition of their status.

Some "authorities" claimed that the remaining natives would function best back within a tribal group. Hence, in 1934, the Dawes Act was repealed. From that date until 1953 the government tried to restore tribal life, encouraging Native Americans to earn a livelihood through production of handicrafts. By that time, large numbers of California's natives had left their reservations for good. Some simply disappeared, as measured by census statistics.

Occasional private, state, and national organizations have fortunately made a contribution to the betterment of the condition of American Indians in California. One such institution is the Sherman Institute, near Riverside, founded in 1901 to afford Indian children of southern California industrial and handicraft training.

With a few such exceptions, however, efforts to help the natives have generally failed. A few lusty tribal groups did win favorable land-tenure legal decisions. Beginning in the 1930s, the state sought payment of $1.25 per acre from the federal government for lands previously taken from several tribelets. In 1944, after fifteen years of litigation, the Indians were awarded $5,165,863.46. This sum, however, was placed in the U.S. Treasury. The money became available only by congressional appropriation.

After 1948 the U.S. Supreme Court awarded 3,337 acres of Palm Springs land to 71 surviving members of the Agua Caliente band of the Cahuilla Indians. Because these natives remained unsatisfied with that allotment, Congress in 1959 passed a law on their behalf. They achieved a commanding position in real estate ownership at the popular resort town, receiving in excess of thirty thousand acres. In addition, hearings before a federal Indian Claims Commission during the 1950s and 1960s determined that California's Native Americans held title to 64 million acres for which they were entitled to compensation of approximately $29 million, which the government eventually paid. By then, however, their aggrieved native ancestors were all dead.

Selected Readings

A basic work is R. F. Heizer and M. A. Whipple, eds., *The California Indians: A Source Book* (1951). See also Sherburne Cook, *The Population of the California Indians 1769–1970* (1979); Helen Hunt Jackson, *A Century of Dishonor,* Andrew Rolle, ed. (repr., 1965); George E. Anderson, *Treaty Making and Treaty Rejection by the Federal Government* (1978); William H. Ellison, "The Federal Indian Policy in California," *Mississippi Valley Historical Review* 9 (June 1922), 37–67. Avowedly emotional over the mistreatment of the American Indian is Rupert and Jeanette Costo, *Natives of the Golden State: The California Indians* (1995).

On reservation problems see Imre Sutton, *Indian Land Tenure* (1975) and Sutton's *Irredeemable America* (1986); Stephen Bonsal, *Edward Fitzgerald Beale: A Pioneer in the Path of Empire, 1822–1893* (1912); Helen S. Giffen and Arthur Woodward, *The Story of El Tejón* (1942); Richard E. Crouter and Andrew Rolle, "Edward Fitzgerald Beale and the Indian Peace Commissioners in California, 1851–1854," *Historical Society of Southern California Quarterly* 42 (June 1960), 107–32; J. Ross Browne, *The Indians of California* (repr. 1944); John W. Caughey, ed., *The Indians of Southern California* (1952); Lafayette H. Bunnell, *Discovery of the Yosemite and the Indian War of 1851* (1911); Annie R. Mitchell, *Jim Savage and the Tulareno Indians* (1957) and C. Gregory Crampton, ed., *The Mariposa Indian War, 1850–1851 . . .* (1958).

Other titles include William Edward Evans, "The Garrá Uprising: Conflict Between San Diego Indians and Settlers in 1851," *California Historical Society Quarterly* 45 (December 1966), 339–49; Keith A. Murray, *The Modocs and Their War* (1959); Max Heyman, *Prudent Soldier* (1960), a biography of General E. R. S. Canby; Erwin N. Thompson, *Modoc War: Its Military*

History and Topography (1971); C. T. Brady, *Northwestern Fights and Fighters* (1907); A. B. Meacham, *Wigwam and War-path* (1875); Kenneth Johnson, ed., *K-344, or the Indians of California vs. the United States* (1966); David G. Shanahan, "Compensation for the Loss of the Aboriginal Lands of the California Indians," *Southern California Quarterly* 57 (Fall 1975), 297–320; George H. Phillips, *Chiefs and Challengers: Indian Resistance and Cooperation in Southern California* (1975), also Phillips, *Indians and Intruders in Central California* (1993) and his *Indians and Indian Agents: The Origins of the Reservation System in California, 1849–1852* (1997). See also William F. Strobridge, *Regulars in the Redwoods: The U.S. Army in Northern California* (1994) and Joan Weibel-Orlando, *Indian Country, L. A.: Maintaining Ethnic Community in a Complex Society* (1991).

Labor, the Farmers, and the New Constitution

////////// CHAPTER 25

In 1873, a nationwide economic panic affected all segments of California society. Tramps slept in abandoned barns and job seekers crowded dusty roads in search of employment. If they were lucky they found jobs that paid $2 per day.

A great railway strike in 1877 plunged the country into violence and turmoil. In San Francisco that year, workers began to demonstrate in favor of an eight-hour day, as a means of sharing a small number of jobs more widely. Their spokesman was a drayman, Denis Kearney, who had arrived from Ireland during 1868. A coarse man, clothed in a low-cut waistcoat, he swayed crowds of workers with intemperate speeches that caused fearful local merchants to boycott his small business.

A rabid exclusionist, Kearney repeatedly harangued his followers with the slogan "The Chinese Must Go!" As unemployment increased, 22,000 Chinese arrived in California's ports in 1876 alone, which added fuel to the flames of social unrest Kearney lit. His "shoulder-striking hoodlums," recruited among disgruntled workers, physically abused the Chinese.

Below the palaces of the Nob Hill millionaires, unemployed workers prowled San Francisco's streets looking for hapless Chinese. In July 1877, anti-Chinese riots broke out, posing an emergency that the police could not handle. As a result, a new Committee of Safety was formed by aroused citizens under the leadership of William T. Coleman, the former vigilante chieftain. Coleman's new law-enforcement group equipped itself with 6,000 hickory pick handles with which to quell rioters along the turbulent waterfront. At the docks a two-hour fight occurred before

Coleman's vigilantes could subdue rioting laborers who sought to prevent the landing of more Chinese immigrants who were wanted by merchants.

Amid these violent conflicts, Kearney founded the Workingmen's Party of California. With 15,000 men unemployed in San Francisco, he easily stirred up disgruntled workers with talk of violence in open-air meetings in a vacant lot in front of San Francisco's city hall. The fiery Irishman suggested "a little judicious hanging" of employers whom he labeled "robber-capitalists." One of Kearney's largest meetings took place during October 1877, with three thousand workers in the crowd. Kearney and six associates were subsequently arrested. After two weeks in prison, however, he resumed unrestrained attacks upon public officials.

In January 1878, a group of the unemployed took to the streets demanding "work, bread, or a place in the county jail." As their numbers swelled to 1,500, local authorities were powerless to help them. With marching laborers threatening further trouble, at another mass meeting the workers boasted that they could "blow up the Pacific Mail Steamship Company's dock and steamers," and bomb the Chinese quarter. In this charged atmosphere, a U.S. Navy man-of-war arrived to protect the government mail docks. More of Kearney's firebrand followers were then thrown into prison by the police, as it was illegal to commit acts of violence. An alarmed legislature made it a felony to incite a riot.

On January 21, 1878, the noisy Workingmen's party held its first formal convention, inveighing against a government that "has fallen into the hands of capitalists and their willing instruments." By this time the Workingmen had become a force in state politics. Suggesting relatively modest reforms, by 1879 they had elected a mayor of San Francisco, several state supreme court judges, eleven state senators, and sixteen assemblymen.

But disintegration began to appear in the labor party's ranks after a rumor spread that Kearney had accepted railroad money and was personally corruptible. Both his integrity and loyalty to his workers continued to be impugned in a whispering campaign that led to his removal from leadership of the Workingmen. Kearney's opponents within his party, which also acted as a union, thereby hoped to combat charges of labor recklessness with which his leadership had been tarred.

The Workingmen, in an age when business felt little need to apologize for its abuses, were considered dangerous radicals. Yet many of the reform measures Kearny advocated later became law. These included the eight-hour workday, establishment of a statewide public school system, reform of the banking system, and restrictions upon business and land monopolies.

Accompanying the Workingmen's demands, Californians moved toward revision of their 1849 constitution. That document had met the needs of a frontier area that had been anxious for admittance to the Union. The constitution, however, contained outmoded provisions for public finance, safeguarding of public lands, and improving labor conditions. Also, it offered Californians no real public controls against violence at a time when discontent of both farmers and workers with the practices of the railroads was increasing.

On September 28, 1878, California's second constitutional convention convened with 152 delegates assembled. The largest group of delegates were lawyers. Farmers had the next largest representation. Thirty-five delegates were of foreign birth. No Native Americans attended.

As the state desperately needed more revenue, a topic of major importance was taxation. Some favored a poll tax. Others advocated a tax on all property, a state income tax, a graduated tax on the largest estates, and suspension of taxes for citizens already in debt. An Independent Taxpayer's party achieved adoption of a California State Board of Equalization to "equalize the valuation of taxable property in the several counties, and also assess the franchise, roadway, roadbed, rails and rolling stock of all railroads. . . ."

Numerous delegates held the railroads responsible for racial and labor conflict by their importation of thousands of Chinese. Members of local "farmer clubs," or Grangers, at the convention charged the railroads with hurting small farmers by fraudulently influencing elections, conspiring among themselves to fix high freight rates, and favoring large shippers through secret rebates. The Grangers, aided by such reformers as the writer Henry George, charged that such monopolies were seriously damaging the poor. Dissatisfied farmers further felt that California, dominated by monopolies, was at the service of powerful landowners. After 1867 the Granger movement had stepped up its activities, sponsoring political forums to protest economic abuses against farmers. By forming new cooperative enterprises, they also established their own grain elevators, mills, and supply centers. Hence the Grangers were bound to be heard at California's second constitutional convention.

Although the constitutional convention created a State Railroad Commission, individual commissioners bowed to the railroads. And railroad attorneys, working with sympathetic judges, kept the railroads from paying proper taxes. When challenged, railroad attorneys were able to tie up such legal proceedings for years on end. Finally, government reforms did not cut deeply, and railroad abuses continued for many years after the 1879 constitutional convention.

In 1880, a highly inflammatory dispute between farmers and the Southern Pacific occurred at Mussel Slough, near the town of Hanford in Kings County. After improving land along the slough, as well as having built an elaborate irrigation system, settlers there encountered repeated delays in the conveyance of titles to the land "sold" to them by the railroad. Enraged homesteaders, who felt cruelly deceived, claimed they had bought the land under irrevocable conditions, only to have railroad officials change the terms of the sale once the land had been rendered more valuable. When S.P. representatives tried to evict the settlers, a battle ensued between the two groups. Seven persons were shot to death and an eighth badly wounded. The S.P., backed by the courts, had five of the settlers imprisoned for a period of eight months, in part because they had resisted a federal official who tried to control their outrage.

Although reform-minded delegates at the constitutional convention were united in opposition to such railroad abuses, they split over proposals to control the banks. As the credit of local banks was vital to farmers, the Grangers sided with country bankers who opposed too much reform of banking practices. Both the banks and the railroads favored the status quo, which they had created.

Labor delegates clamored for insertion in California's new constitution of exclusionist clauses embodying the slogan, "The Chinese Must Go!" A number of tired anti-Chinese clauses were indeed adopted. Condemnation of Asiatic "coolieism," or contract labor, as "a form of human slavery" became part of the new document. These prohibitions against employment of Chinese were later held to be in conflict with the U.S. Constitution.

The 1879 convention gave California's public school system its basic shape. Under it the University of California was accorded the legal status of a corporation. Other matters determined by the convention concerned the granting of divorces and rights of eminent domain. A section of the new constitution concerning waters and shorelines would later be cited to support state claims to tideland oil deposits.

The convention continued its deliberations for 157 days. Lobbying by so many pressure groups actually hindered some reforms. Though some delegates pleaded for political equality of the sexes, this group met with little immediate success. California was not to achieve women's suffrage until 1911. In the end, after restraints upon corporations were watered down, reform-minded delegates like George considered the power of the state's land monopolists unbroken.

The vehemence with which the Workingmen put forth their demands had scared off their potential supporters, especially the farmers. Although unsuccessful in achieving some reforms, the new constitution's restrictions against monopolies, though limited, had been gained partly because of the energies of the Workingmen. Unfortunately, the Workingmen were also racists who had pushed for passage of the federal Exclusion Act of 1882 aimed at Asian immigrants. The Workingmen's demands for an eight-hour day, fixed salaries for government jobs, and the creation of a bureau of labor affairs eventually influenced the two major parties.

As for the Constitution of 1879, it remained a catalogued code of laws, rather than a working framework of government. California's original constitution probably need not have been totally scrapped. Its worst deficiencies could have been fixed by a series of amendments. As a result, today's constitution remains a wordy compendium.

Selected Readings

Regarding labor see Daniel Cornford, ed., *Working People of California* (1995); Jules Tygiel, *Workingmen in San Francisco, 1880–1901* (1992); Ralph Kauer, "The Workingmen's Party of California," *Pacific Historical Review* 13 (September 1944), 278–91; J. C. Stedman and R. A. Leonard, *The Workingman's Party of California* (1878); Ira B. Cross, *Frank B. Roney: Irish Rebel and California Labor Leader* (1931); and Cross, *History of the Labor Movement in California* (1935); Arthur N. Young, *The Single Tax Movement in the United States* (1916) and Henry George, Jr., *Life of Henry George* (1900).

About the first constitutional convention see *Debates and Proceedings of the Constitutional Convention of the State of California* (3 vols., 1880): Winfield J. Davis, *History of Political Conventions in California* (1893) and Carl B. Swisher, *Motivation and Political Technique in the California Constitutional Convention, 1878–1879* (1930).

Criticism of the railroads is in Gordon W. Clarke, "A Significant Memorial to Mussel Slough," *Pacific Historical Review* 18 (November 1949), 501–4; Irving McKee, "Notable Memorials to Mussel Slough," *Pacific Historical Review* 17 (February 1948), 19–27; John A. Larimore, "Legal Questions Arising From the Mussel Slough Land Dispute," *Southern California Quarterly* 58 (Spring 1976), 75–94.

California Culture,
1870-1918

//////// **CHAPTER 26**

By 1870, the pioneer phase of California's history was over. At San Francisco, wealthy patrons set about to encourage poetry, art, theatrics, and learning. Other towns too founded museums, opera houses, and symphony orchestras.

Especially notable was the emerging role of women in California society. Among those who contributed significantly to California's new culture was Helen Hunt Jackson, originally a writer of children's stories. Later, as noted, she combined an interest in raising the public consciousness of the mistreatment of Indians with a concern for the neglect of California's Hispanic past. Indeed, her articles in *Century Magazine* and her book *A Century of Dishonor* (1881) stirred up national interest in California's abused natives. However, her novel *Ramona* (1884) did not achieve the desired effect; it was instead taken as a true picture of California's idyllic Arcadian past. This romantic stereotyping would later be perpetuated in an annual "Ramona Pageant."

Another talented woman of the era was Helena Modjeska, a Polish actress. In 1876 she established a short-lived Utopian colony near Anaheim. Isadora Duncan, a San Franciscan, went on to world fame as a flamboyant dancer. A quite different, yet also remarkable woman was a former Georgia slave, Biddy Mason.

Mason crossed the plains in 1851 with three daughters, driving a herd of sheep. She found work as a nurse in Los Angeles at $2.50 per day. With her savings she purchased several parcels of land. She lived to see property she had bought for $250 soar in value to $200,000 during the real estate boom of 1887. She used her wealth to found a nursery school and frequently visited the city jail, also paying the expenses and taxes for her church, and providing a home for indigents. She died in 1891 as one of the most affluent property owners in California.

Another former slave, but of a different nature, was "Mammy" (Mary Ellen) Pleasant, the operator of a San Francisco boarding house in the 1850s. She has been remembered alternately as a procuress and a blackmailer. She was also a financial backer of John Brown's famous raid upon Harpers Ferry. By lending her fellow blacks money at reasonable rates of interest, she built a fortune, which she used to aid the fight to secure rights of testimony in the courts, which was gained by a legislative act of 1863. That year Pleasant successfully sued two San Francisco streetcar companies that barred blacks from riding their cars. And at a time when black female literary figures were rare, Charlotta Bass was editor of the *California Eagle,* southern California's first black newspaper.

White women writers encountered fewer hurdles to success than did their black counterparts. In 1893 the state legislature named Ina Coolbrith California's first poet laureate. The eccentric Gertrude Stein, later an expatriate writer and critic, lived in Oakland from 1879 to 1892 before settling in Paris. In 1903, she was joined there by a young San Franciscan, Alice B. Toklas, with whom she was to share the rest of her life.

In 1899 another writer, Mary Austin, traveled west from Illinois with her family. While she taught school in the Owens Valley, Austin wrote stories and articles for Charles Lummis's magazine and also produced *The Land of Little Rain* (1903), her best-known book. It sympathetically describes the natives, animals, and land south of Yosemite and north of Death Valley. In *The Basket Woman* (1904), *The Flock* (1906), and *California, Land of the Sun* (1914), she continued to evoke appreciation of a land of sagebrush and sand.

Among other women writers attracted to California was Gertrude Atherton, who spent most of her life in her native San Francisco. Her heavily romanticized best sellers included *The Splendid Idle Forties* (1902) and *The Californians* (1898). Both books idealized the Hispanic past. The autobiographical writer Charlotte Perkins Gilman, who lived and worked in Pasadena, is best known for her intensely personal essay *The Yellow Wallpaper* (1899).

Yet another female author, Kate Douglas Wiggin, combined a life of public service with writing. After training the majority of California's first kindergarten teachers, she went on to New York to pursue her writing career; but she remains famous for the free kindergartens she established for poor children. She wrote books for girls, among them *A Sum-*

mer in a Cañon (1889). By 1895, a devotee of Mrs. Wiggin, Sarah Brown Cooper, established 287 kindergartens throughout America.

A less orthodox woman of the period was a one-eyed, high-spirited stagecoach driver named "Charley" Parkhurst. As a teenager, Charlotte had fled westward from a Massachusetts orphanage masquerading as a man. On the job Parkhurst wore rough trousers and a patch over her left eye; she chewed tobacco; her skin was tanned and leathery. "Charley" became a highly respected "jehu," or stage driver, who regularly toted a six-shooter, which she did not hesitate to use to shoot and kill highway robbers. Upon her death in 1879, an autopsy finally revealed the secret that "Charley" had kept for most of her life.

In 1875 Caroline Severance, a pioneer reformer, came from Boston to Los Angeles with ideas for changing the sleepy pueblo environment. She established Los Angeles's first book club and, indeed, the city's public library. Severance also founded the Friday Morning Club, whose members advocated reform of the juvenile detention system and led a campaign to keep politics out of school board elections. Severence and her group also sought to save the giant Sequoias, established "El Camino Real" signposts to mark the route between missions, helped develop the Los Angeles Philharmonic Orchestra, and worked to bring a branch of the University of California to Los Angeles (later UCLA).

Women's clubs captured the attention of many women, giving them the opportunity to step outside their proscribed spheres of church and home. Six-hundred of these organizations in California served as social and intellectual centers for women, also encouraging political action. Despite societal limitations, women repeatedly demonstrated real leadership qualities. After women won the right to vote, many were lured away from the clubs by other activities, but in their time these clubs were an important means of personal transcendence and mutual reinforcement for women.

A founder of the Wilshire-Ebell Club in 1894, Harriet Williams Russell Strong also became an agriculturist and a civic leader. Her husband, Charles Strong, had purchased the Rancho del Fuerte, near the present city of Whittier, from Pío Pico, the last Mexican governor. After Charles died, Harriet studied marketing, as well as irrigation and flood control. From 1887 to 1894 she took out patents on a sequence of storage dams and various farm and household inventions. Strong became known as the "walnut queen" and "pampas lady" (for she grew pampas grass), won election as the first woman member of the Los Angeles Chamber of Commerce, and gained national fame by her agricultural product exhibits at the 1893 Columbian Exposition at Chicago. She was also a persuasive advocate of flood control and water supply development, supporting the federal aid program to dam the Colorado River.

Another woman of distinction was Alice Constance Austin, who in 1918 designed and helped develop a utopian city known as Llano del Rio. Tied to the California "arts and crafts" approach (a back-to-the-basics movement inspired by England's William Morris), she devised an innovative architectural scheme in which a central kitchen and laundry facility would be connected to outlying homes via an underground railway!

In late-nineteenth-century California, women slowly entered male-dominated professions. The Los Angeles city directory for 1890 listed 287 physicians, 27 of whom were women. One woman who had an ongoing effect upon the legal profession was Clara Shortridge Foltz. She studied law on her own and eventually procured passage of a legislative act that permitted women to practice law. In fact, she was the first female admitted to the state bar and also the first woman attorney to plead cases before the California Supreme Court.

Other women entered politics, including Katherine Phillips Edson. After the turn of the century, Edson helped to transform California into a leading Progressive party center. Still later, Elizabeth Snyder became the first woman to chair a state political party, becoming a leading force in Democratic party circles.

The period also witnessed the rise of a second generation of male writers and social reformers. Among them were Henry George, Frank Norris, Jack London, Josiah Royce, Ambrose Bierce, and Thorstein Veblen, creator of a "theory of the leisure class." George, restless and unorthodox, had held half a dozen jobs along the San Francisco waterfront before he turned to economic theorizing. In an atmosphere of labor turbulence and high unemployment, George's printed tracts, supporting land reform as well as an eight-hour working day, attracted worldwide attention. He evolved an appealing "single-tax" theory in his book *Progress and Poverty* (1880), which made him world famous. George charged that absentee monopolists were unfairly collecting an "unearned increment" from their vast rural properties.

Yet another thinker who wrote in a reformist vein was Josiah Royce. Born in 1855 at Grass Valley, Royce, like Henry George, published his initial writing in California. Royce too was incensed at abuses of the land monopolists and the railroads. As a member of the Harvard University philosophy faculty, he became an influential idealist nonconformist, writing *California . . . A Study of American Character* (1886).

A spiritual ally of Royce and George was Frank Norris, a talented writer impressed by Europe's naturalist authors. His most famous book was *The Octopus* (1901). Based on the Mussel Slough tragedy, it featured the continuing clash between the railroad monopoly and the farmers. Together with Norris's other reform novels, including *McTeague* (1899) and *The Pit* (1903), *The Octopus* won him national acclaim.

Norris also exerted a deep influence upon another highly productive writer, Jack London. London's realism combined a strong romantic strain with a sense of social conscience. In *The Call of the Wild* (1903) and *The Sea Wolf* (1904), he celebrated the elemental interaction of man and nature. His early struggle to make a living as a writer is the subject of the autobiographical novel, *Martin Eden* (1909). His later works led him toward Marxism as an economic and political alternative to democracy. In seventeen years, London turned out some fifty books filled with adventure, primitive violence, and class struggle before dying in 1916 at the age of forty.

A writer of a different sort, the acid-tongued Ambrose Bierce, dominated the California literary scene for decades with opinionated diatribes. From the late 1880s onward, his targets were many, from disreputable politicians to untalented young authors. Bierce delivered contemptuous judgments with gusto in *The Devil's Dictionary*. In his ghost and horror stories he used satire that was both gruesome and amusing. His criticisms of society also appeared in the columns of young William Randolph Hearst's San Francisco *Examiner*. Bierce's 1913 disappearance, probably into Mexico, remained as mysterious as his controversial writings.

Participants in the dramatic events of California's past frequently recorded their reminiscences. Among these was William Heath Davis, whose *Seventy-Five Years in California* (repr. 1929) gives one a view of the formerly provincial society that adjusted to urbanism. Often such chroniclers highlighted their personal participation in momentous events like California's American conquest and gold rush. Harris Newmark's *Sixty Years in Southern California* (1916) likewise presented a view of urban social and commercial life through the eyes of a pioneer Jewish merchant.

Among those writers who overglorified the Hispanic heritage was Charles Fletcher Lummis, eccentric litterateur and Harvard classmate of Theodore Roosevelt. Lummis's *The Land of Poco Tiempo* (1893) and *The Spanish Pioneers* (1893) set the trend for books of adulation about the leisurely existence that supposedly prevailed in early California. Lummis cut a striking figure, often wearing a green corduroy suit, with a Spanish sombrero on his head and a red sash wrapped around his middle. He further illustrated his distinctively Bohemian interpretation of Spanish colonial life in El Alisal, the house he constructed from boulders on the edge of Los Angeles's Arroyo Seco. Lummis also helped to restore the crumbling missions and preserved Indian-Spanish folk traditions in his magazine (1895–1902) *The Land of Sunshine.*

Also writing prior to World War I, were two authors whose works were rooted in natural history: George Wharton James and Charles Francis Saunders. James was for years employed by the Southern Pacific Railroad, and the books he wrote praised the wonders of nature, disseminated Indian lore, and promoted California as a unique place to live. Among his most widely read books were *In and Out of the Old Missions* (1905) and *Through Ramona's Country* (1907). Saunders, a Quaker naturalist fascinated by the southern California backcountry, wrote such charming books about the state as *Finding the Worthwhile in California* (1916).

A prolific spinner of narrative yarns was Stewart Edward White. Among White's books, which were serialized in the Saturday Evening Post and other national journals, were *The Blazed Trail* (1902), *Gold* (1913), and *The Forty Niners* (1918). White wrote both historical and fictional works that catered to a public yearning for adventurous fiction about California's deserts, mountains, and past heroes and heroines.

Lummis and White, though incurably romantic, achieved popularity because their picturesque qualities suited the taste of the reading public of their times. The theme of California as a pastoral paradise also dominated the writings of John Steven McGroarty whose *Mission Play* was staged annually at San Gabriel after 1912. During the same era, a rough-hewn character, Joaquin Miller (Cincinnatus Hines Miller), dubbed himself "Poet of the Sierra." Miller was later acclaimed in England as a "frontier poet." At British literary soirées Miller read his long-winded poetry dressed in chaps, sombrero, a red shirt, baggy trousers complete with suspenders, cowhide mining boots, and a sealskin coat.

Two other California poets of note were Edward Rowland Sill and Edwin Markham. Sill stressed the California locale in both poetry and prose, as in his *Christmas in California* (1890). Markham, like Sill, bespoke the state's praises, as his *California the Wonderful* (1914) attests. His best-known work is *The Man with the Hoe and Other Poems* (1899). Markham lived to see this protest against the brutalization of downtrodden farmers and laborers translated into forty different languages.

Less serious in tone was the doggerel of Gelett Burgess, originally a surveyor for the Southern Pacific Railroad. By the turn of the century his verse "The Purple Cow" was being recited all over the country:

> I never saw a purple cow
> I never hope to see one
> But I can tell you anyhow
> I'd rather see than be one.

Burgess later wrote, regretfully:

> Oh, yes, I wrote the Purple Cow
> I'm sorry now I wrote it
> But I can tell you anyhow
> I'll kill you if you quote it.

This playful verse aside, his "Ballad of the Hyde Street Grip" reveals that Burgess actually was a poet of considerable ability.

A number of writers of nonfiction focused upon California's natural wonders. The most popular of these naturalists was John Muir. No writer has shown such feeling for the majesty of the Sierra peaks, or the great Yosemite Valley. Scottish-born, but educated in the United States, Muir spent much of his life hiking through the California backcountry; he became a defender of its forests, mountains, and wildlife. Partly because President Theodore Roosevelt listened to Muir's advice, government preservation of wilderness areas increased in the state and the nation. Muir left behind works of natural history that are still widely read. Among the best of these are *The Mountains of California* (1894) and *The Yosemite* (1912). In 1892 he was one of the founders of the Sierra Club.

Other naturalists included the brothers Joseph and John Le Conte, who produced geographical writings and Sierra mountain sketches. The Le Contes were joined in the writing of natural history by David Starr Jordan, later president of Stanford University, whose *Alps of the King*

The naturalist, John Muir. Photography by Bradley and Rulofson, San Francisco [no date]. Courtesy of The Bancroft Library, University of California, Berkeley.

and Kern Divide (1907) ranks with Clarence King's *Mountaineering in the Sierra Nevada* (1872). King was a geologist and naturalist who tramped the California backcountry.

By the end of the nineteenth century, several amateur compilers of history were moving that discipline toward professionalization. These included Zoeth Skinner Eldredge and Theodore H. Hittell. Both produced multivolume histories of the state, as did Hubert Howe Bancroft, the best organized and most prolific of California's amateur chroniclers. Bancroft was originally a San Francisco bookseller and publisher who, during 1875–1890, compiled thirty-nine stout volumes that spanned the record of the Pacific Coast from Latin America to Alaska. In doing so he set up a virtual "history factory" production system, with a staff of assistants to interview early residents. At the heart of the Bancroft series were seven heavily footnoted volumes on California. His invaluable manuscript and book collection was ultimately sold to the University of California at Berkeley, where it forms the core of today's Bancroft Library.

After World War I, a band of scholars took on the task of structuring the history of California in a more systematic manner. At the state university in Berkeley, anthropologist Alfred L. Kroeber turned his attention to the Indian past. Historians Herbert E. Bolton, Charles E. Chapman, and Herbert I. Priestley dealt with the Spanish period.

A writer who had focused international attention upon California was the visiting Scotsman Robert Louis Stevenson. In 1880 he published "The Old Pacific Capital" in London's *Fraser's Magazine*. This dealt with Monterey and, along with his *The Silverado Squatters* (1884), recalled his short but idyllic stay in California, where he found his future wife. Some of Stevenson's accounts were printed in newspapers.

These California newspapers of the late nineteenth century were mostly four-page publications, containing five to seven columns of small type. On the front page they ran several columns of advertisements, including patent-medicine claims, notices by quack doctors who promised to alleviate severe bodily aches and pains, and ads for high-buttoned shoes, canvas sails, pink velvet vests, ten-penny nails, and "long-nine" cigars. The rest of the front page was generally devoted to brief news clippings from the outside world. Before the completion of the transcontinental telegraph in 1861, such news was weeks, even months, behind the times.

By 1854, San Franciscans published twenty-two different papers. The best known of these was the *Chronicle*, founded in 1865 by Michael and Charles De Young. The San Diego *Union* and Los Angeles *Times* were the major papers of southern California. General Harrison Gray Otis acquired the *Times* in 1881, becoming embroiled in the Free Harbor struggle, the Owens River water controversy, and severe union confrontations.

At Sacramento, after 1883, Charles McClatchy gave new life to the Sacramento *Bee,* founded in 1857. For several generations it was to remain, along with the Fresno and Modesto *Bees,* both members of the same hive, an authoritative voice in the Sacramento Valley.

At Santa Barbara, Thomas Storke's *News Press* virtually became the official oracle of that community. Significant "newspaper families" gradually assumed control of most California dailies. The De Youngs, the Hearsts, the McClatchys, the Storkes, and the Chandlers all built powerful newspaper chains, some outside the state.

After 1870, musical performances also increased. San Francisco's Tivoli Theater and Opera House offered a year-round schedule of opera performances. In 1890 these included the first performance of Pietro Mascagni's *Cavalleria Rusticana.* At the last musical performance to be held in the Tivoli, on November 23, 1913, another Italian composer, Ruggiero Leoncavallo, personally conducted his new opera, *I Pagliacci.*

Before World War I, performers of international stature were attracted to the state. Among them was Adelina Patti, the most celebrated soprano from the end of the Civil War to the turn of the century. Opera singers Ernestine Schumann-Heink and Lotte Lehman liked California so much that they settled there permanently. Other popular divas, including Nellie Melba, Luisa Tetrazzini, and Amelita Galli-Curci, were feted in California. Tetrazzini became the darling of San Francisco opera fans. On the very night of its earthquake and fire of 1906, the great Italian tenor Enrico Caruso sang in Bizet's *Carmen,* while elsewhere in the city the young Shakespearean actor John Barrymore was giving one of his earliest performances.

Drama, like music, was also warmly supported. Shakespearean plays produced in San Francisco after 1870 included *The Merchant of Venice, Othello,* and *Macbeth.* The most outstanding actor to appear in California during this period was Edwin Booth, whose name was synonymous with that of Hamlet in the minds of theater fans. In 1876 Booth smashed all attendance records; hundreds were turned away each night from the theater in which he played. That season a young San Francisco boy managed to get a walk-on part alongside Booth. His name was David Belasco. With San Francisco as his base he played more than 170 parts in 100 plays before going on to further national prominence.

An entirely different type of performer, Lillian Russell, came to California in 1881. The blond Miss Russell appeared in the revue *Babes in the Woods* attired only in a blouse, purple tights, and high-buttoned shoes. Although female tongues wagged, hundreds of males applauded her per-

Market Street from Third Street, San Francisco, looking east, before the earthquake and fire of 1906. H. G. Hills Collection; courtesy of The Bancroft Library, University of California, Berkeley.

formances. After the turn of the century Maude Adams too packed large audiences into San Francisco's theaters to see her performances of J. M. Barrie's *Peter Pan.*

In 1872, San Francisco's exclusive Bohemian Club began to admit a select number of actors and artists to its *al fresco* outings, events held annually on the club's 2,700 acres amid a redwood forest along the Russian River.

Aside from literary, musical, and dramatic activity, the cultural growth of California during the late nineteenth century can also be measured by educational advances. The first institutions of collegiate rank were founded by church endowment. The Catholics established Santa Clara University in 1851. Later Loyola University, the University of San Francisco, Saint Mary's, and Immaculate Heart College were also begun by Catholic religious orders.

Among other private institutions was the College of the Pacific, today located in Stockton, which was begun at San Jose by the Methodists in 1851 as the University of the Pacific. In 1879 the Methodists also founded the University of Southern California. Mills College, situated in the Oakland suburbs, traces its history to 1852 and is now the oldest women's college in the Far West. In recent years it has become co-educational. At Palo Alto, Stanford University was founded in 1890 by Leland Stanford as a memorial to his only son.

In 1868 the University of California was formally created by the state legislature as a public institution. The year 1887 saw the founding of both Occidental College, by Presbyterians, and Pomona College, by Congregationalists. In 1901 the Quakers established Whittier College, and in 1909 the Baptists founded a college at Redlands. Before mid-century, most of these colleges had given up their sectarian connections.

Californians also proudly measured their achievements through a variety of popular celebrations. The Panama-Pacific Exposition of 1915 was a symbolic highlight of the state's pre–World War I era. Although half the world was plunged into war as its exhibits neared completion, this exposition (and another held the same year at San Diego's Balboa Park) trumpeted California's progress since the turn of the century as well as the new sea connection with America's East Coast via the Panama Canal.

Before the great fire of 1906 absorbed San Francisco's energies in reconstruction, and before prohibition and civic reform chastened that city, it hosted no less distinguished visitors than Presidents Grant, McKinley, and Theodore Roosevelt. Each enjoyed gold-service banquets in its Palace Hotel. In that same hostelry, the flamboyant "Diamond Jim" Brady once downed six dozen oysters before astonished onlookers. After 1900, in a golden age of *gourmandiserie,* it was possible to obtain a good meal, with the best Napa Valley claret, at Papa Coppa's for less than fifty cents. Visitors could find other brands of hospitality at other popular restaurants such as Leveroni's Cellar, the Bella Union Saloon, or the Bank Exchange Saloon, or at Jack's Restaurant, while the Cliff House offered an incomparable view of the Pacific.

The generation that lived in California between the Civil War and World War I possessed an unshakeable faith in progress. Writers, visual artists, and actors all found the Golden State congenial. One result was that California's romantic chroniclers had won out over its peddlers of gloom and discord. As time passed, a cosmopolitan culture had begun to flourish.

Selected Readings

An overview of the period is Kevin Starr's *Americans and the California Dream, 1850–1915* (1973), also Starr, *Inventing the Dream: California Through The Progressive Era* (1985) and David Wyatt, *The Fall Into Eden: Landscape and Imagination in California* (1986). An anthology of California writing is Joseph Henry Jackson's *Continent's End: A Collection of California Writing* (1944); also see Lawrence Clark Powell, *Land of Fiction* (1952) and his *California Classics* (1971); as well as Franklin D. Walker, *A Literary History of Southern California* (1950) and Walker's *San Francisco's Literary Frontier* (1939).

Regarding specific writers, see Jacob Oser, *Henry George* (1974), and Kenneth M. Johnson, "Progress and Poverty—A Paradox," *California Historical Society Quarterly* 42 (March 1963), 27–32; Stephen Fox, *John Muir and His Legacy* (1981); Walter Neale, *Life of Ambrose Bierce* (1929); Paul Fatout, *Ambrose Bierce: The Devil's Lexicographer* (1967); Franklin Walker, *Frank Norris* (1932); Ernest Marchand, *Frank Norris: A Study* (1942); Earle Labor and Jeanne Reesman, *Jack London* (1994); Joan London, *Jack London and His Times* (1939); Richard O'Connor, *Jack London* (1964) and John W. Robinson, "Charles Francis Saunders: A Quaker Botanist in Southern California," *Southern California Quarterly* 60 (Summer 1978), 143–53.

Regarding women leaders see Jacqueline R. Braitman, "A California Stateswoman: The Public Career of Katherine Philips Edson," *California History* 65 (June 1986), 82–96 and Braitman, "Elizabeth Snyder and Role of Women in the Postwar Resurgence of California's Democratic Party," *Pacific Historical Review* 62 (May 1993), 197–220; Elinor Richey, *Eminent Women of the West* (1975); Dorothy Gray, *Women of the West* (1976); Joan Hoff Wilson and Lynn Bonfield Donovan, "Women's History: A Listing of West Coast Archival and Manuscript Sources," *California Historical Quarterly* 55 (Spring 1976), 74–83; Christiane Fischer, "Women in California in the Early 1850s," *Southern California Quarterly* 60 (Fall 1978), 231–54; David J. Langum, "California Women and the Image of Virtue," *Southern California Quarterly* 61 (Fall 1977), 245–50; Thelma Lee Hubbell and Gloria R. Lothrop, "The Friday Morning Club: A Los Angeles Legacy," *Southern California Quarterly* 50 (March 1968), 59–90 and Lothrop, "Three Southern California Heroines," Brand Book XV, *The Westerners Los Angeles Corral* (Los Angeles, 1978) also Lothrop, "Westering Women and the Ladies of Los Angeles," *South Dakota Review* (Summer 1981), 41–67; Helen Holdridge, *Mammy Pleasant* (1959); Valerie Mathes, "Helen Hunt Jackson: Official Agent to the California Mission Indians," *Southern California Quarterly* 63 (Spring 1981), 63–77; Ruth Odell, *Helen Hunt Jackson* (1939); Emily Leider, *California's Daughter: Gertrude Atherton* (1991); Doyce B. Nunis Jr., "Kate Douglas Wiggin: Pioneer in California Kindergarten Education," *California Historical Society Quarterly* 61 (Fall 1962), 291–307.

Other writers are in Thomas M. Pearce, *The Beloved House* (1940); Mary Austin, *Earth Horizon* (1932); Helen M. Doyle, *Mary Austin: Woman of Genius* (1939); Edwin Bingham, *Charles F. Lummis, Editor of the Southwest* (1955); Turbese Lummis Fiske, *Charles F. Lummis: The Man and His West* (1975); Martin S. Peterson, *Joaquin Miller: Literary Frontiersman* (1937); Anne Roller Issler, *Our Mountain Heritage, Silverado and Robert Louis Stevenson* (1950); Katharine D. Osbourne, *Robert Louis Stevenson in California* (1911).

Historiography is in Harry Clark, *A Venture in History: The Production, Publication, and Sale of the Works of Hubert Howe Bancroft* (1973); John W. Caughey, *Hubert Howe Bancroft: Historian of the West* (1946), and Doyce Nunis Jr., *The Historians of Los Angeles* (1988), a brochure.

Newspapers are examined in Edward C. Kemble, *A History of California Newspapers* (1927). John P. Young's *Journalism in California* (1915), and John Bruce's *Gaudy Century: The Story of San Francisco's Hundred Years of Robust Journalism* (1948) and *History of the Los Angeles Star* by William B. Rice (1947); also Marshall Berges, *The Life and Times of Los Angeles, a Newspaper, A Family, and a City* (1984); R. L. Duffus, *The Tower of Jewels: Memories of San Francisco* (1960), and Mrs. Fremont Older, *San Francisco, Magic City* (1961).

Drama forms a part of *Memories and Impressions of Helen Modjeska: An Autobiography* (1910); *Portrait of America: Letters of Henry Sinciewicz*, trans. and ed. by Charles Morley (1959); William Winter, *The Life of David Belasco* (2 vols., 1918); Constance Rourke, *Troupers of the Gold Coast* (1928) and Parker Morell, *Lillian Russell: The Era of Plush* (1940).

Higher education is in William W. Ferrier, *Origin and Development of the University of California* (1930) also his *Ninety Years of Education in California* (1937) and Verne A. Stadtman, *The University of California, 1868–1968* (1970); Albert G. Pickerell and May Dornin, *The University of California, A Pictorial History* (1969); Andrew Rolle, *Occidental College: A Centennial History* (1987); Charles W. Cooper, *Whittier: Independent College in California* (1967); Charles Elliott Jr., *Whittier College: The First Century* (1986); Helen Raitt and Bernice Moulton, *Scripps Institution of Oceanography: First Fifty Years* (1967); Edith R. Mirrielees, *Stanford: The Story of a University* (1959); Charles Burt Sumner, *The Story of Pomona College* (1914); Manuel P. Servin and Iris A. Wilson, *Southern California and its University, A History of U.S.C., 1880–1964* (1969); John R. Thelin, "California and the Colleges," *California Historical Quarterly* 56 (Summer 1977), 140–63 and (Fall 1977), 230–49; *The Memoirs of Ray Lyman Wilbur*, edited by Edgar Eugene Robinson and Paul Carroll Edwards (1960); Benjamin Ide Wheeler, *The Abundant Life* (1926); Lester Stephens, *Joseph Le Conte: Gentle Prophet of Evolution* (1982).

Other useful references include: Judith Raftery, *Land of Fair Promise: Politics and Reform in Los Angeles Schools, 1885–1941* (1992); Richard W. Fox's *So Far Disordered in Mind: Insanity in California, 1870–1930* (1978); Robert Griswold, *Family and Divorce in California, 1850–1890* (1982) and Stephen Vincent, ed., *O California! Nineteenth and Early Twentieth Century California Landscapes* (1989).

Progressive Politics

//////// CHAPTER 27

In California, as throughout the nation, the period between 1900 and the outbreak of World War I stands out as one during which the discontent of farmers was directed at the railroad and meat-packing monopolies as well as banking, finance, and manufacturing trusts. City workers opposed the influence of big business over government and focused their anger upon corrupt machine politics at the municipal level. A group of reform-minded journalists, who came to be known as "muckrakers," joined these agrarians and city workers in exposing shady big-business practices and in championing close control of large trusts, or industrial combinations.

The beginning of the new century had seemed to forecast no sharp political or economic changes. No state or national leader had yet arisen to head the crusade for reform. In the presidential campaign of 1900, California voted for the conservative William McKinley over William Jennings Bryan, as did the nation as a whole. By 1904 the national mood had shifted toward liberalism, however, and the state again followed a prevailing political pattern. For the presidency it supported Theodore Roosevelt, who had become the standard-bearer of reform. But in the ensuing gubernatorial campaign, it elected Republican James N. Gillett, a machine candidate. The popular belief was that political control of the state lay behind the scenes, rather than with either of the major parties. The real power was the Southern Pacific Railroad.

For half a century, indeed, beginning with the construction of the railroad, its political activities were closely involved with the course of California history. At first the purpose of the railroad's founders in entering practical politics was to maintain their monopoly as to rates and services. Railroad lobbyists and emissaries—principally William F. Herrin of San Francisco and Walter Parker of Los Angeles—were adroit dispensers of money on behalf of their cause. At Sacramento, when the legislature was in session, Herrin, as the S.P.'s chief counsel, saw to it each week that a round-trip ticket to San Francisco was left on the desk of every member. Annually also the railroad bribed a sizable number of the forty members of the state senate and even more members of the assembly. The railroad also regularly subsidized newspaper editors with monthly payments, hoping to obtain favorable publicity in a state where a kind word for the railroad had become a rarity.

The Mussel Slough tragedy only added ugliness to the railroad's reputation. The reform-writers, George, Norris, and Royce, had complained in their books that the power of the railroad was free from regulation and control. Even before development of the S.P., the Central Pacific Railroad had been charged as the "third party" in state politics. "Its leaders, its managers, its editors, its orators, its adherents" were everywhere, bearing no allegiance to the people of the state. Especially resented was the notion that the railroad was outside the law. The constitution of 1879 had made provision for a Board of Railroad Commissioners; but this measure had been ineffective in regulating freight and passenger rates. The railroad had gained so powerful a grip on the press that opposition seemed futile. Such independent newspapers as the Sacramento *Union* were subjected to relentless opposition, because of their criticisms of the railroads.

Farmers had long been hostile to the railroad because of its discrimination against small customers and its under-the-table rebates to favored shippers. Ranchers resented the failure of the state to control the railroad's power. And, in general, public antipathy toward the railroads was reaching new heights.

Then, during 1883, an exposé of railroad politics, known as "The Colton letters," became public knowledge. David D. Colton had been a close associate of Huntington, Stanford, and Crocker when they were lobbying for government subsidies to establish the Southern Pacific network eastward from Yuma. After Colton died suddenly, his widow was dissatisfied with the settlement she received from her husband's selfish colleagues. In retaliation, the unhappy Mrs. Colton released to the public several hundred incriminating letters that Huntington had written to her late husband. These letters provided a sordid picture of backroom political manipulations in Sacramento as well as in Washington.

Long lists of potentially corruptible officeholders came out of Colton's correspondence, in which Huntington had indiscreetly discussed the costs of assuring passage of legislation that would be in the railroad's interest. The Colton letters, by providing an inside view of Huntington's power to influence legislation, supported the popular conviction that the railroad had established a government within a government. Furthermore, Huntington was in no mood to apologize. When he appeared before the U.S. Railway Commission, he admitted that he considered it perfectly proper to pay the salaries and expenses of the entire Arizona territorial legislature in order to get favorable legislation passed.

After revelation of the incriminating Colton letters, Huntington came in for further notoriety. Congressional legislation called for the railroads to return money loaned them as thirty-year bonds as scheduled. As public knowledge increased, Huntington used every means to prevent repayment of the outstanding bonds at 6 percent interest. He wanted these replaced by ninety-nine-year obligations at 1.5 percent interest. Each of the "Big Four" had, meanwhile, amassed great fortunes. Huntington personally owned enough railroad trackage to connect the North and the South Poles; he could travel from Newport News, Virginia, to San Francisco without ever riding on anyone else's rails. He also owned timber stands, saw mills (in which he employed his nephew, Henry E. Huntington), steamship lines, and coal mines.

The San Francisco *Examiner,* owned by young William Randolph Hearst, kept up a barrage of criticism against Huntington. In 1896 Hearst sent Ambrose Bierce to Washington to cover Huntington's activities. Bierce wired his paper daily descriptions of Huntington's testimony before congressional committees. Bierce fiercely exposed Huntington's dishonesty, his articles accompanied by cartoons that showed Huntington leading the governor of California around on a leash.

Another controversy that dogged Huntington's career was his involvement in the Los Angeles "Free-Harbor" fight. By 1890 that city, with a population of over 50,000 persons, was on its way toward becoming the largest in California. Only one deficiency threatened to halt this expansion—the lack of a harbor. Ships still docked a short distance away at the open roadstead of San Pedro–Wilmington.

It became clear that only federal funds could build the expensive docks, sea walls, slips, and passages necessary to convert muddy flats into a modern harbor. Two sites—San Pedro and Santa Monica—were available. A bitter fight developed over which of these would become the future expanded harbor. The Huntington interests favored construction at Santa Monica because the Southern Pacific controlled the approaches to that location. Angeleños, however, knew that if Congress should select Santa Monica, it would be a port constructed for the benefit of Huntington and his company.

An aroused Los Angeles public organized a "Free Harbor League" to secure the federal appropriation for San Pedro instead, the term "fee harbor" springing from the feeling that the new port should not be dominated by the railroad. Critics of the Southern Pacific felt that at Santa Monica the hailed S.P. would naturally set whatever freight rates it wanted, as well as govern the loading and unloading of ships' cargoes. Senator Stephen M. White, a persuasive public figure, allied himself with the Free Harbor Leaguers, as did the Los Angeles *Times* and the city's chamber of commerce. Senator White, a persuasive orator, battled for three years, from 1893 to 1896, to prevent Huntington from having federal funds allocated to Santa Monica. The free-harbor fight ended with the designation of San Pedro as the site of Los Angeles's future port.

Shortly after Huntington's death in 1900, his nephew, Henry, sold control of the Southern Pacific to E. H. Harriman. Out of seventy-three local lines Henry Huntington formed a new interurban railway system to serve the Los Angeles area. But he found it difficult to rid himself of the stigma of his uncle's primitive capitalism. Only when the magnificent Henry E. Huntington Library and Art Gallery was founded in San Marino, after the turn of the century, did the memory of the Huntington name begin to mellow in public esteem.

The Southern Pacific remained so strong a power in state politics that even the progressive movement found it hard to challenge. Yet the tide of national reform was swelling as a reform-minded president, Theodore Roosevelt, entered the White House. By 1910 he helped to force the railroads to capitulate to greater government regulation.

Meanwhile, the "muckrakers," began to agitate for even more rigid control of monopolies. Lincoln Steffens, the best known of these determined journalists, had spent his boyhood in Sacramento. His collected articles, which boldly addressed the corrupt alliance of business and politics, were published in his book, *The Shame of the Cities.*

In 1902 San Francisco was especially ripe for Steffen's type of investigations. That year a labor-backed political machine, the Union Labor party, installed a theater musician, Eugene E. Schmitz, as mayor. But Abraham Ruef, a clever attorney with a handlebar mustache, was the real power behind the throne. Ruef blackmailed legitimate businesspeople and extorted them through protection rackets. His political machine further forced business owners to purchase licenses to operate liquor, cigar, and gambling establishments and bilked "French restaurants," establishments known to operate prostitution cribs upstairs.

In 1905 the San Francisco *Bulletin* began publishing articles by Fremont Older, its reformist editor, excoriating the city regime. Older, former mayor James D. Phelan, and sugar magnate Rudolph Spreckels were

Top: Earthquake damage, San Francisco, City Hall from Larkin Street, April 23, 1906.
Bottom: Earthquake damage, San Francisco, Valencia Street, between 17th and 18th streets,
April 23, 1906. Both pictures from the H.G. Hills Collection, photography by T. E. Hecht. Courtesy
of The Bancroft Library, University of California, Berkeley.

about to begin a campaign to overthrow Ruef and Schmitz when disaster struck corrupt San Francisco.

At 5:16 A.M. on April 18, 1906, a massive earthquake shook the ground along the San Andreas Fault from Salinas in the south to Cape Mendocino in northern California. A rumbling noise, which awakened thousands at San Francisco, was followed by a terrifying sound as flimsy buildings were twisted off their foundations. As multistoried brick structures also cascaded into the streets, fissures opened up in the earth. Almost every chimney in the city was so cracked that passersby were in danger. Short-circuited electric wires, which fell into the city's streets, set off fires that swept through block after block of residences.

When volunteer firemen attached their hoses to hydrants, little or no water came out of the mains. Not only were pipes broken, but in some instances the city's fire hydrants, thanks to the irresponsible city government, had never been hooked up to its water system. Firemen, thus, fought frantically without water to stamp out advancing flames.

General Frederick Funston, commandant of the Presidio of San Francisco, charged into the city and foolishly proceeded to dynamite more than a quarter mile of mansions along Van Ness, one of its most beautiful streets. The fire raged for days before it burned itself out. Both Nob Hill and Chinatown were left in ruins; almost the entire northeastern part of the city—four square miles extending from the Southern Pacific Depot to Telegraph Hill—lay in debris.

Despite relief shipments sent from all over the world, 300,000 homeless people were forced to live for weeks in army tents pitched on vacant lots and in Golden Gate Park. Campers, some clad in their best Sunday clothes, sadly munched on rations of shredded-wheat biscuits and drank beef tea. Hundreds of tins of corned beef were distributed by the Red Cross.

Even as the work of rebuilding the devastated city began, the destruction of the Ruef-Schmitz machine became the goal of Older, Phelan, and Spreckels. Joining them was a young attorney, Francis J. Heney, who, as a United States prosecutor, had indicted fraudulent timber operators in Oregon. By November the great "San Francisco graft prosecution" began indictments of Ruef and Schmitz for extortion. Masses of incriminating evidence were piled up, in addition, against executives of the city's public utility corporations. Whereas the bribe takers, Ruef and Schmitz, were condemned for their crookedness, the bribe givers were regarded differently. Newspapers argued that members of the business community had been blackjacked into filtering funds to the politicians who ran the city.

During the graft trials, Older and his fellow reformers not only were subjected to numerous indignities, including social ostracism by their peers, but on several occasions experienced near-violence. Older was kidnapped and taken by train to Santa Barbara. After he was later "found," Older was returned to the trial by police officials. Next, the house of the principal witness, a San Francisco supervisor, was blown up. Documents intended for use in the graft prosecutions were stolen out of private homes and offices. On November 13, 1907, a prospective juror who had been challenged by the prosecution because of a criminal record, arose in the courtroom during Ruef's trial, drew a gun, and shot the chief prosecutor in the head, wounding him almost fatally. He was succeeded by local attorney Hiram Johnson who was then on the brink of a long and famous career.

The San Francisco graft trials lasted more than two years. The evasive Abe Ruef, although the political boss of San Francisco, was not technically an officeholder. Yet, of all the defendants, only he went to the penitentiary, sentenced to fourteen years for bribery. After four years and seven months at San Quentin, he was freed.

The spirit of municipal reform, meanwhile, was resulting in other reform protests at Los Angeles. In that city a "good government" movement took shape under Dr. John R. Haynes, a wealthy physician and critic of the Southern Pacific monopoly. He fathered a Direct Legislation League which denounced municipal and state "boodlers," seeking to replace them in public office with honestly elected citizens. His ideal

The defense in the great San Francisco graft prosecution of 1906–1907. Henry Ach, one of Abraham Ruef's attorneys, in whispered conversation with Ruef. San Francisco police chief Biggy at left. Carl Hoffman Papers; courtesy of The Bancroft Library, University of California, Berkeley.

was to limit the power of corporations, especially the Southern Pacific, as well as that of wheedling legislators. Haynes also established a foundation bearing his name, with the goal of raising the moral standards of public life.

Through the influence of Dr. Haynes and his civic-minded fellow citizens, Los Angeles became one of the first cities in the nation to adopt initiative, referendum, and recall measures. These three items had been at the heart of the progressive reform program. During 1909 the electorate, using the new recall weapon, forced Mayor Arthur C. Harper to resign after he became involved in a sugar company stock speculation. The fact that Harper had received the support of the Southern Pacific political machine in his bid for office did not bolster his popularity.

Reformers also sought the resignation of graft-tainted officials at Sacramento, Oakland, Fresno, and Santa Barbara. On August 1, 1907, a new political alignment within the Republican party, the California Progressives, formed the Lincoln-Roosevelt League. The founders of the league were liberal Republicans, who fused the names of their greatest party leaders into a symbol for freeing the Republican party from domination by corrupt interests.

In 1910 the Lincoln-Roosevelt League ran Hiram W. Johnson—a stocky little man in a tight vest with the gleam of reform in his eye—as its candidate for governor. Johnson had achieved fame in the last days of the San Francisco graft prosecutions. Now forty-four, this stubborn and steel-nerved politician undertook a 20,000-mile automobile campaign over rocky, unpaved roads. He won the governorship against four candidates and led progressive Republican legislators to Sacramento.

The Lincoln-Roosevelt League succeeded in an objective that neither the Republicans nor the Democrats had been able to accomplish in a generation—the overthrow of one of the nation's most entrenched political systems. The legislature of 1911 racked up a record that was the envy of progressives in every state of the Union. A direct primary law assured the nomination of candidates by the voters themselves: previously the Republican and Democratic parties had nominated senatorial candidates within politically safe conventions. The state legislature also adopted initiative, referendum, and recall measures. These bills were designed to cut down on the prerogatives of big-city political machines and their bosses.

The 1911 legislature also added a total of twenty-three amendments to the constitution that concerned control of public utilities, workmen's compensation, regulation of weights and measures, conservation of natural resources, income-tax provisions, and women's suffrage. Other pro-

Hiram Johnson, (Republican) governor, 1910–1917; United States senator, 1917–1945. Courtesy of California State Library.

gressive measures included a "blue-sky" law for protection of the securities investor, a civil-service law, laws providing for mothers' pensions, and establishment of a minimum wage for women and minors.

Despite the major innovations of the California progressives, a black spot on the record of these reformers was their insistence upon Asiatic exclusion. One writer has called Johnson and his retinue racists whose liberalism did not extend to minority groups. But this is present-mindedness. One should remember that both liberals and conservatives would be labeled racists by today's standards. Before World War I, large segments of society were opposed to unrestricted immigration.

The major achievement of the California progressives was the defeat of the entrenched Southern Pacific political machine. As governor, Hiram Johnson worked with the legislature to make sure that the railroads would henceforth become the servants and not the masters of the people. Passage of a cross-filing law in 1913 ensured that progressive candidates could henceforth become the nominees of more than one party. This allowed progressives to retain Republican registration and to control that party's future.

By 1912 the progressives had become involved in founding a third national political party under Theodore Roosevelt. He was nominated for the presidency on its "Bull Moose" ticket, with Governor Hiram Johnson as his running mate. The pair carried the state that year, but lost the national election. After Johnson's defeat, the California progressives lost much of their drive. In 1914 he was, nevertheless, returned to the governorship under the Progressive party banner.

Governor Johnson would, however, play a key role in the presidential campaign of 1916. That year Charles Evans Hughes ran on the Republican ticket against President Woodrow Wilson. Though a Democrat, Wilson's reelection by only 3,700 votes was partly due to Johnson's antipathy to Hughes. In August 1916 Hughes visited California but kept in poor contact with Governor Johnson. At one point both men stayed in the same hotel without even meeting. Hughes scarcely realized the extent of Johnson's power in his home state. And Johnson clearly felt snubbed by Hughes.

Johnson, therefore, failed to campaign for his fellow Republican. Had he done so, he might have swung the state toward Hughes. Instead, California's electoral votes went to Wilson, leaving Hughes only twelve votes short of the presidency. Some asserted that it was the California vote that lost Hughes the election, but other important "swing" states such as Ohio also voted for Wilson. Johnson's own race for the Senate in 1916 resulted in his victory by almost 300,000 votes. He stayed in the Senate until his death in 1945.

Our generation, having largely forgotten the pioneering efforts of the progressives to rein in corporations, is less grateful for the progressive legacy. But the progressives not only had cleaned up state and local government, they had improved its efficiency. Their goal, "to kick the Southern Pacific out of state politics forever," was attained. Had the Republican party in 1912 not split into conservative and reform wings, the Progressive campaigns might have gone even further.

Selected Readings

Labor and railroads are in J. L. Brown, *The Mussel Slough Tragedy* (1958); Irving McKee, "Notable Memorials to Mussel Slough," *Pacific Historical Review* 17 (February 1948), 19–27; David Lavender, *The Great Persuader* (1970); Ralph N. Traxler, "Collis P. Huntington and the Texas and Pacific Railroad Land Grants," *New Mexico Historical Review* 34 (April 1959), 117–33; James Thorpe, *Henry Edwards Huntington* (1994) and William Friedricks, *Henry E. Huntington and the Creation of Southern California* (1992).

Railroad involvement in the free-harbor controversy is in Charles D. Willard, *The Free Harbor Contest at Los Angeles* (1899); Edith Dobie, *The Political Career of Stephen Mallory White* (1927); William Deverell, "The Los Angeles Free Harbor Fight," *California History* 70 (Spring 1991), 13–

29; Charles Queenan and Stephen Sato, *Long Beach and Los Angeles: A Tale of Two Ports* (1986) and Franklyn Hoyt, "The Los Angeles Terminal Railroad," *Historical Society of Southern California Quarterly* (September 1954), 185–91.

Other pertinent references include Norman E. Tutorow, *Leland Stanford, Man of Many Careers* (1971); Ward McAfee, *California's Railroad Era, 1850–1911* (1973); Morley Segal, "James Rolph and . . . the San Francisco Municipal Railway," *California Historical Society Quarterly* 43 (March 1964), 3–18; Judd Kahn, *Imperial San Francisco: Politics and Planning, 1897–1906* (1980) and Philip Ethington, *The Public City . . . San Francisco, 1850–1900* (1994).

One of the great books of its time is J. Lincoln Steffens, *The Autobiography of Lincoln Steffens*, 2 vols. (1931); see also George E. Mowry, *The California Progressives* (1951); William Deverell and Tom Sitton, eds., *Progressivism Revisited* (1994) and Sitton, *John Randolph Haynes, California Progressive* (1992) as well as Sitton, "Promoting the Well-Being of Mankind: The John Randolph and Dora Haynes Foundation," *Southern California Quarterly* 67 (Spring 1988), 95–106.

On the Progressives see Richard Lower, *A Bloc of One: The Political Career of Hiram Johnson* (1993); Spencer C. Olin, *California's Prodigal Sons: Hiram Johnson and the Progressives, 1911–1917* (1968); Walton Bean, *Boss Ruef's San Francisco* (1952); Fremont Older, *My Own Story* (1919); Evelyn Wells, *Fremont Older* (1916); Bruce Bliven, "The Boodling Boss and the Musical Mayor," *American Heritage* 11 (December 1959), 8–11, 100–104 and James P. Walsh, "Abe Ruef Was No Boss," *California Historical Quarterly* 51 (Spring 1972), 3–16.

Regarding the San Francisco earthquake and fire of 1906 see William Bronson, *The Earth Shook, The Sky Burned* (1959); Monica Sutherland, *The Damndest Finest Ruins* (1959); John C. Kennedy, *The Great Earthquake and Fire, San Francisco 1906* (1963) and Gordon Thomas and M. M. Witts, *The San Francisco Earthquake* (1971).

Regarding the Hughes-Johnson misunderstanding see Edward A. Dickson, "How Hughes Lost California in 1916," *Congressional Record* (August 19, 1954); F. M. Davenport, "Did Hughes Snub Johnson?" *American Political Science Review* 40 (April 1949), 321–32 and J. Gregg Layne, "The Lincoln-Roosevelt League," *Historical Society of Southern California Quarterly* 25 (September 1943), 79–101.

Regarding other elections see A. Lincoln, "Theodore Roosevelt, Hiram Johnson, and the Vice Presidential Nomination of 1912," *Pacific Historical Review* 28 (August 1959), 267–83; H. Brett Melendy, "California's Cross-Filing Nightmare: The 1918 Gubernatorial Election," *Pacific Historical Review* 33 (August 1964), 317–30; Franklin Hichborn, "The Party, the Machine, and the Vote: The Story of Cross-filing in California Politics," *California Historical Society Quarterly* 38 (December 1959), 349–57; James C. Findley, "Cross-filing and the Progressive Movement in California Politics," *West-*

ern Political Quarterly 12 (September 1959), 699–711 and Fred Viehe, "The First Recall: Los Angeles Urban Reform or Machine Politics," *Southern California Quarterly* 57 (Spring, 1988), 1–28; Jackson K. Putnam, "The Persistence of Progressivism in the 1920's: The Case of California," *Pacific Historical Review* 35 (November 1966), 395–411; Thomas G. Patterson, "California Progressives and Foreign Policy," *California Historical Society Quarterly* 47 (December 1968), 329–42; Eric Falk Petersen, "The Adoption of the Direct Primary in California," *Southern California Quarterly* 54 (Winter 1972), 363–78 and John L. Shover, "The California Progressives and the 1924 Campaign," *California Historical Quarterly* 51 (Spring 1971), 17–34.

Material
Growth

The San Francisco earthquake and fire, the most cataclysmic event in the history of California, sharply set back the growth of the city's population. On the other hand, the heavy damage produced many years of booming employment in the building trades and supporting businesses. Civic leaders demanded a rebuilding of the city on a grander scale than ever before.

Further south, the citizens of Los Angeles set about to develop their great new port. In 1909, legal consolidation of the coastal towns of San Pedro and Wilmington with Los Angeles was accomplished through an intricate piece of political gerrymandering. A narrow "shoestring" of land, only five hundred feet wide and stretching more than fifteen miles, had been annexed to Los Angeles to provide an extended harbor district that represents a significant engineering achievement for its time. Because the harbor was shielded only haphazardly from the sea by Point Fermin, War Department engineers had to construct an elongated breakwater to protect both shipping and wharves.

The new port facilities, the construction of which was soon followed by the opening of the Panama Canal in 1914, made Los Angeles one of the world's most important port cities. By 1924 Los Angeles had eclipsed San Francisco in total annual tonnage and had become the biggest port on the Pacific Coast. Situated on the great circle route to the Orient, Los Angeles harbor continued to enjoy significant growth in the 1920s.

Meanwhile, the city was becoming a new labyrinth of steel and concrete, expanding rapidly as a population shift occurred from northern California southward. Los Angeles pushed its boundaries over the Hollywood Hills toward the San Fernando Valley. On the west it came to bound Culver City and northward to adjoin Burbank, Glendale, Pasadena, Alhambra, Vernon, Huntington Park, South Pasadena, Torrance, Inglewood, Gardena, Hawthorne, El Segundo, and Long Beach. From the foothills of the Santa Monica Mountains, the city encompassed the Verdugo Hills and eventually included more than 450 square miles of land. Soon "L.A." was referred to by some as "a group of suburbs in search of a city."

Urban transportation was vital to the growth of both San Francisco and Los Angeles. After 1915, as the northern city also increased in size, Francis Marion Smith, "the borax king," developed the Key Route Electric Railway to supplement the city's Peninsular Electric Railway, similar to Henry E. Huntington's network of "big red electric cars" at Los Angeles. Huntington's Pacific Electric rail system operated over eleven hundred miles of track. By the 1920s, however, Los Angeles County contained more than forty incorporated cities, and its transport services already were strained.

At San Diego John and Adolph Spreckels poured millions of dollars into development of the city, including its renowned Hotel del Coronado (1887). After the turn of the century, Katherine Tingley and a group of Theosophists began a utopian colony at nearby Point Loma. As the Horton House of the 1870s gave way to the U.S. Grant Hotel, few even remembered William Heath Davis's pioneering attempts to build San Diego in the 1850s. The city's 1908 welcome of President Theodore Roosevelt's "Great White Fleet" ushered in a new future for San Diego as a major naval center. By 1915 a Hispanic architectural boom accompanied the opening of the city's Panama-California Exposition. Later San Diego's Ryan Aeronautical Corporation built Charles E. Lindbergh's renowned airplane, the *Spirit of Saint Louis*.

Before World War I, California employment had centered around food processing, including packing and canning, as well as lumber, fishing, and mineral and oil production. These activities flourished with renewed vigor while the war encouraged diversification. Demand for San Joaquin Valley cotton grew because of its use in the millions of new uniforms that had to be supplied to soldiers. Taking up the slogan "Food Will Win the War!", the state sent huge quantities of grains, fruits, meats, and vegetables into government federal storehouses. California also contributed more than 150,000 soldiers to the Allied forces, especially to the Ninety-first Division, which saw service in the Battle of the Argonne in France. As it had in the Civil War, California also gave generously to Liberty and Victory Loan drives, in each case exceeding the state quota.

When peace came, the economy of California had been lifted onto a new plateau. By the 1920s, the state ranked second among the states in total mineral production, despite its lack of coal and iron deposits. The

The Hotel del Coronado, built in 1887, is now a historic landmark. Courtesy of the San Diego Convention and Visitors Bureau.

war had stimulated demands for gold and silver, as well as for soda, potash, and quicksilver. Hydraulic mining, which had devastated hundreds of square miles of rich agricultural lands, was replaced by yet another injurious system. This was dredging, which created desolate wastes by sluicing out great piles of sand and rock.

The development of better roads required increasing quantities of asphalt and cement, virtually creating a new industry. Another product, Borax, or sodium borate, had been mined commercially since 1885, when twenty-mule teams began to haul this mineral, used as a cleanser, out of Death Valley. Far more important was a mineral that would change California's economy, petroleum.

From the Mexican period onward, Angeleños had used asphalt, a sticky form of petroleum, for roofing. The first usable oil was found at Pico Canyon near San Fernando, but the earliest verifiable oil well in California was drilled in 1861 in Humboldt County. Wildcatters also dug shallow wells all over the Santa Susana Mountains near Ventura, as well as at Santa Barbara and further north in the Humboldt Bay region.

Meanwhile, the first actual oil production west of Pennsylvania occurred in California's Ventura County, and without the actual drilling of wells. This operation originally had begun in 1859, after a whale-oil merchant investigated some oil seepages near Los Angeles. On property belonging to Major Henry Hancock, he erected a small pot-still with which he produced semiliquid asphaltum. When Hancock drove him off the ranch, the entrepreneur set up a second still along the Ventura River.

By 1864 a touring professor of chemistry from Yale College, Benjamin Silliman, Jr., after examining the oil seepages in Ventura County, wrote glowing reports on their commercial possibilities. One result of his account was the formation of two companies to exploit California oil resources. Both firms were controlled by the Pennsylvania Railroad. A combine, the Philadelphia & California Petroleum Company, drilled a well near the Camulos Ranch and seven other wells in the Ojai region between 1865 and 1867. One of the latter was California's first gusher.

Not until after the turn of the century were techniques developed for making a satisfactory illuminant from California crude oil, which is heavy and asphalt-based. In the mid-1860s, crude oil was sold as fuel, without refining, as it came from the wellheads. After this initial frenzy of the 1860s died away, the oil industry entered a dormant period that was not to be interrupted until the mid-1870s, when the California Star Oil Company began drilling in southern California's Newhall Basin.

Scores of other small firms followed the lead of the California Star Oil Company. In no industry was competition fiercer than in oil refining. Because so many new wells were dug and refineries set up, the oil market became glutted, and prices fell. The frenzied rush to new sites was reminiscent of the gold mania of 1848–1849. Few operators survived this experimental and exciting period of speculative enterprise. Despite the production of kerosene for illumination, tar for roofing, and oil for lubrication, the petroleum industry in those years before the invention of the internal-combustion engine still suffered from limited markets and primitive operational techniques. In 1879 California Star became the Pacific Coast Oil Company, corporate ancestor of the Standard Oil Company of California. Pacific was then the dominant oil company of the state. By 1884 many companies had failed or been absorbed by larger operations.

Two oil pioneers were to profit greatly from the state's vast underground reserves. These were Lyman Stewart and Edward L. Doheny. In 1883 Stewart, who had made his fortune in an oil rush at Titusville, Pennsylvania, headed west to begin a new career. By 1890 he formed the Union Oil Company. Two years later that company sank a well in Adams Canyon, Ventura County which overflowed into the Santa Clara River until it could be capped. This gusher produced 1,500 barrels of oil per day.

"Spudding in" ceremonies in Compton, September 21, 1926. Courtesy of the Historical Collections, Security Pacific National Bank.

The career of Doheny is one of the most colorful in the history of American capitalism. Born in Wisconsin in 1856, he started work as a government surveyor. In 1876, as a youth of twenty, he drifted into the Black Hills just as Dakota Territory was experiencing a silver and gold rush. Doheny next headed for Arizona and then Kingston, New Mexico, where another rush was under way. He worked as a mucker and hard-rock miner along the Mexican border, then as a miner in the Mojave Desert of California. With this experience and some money behind him, in 1892 Doheny came to Los Angeles where he noticed that brea, a tar-pitch, clung to the wheels of carriages and carts. After tracing the source of the substance to a seepage near Westlake Park, Doheny leased a city lot and began to dig, striking a pocket of gas. At 600 feet, Doheny's workers next brought in a well with a capacity of forty-five barrels a day. This started an oil boom. In the next five years 2,300 wells were dug in the Los Angeles basin.

A strange new skyline sprang up in that former pueblo. Wooden derricks were erected in both front and back yards, and greasy little refineries were noisily hammered together. Some Angeleños became wealthy, but others got little for their trouble other than expensive drilling bills, uprooted gardens, and clouds of dry dust that coated their houses. A rich oil field surrounded La Brea pits where, in 1875, amateur paleontologists found the first remains of prehistoric animals—the skeleton of a saber-tooth cat that had been trapped in the tar seeps. By 1897, oil production in the Los Angeles area, including nearby Puente and Fullerton, had risen to 1,400,000 barrels per year. Five years later the figure reached 9,000,000 barrels.

But Doheny and his competitors were having trouble marketing surplus oil. They sold some of it for spraying dusty streets and also persuaded manufacturers of pipe to use an oil coating to prevent rust. Eventually, however, a new market for oil was created after railroad managers realized that they could save a substantial amount in fuel costs by adapting locomotives from the burning of coal to oil. By 1901, the Southern Pacific Railroad bought five hundred tank cars and built fifty storage tanks after converting its engines to use oil.

Encouraged by this new market, the oil industry stepped up its efforts to discover new reserves, an enterprise further spurred as use of the automobile skyrocketed. During the 1920s further oil deposits were found in the San Joaquin Valley and in the Midway-Sunset, Lost Hills-Belridge, Elk Hills, Wheeler Ridge, and Kettleman Hills areas. New wells were also brought in at Whittier, Fullerton, Puente, Coyote Hills, Montebello, Richfield, Compton, Torrance, and Inglewood. Along the coast, wells were drilled at Watsonville, and Santa Maria as well as at Coalinga in Fresno County, at Bakersfield, and near the Kern River.

But the greatest oil strikes were made in 1920 at Huntington Beach and the next year at Santa Fe Springs and Signal Hill. These three fields contained such vast pools of oil that their discovery upset national prices and glutted storage facilities. By 1922, the Signal Hill fields alone reached a production of 244,000 barrels daily from 265 wells. Two years later California ranked first among the states in the production of petroleum.

By the 1920s, moving beyond such by-products as kerosene and axle grease, Lyman Stewart also encouraged development of an oil burner for marine engines. His Union Oil Company commissioned tanker vessels to transport oil to overseas markets, making California's oil industry a global one. The ever ambitious Doheny, who in that decade branched out to Peru and Mexico, would, however, soon attract national notoriety.

His eagerness to obtain certain Elk Hills reserves produced charges of corruption that led all the way into the cabinet of President Warren G. Harding when Doheny's secret operations were revealed. In November of 1921 he had sent a satchel containing $100,000 to Secretary of the Interior Albert B. Fall, "an old prospector friend" who happened to control the Elk Hills reserves as well as those at Teapot Dome, Wyoming. In 1923, both Fall and Doheny were indicted for conspiracy to corner federal oil resources. Fall went to prison, but Doheny managed to escape punishment.

The pioneering oil speculators of Doheny's generation lived in an age when great opportunities for corruption existed. In 1921 Courtney Julian, an oil supersalesman, advertised for funds in Los Angeles newspapers and raised $175,000 in one fortnight. He organized the Julian Petroleum Company, known as "Julian Pete," on the basis of a few wells leased on the edge of Signal Hill. After satisfying a few of the original stockholders, Julian was able to talk new investors into buying bogus stock in his dummy corporation, a scam through which Julian made several million dollars. In 1925, after a public audit of his operations was demanded by outraged holders of worthless stock, he fled the state, eventually sail-

Oil field in the Central Valley. Courtesy of the Chevron Corporation.

ing for Shanghai—one step ahead of the law—where he committed suicide in 1934.

Other oil producers who continued to curtail production were accused of price fixing. In later years, dwindling reserves encouraged better regulation. Yet the oil industry was able to maintain unique tax deductions based on high exploration costs and depletion allowances. The average life of the best-producing wells was only twenty-five to thirty years; as oil wells reached maturity, others had to be drilled deeper than 1,000 feet. In the 1930s, in the quest for new reserves, drillers tapped offshore pools from rigs anchored onto the ocean floor. The development of the port of Long Beach, which was begun in 1938 and financed in large measure by proceeds from drilling a rich field along its waterfront, created a new legal question: Did the state or the federal government own tideland oil resources? Final determination would have to await future legal decisions. Then, due to overdrilling, sea water began to leak under that city.

From 1900 to 1930, California's oil industry had been dramatically spurred by the discovery of large new pools and by the development of better refining techniques. These included the catalytic cracking process which accompanied new fuel demands for factories, automobiles, trucks, and airplanes.

There were not many cars on western highways in the first years of the twentieth century. By 1919 there were fewer than 7 million passenger cars registered in the entire United States. Then, in the 1920s, the auto underwent a transformation from a sputtering plaything of the rich, which frightened ladies and horses, to a necessity of the working masses. Quantity production of the inexpensive Model T Ford, the price of which dropped to $280, increased the number of cars nationally to over 23 million by 1929. Just under 2 million of these were the property of Californians. Numerically, this far exceeded that of other western states (Nevada, 31,915; Arizona, 109,013; Utah, 112,661; Oregon, 269,007). On a per capita basis, California's automobile registration was the largest in the United States. Meanwhile, as tractors replaced horses on farms, and buses took the place of trolleys in the larger cities, mechanized transportation of all forms became common.

The rise of the automobile also stimulated roadside enterprise. Service stations sprang up everywhere, providing—in addition to gasoline and minor adjustments—free air, road maps, and restrooms for the convenience of dusty motorists. Repair shops and garages fixed stubborn self-starters, inert spark plugs, and faulty brakes, relieving drivers of such anxieties as the need to know such terms as "magneto," "differential," and "generator." Supply houses too installed seat covers, batteries, and side curtains. The growth of tourism led to the development of locally owned motels until national hotel chains arrived in California. The manufacturers of windshields, rubber tires, tubes, and automobiles themselves remained centered in the large cities of the East. Only as demands markedly increased did they move facilities to California. Its motorists sometimes felt that the state was functioning as a colonial appendage of large Eastern corporations.

Along with the phonograph, radio, and movies, the auto broke down the isolation of those who lived on farms and ranches. It also emancipated city workers, who came to use "the machine" for pleasure trips on weekends and during holiday periods. Gradually, too, automobiles stimulated the decentralization of cities, making it possible for laborers to live at some distance from their work. In the years from 1910 to 1930, California began to pull itself out of the mud, as rutted country lanes were converted into two-laned ribbons of concrete. These, in turn, gave way after the 1930s to four-lane macadamized highways, which remained in use until the advent of still larger freeways in the 1940s. The $18 million appropriation voted for road construction in 1910 seemed like a pittance a few years later. Highway routes 66, 70, 99, and 101, major arteries, were built in part with federal funds. These highways changed the face of the California countryside, aiding the development of raw settlements in sometimes wild and empty deserts.

The automobile made for a new type of landscape. Railroad towns were displaced by crossroads with garages, filling stations, hot dog stands, and tourist bungalows. Gypsy fortune tellers joined concessionaires desirous of doing business with unwary Easterners who drove past neon-lighted stucco booths shaped like a half orange. From these glared such highway signs as "All the Orange Juice You Can Drink for 10 Cents" and "Palmistry Will Tell Your Future in California."

Favorable climatic conditions, low gasoline prices, and ready access to desert, beach, and mountain helped to make Californians automobile-minded. Thousands of tourists were brought to the state each year by advertising that emphasized California's constant sunshine. The most popular resorts were the beaches from Santa Barbara to San Diego, Catalina Island, Lake Tahoe, Sequoia and Lassen National parks, the Yosemite Valley in the High Sierra, the Russian River area above San Francisco, Palm Springs on the desert, and Big Bear and Lake Arrowhead in the San Bernardino Mountains. Death Valley too became a winter tourist attraction.

The control of traffic was a matter of great complexity, especially at Los Angeles and San Francisco, where congestion was heaviest. Meanwhile, public transportation suffered a decline. At Los Angeles the interurban system established by the Pacific Electric Company eventually

Top: Broadway, looking south from Second Street, Los Angeles, June 8, 1889, at the opening of the cable car route. C. C. Pierce Collection; courtesy of The Huntington Library, San Marino, California. Bottom: Pasadena Freeway, one of the first in the nation, mid-1950s; courtesy of the Historical Collections, Security Pacific National Bank.

perished in the interwar years. Railroads were forced to close down branch lines as buses and trucks took advantage of shorter routes between cities. Though accidents and highway fatalities continued to mount, so did the demand for new cars. Whole boulevards, notably Figueroa and Alvarado streets in Los Angeles, and Van Ness Avenue in San Francisco, came to be monopolized by auto dealers.

In the 1920s and 1930s, despite a national economic depression, California's domestic and foreign trade expanded. Increases in tourism and the growth of the mining, hydroelectric power, and film industries all helped to gain prominence for the state. The automobile and its subsidiary industries were largely responsible for all this expansion. The assembly plants of Ford, Chrysler, and General Motors, the tire-production establishments of Firestone and Royal, and such firms as Libby-Owens-Ford Glass and Exide Batteries gave employment to thousands of Californians. Throughout the depression years, 1930 through 1937, automobile production remained surprisingly stable.

Accompanying a shift of population to such suburbs as Oakland and Long Beach, there arose a need to finance new residential and manufacturing construction. Banks were now consolidated into stronger institutions capable of loaning millions of dollars annually. In 1929, a merger created the Security First National Bank of Los Angeles. This gave southern California one of the country's largest banks. The largest of all was the Bank of Italy, later the Bank of America. Founded in 1904 at San Francisco by Amadeo Pietro Giannini, son of an Italian immigrant, it developed a system of branch banking that came to dwarf other banks. Geared to the needs of the small depositor, Giannini's system spread beyond the boundaries of the state, and even of the nation. For a time the Bank of America became the largest bank in the world, having begun in San Francisco, where its headquarters still remain.

The growth of California during the interwar period is mirrored in the record established by its largest city. In 1921 Harry Chandler, who had become the publisher of the Los Angeles *Times*, called a crucial conference to examine ways by which the tourist trade might be increased. The businessmen and real estate boosters who attended that meeting helped him form the "All-Year Club of Southern California," designed to advertise the wonders of Los Angeles in Eastern newspapers. In the heady spirit of the 1920s, this organization did much to attract new residents as well as visitors.

By 1930, 2,300,000 people lived within a thirty-mile radius of the city. Yet, only in the early thirties did "L.A." develop a genuine civic center, with its new Spanish-style Union passenger railroad terminal and nearby complex of government buildings. Between 1930 and 1940

Opening ceremonies, 1932 Olympics. Courtesy of Citizens Savings Athletic Foundation.

the city also celebrated its 150th anniversary. In those years it hosted the Tenth Olympiad in a new coliseum, saw the arrival of the first streamlined transcontinental trains, built an observatory at Griffith Park, constructed a new metropolitan water system, and laid the groundwork for its future wartime aircraft industry.

San Francisco too improved its metropolitan facilities, strengthening its opera, symphony orchestra, and museums, improving Golden Gate Park, and building the remarkable Bay bridges to supplant ferry boats previously in operation. On May 27, 1939, the day the Golden Gate Bridge opened, 200,000 people proudly walked across the span. That same year San Francisco was host to the Golden Gate International Exposition, the "World's Fair of the West." Exactly 17,041,999 persons paid the entrance fee for this largest exposition ever held west of Chicago. The island in the middle of San Francisco Bay, site of the fairgrounds became a naval base during World War II.

San Francisco remained a tourist mecca, with its exotic Chinatown, cable cars, restaurants, Coit Tower, and Golden Gate, through which ships stream in a constant procession. During the 1930s the city's shipyards, drydocks, and canneries continued expansion; but this was also a period of experimentation. Captain Robert Dollar made San Francisco

200,000 people walk north across the Golden Gate Bridge at its opening on May 27, 1939.
Courtesy of the San Francisco Chronicle.

the home port of steamship companies, while the city was becoming an air center. On November 22, 1935, Pan American Airways' "China Clipper" soared off to establish the first air link between North America and the mainland of China.

The spectacular growth of California's population during the twenties and thirties was part of a larger pattern. This increase had gone on unabated since the gold rush. By 1940, on the eve of World War II, the state's population numbered 6,907,387. Los Angeles was then a metropolis of 1,504,277 persons, and San Francisco one of 634,536. Outside San Francisco, commuters found new "bedrooms" in the suburbs of Alameda, Oakland, Berkeley, and Burlingame. With the promise of further expansion ahead, the contrast between the nineteenth and twentieth centuries was to become even more marked. Like other urban centers, California would become overdeveloped as to population but underdeveloped in the means for dealing with its future pressing problems. These would become increasingly complex.

Selected Readings

Regarding society and urbanization see Michael E. Engh, *Frontier Faiths: Church, Temple, and Synagogue in Los Angeles, 1846–1888* (1992); Oscar Osborn Winther, "The Rise of Metropolitan Los Angeles, 1870–1900," *Huntington Library Quarterly* 10 (August 1947), 391–405; Spencer Crump, *Ride the Big Red Cars: How Trolleys Helped Build Southern California* (1962); Andrew Rolle, *Los Angeles: From Pueblo to City of the Future* (1995); Charles A. Matson, *Building a World Gateway* (1945); William Issel and Robert Cherny, *San Francisco, 1865–1932: Politics, Power, and Urban Development* (1986) and Issel, "Citizens Outside the Government, Business and Urban Policy in San Francisco and Los Angeles, 1890–1932," *Pacific Historical Review* 57 (May 1988), 117–45, as well as Roger Lotchin, *Fortress California: From Warfare to Welfare* (1992) and his "The City and the Sword in Metropolitan California, 1919–1941," *Urbanism Past and Present* 7 (Summer 1982), 1–16, and Michael Kazin, *Barons of Labor: The San Francisco Building Trade and Urban Power in the Progressive Era* (1987).

Regarding commercial developments see Marquis James, *The Biography of a Bank: The Story of Bank of America* (1954); Frank F. Latta, *Black Gold in the San Joaquin* (1949); Frank J. Taylor and Earl M. Welty, *Black Bonanza* (1950); R. G. Percy, "The First Oil Development in California," *California Historian* 6 (December 1959), 29–30; I. F. Marcosson, *The Black Golconda* (1924); Ruth S. Knowles, *The Greatest Gamblers* (1959); Gerald T. White, *Formative Years in the Far West, A History of Standard Oil Company of California and Predecessors Through 1919* (1962); W. H. Hutchinson, *Oil, Land, and Politics: The California Career of Thomas Robert Bard* (1965) and Walker A. Tompkins, *Little Giant of Signal Hill* (1967).

Regarding "the automobile era" see Scott Bottles, *Los Angeles and the Automobile* (1987); Jules Tygiel, *The Great Los Angeles Swindle: Oil, Stocks, and Scandal During the Roaring Twenties* (1994); Phil T. Hanna, "The Wheel and the Bell," *Westways* 42 (December 1960), 41–56; Mark S. Foster, "The Model-T, the Hard Sell, and Los Angeles's Urban Growth . . . ," *Pacific Historical Review* 44 (November 1975), 459–84; Fred Viehe, "Black Gold Suburbs: The Influence of the Extractive Industry on the Suburbanization of Los Angeles, 1890–1930," *Journal of Urban History* 8 (1981), 3–26; Bruce Henstell, *Sunshine and Wealth: Los Angeles in the Twenties* (1985); David Gebhard and Hariette Von Breton, *Los Angeles in the Thirties* (1975); Willis Miller, "The Port of Los Angeles–Long Beach, 1929–1979 . . . ," *Southern California Quarterly* 65 (Winter 1983), 341–78 and Judith Elias, *Los Angeles: Dream to Reality, 1885–1915* (1983).

Water, Conservation, and Agriculture

//////// **CHAPTER 29**

The new migration into the state spurred on by the automobile could not have been supported without water. From 1900 onward, its cities and counties alike spent millions of dollars on new dams, reservoirs, and aqueducts to conserve that precious commodity.

In semi-arid southern California, farmers welcomed the unique irrigation experiments of a Canadian, George Chaffey, who successfully diverted streams, created artificial lakes, and stored subsurface water efficiently. Thirsty Los Angeles, located amid a dry belt of expanding suburbs, was dependent upon the meager Los Angeles River (an uncertain underground stream) and a shrinking water table. By 1904 its reservoirs were barely able to take in enough water to equal their outflow. At this point City Chief Engineer William Mulholland argued that the city could no longer rely upon the Los Angeles River as its main water source. He recommended that an attempt be made to tap the distant Owens River in the southern Sierra mountain range.

A bond issue was subsequently put on the ballot to provide construction of a $25 million aqueduct that would traverse the 238 miles from the Owens Valley to Los Angeles. Construction of a pipe and flume system across the Mojave Desert, to catch the melted snow of the southern Sierra range, began in 1908. Utilizing several thousand workers, Mulholland completed his complex network of tunnels and trenches in less than five years. Though it was a highly acclaimed feat of engineering, controversy soon developed over the project. Violent criticisms of Mulholland and the Los Angeles elite came from ranchers and farmers forced to evacuate their Owens Valley homes under threat of eviction.

People who loved to fish in the valley, as well as other outdoor recreationists and naturalists, joined in the protest.

Critics also charged that Los Angeles bankers and real estate operators who owned tracts in the Van Nuys area would be the real beneficiaries of water development. It was further alleged that their syndicate had bought up fallow land throughout the San Fernando Valley in order to make a financial killing after the successful importation of Owens River water. These charges were disputed because of involvement, and perhaps connivance, by the U.S. Reclamation Service, in whose judgment the Owens Valley Project was a pressing necessity.

Residents of the four Owens River towns of Big Pine, Lone Pine, Bishop, and Independence, however, believed that only a distant syndicate could draw upon huge reservoirs outside Los Angeles to store water looted from the Owens Valley. Pathetic stories in the national press dwelt upon the privations inflicted upon a pastoral paradise by the beastly aqueduct. Owens Valley residents appealed to the Chief Forester of the United States, Gifford Pinchot, and to President Theodore Roosevelt. But both men sided with Los Angeles, and in 1913 the city's new aqueduct was completed.

Years later, in 1923, disgruntled ranchers, armed with rifles, stood guard at the headgate of Big Pine Ditch to prevent further diversion of water from the Owens River into the aqueduct. Then a spillway near Lone Pine was dislodged by dynamite and large pieces of the aqueduct were torn away. Once more, in 1924, protestors opened up the Alabama Wastegates, north of Lone Pine, turning the flow of the aqueduct back into the Owens River. After these shows of force, and revelations of corruption by valley bankers and businesspeople, local opposition collapsed. But the slogan "Remember the Owens Valley" reminded Californians for years to come of the seizure of land for water by an avaricious Los Angeles. And the reputation of Los Angeles, whether deserved or not, as a looter of water has persisted to the present day. Some critics remain convinced that private L.A. interests benefitted most from the Owens Valley Project.

In 1928 more criticisms of William Mulholland arose when a dam he had constructed in San Francisquito Canyon, part of the Owens Aqueduct, collapsed. Close to midnight on March 12 of that year, an avalanche of water cascaded down the narrow Santa Clara Valley to Santa Paula, fifty miles away. Houses, trees, telephone poles, bridges, and railroad tracks were swept away, with 385 people losing their lives. Mulholland stoically accepted the blame for having built his dam on a weak clay substratum, and thus ended his career of public service.

The Owens Valley Project's many defenders emphasized its contributions to Los Angeles and to the valley itself. Supporters pointed to new roads in the Owens Valley, constructed and improved in connection with building the aqueduct. Valley residents who once sold alfalfa were able to start roadside businesses to serve a growing tourist trade. Furthermore, the city of Los Angeles reimbursed those whose homes and farms had been confiscated, in addition to paying for the lands of owners willing to sell out. The aqueduct was recognized as a major achievement that would provide hydro-electric power as well as water to much of southern California. It also assured the region's continued rapid growth.

San Francisco too had to cope with a water shortage in the early years of the twentieth century. Although located in an area of heavier rainfall, the city's demands for water soon exceeded the supply. Civic leaders had long been eyeing the Hetch Hetchy Valley near Yosemite National Park as a new water source for San Francisco. Naturalists, however, objected strongly to San Francisco's plan to build a dam that would inundate a scenic valley and, also, to divert water from the Tuolumne River. Despite their protests, which retarded construction of the proposed dam for years, federal authorization for the project came in 1913. That year, Franklin K. Lane, former city and county attorney of San Francisco, became Secretary of the Interior. Despite heavy opposition by the Sierra Club, San Francisco finally completed its Hetch Hetchy aqueduct and power network in 1931. Although the project cost the then-phenomenal sum of $100 million, it still did not fully meet the city's growing water shortages.

By 1923, while controversy over the Owens Valley Project remained a public issue, Los Angeles again faced water shortages. The city was adding 100,000 new residents per year. And its population was approaching 2 million persons. To solve the disparity between daily intake and outflow of city reservoirs, its engineers went so far as to consult with occult rain makers, Indian medicine men, and water dowsers before concluding that new dams were the only solution to the water shortage.

Meanwhile, representatives of Colorado, Wyoming, Utah, New Mexico, Arizona, Nevada, and California signed a Colorado River Water Compact. This document provided for cooperative development of that river's resources. The project was to be undertaken jointly by the federal government, the participating states, and certain municipalities. Its aims were to protect the Imperial Valley against recurrent threats of flooding, to provide multistate water reserves, and to generate hydroelectric energy for an expanding Southwest.

Not, however, until 1928 was the Swing-Johnson Bill passed by the U.S. Congress to permit construction of a dam in Boulder Canyon that was basic to the proposal. Another federal bill of 1930 allocated almost $11 million to begin construction. Most of the major cities of Los Angeles County then formed a Metropolitan Water District to coordinate water and power distribution for southern California. In 1931 the district floated a bond issue of over $200 million to complete construction. Since the effects of the Great Depression blunted sale of the bonds, the federal government's new Reconstruction Finance Corporation assumed a share of the financing of the Boulder Canyon Project.

With Hoover Dam (in Boulder Canyon) as its dominant structure, this massive project was one of the largest construction jobs in the world. The dam, 1,282 feet high, required the combined efforts of six construction companies employing 10,000 workers, who were housed in a new town, Boulder City, built expressly for the purpose. An artificial lake 242 miles long, Lake Mead, was constructed in connection with the dam, as well as a complicated system of conduits, reservoirs, and pumping plants to transport water from the lake.

Hoover Dam, with its accompanying storage facility, Parker Dam, was completed on March 1, 1936. Huge generators pumped electrical energy into homes, farms, and industrial plants throughout the Southwest. Piercing its way through six mountain ranges, the aqueduct provided a lifeline to the communities drawing upon it. The Metropolitan Water District erected a costly diversion dam to deflect water westward for 242 miles to Los Angeles. Water was also diverted above Yuma, Arizona, and transported 80 miles along the All-American Canal, to the Imperial Valley. A 125-mile extension of this canal, to serve the Coachella Valley, was completed in 1948.

Without the Boulder Canyon Project, southern California could not have expanded commercially and industrially. Hoover Dam, furthermore, safeguards the Imperial Valley and communities surrounding the Gulf of California from spring floods, storing water to be released during periods of shortage.

Farther north, the 1930s saw California's farmers concerned over water supplies. One of the most obvious sources of water was the 400-mile-long Sacramento River, with its average annual runoff of 22,230,000 acre-feet. (An acre-foot of water is the amount that will cover one acre to a depth of one foot—or 43,560 cubic feet.) The Sacramento's drainage area covers almost 30,000 square miles. Many tributaries help swell that river along its way; among them are the McCloud, Pit, Feather, Yuba, Bear, and American rivers, which flow out of California's Sierra and northern Cascade ranges.

Because of the damage done by hydraulic mining, by 1884, when the practice was banned by the courts, the channel of the Sacramento had become so silted that navigation was closed to all but vessels of the shallowest draft. This situation only worsened matters whenever the Central Valley's rivers went on a flooding rampage, with the cities of Stockton, Visalia, Oroville, Yuba City, and Marysville sustaining millions of dollars in damage. It was difficult to harness the San Joaquin River, a twisting stream that flows into the Sacramento out of California's southern Central Valley.

In 1933 the state legislature voted in the Central Valley Project to impound water from the Sacramento, San Joaquin, and lesser streams. When a construction bond issue of $170 million could not be sold, the state appealed to the federal government for assistance under the National Industrial Recovery Act (NIRA). Congress responded with a Rivers and Harbors Bill of 1935, which authorized starter funds for construction of Shasta Dam as a first step of the Central Valley Project. The Friant and other dams of this project would eventually store almost as much water as all of California's 600 reservoirs. The Friant-Kern Canal and the Delta-Mendota Canal, were to channel water throughout the San Joaquin Valley.

Completion of the Central Valley Project was delayed by controversies that continued to rage as to who should build and control its water and power facilities. The struggle involved the Bureau of Reclamation, the Army Corps of Engineers, the state Department of Public Works, municipal water systems, and private utilities—the power companies then branded most public works programs as heady socialistic experiments. Further opposition to government participation in the project also came from large landowners. They fought a 160-acre limit on ownership for anyone receiving water from Bureau of Reclamation projects. Some large farm operators feared the prospect of not qualifying for federal subsidies.

"No state has gained more than California from the artificial application of water, or has more at stake in the extension of its use," once wrote Elwood Mead, the pioneer conservationist after whom Lake Mead was named. Irrigation is essentially a form of conservation, Mead believed, as did Theodore Roosevelt and other early conservationists. The reclamation of water resources early in the twentieth century came to be accompanied by a belated concern over depletion of the timber and mineral wealth of the Far West.

Although the idea of conservation had grown through the years of the progressive movement, effective regulatory steps had yet to be taken. Within only a few generations whole forests had been denuded by fire and ax. A fortunate exception had occurred in the case of the Muir Woods, one of the world's greatest redwood stands, which was spared through the efforts of the nature-lover William Kent. Located on the

Giant redwood trees overwhelming visitors on one of many inviting pathways. These trees are in Stout Memorial Grove, Del Norte County. Courtesy of Redwood Empire Association.

side of Mount Tamalpais, in Marin County, this timber was about to be logged in 1903, when Kent borrowed money to buy the land and then turned it over to the government as a national preserve.

In general, however, lumber companies had been permitted to exploit forest resources, with no provision for replacement or selective cutting. By the early twentieth century, the close connection between overcutting and periodic floods had become clear. By then, some of the choicest lands in the state already had been ruined by man-made erosion. Populations of native animals, like the bighorn mountain sheep, had been reduced to a few scraggly specimens in zoos. John Muir and John Burroughs fortunately demanded the creation of parks to protect the magnificent sequoias and coast redwoods, as well as the wildlife of the countryside.

Only after California had created state conservation and water commissions did these agencies begin to enforce advances in scientific forestry. Lumber companies, which had resisted management of forest preserves, came to see the merits of reforestation, if only out of the need to protect their own future. The California Forest Protective Association planted millions of replacement redwoods, as well as Douglas firs, spruce, and cedars, on logged or cutover lands. During the Depression years of the 1930s, the Civilian Conservation Corps (CCC) also carried on extensive replanting along wilderness trails. The National Park Service and the California State Division of Beaches and Parks likewise preserved wilderness sites, as did privately funded agencies like the Sierra Club.

Agriculture, meanwhile, reaped inestimable benefits from California's new water and power supplies. Reclamation too helped agricultural yield

Rio Nido Beach in the Russian River district in Sonoma County. Courtesy of Redwood Empire Association.

spiral upward at a time when the acreage of the average farm decreased nationally. By 1920, there were 117,670 farms in the state. Huge corporations would gobble up many of these in forthcoming years.

A major problem of the interwar period was not agricultural production but, rather, finding the means to increase consumption of the many crops that California grew. Some of these were plowed under during the Depression of the 1930s, at the very time when refugees from the Dust Bowl regions of the Midwest were going hungry. The Golden State alone still produces 97 percent of the grapes grown in the nation. Vineyardists, orange-grove owners, and ranchers redoubled their search for markets to absorb the greater yields that resulted from the application of improved agricultural techniques.

By the 1930s, in order to achieve greater efficiency, large "agribusinesses" began to appear. Fresno and Bakersfield, in the San Joaquin Valley, became new centers for the distribution of petroleum products, fruit and vegetables, cotton, livestock, wine, and raisins and other dried fruit. In addition, these cities supplied nearby mountain recreation sites. Other key valley towns—Stockton, Visalia, Madera, Merced, and Modesto—also grew into important market centers that had benefited from the development of new water sources.

Selected Readings

Regarding conservation see John Muir, *The Mountains of California* (1894) and Muir, *Our National Parks* (1901); Linnie M. Wolfe, ed., *John of the Mountains* (1938); Holway R. Jones, *John Muir and the Sierra Club: The Battle for Yosemite* (1966); Michael S. Smith, *Pacific Visions: California Scientists and the Environment* (1988); Francis P. Farquhar, *History of the Sierra Nevada* (1965) also Farquhar, *Place Names of the High Sierra* (1926); Douglas Strong, *Tahoe: An Environmental History* (1984); W. Storrs Lee, *The Sierra* (1962); Norman Taylor, *The Ageless Relics* (1962), Susan Schrepfer, *The Fight to Save the Redwoods* (1983) and Roderick Nash, *Wilderness and the American Mind* (1967).

Concerning the Owens Valley controversy see Robert A. Sander, *The Lost Frontier: Water Diversion in the Growth and Destruction of Owens Valley Agriculture* (1994); William L. Kahrl, *Water and Power: The Conflict Over Los Angeles' Water Supply in the Owens Valley* (1982); Abraham Hoffman, *Vision or Villainy: Origins of the Owens Valley-Los Angeles Water Controversy* (1981) and Hoffman, "Origins of a Controversy: The U.S. Reclamation Service and the Owens Valley . . . ," *Arizona and the West* 19 (Winter 1977), 333–45.

On water and reclamation see John Walton, *Western Times and Water Wars . . . in California* (1992); Catherine Mulholland, *The Owensmouth Baby*

(1987); Robert Matson, *William Mulholland, A Forgotten Forefather* (1978); Charles Outland, *Man-Made Disaster: The Story of the Saint Francis Dam* (1962); Doyce Nunis, ed., *The Saint Francis Dam Disaster Revisited* (1995); Joseph Stevens, *Hoover Dam: An American Adventure* (1988); George A. Pettit, *So Boulder Dam Was Built* (1935); David O. Woodbury, *The Colorado Conquest* (1941); P. L. Kleinsorge, *Boulder Canyon Project* (1941); Norris Hundley, *Water and the West: The Colorado River Compact and the Politics of Water* (1975) and Hundley, *The Great Thirst...* (1991); Donald J. Pisani, *To Reclaim A Divided West: Water, Law, and Public Policy, 1848–1902* (1992); Philip Ross May, *Origins of Hydraulic Mining in California* (1970); John Upton Terrell, *War for the Colorado River* (2 vols., 1965); Robert de Roos, *The Thirsty Land: The Story of the Central Valley Project* (1948); S. T. Harding, *Water in California* (1961); Kenneth Thompson, "Historic Flooding in the Sacramento Valley," *Pacific Historical Review* 39 (November 1960), 349–60 and Robert Kelley, "Taming the Sacramento...," *Pacific Historical Review* 34 (February 1965), 21–49.

Labor in an Industrial Age

////// **CHAPTER 30**

California's massive population growth did not occur without serious societal problems. The blue-and-gold tourist folders that urged visitors to spend winters in "the Golden State" scarcely hinted that severe issues continued to brew beneath the surface of its outwardly easy-going way of life. Real estate advertisements that extolled the state's attractions stood in stark contrast to the ferment of social unrest.

After the turn of the century, tensions between laborers and employers grew even more pronounced than in Denis Kearney's time. Now workers, through a new Union Labor party, spoke out even more forcefully against powerful financiers and shipping tycoons. Labor had also raised a strong voice of protest during the Ruef-Schmitz scandals in San Francisco. That city became a labor stronghold from which agitators penetrated the state's rural areas.

After 1905 a national labor organization, the Industrial Workers of the World (IWW), turned its attention to California. The IWW hoped to organize its seasonal and part-time workers into "One Big Union." Among these migratory laborers were field hands, lumberjacks, and cannery workers not welcome to join the American Federation of Labor (AFL), which had been organized along craft lines. Furthermore, the use of farm machinery annually lessened the need for harvest workers.

The work day on farms and ranches remained long and the pay extremely low. Furthermore, sanitary conditions in farm labor camps were deplorable. These conditions drew the attention of IWW leaders. From 1908 to 1913 its organizers recruited about one thousand migratory farm laborers as new members of a dozen local chapters.

230

The IWW, the first labor group to reach out to migrant workers, urged radical reform of the economy. Its members were referred to contemptuously in rural newspapers as socialist "Wobblies" who belonged to an "I Won't Work" movement. Frequently local police officials regarded the volatile organization as an outlaw labor group. IWW soapbox orators were arrested at rallies, fire hoses were turned on its members, and field workers were warned not to join the organization.

In spite of such harassment, the IWW persisted. After labor strife broke out at Fresno and San Diego, these and other municipalities adopted stiff regulations against the IWW. The terror in which municipal officials held the organization was based on its radical ideology. Subscribing as it did to the Marxian concept of class struggle and to syndicalist and anarchist ideas, the organization posed a clear threat to California's status quo.

Even some workers distrusted the "Wobblies" because of their attempts to obtain equal employment status for Chinese and Mexican laborers. Most employers too hated IWW on-the-job recruiting and unannounced strikes. Though its leaders were jailed, clubbed, and even killed, the "Wobblies" continued their campaign to organize migratory workers.

Conflict reached a peak of violence on August 3, 1913, at the Durst Ranch, a large hop farm in the Sacramento Valley. In contention were the conditions under which itinerant laborers—men, women, and children—were forced to work and live on the ranch. Only eight toilets were available for the use of 2,800 itinerant workers. Also, the owners of the ranch had advertised for many more laborers than they could actually use, paying those they selectively hired as little as 75 cents per day. Finally, a ranch-owned store held back 10 percent of these meager wages, forcing field hands to purchase food and supplies at inflated prices. The workers, under the leadership of Blackie Ford, the head of the IWW local, called a strike.

When a sheriff's posse sought to arrest Ford, a pistol was fired, and a violent riot ensued. The sheriff and the local district attorney, as well as several workers, were killed. Governor Hiram Johnson called out the National Guard to quell the disturbance and brought in private detectives to investigate its cause; as a result of the incident the IWW organization was virtually dismantled in the Sacramento Valley. Although the actual "shooter" was never found, Ford and a colleague were convicted of murder and sentenced to life imprisonment.

The Wheatland Riot, nevertheless, ultimately improved the welfare of migratory workers. Its attention drawn to the plight of the field hands, the California legislature subsequently passed several bills to control labor conditions for seasonal workers, though these measures were not effective. A new Commission on Immigration and Housing also pushed for better working conditions, but it was hampered by lack of power. Those ranchers who imported thousands of excess workers each season to pick peaches, grapes, cotton, and hops, still claimed they could not afford to furnish individual dwellings to part-time laborers. They argued that because the harvesting lasted only a few weeks, such housing, vacant much of the year, was impractical to maintain. Critics contended that this was a poor excuse for the continued inhumanity with which workers were treated.

Depressed labor conditions cried out for leadership. Late in 1913, a local agitator, who called himself "General" Kelley, marched an "army" of several thousand unemployed workers to Sacramento. He demanded better treatment for all pickers. Kelley's adherents resembled Jacob Coxey's ragamuffins, who, in 1895, had marched to Washington with similar demands. But Kelley's men were driven off by armed guards after attempting to camp near the state capitol building.

In 1910, several years before Kelley's march, the labor movement became involved in another ill-conceived effort. This was the bombing of the Los Angeles *Times,* which would set back the labor movement in California for many years. The fateful blast occurred at 1:07 A.M. on October 1, just as the newspaper's mechanical force was getting the paper to press; twenty persons were killed and many more injured. The *Times* building was reduced to a mass of rubble.

After the bombing, mutual suspicion between management and the workers increased in Los Angeles. The owner of the *Times,* General Harrison Gray Otis, blamed irresponsible labor leaders for the bombing, particularly the International Association of Bridge and Structural Iron Workers, then involved in a local strike. Conversely, labor accused the *Times* of criminal negligence in operating a plant which union spokesmen called a gas-leaking firetrap.

In 1911 three labor agitators—Ortie McManigal and James B. and John J. McNamara—were brought to trial, accused of organizing the bombing. Labor retained the attorney Clarence Darrow, known for his vigorous opposition to both violence and capital punishment. The testimony against the McNamara brothers was far too incriminating for Darrow to win their acquittal. Acting on his advice, the defendants changed their pleas from not guilty to guilty and, after a compromise with both prosecution and judge, were sent to the state penitentiary. James McNamara drew a sentence of life imprisonment and John one of fifteen years. McManigal was freed because he had "turned state's evidence." This may have been Clarence Darrow's only hope of saving the lives of the McNamara brothers, who confessed to the *Times* dynamiting.

Destruction by bombing of the Los Angeles Times *Building, 1910. C. C. Pierce Collection, photograph by C. C. Tarter; courtesy of The Huntington Library, San Marino, California.*

The bombing blackened the reputation of all union leaders. In 1911 Samuel Gompers, President of the AFL, had backed a reform-minded attorney, Job Harriman, for mayor of Los Angeles on the Socialist party ticket. His chances of winning the election had looked promising until the bombing occurred. Harriman lost the election by 34,000 votes. A coalition of powerful business and civic leaders insured that no one associated with labor violence could ever control local politics. Harriman abandoned his political ambitions in order to found a utopian colony. After the outbreak of World War I, any form of labor unrest came to be linked with lack of patriotism.

The war was to create a heavy demand for both skilled and unskilled workers, which raised wages, particularly in urban areas. Apprehensive about the spread of union activity, management urged upon labor the "open shop" as a temporary war measure. As public enthusiasm for the open shop increased, so did the level of antagonism between capital and labor. In 1916 violence again erupted, this time in San Francisco.

President Wilson had proclaimed July 22 of that year "Preparedness Day," when the nation was to demonstrate its unity in case war were declared. At San Francisco advocates of the open shop helped organize a patriotic parade as a Preparedness Day demonstration. Meanwhile, a serious longshoremen's strike was under way. The combination was

enough to make employers and union organizers edgy about their differences. In the midst of this uneasy situation a suitcase containing a
bomb, left by someone on a city sidewalk, exploded at 2:06 P.M., killing
nine persons and injuring forty others.

Two San Francisco union leaders, Thomas J. Mooney and Warren K.
Billings, were arrested and accused of the crime. In 1913 Billings had
been convicted of carrying explosives, for which he spent two years in
Folsom Penitentiary. Newspapers joined in public protests over the Preparedness Day bombing and the Mooney-Billings trial, which dealt in
rumor and innuendo. The press circulated a story on January 3, 1917,
the day the trial began, that Mooney and Billings, both anarchists, had
been part of a conspiracy that plotted to assassinate Governor Hiram
Johnson. There was also talk connecting the two men with "Reds" from
abroad, supposedly converging on California to spread the new doc-
trine of bolshevism.

Both Billings and Mooney presented alibis to clear themselves. Mooney
produced three photographs of himself and his wife on the roof of a
Market Street building viewing the parade. In these photos a streetside
clock, visible in the background, showed the time to be 1:58, 2:01 and
2:04 P.M. respectively, just prior to the bombing. Despite such evidence
for the defense, Mooney was convicted and sentenced to be hanged,
and Billings received a life term in the state penitentiary.

Their case attracted attention all over the world. A rally in Petrograd,
Russia, occurred as the White House was deluged by protests from world
leaders. In response to the international outcry, President Woodrow
Wilson appointed an investigative committee to review the case; it concluded was that there was insufficient evidence to find anyone guilty. In
the interest of wartime unity, President Woodrow Wilson requested
Governor William Stephens to commute Mooney's sentence to life
imprisonment. Nevertheless, the public remembered that during the trial
the prosecution had readily proved Mooney's association with the
McNamara brothers—convicted earlier of the explosion of the Los
Angeles *Times*.

After Mooney and Billings went behind the bars of San Quentin Penitentiary, labor interests embarked upon a determined twenty-year campaign to free the two men. Their sympathizers maintained that they
had been found guilty only because of association with anarchistic anti-
war exiles. Finally, in 1939, after repeated petitions and appeals, Mooney
was released, but he died soon thereafter. Later, Governor Culbert Olson
also persuaded the California Supreme Court to commute Billings' sentence to time served, and he too was eventually released.

Partly because of the 1916 Preparedness Day bombing, the open shop reigned in California for a number of years. In 1919, during the repressive atmosphere of the postwar years, California adopted a Criminal Syndicalism Law to control labor leaders. The act, resulting from the nation's first "Red Scare," public fear of the spread of communism after the Russian Revolution of 1917, forbade any form of violence in labor disputes. Anyone convicted of "labor violence" could be sentenced to as much as fourteen years' imprisonment. Radical ideas of foreign origin were not to be welcomed in postwar California, which gave its full support during this period to Prohibition and "100 percent Americanism."

The Criminal Syndicalism Law was repeatedly invoked to discourage union agitators in such tense situations as the 1923 San Pedro waterfront strike, various cannery strikes during the 1930s, and work stoppages from 1933 to 1934 among vegetable, fruit, and cotton pickers of the Imperial and San Joaquin valleys. At Salinas in 1936, growers recruited a "citizen's army" to put down a strike by migrant lettuce pickers. Equipped with shotguns and pick handles, the army "got the lettuce picked," broke the strike, and disbanded offending unions.

The fierceness of California's Criminal Syndicalism Law was illustrated by the arrest of the writer Upton Sinclair for reading the U.S. Constitution aloud in public! At San Pedro a 1923 strike, led by the IWW, had elicited the sympathy of the young, reform-minded Sinclair. His confrontation with the Los Angeles commercial establishment helped Sinclair to launch the American Civil Liberties Union in southern California. The major punitive effect of the law, however, fell squarely where its advocates had intended—upon radical labor leaders. This legislation, as well as municipal ordinances and continuing public pressure, combined in a few years to kill off what remained of the IWW and other extremist groups in California. They would not re-emerge for decades. For Californians wanted no further bombings or other acts of violence.

Selected Readings

Labor struggles are in Gregory Woirol, "Men on the Road . . . ," *California History* 70 (Summer 1991), 192–204; Martin Zanger, "Politics of Confrontation: Upton Sinclair and the Launching of the ACLU in Southern California," *Pacific Historical Review* 38 (November 1969), 383–406; Carleton Parker, *The Casual Laborer and Other Essays* (1920); William D. Haywood, *Bill Haywood's Book* (1929); Robert L. Tyler, "The I.W.W. and the West," *American Quarterly* 12 (Summer 1960), 175–87; Stewart Holbrook, "The Last of the Wobblies," *American Mercury* 62 (April 1946), 467–68; Louis

Adamic, *Dynamite: The Story of Class Violence in America* (1935); William J. Burns, *The Masked War* . . . (1913) also Robert K. Murray, *Red Scare: A Study in National Hysteria, 1919–1920* (1955).

On the Preparedness Day bombing see Ernest J. Hopkins, *What Happened in the Mooney Case* (1932); Thomas J. Hunt, *The Case of Thomas J. Mooney and Warren K. Billings* (1929); Curt Gentry, *Frame-Up: The Incredible Case of Tom Mooney and Warren Billings* (1967) and Richard H. Frost, *The Mooney Case* (1968).

Regarding other labor strife see Herbert Shapiro, "The McNamara Case, A Window on Class Antagonism in the Progressive Era," *Southern California Quarterly* 70 (Spring 1988), 69–94; Adela Rogers St. Johns, *Final Verdict* (1962); James P. Kraft, "The Fall of Job Harriman's Socialist Party," *Southern California Quarterly* 70 (Spring 1988), 43–68; Louis B. and Richard S. Perry, *A History of the Los Angeles Labor Movement* (1963); Bernard C. Cronin, *Father Yorke and the Labor Movement in San Francisco, 1900–1910* (1943); Grace H. Stimson, *Rise of the Labor Movement in Los Angeles* (1935); Paul S. Taylor, *The Sailors' Union of the Pacific* (1923); Gerald D. Nash, "The Influence of Labor on State Policy: The Experience of California," *California Historical Society Quarterly* 62 (September 1963), 241–57; Norris Hundley, "Katherine Philips Edson and the Fight for the California Minimum Wage, 1912–1913," *Pacific Historical Review* 29 (August 1960), 271–86; David Selvin, *A Terrible Anger: The 1934 Waterfront* . . . *Strike* (1915) and Selvin, *A Place in the Sun: A History of California Labor* (1981) as well as Alexander Saxton, *The Indispensable Enemy: Labor and the Anti-Chinese Movement in California* (1971).

The Depression Years

[handwritten notes:] 1930's Progression action rise of urbanization Industry Devp trade, Free nabo league flumingtan articities Ind Cal biggers Growth of Pres Rose

After a national collapse of the stock market in October 1929, jobs grew increasingly scarce. Labor leaders were no longer in a position to demand the closed shop, or to insist upon better working conditions.

Californians now sought more direct political solutions to their economic distress. In the presidential elections of 1932, the Democratic party nominated a new type of candidate. This was Franklin Delano Roosevelt, the highly popular governor of New York. Roosevelt's campaign took him to the major cities of the Far West, which responded to his magnetic appeal. He offered genuine hope the downhearted and discouraged. Californians had tired of hearing that speculation in the stock market was the primary cause of the Depression. They were more interested in the solution of local problems than in national issues.

At the Commonwealth Club in San Francisco on September 23, 1932, Roosevelt described in somber terms the concentration of private enterprise in the United States into large business concerns: "Put plainly, we are steering a steady course toward oligarchy, if we are not there already," he said. Roosevelt went on to speak of every man's right to life and to a comfortable living, and declared, "Our government, formal and informal, political and economic, owes to everyone . . . a portion of that plenty sufficient for his needs, through his own work." When election day came, California voted overwhelmingly for Roosevelt.

But while he campaigned, the state's economy was growing worse. Overproduction of both agricultural and commercial commodities caused unemployment to spread. Once-prosperous industries, farms, and real estate developments were mired down by a national depression. Within a few months banks, following runs on their holdings by worried depositors, were threatened with collapse. To allow time for the state legislature to devise protective legislation, California Governor James "Sunny Jim" Rolph, Jr., ordered a three-day bank holiday on March 2, 1933. By March 4, the day of President Roosevelt's inauguration, almost every state governor had imposed severe restrictions on the withdrawal of funds. On the same day, Rolph extended the California bank holiday for three more days.

The country faced economic paralysis, with the scarcity of money in some cases reducing business to a barter system. Hope ran high that Roosevelt's "New Deal" would quickly be effective. Because the new president demonstrated that he viewed the crisis as far from insoluble, Californians looked to him for crucial leadership.

California's relief activities—now carried on through a State Relief Administration—were far from adequate to meet emergency conditions. At this very time thousands of new migrants descended upon the state, though they were warned not to come in search of jobs. Rumors of high wages "out West" nonetheless caused many to make a cross-country trip they were later to regret. Among the newcomers were 350,000 farmers from the parched Dust Bowl areas of the Middle West, known as "Okies" or "Arkies," from their origins in Oklahoma or Arkansas. Their trek overland in rickety "flivvers," with brooms and pails tied onto their old jalopies, also heaped with mattresses, children, and blankets, has been described in John Steinbeck's novel *The Grapes of Wrath.* 1934

Most of these migrants arrived during 1935 and in the four years thereafter. Because the labor situation was so gravely depressed, even responsible citizens supported legislation to close the border to indigents. (Later, in 1941, the U.S. Supreme Court declared such laws unconstitutional.) Farm owners became accustomed to paying starvation wages that desperate migrants were forced to accept. Faced with bankruptcy, employers claimed they could not possibly spend money they did not have to improve the working conditions of California's new refugees.

Both the AFL and Congress of Industrial Organizations (CIO), two rival labor groups, battled in the orchards of Marysville. In the packing sheds of Bakersfield and in Fresno's canneries each sought to organize migrant workers. To combat them, in 1934, after a wave of field strikes, a group of farm owners formed the Associated Farmers of California. This anti-union group came to number forty thousand members. It proved more than a match for the United Cannery, Agricultural, Packing and Allied Workers of America, part of the CIO.

Governor Rolph had little idea of how to cope with the state's massive unemployment, especially among migrant workers. He opposed almost

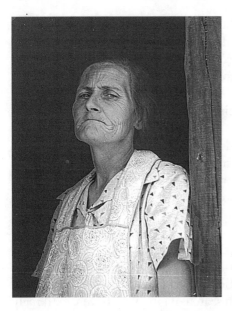

Migrant Arkansas woman living in contractor's camp near Westley, California, approx. 1939. [Lange photo] Courtesy Library of Congress # 19488.

any reform of California's tax structure and signed legislation that caused taxes to fall unfairly upon persons of the lowest income. A sales tax on all retail items, including food, came to be blamed upon Rolph. He also vetoed a progressive income tax bill and made the mistake of endorsing a brutal jailbreak lynching. When he died in 1934, "Sunny Jim" was succeeded by the lieutenant governor, Frank Merriam, who was more conservative in his rhetoric than in his actions.

Folksinger Woody Guthrie mocked Merriam in one of his ballads about official indolence over just what to do about the Okies and Arkies. Public prejudice against these migrants was born of a combination of insecurity and shame concerning the tragic plight of fellow Americans. Guthrie, like Steinbeck, captured the spirit of the Great Depression. Born in Oklahoma, he spent several years in Los Angeles, where he sang on a radio station for "the little man" and "drifting families," voicing both strength and bitterness in his "talking blues":

> We got to old Los Angeles broke,
> So dad-gum hungry we thought we'd choke,
> And I bummed up a spud or two
> And my wife cooked up potater stew . . .
> Fed the kids a big batch of it,
> But that was mighty thin stew . . .
> So dad-gum thin you could pretty nearly
> Read a magazine through it . . .

If it had been just a little thinner,
I've always believed,
If that stew had been just a little bit thinner,
Some of our senators could have seen through it.*

Guthrie felt that California was being misused by selfish, scared people:

California's a Garden of Eden
A paradise to live in or see . . .
But believe it or not,
You won't find it so hot
If you ain't got the Do-Re-Mi.†

Guthrie, who composed over a thousand songs, is best remembered by his "folk national anthem" entitled *This Land Is Your Land*.

In addition to the influx of Arkies and Okies, a growing number of Mexicans slipped over the border in search of jobs, which were extremely hard to come by. Serious problems of education, housing, and assimilation subsequently developed around California's Mexican minority. Forced to accept unpleasant jobs at low wages or to remain unemployed, they clung to their Spanish language, clustered in their own organizations, and retained largely separate tastes. At Los Angeles, Mexican newcomers formed the largest Mexican community in the world outside Mexico. One Mexican immigrant, Ignazio Lozano, founded *La Opinión*, which became the nation's largest Spanish-language newspaper.

Members of another minority group, the Filipinos, also competed for jobs as houseboys, laundry workers, dish washers, and fry cooks. Sentiment against Filipino farm laborers led to the Watsonville riot of 1930, and to another disturbance at Salinas in 1934, in which many Filipinos were manhandled. By the mid-1930s, proposals for the exclusion of Filipinos were heard in the California legislature. The state eventually offered them free transportation home if they promised not to return to California.

Thousands of older people, many of them no longer able to work and dependent on curtailed incomes, seemed to believe that life in sunny California would rejuvenate them. During the Depression many of these elderly folk were attracted to schemes that promised to alleviate their hardships by redistributing the uneven wealth. Among such plans in

---

Talking Dust Bowl, words and music by Woody Guthrie. TRO copyright 1961 Ludlow Music, Inc., New York, N.Y. Used by permission.
†*Do-Re-Mi*, words and music by Woody Guthrie. TRO copyright 1961 and 1963 Ludlow Music, Inc., New York, N.Y. Used by permission.

circulation at the time was a movement known as "Technocracy." Its chief advocate was Howard Scott, an engineer who wanted to create a utopian society by eliminating poverty. Equipped with elaborate blueprints, he explained his proposed civilization in abandoned drug stores, garages, and unrented buildings. His ideas did not endure.

Like Technocracy, other utopian plans during the depression years were identified with a particular personality. One of these was Upton Sinclair, who had been, since the Progressive era, a crusading author and journalist. In 1920 he unsuccessfully sought a congressional seat for the first time. Two years later he ran unsuccessfully for the Senate, and in 1926 and 1930 he was the Socialist party candidate for governor. Sinclair's last attempt at public office was in 1934, when he sought the Democratic nomination for governor. Sinclair's experimental EPIC ("End Poverty in California") plan was tailor-made for the downhearted. He advocated a monthly pension of $50 for widows, the aged, and the handicapped. In earlier times of distress, Henry George had championed a heavy tax on idle land. Sinclair similarly believed that homeowners should be totally exempt from taxation. His "production for use" scheme called for the state to buy up idle land and factories. This would somehow help the unemployed. Sinclair also wanted the legislature to issue "scrip currency" to take the place of scarce dollars.

Although Sinclair's plan held much the same appeal for the unemployed as Roosevelt's New Deal, the president considered Sinclair's program impractical. Other democratic party leaders also regarded Sinclair as an extremist whose idealistic notions were unworkable. In 1934, during that year's bitterly contested gubernatorial elections, the press, radio, and film industry (then in conservative control) united against Sinclair. His opponent, Governor Merriam, defeated him soundly.

Sinclair, however, was followed by even more radical messiahs. His was an age when pundits of every description gained huge audiences of discontented citizens. Among these was Dr. Francis E. Townsend, a retired physician who sold real estate at Long Beach. With the slogan "Youth for work and age for leisure," in 1934 he proposed his Townsend Old Age Pension Plan. This scheme would provide a monthly pension of $200 for every person over the age of sixty. Recipients, however, would have to retire from work completely and spend these payments within one month. A 2 percent federal tax upon business transactions was to support the plan.

Townsend led a "crusade" via his newspaper, *The Townsend Weekly*, and 5,000 clubs organized in his name. By 1937, national Townsend Club membership was estimated at from 3 to 10 million persons. But even Upton Sinclair considered Dr. Townsend's plan economic madness. Only slowly did Townsend's followers give up on his ideas, even after Congress passed the 1935 Social Security Act.

In 1938 yet another visionary plan, the "Thirty Dollars Every Thursday" or "Ham and Eggs" proposal emerged. Its proponents wanted to award a pension to every unemployed person over the age of fifty. Payment of pensions and state taxes would be by scrip or warrants financed by a compulsory stamp purchase system. In the state elections of 1938 and 1939 the measure actually came close to adoption, despite the fact that critics labeled it economically irresponsible.

This movement, like Sinclair's EPIC plan and Townsend's pension scheme, can best be understood in terms of the despair and confused thinking of the depression years. President Roosevelt's unwillingness to enclose such locally improvised plans doubtless contributed to their end. Passage of the more realistic federal Social Security Act of 1935 was, however, influenced by and partly in response to California's experimental public welfare schemes.

A series of congressional measures, most of which survived Supreme Court tests of their constitutionality, enabled Roosevelt to deliver on his campaign promises of a New Deal featuring relief, recovery, and reform. Dozens of new federal agencies, with abbreviated alphabetic titles, were established to perform functions designed to bring back prosperity. Some of these organizations worked in partnership with state relief agencies.

Following the use of federal funds to construct Hoover Dam and the Central Valley Project, the federal government helped to finance other power, reclamation, flood-control, and navigation projects. These were to affect markedly the future of California. By the mid-1930s the short-term relief benefits of massive government aid had become everywhere evident. In California, as elsewhere throughout the nation, destitute people depended upon weekly government checks to sustain them until they could get permanent employment. In addition to this direct relief, unemployed young men were given "make-work" jobs in the Civilian Conservation Corps (CCC). This project constructed mountain trails and firebreaks on federal forest lands and in six new state parks established in California during 1933. Other young people in college were aided by National Youth Administration (NYA) money. Their fathers, meanwhile, worked on Works Progress Administration (WPA) or Public Work Administration (PWA) construction projects.

Though resisted by conservatives, these activities helped to alleviate economic hardship. Their costs, moreover, were to seem modest compared to expenditures during World War II and after. No state benefited more from the federal relief programs than did California. There, hundreds of new schools, parks, roads, and beach facilities were built during the Depression. In addition to the larger-scale projects previously mentioned, these new undertakings contributed materially to the state's development.

Although Franklin Roosevelt won the state in four successive national elections, until Culbert L. Olson assumed power in 1938, Californians had not seated a Democratic governor since 1899. In the early years of this century the state Republican party was quite liberal. Its Democratic party, almost defunct through the 1920s, did not make a comeback until after 1932. Governor Olson, an advocate of President Roosevelt's reform ideas, was elected governor when the New Deal was virtually over and public pressure for reform had abated. In supporting migrant laborers and confronting agricultural malaise, he came up against the Associated Farmers, which opposed all government intervention.

Following an upswing of business activity after 1937, the CIO began to attract more unorganized laborers. The labor union renewed its interest in unskilled laborers, once represented by IWW organizers. For years, the Coast Seamen's Union had agitated for better working conditions. Its Norwegian leader, Andrew Furuseth, a pioneer crusader for seamen's rights, had dedicated himself to the extermination of such evils as "the crimp." Sailors were then still forced to pay a fee to a "crimp," or labor broker, in order to join ship crews. Waterfront boardinghouses, providing seamen with beds, meals, and clothing, also charged exorbitant fees. Their operators regularly turned over to shipmasters those unemployed seamen who were deeply in their debt. Furuseth's struggle to obtain seamen's rights eventually was passed on to the Sailors' Union of the Pacific.

To obtain employment, waterfront workers joined the Longshoremen's Association, actually an open-shop company union through which shippers controlled hiring and wages. Worker discontent paved the way for the entrance of radicalism into the maritime labor movement, which now acquired new organizers. Among these was Harry Bridges, a spellbinding Australian-born longshoreman.

Maritime employers labeled the militant Bridges a dangerous alien radical, if not a Communist. But thousands of longshoremen up and down the Pacific Coast stood behind his leadership. By 1934 he staged a massive strike that affected all shipping from San Diego to Seattle. Bridges sought a minimum thirty-hour week for his dock workers at wages of a dollar an hour. He also objected to the hiring of longshoremen by company foremen who selected their favorite workers.

During the great maritime strike of 1934, Bridges tied up traffic at San Francisco for ninety days. In sympathy with longshoremen, other transport workers went out on strike too. Hundreds of ships lay idle, while cargoes rotted and rusted on piers and in warehouses. On July 5, "Bloody Thursday," a violent episode erupted. After the San Francisco police moved against picket lines with tear gas, two union pickets were shot to death, and over 100 men, including police, were wounded. Almost 150,000 workers then walked off the job, paralyzing the San Francisco bay area. When the governor called out the National Guard, this only intensified the resentment of strikers.

The 1934 "general strike" actually damaged the long-term interests of unionism. Eventually the longshoremen agreed to submit their demands to arbitration. Although they won some concessions from management, settlement of this strike by no means brought peace to the San Francisco waterfront. Other labor stoppages, though less intensive, occurred throughout the later 1930s. These caused continuing public criticism.

A jurisdictional altercation between Bridges and other labor leaders ultimately led Bridges to take his longshoremen into the CIO. Because of his power, the Hearst press made demands for his deportation from 1936 onward. Eventually, the congressional Committee on Un-American Activities charged that various CIO unions were under Communist leadership and control. The courts upheld Bridges's radical unionization techniques, however, and he retained considerable power.

Demands for unionization also spread to Los Angeles, the center of the open shop or "American Plan." By 1935, the port of San Pedro had been unionized. After similar pressures filtered back from the city's waterfront into Los Angeles proper, the plasterers, hod carriers, plumbers, typographers, tire workers, steam fitters, and auto workers also made greater demands upon management.

However, by the end of the 1930s a new era of negotiation had begun in the relations between California labor and management. Harry Bridges eventually came to call strikes an "obsolete weapon," while Roger Lapham, chairman of the board of the American-Hawaiian Steamship Company (and later mayor of San Francisco) agreed to participate in collective bargaining through the federal National Labor Relations Board.

Against the background of the grave social dislocations of the depression years, the figure of William Randolph Hearst stands out in particular relief. Born into a wealthy family at San Francisco in 1863—his father, Senator George Hearst, had created a mining fortune—young Will attended Harvard and, in 1887, at the age of twenty-four, was virtually handed the San Francisco *Examiner*. Through his willingness to invest vast amounts of his father's money, Hearst made the *Examiner* the most powerful paper on the West Coast. His reputation as a young and energetic publisher was first made by attacks on the Southern Pacific Railroad. At first Hearst appeared in the role of a reformist crusader, but by the 1930s he bore little resemblance to the liberal of earlier decades. Like many disgruntled businessmen, Hearst came to believe that reform had gone quite far enough and that conservatism must reverse the power of labor unions, of government, and, in particular, of nebulous New Dealers.

Throughout his eighty-eight years, Hearst was an enigma even to close associates. Though outwardly shy, he made his power felt even at the international level through his chain of some thirty newspapers, thirteen magazines, and several radio stations. Hearst came to be associated with a remarkable number of issues and events. Prominent among these were the Spanish-American War (which he almost surely helped cause); hatred of the two Roosevelts (although by one of the choicest ironies of history he had in large measure obtained the presidential nomination of the second one); antivivisection; opposition to United States entry into both World Wars; suppression of radical minorities; and distrust of internationalism. In promoting his prejudices, Hearst achieved mixed results. Thinking persons were offended by his convictions, and nearly always repelled by his personal tastes.

At the heart of Hearst's popular empire were his newspapers. He bought up papers all over the country and, by reckless spending and reporting, made them successful. There was a sameness about their sensational reportage, as well as about their slanted editorials that appealed to a less-than-educated readership. These newspapers became the archetypes of yellow journalism and the despair of Hearst's critics. In California's depression decades, as the "Chief" grew more eccentric, the Hearst press stood in the way of economic and political reform. Even conservatives shunned Hearst. The Hearst machine spewed hate at both President Roosevelt and Governor Olson and fulminated against all attempts to "tinker" with the currency, to "coddle" the unemployed, and to "socialize" the country.

The headquarters of Hearst's domain was his San Simeon estate, on the rocky coast between San Luis Obispo and Monterey. In the interwar years "the Lord of San Simeon" poured $35 million into the construction of an immense castle there. Stocking it with art treasures from all over the world, Hearst made his San Simeon a rendezvous for guests drawn from the fields of the movie industry, art, music, literature, and public affairs.

Hearst, like his mother, Phoebe Apperson Hearst, was given to subsidizing philanthropic and educational institutions. Nevertheless, there were many who felt that he could easily have used more of his annual income for other purposes than to gratify his acquisitive impulse. In

1935 his far-flung personal empire was valued at $200 million. His holdings included seven castles; warehouses full of antique furniture, hundreds of paintings, and tapestries; ranches on which he raised 10,000 beef cattle; several zoos, hunting lodges, and beach homes.

Orson Welles's 1940 film *Citizen Kane* drew a stark picture of the aging autocrat. As times changed, the anachronism of "Citizen Hearst," as one of his biographers calls him, became ever more apparent. After World War II, the Hearst dynasty gradually crumbled. By the mid-1960s his two major papers, the San Francisco *Examiner* and the Los Angeles *Examiner*, gave way to the *Chronicle* and the *Times*. The *Examiners*, both morning papers, had to be merged with the Hearst evening newspapers to meet the competition of suburban as well as radio and television newscasts. Falling circulation led his heirs to enter other fields of endeavor.

Hearst's past opulence dramatized a great gap between him and ordinary working Californians who were more than anxious to leave behind the struggles of their depression years.

Selected Readings

An excellent source is Leonard Leader, *Los Angeles and the Great Depression* (1991). See also William Mullens, *The Depression and the Urban West Coast, 1929–1933* (1991).

On the Dust Bowl migration see James Gregory, *American Exodus: The Dust Bowl Migration and the Okie Culture in California* (1989); Charles J. Shindo, *Dust Bowl Migrants in the American Imagination* (1997); Walter J. Stein, *California and the Dust Bowl Migration* (1973); Dorothea Lange and Paul S. Taylor, *An American Exodus: A Record of Human Erosion* (1939).

Other depression-era sources include Luther Whiteman and Samuel L. Lewis, *Glory Roads: The Psychological State of California* (1936); Jackson K. Putnam, *Old Age Politics in California* (1970); Abraham Holtzman, *The Townsend Movement: A Political Study* (1963) Gilman Ostrander, *The Prohibition Movement in California* (1957); Abe Hoffman, "A Look at Llano: Experiment in Economic Socialism," *California Historical Society Quarterly* 40 (September 1961), 215–36; Upton Sinclair, *I, Candidate for Governor—and How I Got Licked* (1935); Greg Mitchell, *The Campaign of the Century: Upton Sinclair's Race for Governor of California and the Birth of Media Politics* (1992); Fay Blake and H. M. Newman, "Upton Sinclair's Epic Campaign," *California Historical Quarterly* 63 (Fall 1984), 305–19; Judson Grenier, "Upton Sinclair: A Remembrance," *California Historical Society Quarterly* 47 (June 1969), 165–69; and Grenier, "Upton Sinclair: The Road to California," *Southern California Quarterly* 56 (Winter 1974), 325–36.

On reform and labor consult Tom Sitton, "Another Generation of Urban Reformers: Los Angeles in the 1930s," *Western Historical Quarterly* 18 (July 1987), 315–32; Woodrow C. Whitten, *Criminal Syndicalism and Law in California* (Philadelphia, 1969); Philip Taft, *Labor Politics American Style: The California State Federation of Labor* (1968); Robert W. Cherny, "The Making of a Labor Radical: Harry Bridges, 1901–34," *Pacific Historical Review* 64 (August 1995), 363–88; Hyman Weintraub, *Andrew Furuseth: Emancipator of the Seamen* (1959); Robert Knight, *Industrial Relations in the San Francisco Bay Area, 1900–1918* (1960); Paul S. Taylor, *The Sailors' Union of the Pacific* (1923); Alexander Saxton, "San Francisco Labor and the Populist and Progressive Insurgencies," *Pacific Historical Review* 34 (November 1965), 421–38; Ira Cross, *History of the Labor Movement in California* (1935); Mike Quin, *The Big Strike* (1949) and Paul Eliel, *The Waterfront and General Strike . . .* (1934).

H. Brett Melendy and Benjamin F. Gilbert's *The Governors of California* (1965) is a study of governors. See also Robert E. Burke, *Olson's New Deal for California* (1952).

Concerning Hearst see Oliver Carlson and Ernest S. Bates, *Hearst: Lord of San Simeon* (1937); John Tebbel, *The Life and Good Times of William Randolph Hearst* (1952); John K. Winkler, *William Randolph Hearst: A New Appraisal* (1955) and W. A. Swanberg, *Citizen Hearst: A Biography of William Randolph Hearst* (1961).

Concerning competition between farm workers see Gilbert Gonzalez, *Labor and Community: Citrus: Worker Villages . . .* (1994); Camille Guerin-Gonzalez, *Mexican Workers . . . and California Farm Labor* (1994); Wayne Cornelius, *Leo Chavez, and Jorge Castro, Mexican Immigrants and Southern California* (1982); Richard Griswold del Castillo, *The Los Angeles Barrio, 1850–1890* (1980); Vicki Ruiz, *Cannery Women, Cannery Lives . . . 1930–1950* (1987) and Devra Weber, *Dark Sweat, White Gold: California Farm Workers . . .* (1994); Daniel E. Cletus, *Bitter Harvest: A History of California Farm Workers . . .* (1981) and Harold A. De Witt, "The Watsonville Anti-Filipino Riot of 1930," *Southern California Quarterly* 61 (Fall 1979), 291–302.

Twentieth-Century Culture

////// **CHAPTER 32**

After 1900, California attracted a wide variety of individualists. Social improvisation took many forms that seemed bizarre to the rest of the country. Religious fundamentalists were particularly popular. These included the Reverend Robert P. Shuler, a shouting radio evangelist. Denominational gurus of every sort were joined by Yogi mystics, Swami palm readers, rainmakers, Hindu fakirs, and occultists. Theosophy, which was based upon Buddhist and Brahman spiritual beliefs, also gained ready adherents.

In the 1920s, at Point Loma near San Diego, "The Purple Mother," Katherine Tingley, established a theosophical community. Another theosophist, Annie Besant, settled in the quiet Ojai Valley below Santa Barbara. There she brought "The New Messiah," one Krishnamurti, from India, to preside over her flock of converts.

The best-known faith-healer was Aimee Semple McPherson, a dynamic pentecostal evangelist who founded the Four Square Gospel Church in Los Angeles. In the interwar years, "Sister Aimee" remained full of verve and loud of voice. On one occasion she scattered religious tracts from an airplane; at other times she held prayer meetings in a boxing arena. A talented showwoman, she sometimes wore the white uniform and gold braid of an admiral. From the platform of her Angelus Temple, Sister Aimee combatted the devil on behalf of the downhearted and lonely, for many of whom she had a potent appeal.

For twenty years she broadcast services via her own radio station. In 1925 the station wandered off its assigned wave length. When Herbert Hoover, then secretary of commerce, ordered her broadcast license sus-

pended, Sister Aimee cabled him: "PLEASE ORDER YOUR MIN-
IONS OF SATAN TO LEAVE MY STATION ALONE . . . YOU
CANNOT EXPECT THE ALMIGHTY TO ABIDE BY YOUR
WAVE LENGTH NONSENSE . . . ." On another occasion Sister
Aimee walked into the ocean and was presumed to have drowned. Eight
days later she reappeared under suspicious circumstances, saying that
she had been kidnapped. McPherson founded more than two hundred
branch churches. She offered her followers not only the entertainment
of bell ringers and xylophone bands, she also gave material aid to the
sick and needy.

Sister Aimee was a notable expression of that occultism for which
southern California was becoming known. One sees a similar phenomenon in the rise of the "funeral park." These establishments advertised
themselves as happy vales for the departed. Unlike the mundane cem-
eteries and graveyards of the past, their slick advertisements glossed over
death. Swaddled in spongy euphemisms, mourners were offered a glowing vision of the hereafter.

For their rather crude, commercial campaigns, the funeral park morti-
cians were lampooned by Aldous Huxley and Evelyn Waugh, two sa-
tiric English critics. Christopher Isherwood also used California as a
playground in which to exercise his sarcasm. Huxley, in his *After Many a
Summer Dies the Swan,* mocked the ostentation and hollowness he
claimed to see in Los Angeles. Although Huxley hated the grotesque
residences of Hearst and of the movie magnates as well as the funeral
parks ("the Beverly Pantheon, a Personality Cemetery"), he remained
content to live in southern California. Huxley never returned to his native Britain, experimenting with LSD and other drugs.

American writers too continued to be attracted to California: some
more distinguished by their industry than by their literary finesse. Zane
Grey, a former baseball player and Ohio dentist, made a fortune publishing pulp westerns. Settling in Altadena, where he built a Zuni-style
terraced house, Grey, like Jack London before him, sometimes wrote
two novels per year. The most popular of these was his *Riders of the
Purple Sage* (1912). Another pulp writer, Harold Bell Wright, was the
author of several dozen novels set in the West. His *The Winning of Barbara Worth* (1911), which focussed upon reclamation of the Imperial
Valley from the desert, sold more than a million and a half copies.

Among poets was the eccentric George Sterling who produced his
romantic sonnets at Carmel. Sterling, in Jack London's words, "looked
like a Greek coin run over by a Roman chariot." His *Testimony of the
Suns* (1903) was both imaginative and honest. In 1926 Sterling killed
himself in San Francisco's Bohemian Club. A much greater poet was

Robinson Jeffers who, after graduation from Occidental College, also went to live at Carmel. There he built with his own hands a stone residence named Tor House. Jeffers contrasted human depravity with the nobility of California's still pristine coastline. Jeffers once wrote, "Cut humanity out of my being, that is the wound that festers." His respect for the primeval and for the wonders of the universe itself were what first drew readers to his stark poetry and what kept them reading his work. He was at his best in such long narrative poems as *Roan Stallion* (1925) and *Be Angry at the Sun* (1925).

Among new reformist writers was the aforementioned Upton Sinclair, who came to California after having written *The Jungle* (1906) and *The Money-Changers* (1908). There is no question that his literature, which attracted worldwide attention, achieved specific reform. Less blatantly reformist was the best known of California novelists, John Steinbeck. In his *Pastures of Heaven* (1932), *Tortilla Flat* (1935), and *In Dubious Battle* (1936), he too reflected anger with all forms of social injustice. Steinbeck's most important novel, *The Grapes of Wrath* (1939), chronicled the plight of Oklahoma Dust Bowl farmers forced to move westward to California.

William Saroyan, of Armenian origin, discovered a rich literary lore in the San Joaquin Valley of his boyhood. His *My Heart's in the High-*

Jagged stretch along the coast of Sonoma County in Northern California. Courtesy of Redwood Empire Association.

lands (1939), *My Name is Aram* (1940), and *The Beautiful People* (1942) are peopled by attractive eccentrics who inhabit a dream world. Saroyan is best remembered for his short stories and occasional plays, which do not venture far from the Fresno of his youth.

Because so many European refugees arrived, southern California came to be called a boneyard for aging foreign intellectuals. Among them the English philosopher Bertrand Russell spent part of his World War II years teaching at UCLA. He ungratefully called Los Angeles "the ultimate segregation of the unfit." The German novelist Thomas Mann was another European refugee, in his case from Nazism. Between the wars Sadakichi Hartmann, a Japanese-born historian of art and an aesthete, also wrote screenplays and exotic poetry in Hollywood and San Francisco.

Following World War II much good writing began to come out of the state's colleges and universities. At Stanford, Wallace Stegner was earning acclaim for his books set in the American West, among them *Mormon Country* (1942), and *The Big Rock Candy Mountain* (1943). At Berkeley, Mark Schorer (*The State of Mind*, 1947) and Henry Nash Smith (*Virgin Land*, 1950) combined writing with teaching. Richard Armour, on the faculty of Scripps College, made a name for himself as the "playful poet," with light verse reminiscent of Gelett Burgess.

At Occidental College, historian Robert Glass Cleland produced entertaining narratives on the fur trade, the California ranches, and the American West. At the University of California, George R. Stewart spanned both history and literature in his *Ordeal by Hunger* (1936) and *Storm* (1941). Walter Van Tilburg Clark, at San Francisco State College, wrote *The Ox-Bow Incident* (1940) and *The Track of the Cat* (1949).

The best-known novel of Niven Busch, *California Street* (1959), concerns a San Francisco newspaper dynasty while James Edmiston's *Home Again* (1955) reflected poignant criticism of the government's removal of Japanese Americans from the Pacific Coast during World War II. A related theme runs through Abraham Polansky's *A Season of Fear* (1956). San Francisco's Chinese form the backdrop of C. Y. Lee's *The Flower-Drum Song* (1956), which became a musical play and film.

Other prominent postwar writers include Jessamyn West, whose *The Friendly Persuasion* (1945) was also transformed into a prize-winning film script. Her *South of the Angels* (1960), like James M. Cain's *The Postman Always Rings Twice* (1934) and *Mildred Pierce* (1941), are set in southern California. Similarly, Judy van der Veer evoked the San Diego backcountry in *Brown Hills* (1938) and *November Grass* (1940). Both John Fante, in *Ask the Dust* (1940) and *Dago Red* (1940), and Joe Pagano in *Golden Wedding* (1943), portrayed Italian-American life in the Far West.

Among popular mystery authors who did some of their best writing in California were Raymond Chandler, Dashiell Hammett, Ross McDonald, and Erle Stanley Gardner. Admitted to the California bar in 1911, Gardner became best known as the creator of Perry Mason, a fictional supersleuth. Edgar Rice Burroughs, originator of the banal Tarzan stories, also kept up a voluminous production. Outpacing even these prolific writers was Louis L'Amour who, beginning with his book *Hondo* (1952), sold millions of copies of his several dozen western stories.

A totally different type of writer was Henry Miller, born in Manhattan in 1891. Most of his work was autobiographical; his best-known books are *Tropic of Cancer* (1934) and *Tropic of Capricorn* (1938), written during his expatriate period abroad. For many years Miller lived on a mountaintop overlooking the Pacific Ocean at Big Sur. His book *Big Sur and the Oranges of Hieronymus Bosch* (1956) describes his life in California. He takes his reader on a firsthand tour of human depravity, and his central statement is that man has lost the art of living and that "until this collosal, senseless machine which we have made in America is smashed and scrapped there can be no hope."

A group reflecting Miller's influence grew up in the 1950s. Prominent among these spokesmen of the "Beat Generation" were Jack Kerouac and Allen Ginsberg, who made San Francisco their headquarters. Both expressed the frustrations of impatient young people who abhorred postwar society. Kerouac coined the phrase "Beat Generation" to describe the disillusionment he portrayed in his writings. Ginsberg joined Kerouac in publishing his writing in *Neurotica*, a journal built on "beat" compositions that reflected a rebellion against "squares"—those mediocre conformists who lived a safe but dull existence. Defying society's conventions, the "beatniks" clustered about the *café espresso* houses of San Francisco and at Venice on the west side of Los Angeles.

These bearded bohemians aroused their critics, who felt they deserved the unpopularity they sought. As if to anticipate the Hippie rebellion of the 1960s, their poetry readings, music sessions, and "kookie" artistic displays at Sausalito generated mild interest among the young of the 1950s. The "beatniks" thought they were modern and avant-garde, which perhaps they were for a while. Probably the most representative of their works is Kerouac's *On the Road*. Ginsberg's long poem *Howl* (1956) was called on the one hand a tedious collection of raucous wordiness, but his admirers found ground-breaking effects in the work. Ginsberg's and Kerouac's writings were, however, considered adolescent by America's literary establishment. On occasion, the "beats" could become humorous; they encouraged the social commentary of the comedian Mort Sahl, a former University of California student who made a fortune in such nightclubs as San Francisco's Hungry i and Hollywood's Crescendo, as well as through records and television appearances.

By mid-twentieth century, the California press was also undergoing substantial changes. Syndicated news and editorial opinion, provided by eastern wire-services, replaced home-grown journalism. Local newspapers reflected both a lack of variety and a high degree of monopolization. Even in large cities one or two papers came to control the news media.

As for book production, no national publisher has yet emerged in California, though the University of California Press and Stanford University Press sometimes resemble commercial publishing firms on the eastern seaboard and in the Midwest. Also, a number of typographers and book dealers have established a tradition for fine printing in limited editions, supported by the Book Club of California and the Zamorano and Roxburghe clubs. The performing arts, however, have always flourished in California. San Francisco's Tivoli Opera House closed in 1913, but the San Francisco Opera Company filled the gap; after 1932 it was given a permanent home, the War Memorial Opera House. The San Francisco Symphony was founded in 1911 and the Los Angeles Philharmonic Orchestra in 1919. Open-air concerts, held at the Hollywood Bowl since 1921, encouraged renowned musical artists to appear each summer. George Gershwin personally played his "Rhapsody in Blue" at the Bowl.

Ferdinand Rudolph (Ferde) Grofe, arranger and composer of the *Grand Canyon Suite,* began his career as an "extra" piano player at the Old Hippodrome Theater on San Francisco's Barbary Coast. On the eve of World War II other foreign composers also sought refuge in California, among them Arnold Schoenberg and Igor Stravinsky.

Los Angeles has been a point of origin for musicals that have gone on to long Broadway runs. Among the creators of Hollywood musicals were Jerome Kern, Oscar Hammerstein, Sigmund Romberg, and George Gershwin. The Civic Light Opera Company staged a majority of these performances over a period of more than fifty years. Today the Mark Taper and Ahmanson theaters regularly produce plays before their national runs.

Another unique art form, cinematography, has flourished in California. As early as 1872 Eadweard Muybridge, an English-born photographer, was commissioned by Leland Stanford to take action shots of Stanford's favorite horse. Stanford had bet a friend $25,000 that horses, at the gallop, took all four hooves off the ground at one time. In order to prove this, Muybridge lined up cameras along a race track at Palo Alto. Fine wires were then stretched across the track. As the horse broke these,

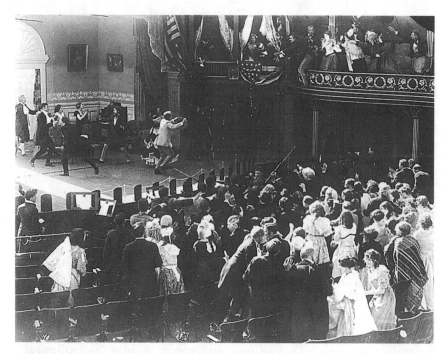

The Birth of a Nation, by D.W. Griffith. Courtesy of The Museum of Modern Art/Film Stills Archives.

a camera shutter was released, with the result that a series of photographic prints were taken at fixed intervals. When projected onto a screen in rapid succession, the exposures created the illusion of a picture in motion. Muybridge's achievement eventually attracted attention to the possibility of designing a motion-picture camera.

Later, Hollywood became the world's film capital. Since then the film industry centered around Hollywood has drawn to California its greatest publicity in modern times, both good and bad. A sleepy village founded by Kansas prohibitionists, its city fathers passed an ordinance in 1903 that forbade driving more than two thousand sheep through the town at any one time. A good climate and variety of scenery made Hollywood an ideal film location. Far from eastern debt collectors and the interference of New York State's motion-picture patent law, Hollywood's pioneer producers operated on a shoestring budget. They rented secondhand equipment, painted their own sets, and improvised lighting techniques.

One of the first California film producers was the Selig Polyscope Company, which in 1908 filmed *The Count of Monte Cristo*. In 1909 the Bison Studios arrived, followed by the Pathé organization and Biograph. In 1913 when Samuel Goldwyn, Jesse Lasky, and Cecil B. De Mille came west to produce *The Squaw Man* in a barn, they had only a few thousand dollars and the talents of an unknown actress, Clara Kimball Young. The producers were amazed when orders for their film poured in from former vaudeville houses and nickelodeons that had been transformed into "movie parlors."

The earliest movie makers were a motley lot. Producer William Fox was originally a cloth sponger on New York's Lower East Side. Marcus Loew moved from dealing in furs to operating a penny arcade. Samuel Goldwyn was originally a glove salesman while Carl Laemmle managed a clothing store. Louis B. Mayer, who became one of the richest and most powerful of these pioneer "cellulords," began as a rag collector.

By 1914, seventy-three firms were grinding out a "Western" every other day. Hollywood soon passed through its megaphone and custard-pie comedy phase of film making. Among directors who came west to "shoot pictures" was David Wark Griffith whose landmark pseudo-historical work *The Birth of a Nation* (1915) grossed $20 million. Outside the marquees of Hollywood's klieg-lighted premières, traffic stopped while fans ogled such silent-movie "stars" as Charlie Chaplin, an English pantomimist. As Chaplin's films captivated audiences throughout the world, his salary skyrocketed from $150 to $10,000 a week.

Also handsomely paid were the cowboy actors William S. Hart, Tom Mix, Ed ("Hoot") Gibson, and Will Rogers. After World War I led to the collapse of movie making in Europe, Hollywood's producers gained control of the world movie market. Their baronial self-confidence led its movie moguls to festoon their studios with pennants that read: "More Stars than There Are in Heaven." This was Hollywood's era of silver-screen idols, equipped with white silk shirts, bevies of aspiring starlets, sixteen-cylinder racing cars, and thirty-room white-stucco palaces.

Eventually the private lives of Hollywood actors, however, drew national criticism. In 1921, the career of comic Roscoe ("Fatty") Arbuckle was shattered by a scandal concerning the death of a would-be actress in the course of a wild party in San Francisco. Not only were Arbuckle's comedies thereafter banned from the screen, but public calls for censorship grew so strong that in 1922 the major producers formed the Motion Picture Producers and Distributors Association. This office was headed by former Postmaster General Will H. Hays, who encouraged the "moral ending" to films, transforming most controversial pictures into pious platitudes.

No one had yet foreseen that a sudden technological innovation would greatly increase the size of theater audiences: this was the development of sound to accompany the formerly silent films. In 1927, *The Jazz Singer* was the first motion picture with a sound track. In 1927 this "talkie" revolutionized the movie industry. Actors with squeaky, high-pitched voices vanished and were replaced by the Clark Gables, Claudette Colberts, and Joan Crawfords. By the late 1920s, for twenty-five cents, in a carpeted atmosphere of popcorn and Coca Cola, America's movie-goers numbered at least 50 million each week.

Director-producer Cecil B. De Mille created pretentious productions such as *The King of Kings* (1927) and *Cleopatra* (1934). De Mille's films, with hundreds of paint-bedaubed extras, chariot races, and papier-mâché monuments, featured elephantine epics in which showmanship regularly triumphed over art. Boy-meets-girl plots, big-laugh comedies, and song-and-dance extravaganzas furnished an escape to viewers, especially during the 1929–1932 depression years. As film became an ingrained feature of popular culture, Hollywood set the fashion for young people in dress, home furnishings, and even married life.

Many films, even in this relatively early period, were subject to the charge of glorifying violence, corruption, and sex. Some representative titles included *Ladies Must Dress, Parlor, Bedroom, and Bath, The Love Flower, Old Wives for New, Paid to Love,* and *Theodora Goes Wild.* One newspaper ad of the 1930s spoke of a movie featuring "beautiful jazz babies, champagne baths, midnight revels, petting parties in the purple dawn, all ending in one terrific smashing climax that makes you gasp."

On the eve of World War II, Hollywood attracted a number of talented European refugees. In 1940 Jean Renoir, son of France's impressionist painter, escaped from the Nazis in order to direct Hollywood films. Foreign composers Igor Stravinsky, Arnold Schoenberg, Kurt Weill, and Bertholt Brecht were joined there by director Billy Wilder and writers Lion Feuchtwanger, Thomas Mann, and Franz Werfel. Hollywood also attracted composers Dmitri Tiomkin and Miklós Rózsa.

Also drawn to Hollywood were novelists, journalists, and playwrights, among them Sinclair Lewis, Theodore Dreiser and William Faulkner. Nathanael West wrote about the ways in which Hollywood wasted such talent in his novel *The Day of the Locust.* L. Frank Baum, a former castor oil salesman who had written *The Wonderful Wizard of Oz,* took the name "Oz" from the bottom drawer of his file cabinet, which he had labeled o to z. In 1940 a much better writer, Ernest Hemingway, sold a screenplay of his *For Whom the Bell Tolls* to the movie makers, but he hated the Hollywood experience, as did his contemporary F. Scott Fitzgerald.

Occasionally Hollywood produced excellent films, like *All Quiet on the Western Front* (1930), *The Informer* (1935), and Orson Welles's *Citizen Kane* (1940). With *Citizen Kane* the young Welles took the industry by storm, directing, writing, and acting in the film. Welles was one of the first directors to use long, fluid tracking shots and the innovative technique of sound montage. Eventually a new generation of producer-directors combined both acting and writing. In the 1950s, director Elia Kazan and Marlon Brando, a new "method actor," exemplified a more vital and realistic approach in films like *On the Waterfront*.

Film versions of classical literature such as *Anna Karenina, Wuthering Heights*, and *War and Peace* made these works familiar to many who never had, or would have read them. The world of cinema also attracted the talented animator Walt Disney who, in 1955, founded Disneyland in Anaheim. It became the largest tourist attraction in the world.

After 1948, antitrust suits forced the major "Big Five" studios to divest themselves of lucrative theater chains. It was then argued that independent theater owners did not stand a chance against studio-owned theaters, which showed the best films first, even exclusively. Gloom settled over the film industry. Beset by burgeoning production costs, and hard hit by the growing competition of television, survival of the film studios in some cases came to depend upon the production of "made for TV" movies. Indeed, Hollywood and Burbank became West Coast television production and transmission centers.

Marilyn Monroe in
Gentlemen Prefer Blondes.
Courtesy of Photofest.

A variety of twentieth-century artists have also had their effect upon modern California. Among its painters were Phil Dike, Barse Miller, Rex Brandt, Millard Sheets, and sculptor Gutzon Borglum, who began his career at San Francisco. Ultimately Borglum was commissioned to carve and drill out the features of four outstanding U.S. presidents in the granite cliffs of Mount Rushmore in South Dakota. Another California sculptor and book illustrator, Joe Mora, also became well known outside the state, as did printmaker and painter Edward Borein.

Outstanding among California photographers, in addition to Muybridge, was Carleton E. Watkins. Mount Watkins, a massive granite peak atop the Yosemite Valley, is named after him. An equally distinguished photographer was the German-born Arnold Genthe. After the 1906 San Francisco fire and earthquake, he wandered along its streets documenting the devastation in light and shadows.

The best-known modern California photographers include Edward Weston and Ansel Adams. Adams's Yosemite photos are especially sharp and vivid in tone while Weston achieved an international reputation with his black-and-white depictions of nature and humans alike. Both men lived near Carmel, endlessly photographing its unique surrounding scenery.

As early as the 1920s, art colonies at Carmel, Santa Barbara, and Laguna Beach reflected deepening interest in sculpture, painting, mosaicwork, and architectural design. Art institutes located in Los Angeles included the Otis, Chouinard, and Art-Center schools. Museums too grew in the richness of their holdings. The Huntington Art Gallery in San Marino obtained increasing numbers of paintings in the English Renaissance style. The Crocker Art Gallery at Sacramento and the De Young Museum in San Francisco also enlarged their collections. The Southwest Museum at Los Angeles likewise steadily improved its holdings of Native-American art and artifacts.

One of the most bizarre architectural phenomena in modern California was the artistry of an Italian immigrant, Simon Rodia, builder of the Watts Towers. Located near Los Angeles, these novel creations were fashioned out of bits of glass, tile, and artifacts garnered from junk heaps. Rodia built the first tower in 1921. By the 1960s, after thirty-three years, he had erected gigantic structures made out of concrete, steel, and rubble. These have been called enduring marvels of folk art.

After the turn of the century, the Mexican adobe ranch house inspired a "mission revival" architecture. A prime example is Riverside's Mission Inn. Its style shared popularity with the mauve wooden California bungalows of Charles Sumner Greene and Henry Mather Greene, which derived from the arts and crafts movement. These dwellings combined European chalets with Asian-inspired ornamentation.

More modern architects, among them Frank Lloyd Wright, Rudolph M. Schindler, and Richard Neutra, built some of their first experimental structures in California. But they hardly replaced the hodgepodge of styles that included Queen Anne, Hawaiian, Oriental, Tudor, Jacobean, French chateau, Georgian, Mount Vernon colonial, Egyptian and Mayan, Cape Cod fishermen's cottages, or Hopi Indian dwellings replete with rope ladders.

In the interwar period no architect was more popular than Wallace Neff. He was heavily influenced by Spanish and Italian building design. Neff built residences throughout the wealthy enclaves of San Marino and Beverly Hills. He also was a favorite designer of mansions for movie stars, including Mary Pickford and Douglas Fairbanks. Other architects also utilized Neff's Spanish white-stucco walls, Tuscan red-tile roofs, and Romanesque arches; three of these who became popular from the 1920s to the 1940s were Reginald Johnson, Gordon Kaufmann, and Roland Coate.

At San Diego, Irving Gill became its best-known architect. Also popular was Bertram Goodhue, who also used white stucco and red tile in his buildings. Except for his leaner, more angular, Los Angeles Public Library, Goodhue's designs utilized motifs found in early Spanish and Mexican architecture.

In San Francisco, between the two world wars, architects Willis Polk, Bernard Maybeck, and John Galen Howard also became popular. Polk had designed the Ferry building and was one of the planners of the city's Civic Center. He also constructed the Hallidie Building, the world's first glass skyscraper.

By the mid-1930s, Richard Neutra, a Viennese, introduced functional houses in the Los Angeles area. His style evoked elements of Frank Lloyd Wright's modernism. Both Neutra and Wright stressed the practical in residential construction: their split-level houses offered increased living space, wide windows, and enclosed recreation areas.

Two unique women also made their mark in California landscape architecture. Beatrix Farrand and Florence Yoch created dozens of unique designs for private residences, public courtyards, and educational institutions. Yoch also became known for designing sets for such ambitious films as *Gone With the Wind*. Both women adapted traditional landscape and garden plans to California. Farrand landscaped both the Caltech and Occidental college campuses.

Varying styles of architecture found expression in the founding of state collegiate institutions. The first of these to require an entire new campus plan was the former State Normal School at Los Angeles; it ultimately became the University of California at Los Angeles, or UCLA, in Westwood. The legislature created other campuses of the university

University of California, Berkeley, central campus dominated by its "campanile." University of California. Photograph by Dennis Galloway.

as well as new state college campuses. Also participating in public education are some ninety city colleges.

The California Institute of Technology (Caltech) in Pasadena, founded as the Polytechnic or Throop College of Technology, specializes in the hard sciences. In the 1950s its world-renowned Jet Propulsion Laboratory, or JPL (operated for the National Aeronautics and Space Administration, or NASA) supervised the manufacture of the United States's first artificial earth satellites. Then, on June 2, 1966, a JPL lunar module achieved the first soft landing on the moon. Many other space launches followed this initial probe.

Another research center is the Lawrence Radiation Laboratory of the University of California at Livermore. Cyclotrons exist at both the Berkeley and Los Angeles campuses of the university. Its law schools, medical facilities, observatories, and institutes all expanded rapidly. The Scripps Institute of Oceanography at La Jolla operates research vessels throughout the Pacific area. Also at La Jolla is the Salk Institute for Biological Studies, named for the discoverer of poliomyelitis vaccine.

In the field of astronomy the Lick Observatory at Mount Hamilton near San Jose—technically also a campus of the University of California—has been in operation since 1874. Better known is the Mount Wilson Observatory, whose 100-inch telescope operated from 1917 to 1985. Located at Mount Palomar Observatory in San Diego County is a 200-inch telescope, in operation since 1948.

Associated with California's educational and scientific institutions are other cultural institutions. California possesses two major historical societies. The California Historical Society, at San Francisco, and the Historical Society of Southern California, at Los Angeles, both print quarterlies. The Bancroft Library of the University of California at Berkeley and the Hoover Library of War, Revolution, and Peace at Stanford have become internationally-known research centers.

More eclectic are two museums near Westwood and Malibu built by the J. Paul Getty trust. Getty, who had made his first fortune in southern California's oil fields, appropriately established his first museum in Malibu. In 1991 his executors, holding an endowment of $2 billion, four times that of the Metropolitan Museum of Art in New York City, began construction of a new site in Brentwood.

Today the "Getty's" collections complement the Huntington's, which also houses thousands of rare books and manuscripts. Its renowned "Blue Boy," painted by Thomas Gainsborough, and "Pinkie," by Thomas Lawrence, form the centerpieces of the finest group of full-length British portraits that exist anywhere. The Huntington also provides visitors with views of English, Japanese, and Australian botanical gardens.

Sports also continue to attract extravagant public support. In 1932 the Los Angeles coliseum was the site of the Olympic games, in which Mildred (Babe) Zaharias, then the greatest woman athlete in the world, performed. California was host to the Olympics again in 1984. Pasadena's Rose Bowl, known as the granddaddy of all the annual bowl games, was the site that year of the Olympic soccer matches.

In addition to the Los Angeles Dodgers and the San Francisco Giants, other professional baseball teams include the San Diego Padres, the Angels at Anaheim, and the Oakland Athletics. Based in Los Angeles are the Lakers of the National Basketball Association (NBA) and, in the same league, the Los Angeles Clippers. The Bay area is represented on the basketball court by the Golden State Warriors, and Sacramento is the home city of the Kings. Californians also are football enthusiasts, and the San Francisco Forty-niners dominated the National Football League (NFL) in the 1980s; overall the "Niners" played in and won an impressive five Superbowls, and they continue as a powerhouse. Other professional football teams include the three-time Superbowl champion Oakland Raiders and the Chargers of San Diego.

Among golfers, Billy Casper, Gene Littler, Johnny Miller, and Ken Venturi became international champions. In tennis, California has produced Richard "Pancho" Gonzalez, Jack Kramer, Pete Sampras, Michael Chang, and two outstanding women tennis players, Billie Jean King and Tracy Austin. In horse racing, Santa Anita, Hollywood Park, Del

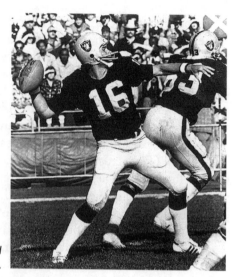

Jim Plunkett, Quarterback of the Oakland
Raiders in two of their Superbowl wins.

Mar, and the Bay Meadows tracks continue to attract thousands of fans annually.

Finally, even professional hockey found its way to California in the twentieth century, with fans flocking to see the Los Angeles Kings, the San Jose Sharks, and the Anaheim Mighty Ducks, a team-name inspired by a Disney movie.

Although the national press has intermittently satirized California as a "land of pop and honey," its culture takes varying forms. For example, today's Rand (Research and Development) Corporation at Santa Monica, a semipublic agency initially created to carry on strategic studies, brings together political scientists, physicists, and mathematicians. Other unique "think tanks"—from the Silicon Valley in the north to San Diego on the Mexican border—engage in cutting-edge research, the scope of which is universal.

Selected Readings

Regarding novelists see Brian St. Pierre, *John Steinbeck: The California Years* (1984); Harry T. Moore, *The Novels of John Steinbeck* (1939); Nelson Valjean, *John Steinbeck, The Errant Knight* (1975) and Martin Stoddard, *California Writers* (1984). William Saroyan's *My Name is Aram* (1940) and *The Human Comedy* (1943) are partly autobiographical. On Jeffers see Lawrence Clark Powell, *Robinson Jeffers: The Man and His Work* (1940); Frederick J. Carpenter, *Robinson Jeffers* (1952); Radcliffe Squires, *The Loyalties of Robinson Jeffers* (1956) and Melba Berry Bennett, *The Stone Mason of Tor House* (1966).

On architecture see Frank J. Taylor, *Land of Homes* (1929); Richard Neutra, *Mystery and Realities of the Site* (1951); Kurt Baer, *Architecture of the Cali-*

fornia Missions (1958); Karen Weitze, *California's Mission Revival* (1984); Harold Kirker, *California's Architectural Frontier* (1960); Geoffrey E. Bangs, *Portals West: A Folio of Late Nineteenth Century Architecture in California* (1960); Randell L. Makinson, *Greene & Greene: Architecture as a Fine Art* (1977); Reyner Banham, *Los Angeles: The Architecture of Four Ecologies* (1971); Esther McCoy, *Five California Architects* (1960) and McCoy, *Richard Neutra* (1960); Frank Harris, ed., *A Guide to Contemporary Architecture in Southern California* (1951); Joseph A. Baird, *Time's Wondrous Changes, San Francisco's Architecture, 1776–1915* (1962); David Gebhard and Robert Winter, *Los Angeles, An Architectural Guide* (1994) and their *Guide to Architecture in San Francisco and Northern California* (1995) as well as Beth Dunlop, *Building a Dream: The Art of Disney Architecture* (1996).

Regarding printing, see James D. Hart's *Fine Printing in California* (1960); Ward Ritchie, *A Bookman's View of Los Angeles* (1961). Photographic commentary is in Mary V. Jessup Hood and Robert Bartlett Haas, "Eadweard Muybridge's Yosemite Valley Photographs, 1867–1872," *California Historical Society Quarterly* 42 (March 1963), 5–26 and Haas, *Muybridge, Man in Motion* (1976); Joyce R. Muench, ed., *West Coast Portrait* (1946); Edward Weston, *My Camera on Point Lobos* (1950); Charis Wilson Weston and Edward Weston, *California and the West* (1940); Ansel Adams with Nancy Newhall, *This Is the American Earth* (1959), and Adams, *Yosemite Valley* (1959) and Jonathan Spaulding, *Ansel Adams and the American Landscape* (1997).

Regarding art see Carl Oscar Borg and Millard Sheets, *Cross, Sword, and Gold Pan* (1936); Helen Laird, *Carl Oscar Borg and the Magic Region* (1984); Edith Hamlin, "Maynard Dixon, Artist of the West," *California Historical Quarterly* 53 (Fall 1974), 361–71; Patricia Trenton, *California Light* (1990) and Trenton, *Independent Spirits: Women Painters of the American West* (1997); Susan Landauer, *California Impressionists* (1996); Paul Karlstrom, ed., *On the Edge of America: California Modernist Art* (1996); Jeanne Van Nostrand, *The First Hundred Years of Painting in California* (1980); D. C. McCall, *California Artists, 1935 to 1956* (1981) and Harvey Jones, *Masterpieces of the California Decorative Style* (1980).

About Hollywood see Sumiko Higashi, *Cecil B. De Mille and American Culture: the Silent Era* (1994); Charles Clarke, *Early Film Making in Los Angeles* (1976); Tina Lent, "The Dark Side of the Dream: The Image of Los Angeles in Film Noir," *Southern California Quarterly* 69 (Winter 1987), 329–48; Richard Batman, "D. W. Griffith: The Lean Years," *California Historical Society Quarterly* 44 (September 1965), 195–204; Otto Friedrich, *City of Nets: A Portrait of Hollywood in the 1940s* (1986); Leo C. Rosten, *Hollywood: The Movie Colony, the Movie Makers* (1941); Raymond Moley, *The Hays Office* (1945); and novels by Harry Leon Wilson, *Merton of the Movies* (1922); Nathanael West, *The Day of the Locust* (1939) and Budd Schulberg's *What Makes Sammy Run* (1941).

On the movie moguls see Neil Gabler, *An Empire of Their Own: How the Jews Invented Hollywood* (1989); Bosley Crowther, *Hollywood Rajah: The Life and Times of Louis B. Mayer* (1960); A. R. Fulton, *Motion Pictures . . .*

From Silent Films to the Age of Television (1960); Edward Wagenknecht, *The Movies in the Age of Innocence* (1962); Fred J. Balshofer and Arthur C. Miller, *One Reel a Week* (1967); George N. Fenin and William K. Everson, *The Western, From Silents to Cinerama* (1962); Kenneth MacGowan, *Behind the Screen: The History and Techniques of the Motion Picture* (1965); Beth Day, *This Was Hollywood* (1960); Hortense Powdermaker, *Hollywood: The Dream Factory* (1951) and Mervyn Le Roy, *It Takes More Than Talent* (1953).

Regarding evangelism see Daniel Epstein, *Sister Aimee* (1993); Lately Thomas, *The Vanishing Evangelist* (1959) and Robert Bahr, *Least of All Saints: The Story of Aimee Semple McPherson* (1979). A whitewash of southern California's "cemetery culture" is Adela Rogers St. Johns, *First Step Up Toward Heaven* (1959), whereas Evelyn Waugh's *The Loved One* (1948) and Aldous Huxley's *After Many a Summer Dies the Swan* (1939), are both novels that debunk the phenomenon. Regarding utopian colonies see Robert V. Hine, *California's Utopian Colonies* (1953) and Hine, *California Utopianism: Contemplations of Eden* (1981) as well as Emmett A. Greenwalt, *The Point Loma Community in California, 1897–1942* (1955).

For literature see Pearsall and Ursula Erickson, eds., *The Californians: Writings of Their Past and Present* (1960); Richard Lehan, *Los Angeles in Fiction* (1981); Robert Kirsch and William Murphy, *West of the West* (1967); Lawrence Clark Powell, *Land of Fiction* (1952); Cynthia Lindsay, *The Natives Are Restless* (1960) and Jessamyn West, *South of the Angels* (1960).

Two histories of the state's major historical societies are Henry R. Wagner, "California Historical Society, 1852–1922," *California Historical Society* Quarterly 1 (July 1922), 9–22 and Jane Apostol, *The Historical Society of Southern California: A Centennial History* (1991).

On the "Beatniks," consult Gene Feldman and Max Gartenberg, eds., *The Beat Generation and the Angry Young Men* (1958); Thomas Parkinson, ed., *A Casebook on the Beat* (1961); and Lawrence Lipton, *The Holy Barbarians* (1959). More recent are John Maynard, *Venice West: The Beat Generation in Southern California* (1991) and Michael Davidson, *The San Francisco Renaissance* (1989).

Wartime Problems

///////// **CHAPTER 33**

Hitler Na chin

During the years preceding World War II, Californians, like other Americans, had become disturbed over the threat posed by the European dictators and the Japanese military clique. The unexpected attack upon Pearl Harbor in Hawaii by Japanese dive bombers on December 7, 1941, created an aggressive mood statewide. Californians soon also heard of the surrender of Sumatra, Borneo, and the Philippines. A new anxiety ran through California.

The war years brought great economic dislocations and social tensions. Manpower problems, rationing, transportation difficulties, and the need to house defense workers became the order of the day. Military training camps, shipyards, and aircraft factories had to be constructed quickly. Nothing must impede the job of getting planes, tanks, and guns to the fighting front. California's war industries drew workers from all parts of the United States. The state dismantled its border "bum blockade" erected against "Okies" and "Arkies." Now its officials encouraged workers to flock westward for employment in its new war plants. Local chambers of commerce focused attention upon getting industries to move to California, or to establish branch plants in the West.

Even before the Pearl Harbor raid, internal security too had become a paramount consideration. During 1940, the state legislature had already passed the Dilworth Anti-Spy Bill, the Slater Anti-Sabotage Act, and the Tenney Anti-Subversive law. This legislation reflected mounting antipathy against the Japanese.

By 1940 there were 120,000 Japanese in California. Their increasing affluence made them more vulnerable to the old racist bugaboo that

265

Asians were unassimilable. As fishermen, cannery workers, and farmers, they still awakened the hostility of envious whites.

After the attack on Pearl Harbor, apprehension spread to the mainland. During 1942 a lone Japanese submarine surfaced at Goleta, near Santa Barbara, and fired a shell that splintered the end of a wooden jetty. Jittery local residents put their houses up for sale and made plans to flee. On February 25, 1942, the Los Angeles *Times* boldly, and erroneously, reported that Japanese planes had bombed the city, damaging defense installations. Anti-aircraft fire had indeed been shot into the sky, but against wholly imaginary aircraft.

Many of the Japanese living in California were second-generation *Nisei*, Japanese Americans born and educated in the United States. They were thereby full-fledged American citizens. There was no evidence that any were disloyal. But this did not alter sometimes hysterical public demands that all Japanese in the country be interned, lest they somehow manage to collaborate with the enemy. California Japanese were forced to sell their homes, businesses, and land at a fraction of their value—much of this property was snatched up by greedy whites. In addition, their radios, cameras and all "suspicious" personal effects were confiscated by federal agents. On February 18, 1942, President Roosevelt signed Executive Order 9066, placing all resident Japanese under military control.

Although this World War II headline produced widespread hysteria, actual damage by a single bomb was negligible.

Japanese Americans on their way to a relocation camp, 1942. Courtesy of the National Archives.

Next General John L. DeWitt, head of the Western Defense Command, ordered that some 112,000 West Coast Japanese, two-thirds of them American citizens, were subject to relocation. Thousands were taken from their homes and businesses and, in full view of onlookers, were herded onto buses that took them away to internment camps. Among them were *Issei* (persons born in Japan), Nisei, and *Kibei* (American-born but partly educated in Japan). The move to detain these innocent persons was at the insistence of Earl Warren, then California's attorney general, who was running for election as governor. He was influenced by such nativist groups as the State Grange, the American Legion, the Native Sons and Daughters of the Golden West, as well as by the State Federation of Labor. His opponent, Governor Culbert Olson, also had to pay attention to the exclusionist California Joint Immigration Committee.

Some Japanese were given the choice of "relocation" in the Midwest or on the East Coast. Most were evacuated to security camps in California or to outlying internment centers. There they lived in stark conditions, behind barbed wire, and under military guard. Their only "crime" was Japanese ancestry. Even the U.S. citizens among them were considered potential enemies by the Department of the Army.

Few citizens had the courage to speak out against the internment of "enemy" aliens. Because these also included certain Germans and Italians, in 1942 the German-born novelist Thomas Mann protested before the Tolan Committee. Other artists, mostly foreign-born, including Lion Feuchtwanger, Bruno Frank, and Arturo Toscanini, sent telegrams to Washington on behalf of European internees. So did physicist Albert Einstein, writer Cesare Borgese, and the Italian exile Count Carlo Sforza. In an atmosphere of suspicion, their efforts, however, were unpopular.

By 1944 the first Japanese internees were allowed to leave relocation centers for coastal areas. In 1946 their incarceration was ended. But only about 65,000 who had been forced to leave the West Coast ever returned there. Some settled in the Midwest and in the East. Historians who have studied this evacuation in calmer postwar years have concluded that it represented a serious violation of constitutional rights. Only long after the war did the federal government authorize payments of $20,000 to some internees. By then most of the Issei among them were dead.

One should note, however, that a remarkable change eventually occurred in the public attitude toward the Japanese. Some Japanese Americans volunteered for duty in the armed services. These Nisei performed magnificently during the war in their highly decorated 442nd Regimental Combat Team. Ironically, a new respect for Japan flowered after its defeat. American occupation troops acquired a special taste for that country's lifestyle and technological skills. Some returned home with Japanese brides.

Before and after the war, Japanese Americans still constituted but a fraction of the U.S. population, yet their success story is almost unmatched by any other minority. They have "outwhited the whites." Education, a low crime rate, and a high rate of professional attainment have made them model citizens. Only in recent years have angry young Japanese Americans begun to challenge "the system" to which their parents accommodated.

Another minority group attracted headlines during World War II. In 1943, youthful Mexican gang members, known as *pachucos,* got into trouble with the Los Angeles police. Accused of carrying switchblade knives in their pockets and razor blades in their long hair, they became involved in violent confrontations with some navy and marine veterans. White hoodlums too joined in the street fights against the Mexican "zoot suiters" who wore long jackets and baggy pants. Their gang activity embarrassed many of the older, settled Mexican-American residents who, like the Japanese, had fought hard for acceptance by the dominant culture.

Though, as attorney general, Earl Warren had played a role in Japanese internment, he was elected governor in 1943. Warren knew how to stay clear of feuds within his Republican party and became a popular figure. Like old Hiram Johnson, whose picture Warren hung in his Sacramento office, he was a Progressive, and both governors attracted moderate voters of all parties. Informal in manner, Warren projected a reassuring image during the stressful wartime period.

Because of the war, Warren enjoyed a moratorium on political and labor discord. Most labor disputes came to be handled by voluntary arbitration: in some cases the governor himself acted as arbitrator. His judgment and good faith were trusted by all sides. Warren easily won reelection in 1946 and 1950, the only California governor ever to serve three terms.

The myriad activities associated with World War II drew hundreds of thousands of defense workers, soldiers, sailors, and airmen into the state. Military posts became virtual cities, with their own supply, transportation, and postal facilities. One of the largest, Camp Roberts, housed upwards of 50,000 men. Another big army depot was Fort Ord, located along the shoreline between Monterey and Salinas. Camp Pendleton, near Oceanside, became a West Coast base for the marines. San Diego, Long Beach, and Mare Island, already major naval bases, increased their facilities manyfold. And there were air training centers at March Field, the El Toro Marine Air Depot, and the Alameda Naval Air Station. California's ports were converted into huge troop embarkation centers for the Pacific war zone.

On the Richmond, Oakland, and San Pedro waterfronts the Todd and Bethlehem shipyards hammered out hundreds of combat vessels. The United States Maritime Commission also reopened shipyards at Sausalito and Vallejo that had been idle since World War I. The Henry J. Kaiser enterprises established new facilities to build cruisers, destroyers, and cargo carriers. The labor force at Kaiser's Richmond Yard alone numbered more than 100,000. Kaiser controlled the "Calship" corporation and also constructed the largest steel mill in the American West, at Fontana.

Even before 1941, California steel, chemical, and machine tool firms had engaged in "defense production." The population of the state's industrial centers quickly expanded. Vallejo jumped from 20,000 residents in 1941 to 100,000 in 1943. Severe housing shortages forced thousands of workers to crowd into trailer parks; often these people commuted to distant plants engaged in war-related enterprises.

No segment of the booming California economy grew more rapidly than the aircraft industry, though airplanes had been produced in the state many years before the outbreak of World War II. Among pioneer plane designers was Glenn L. Martin. At Los Angeles, Martin had established his own company in 1912 but, in 1929, moved to Baltimore. At San Diego, in 1927, Charles Lindbergh, "The Lone Eagle," commissioned San Diego's Ryan Aeronautical Corporation to build his *Spirit of Saint Louis,* in which "Lindy" became the first person to fly across the Atlantic Ocean.

By 1935 the output of California's aircraft industry reached $20 million annually. By 1941, placement orders for warplanes by foreign governments as well as the U.S. government made California vital to the rearmament program of the "free nations" of the world. The Douglas and Lockheed plants became cornerstones of American airpower.

One of the giants of the aircraft industry, the Lockheed Aircraft Company, was founded by Malcolm and Allan Loughead, who sold their then moribund company in 1932 to investment banker Robert E. Gross. Both Lindbergh and the renowned woman pilot Amelia Earhart were to set flying records in Lockheed aircraft. Gross helped to develop the twin-engined Electra, which earned his company an international reputation. During the height of the war, Lockheed employed a work force of 90,000 persons who built 20,000 planes.

Donald Douglas, who had learned aeronautical engineering from Martin, went on to build a plant of his own at Burbank. In order to meet the heavy demand for planes, Douglas trained workers who had never operated an acetylene welding torch or a rivet gun. These people constructed Havoc Nightfighters for the British, Liberators, Flying Fortresses (B-17s), transports, and dive bombers. Lockheed produced Hudson bombers for Britain, the P-38 fighter, the Ventura, and the 128-passenger Constitution. Other war plants, notably Consolidated Vultee (founded by Gerard Vultee), North American, Northrop, and the Hughes aircraft companies, also expanded spectacularly.

In April 1945, as the war in Europe drew to a close, representatives of forty-six nations met at San Francisco to transform wartime alliances against the Axis powers into a permanent structure for world peace. The United Nations Charter was signed there on October 24, 1945. Incidentally, among the reporters covering this event was a recently demobilized veteran named John F. Kennedy, future president of the United States.

World War II was one of the major turning points of California history. It speeded up industrialization, aided by an outpouring of government funds. The war also accelerated urban growth and, to some degree, greater tolerance toward minority groups. Women, blacks, and Hispanics had been sorely needed in the war effort: on the battlefront and on the home front. Each group had been tested by the experience, and each proved its strength. By war's end the state had emerged as a new portal to the outside world.

Selected Readings

On World War II see Martin J. Schiesl, "City Planning and the Federal Government in World War II: The Los Angeles Experience," *California Historical Quarterly* 59 (Summer 1980), 127–43; Arthur Verge, *Paradise Transformed: Los Angeles During the Second World War* (1993); Roger Lotchin, "California Cities and the Hurricane of Change: World War II in San Francisco, Los Angeles, and the San Diego Metropolitan Areas," *Pacific Historical Review* 63 (August 1994), 393–420; Abraham Shragge, "A New Federal City," *Pacific Historical Review* 63 (August 1994), 333–61; Marilynn Johnson, *The Second Gold Rush: Oakland and the East Bay in World War II* (1993) and Gerald Nash, *The American West Transformed: The Impact of the Second World War* (1985).

Regarding Japanese grievances consult Donald and Nadine Hata, *Japanese Americans and World War II* (1995); Jacobus ten Broek and Edward N. Barnhart, *Prejudice, War, and the Constitution* (1954); Peter Irons, *Justice at War* (1983); Stanley Gerard, "Justice Deferred . . . ," *Southern California Quarterly* 74 (Summer 1992), 181–206. The United States Army version of Japanese relocation is *Japanese Evacuation from the West Coast* (1943). See also Stetson Conn, "The Decision to Evacuate the Japanese from the Pacific Coast, 1942," in Kent Roberts Greenfield, *Command Decisions* (1959), and Stetson Conn, *Guarding the United States and Its Outposts* (1964); Miné Okubo, *Citizen 13660* (repr. 1983); Morton Grodzins, *Americans Betrayed: Politics and the Japanese Evacuation* (1949); Roger Daniels, *Concentration Camps USA: Japanese Americans and World War II* (1971) and his *The Decision to Relocate the Japanese Americans* (1975); Harry Kitano, *Japanese Americans, The Evolution of a Subculture* (1969); Bill Hosokawa, *Nisei, the Quiet Americans* (1969); Jeanne Wakatsuki and James Houston, *Farewell to Manzanar* (1973); Leonard Bloom and Ruth Riemar, *Removal and Return* (1949); Edward N. Barnhart, "The Individual Exclusion of Japanese Americans in World War II," *Pacific Historical Review* 29 (May 1960), 111–30; Audrie Girdner and Anne Loftis, *The Evacuation of the Japanese-Americans During World War II* (1969); Michi Weglyn, *Years of Infamy* (1976); John Modell, *The Economics and Politics of Racial Accommodation: The Japanese of Los Angeles, 1900–1942* (1977) and Earl Warren, *Memoirs* (1977).

Regarding other wartime racial strife see Maurizio Mazón, *The Zoot Suit Riots . . .* (1984); Ralph Banay, "A Psychiatrist Looks at the Zoot Suit," *Probation* 12 (February 1944), 81–85; Harold De Witt, "The Watsonville Anti-Filipino Riot of 1930," *Southern California Quarterly* 61 (Fall 1979), 291–302; and Ricardo Romo, "Southern California and the Origins of Latino Civil-Rights Activism," *Western Legal History* 3 (Summer/Fall, 1990), 379–406.

Concerning aviation see Wayne Biddle, *Barons of the Sky: From Early Flight to Strategic Warfare* (1991); William Schoneberger, *California Wings:*

A History of Aviation in the Golden State (1984); Kenneth M. Johnson, *Aerial California: An Account of Early Flight in Northern and Southern California, . . . 1849 to World War I* (1961); Hugh Knowlton, *Air Transportation in the United States: Its Growth as a Business* (1941); Arlene Elliott, "The Rise of Aeronautics in California, 1849–1940," *Southern California Quarterly* 52 (March 1970), 1–32; and Roger W. Lotchin, *Fortress California, 1910–1961: From Warfare to Welfare* (1992).

California After World War II

As reconversion to a peacetime economy began, the possibility of business mortality among war-born plants worried civic leaders. Domination of manufacturing by companies that had grown big during the war was another threat. A third source of anxiety concerned future employment of the huge number of temporary wartime workers.

After the war ended, California faced a population avalanche. More than 300,000 service personnel returned to a state recently inundated by a human tide of new residents. Fortunately most of the returning veterans obtained postwar employment. The G.I. Bill of Rights paid those who had served to enroll in the college of their choice; emergency relief in this form also helped to better their employment prospects. A California State Reconstruction and Reemployment Commission supervised economic reconversion.

The war not only gave new life to manufacturing; it also helped diversify the economy. This expansion was overdue in California, where economic organization was clustered around too few major industries, among them citrus, film, aircraft, and oil. The war, furthermore, allowed California to benefit from a larger share of national per capita income than ever before.

Some of its products gained new prominence in the postwar era. Among these were wearing apparel (especially sportswear), jewelry, sports equipment, and footwear. Significant expansion also occurred in the manufacture of refrigeration equipment, technical instruments, chemicals, hardware, and cosmetics for national markets. Los Angeles continued as an automobile assembly depot second only to Detroit, as well as

California freeway intricacies. Courtesy of the Chevron Corporation.

a tube and tire center. Before the war, only minor smelting and refining of ferrous metals had occurred. After 1943, Kaiser's Fontana mill began to process iron ore from Eagle Mountain and tungsten from the Rand Mountains.

More permanent apartments, schools, business sites, and public facilities also had to be built, and this required the services of engineers, architects, and all sorts of construction workers. There seemed to be no end to the migration of postwar newcomers who crowded into the state. In 1940 California had a population of 6,907,387; it then ranked fifth among the states. By 1950, when the population reached 10,586,223, California had become the second most populous state in the nation. Schoolrooms were so crowded that teachers were forced to meet their classes in several shifts daily.

In those years of spreading housing tracts, thousands of war veterans formed new family units. Postwar California experienced one of the great construction booms of all time. For mile after mile, cities began to replicate themselves. Acres of raw lumber framework, stacks of bricks, and sacks of cement went into thousands of new dwellings. Large-scale tract development occurred at such "instant" cities as Westchester and West Covina in southern California and at Burlingame and Lafayette in the north.

One day during 1946, salesmen sold 107 homes at Lakewood Village within one hour! Its developers boasted that every fifteen minutes construction crews dug foundation trenches for a new tract home. Lakewood alone covered 3,300 acres of land and 133 miles of paved streets and driveways. Unincorporated communities, such as Saratoga, Campbell, Monte Sereno, Los Altos, and Milpitas in Santa Clara County, as well as Pacifica and Woodside in San Mateo County, incorporated themselves as new cities.

An incomplete freeway system became so jammed that California soon recorded the highest auto accident rate in the nation. In 1947, a ten-year highway construction program was voted upon by the legislature. The state spent more than $1 million per working day on new freeways and highways. Highway engineers planned a 12,500-mile statewide freeway system to link all cities with a population of 5,000 or more persons, and to tie these new roads into the federal highway system.

Automotive industries and services became a key element in all this planning. Organizations like the Automobile Club of Southern California grew politically powerful. By 1967, California had more drivers and cars registered—almost 10 million—and consumed more gasoline than any other state in the union. The Los Angeles area had become the fastest-growing petroleum fuel market in the world.

Meanwhile, traffic grew to be an increasingly critical issue. Although the legislature in 1964 had approved a Southern California Rapid Transit District (RTD) to plan intracity transportation, new road construction could not keep up with demand. Some blamed politicians, auto dealers, tire manufacturers, and threats of higher taxes for delays in developing a mass transport system. For years rapid transit remained in the planning stage as commuters continued to rely upon their personal automobiles. Most voters simply refused to abandon their freeway mentality.

An exception occurred at San Francisco where, in 1964, a freeway revolt stopped construction of its Embarcadero Freeway. The city and conservation groups also struggled to keep the state's Panhandle Freeway out of Golden Gate Park. In place of these roadways, construction of the Bay Area Rapid Transit (BART) system began. This light rail and bus project, built with public approval, proved to be highly successful. It connected most cities of the east bay. Tunnels dug under the bay then linked them to the peninsula via subway lines.

Other freeway revolts occurred at Laguna Beach and South Pasadena where irate citizens sought to prevent new freeways from bisecting residential areas as well as destroying parks and historic sites. Freeways were kept out of such beauty spots as Prairie Creek in Jedediah Smith Redwoods Park and Upper Crystal Springs Lake along the Junípero Serra Freeway.

For years the powerful Automobile Club of Southern California opposed the development of mass transit beyond buses. Other pro-automobile concerns were the major oil companies and car dealers. They reminded the public that subway systems could not be built without some form of government-financed support. Subsidies were especially needed in areas of low population density. Each year's delay led construction costs to grow astronomically, because of steady postwar inflation.

Population growth, meanwhile, forced expansion and reconstruction of civic areas. San Francisco, confined to a peninsula, had to utilize its land space carefully. Thus, the process of building skyward accelerated. The city also built Candlestick Park as a new home of the former New York Giants baseball club. In the postwar years Los Angeles too attracted the Brooklyn Dodgers and constructed a new stadium in Chavez Ravine. L.A. also undertook reconstruction of its central city. Around a central mall that covered 228 acres, new 20- to 40-story federal, state, county, and city government offices sprang up in formerly blighted areas.

Conservationists did not agree that all change meant progress. For example, in order to preserve their tiny community's decor, Carmel's residents refused to install new sidewalks and house numbering, even though this meant no home mail delivery. As the shift from single-family homes to apartments continued, California's urban skyline changed markedly. Much vertical rather than horizontal construction ensued. Rising land costs made it uneconomical to build single-family dwellings in downtown areas. Whether at Los Angeles, San Diego, or

BART commuters in the 19th Street Oakland subway station. The first twelve stations opened in 1972. Courtesy of San Francisco Convention & Visitors Bureau.

Oakland, a new style of supposedly efficient architecture featured multistoried apartments and office buildings, many of them built of "high-rise" lightweight metal and much window glass.

Continuing heavy defense expenditures by the federal government underwrote a large share of California's postwar reconstruction. The state increasingly possessed what amounted to a "nongovernmental civil service." Aircraft, missile, and instrument workers had come to rely upon the government for jobs. This made for employment vulnerability whenever defense expenditures were cut. For years, however, America's cold war and intensifying arms race with the Soviet Union provided juicy federal military contracts.

The establishment in 1954 of the Air Force's Space Technology Laboratory at Inglewood and Canoga Park, and the founding of the IBM Research Laboratory at San Jose and of Astronautics Inc., at San Diego, further immersed California in missile, rocket, and satellite research and development. A significant event of the late 1950s was the activation of the nation's first privately financed nuclear power plant at Vallecitos. In that decade the new Pacific Missile Range also became a major launching site. Meanwhile, after the war Vandenberg Air Force Base changed nearby Lompoc from a rural town, concerned with mining diatomaceous soil and flower raising, to a city of 30,000 inhabitants. Several hundred technological companies, which employed more than 100,000 persons, settled within a mile of Los Angeles's new international airport.

The 1950s also saw the dawn of the jet age. The first such experimental flight was achieved by experimental pilot Chuck Yeager at Edwards Air Force Base, a desolate moonscape on the Mojave Desert. This was followed by the supersonic flight of X-15, a combination of rocket and airplane.

By 1962, 40 percent of the nation's $6.1 billion in contracts for military testing and research went to California. New "university-industrial" campuses housed sophisticated engineering and technology facilities. California overexpanded its reliance upon defense contracts. By 1968 more than one-third of its industrial production was in the defense and space fields.

The state's "defense" industry had become highly inventive in the postwar era. North American's El Segundo plant developed the prototypes of the B-70 bomber and the X-15 airplane as well as the guidance and control systems of the Boeing Company's Minuteman missile. North American's Rocketdyne Division powered the ascent of 36 out of 40 of the first American space probes. Rocketdyne also developed the H-1 Saturn rocket engine. North American coordinated its efforts with those

A B-1 Bomber with its camouflaged paint scheme, Edwards Air Force Base. Official U.S. Air Force Photo.

of NASA, Caltech's JPL, and the Space Technology Laboratories, operated for the Air Force by Thompson, Ramo, Wooldridge, Inc. North American was the prime contractor of the Apollo moonship, while Rockwell International handled development of the Air Force's controversial B-1 bomber as well as NASA's Space Shuttle.

In the nuclear age, the Lockheed corporation of Burbank and Sunnyvale, like North American, remained active both in missile and aircraft production. Lockheed, in addition to producing the Polaris submarine missile for the United States Navy, was the main contractor for the Midas system of detecting ICBM (intercontinental ballistic missile) firings anywhere in the world. Lockheed played a key part as well in the development of the Samos "spy-in-the-sky" satellite.

By the 1970s, Lockheed's L-1011, a wide-bodied passenger jet, was featured in the fleets of major commercial airlines. Competing with that airplane was the McDonnell-Douglas DC-10, repeatedly modified after the war. That firm had successfully converted from production of the Apache and Hornet warplanes, as well as Delta and Tomahawk missiles, to manufacturing commercial airplanes. The best known of these are the MD-11, the MD-80, and the MD-90. In 1997 McDonnell-Douglas merged with the largest airplane company in the world, Boeing of Seattle.

At San Diego, Convair (later General Dynamics), another missile designer, built the F-106 Delta Dart fighter and the 880 jet airliner. Its prize product was the Atlas ICBM, a missile with a range of almost 10,000 miles.

In support of California's plane and missile industry, more than 200 high-tech electronic firms operated plants in the peninsula suburbs south of San Francisco alone. Among these were such national companies as IBM, ITT, Ampex, Hewlett-Packard, Western Electric, Raytheon, Remington Rand, Sylvania, Sperry-Rand, Zenith, Motorola, Philco, and General Electric. Today the phrase *Silicon Valley* connotes electronic specialization worldwide.

More and more invested wealth came to be centered in the state, which moved beyond regional domination into national leadership. Modern California has been described as "America only more so." In recent years the state's "gross product" has been exceeded only by that of the United States itself and a few other countries.

Politically too California's power grew at the national level. In 1953, when President Dwight Eisenhower called Governor Earl Warren to Washington to become chief justice of the United States, California's "Warren era" of politics came to a close. Soon another of its politicians, Richard Milhous Nixon, would rise to national prominence. A former Navy veteran, in 1946 he first ran for the seat held by liberal congressman Jerry Voorhis, a Democrat in Nixon's Yorba Linda home district. Nixon won and four years later ran for the U.S. Senate against Helen Gahagan Douglas, a liberal Democratic congresswoman and wife of film star Melvyn Douglas. In his campaign Nixon, a staunch cold warrior who was quick to point his finger at alleged "Communists," suggested that both Voorhis and Douglas were lacking in their anti-Communist convictions.

During the nation's second Red scare, spearheaded by Republican Senator Joseph McCarthy of Wisconsin, treasonable accusations against numerous public officials—and even against film stars and others connected to the entertainment industry—were rampant. Congressman Nixon's career was furthered by passage of the restrictive anti-Communist Mundt-Nixon Immigration Act. Also, bolstering his image as an internal-security specialist was his membership on the House Un-American Activities Committee, which helped bring to trial former State Department aide Alger Hiss for perjury concerning espionage charges. In these politically tense years, state senator Jack B. Tenney headed a committee that claimed to have detected Communists in California's government and educational circles. In order to uproot these alleged subversives in public life, Tenney recommended that teachers and government employees be required to sign a "loyalty oath." Beginning in 1949, a "test-oath" controversy raged on the campuses of the University of California. Professors who refused to sign an oath stating that they were not Communists and were loyal to the United States were dismissed. Ultimately the state supreme court ruled imposition of this oath invalid. But, in 1950, the legislature's Levering Act required an even more elaborate oath of all state employees. In the meantime, the University of California had lost some of its most talented and independent-minded faculty members. In 1958 yet another California loyalty oath was struck down by the U.S. Supreme Court.

From 1952 until 1960, Nixon, who had become vice president under Eisenhower, occupied the most prestigious position of any California Republican. Nixon, like Earl Warren earlier, benefitted from cross-filing. This unique political device was in force from 1913 to 1958, when it was abolished. While it was permitted, any candidate could file for the nomination of more than one party. In California, where Democratic registration has traditionally been heavier than Republican, cross-filing worked in favor of the Republicans. Successful candidates for public office, especially incumbents, could thereby capture both party nominations. Campaigning as "nonpartisan," any candidate who won the nomination of both parties could capitalize upon the large proportion of voters who were independent.

In California, as well as nationally, candidates also increasingly relied upon professional public relations firms to publicize their campaigns. Since the 1930s, these organizations, by the use of mass-media techniques, learned how to manipulate public sentiment in favor of a particular candidate or ballot proposal. These public relations firms went on to devise many of the campaign posters, slogans, and cliches of America's recent political history.

A less excusable variety of political lobbying involved Artie Samish, the "Mr. Big" of California politics. Throughout the 1940s and into the early 1950s he ran the "Third House" of the California state legislature, receiving fat fees to lobby in the favor of truck and bus lines, liquor interests, race tracks, and other, confidential, clients. Samish romped through the legislature as though he had prerogatives superior to those of its members. His spree ended in 1953, when he was convicted of evading federal income taxes and sent to jail.

By 1958 the Republican hegemony in California had come to an end. A political squabble within the party helped cause its ouster. Republican Senator William Knowland, who wanted the governorship, forced the incumbent, Governor Goodwin Knight, out of the race. Into the breach stepped

Democratic state Attorney General Edmund (Pat) Brown. Like Governor Warren, Brown had conducted nonpartisan political campaigns, avoiding close association with his own party. Also like Warren, Brown was swept into the state's executive office. Immediately he faced controversial and statewide problems, including traffic and smog control, water development, and a debate over capital punishment. Brown, however, was a fighter who injected vigor into state government. From 1959 to 1962 the governor created an optimistic mood in Sacramento. He was a new figure with novel ideas about building a state college system, improving water projects, mandating fair employment practices, streamlining government agencies, and creating modern transportation systems to meet the needs of a rapidly growing California. Jesse Unruh, speaker of the state assembly, aided Governor Brown in bringing needed measures to realization. Later the two men had a serious falling out.

In 1960 Vice President Nixon became the nominee of the Republican party for the presidency. At the Democratic National Convention, held in Los Angeles's new Sports Arena, Brown gave the nominating speech for Massachusetts Senator John F. Kennedy. This despite the fact that Kennedy considered Governor Brown somewhat inept for failing to hold the California delegation together. In the election, Nixon, the native son, won his state by a narrow margin, but this proved insufficient to prevent Kennedy's election as president.

Two years later Nixon challenged Brown for the governorship. Failure to win this contest, political pundits predicted, might impair Nixon's chances of remaining a public figure. The campaign was bitter. Nixon, resorting to old tricks, accused Brown of being soft on Communists and of bungling administration of the state, but the governor was reelected by a wide majority. Now it seemed that Nixon's political career was indeed over. Little did anyone then know that before the decade ended President Kennedy would be murdered and Richard Nixon would go on to a presidential victory—one that would, in turn, be stained by evidence of his personal deceitfulness uncovered during the congressional investigation known as the "Watergate" hearings.

In the early 1960s, the California Democratic Council, which had built up a productive statewide organization, began to disintegrate. The CDC was especially critical of Governor Pat Brown's timid leadership of the party and his allowing factionalism to develop. This infighting resembled the bloodletting that had wrecked California's Republican party by 1958. The state's independent maverick Democrats included Samuel William Yorty, elected mayor of Los Angeles in 1961, who had bolted the party in 1960 to back Nixon against Kennedy. Assembly Speaker Jesse Unruh, who, like Yorty, had ambitions for higher office,

Los Angeles Mayor Tom Bradley.

became a lone wolf who guarded his powerful role in Sacramento, much as Artie Samish had done. But the Democrats had become a fractured party.

Assembly speaker Unruh was for a time a national figure. Had the Kennedy brothers survived, he would have played a major role in their administrations. After losing the speakership he became a critic of the overlapping of state, county, and city governments. Resembling the Populists and Progressives of an earlier age, he voiced complaints against oil companies, housing-tract speculators, and moneyed interests interfering with the political process by the use of lobbyists via a "political ripoff" system. But Unruh had to fight against his own image as a "Big Daddy" politico in an unsuccessful Los Angeles mayoralty race against Tom Bradley, a popular black Democrat who won in 1973. Earlier, in 1970, the New York *Times* had urged the election of Unruh against the incumbent Ronald Reagan in the gubernatorial race that year: "The Reagan-Unruh contest has significance far beyond California," the *Times* said in an editorial. "Ronald Reagan personifies nonissue politics. His approach is based on a contempt for serious discussion of real problems; it relies on glamorized images projected in carefully controlled public appearances and in intensive television advertising."

The special-interest groups that backed Reagan, as Unruh foresaw, were to exert an enormous influence on the state legislature. As we shall see, the Reagan gubernatorial victory of 1967 would usher in a period that threatened to stop many Democratic reform hopes. For Reagan subsequently opposed attempts to stop water pollution and to obtain mass transportation, thereby encouraging the use of inefficient automobiles that befouled the air with smog.

Although the Democrats controlled California politics from 1958 to 1966, the state has been in Republican hands during most of its history. By the late 1960s a new voting pattern had emerged in California. It featured two political extremes—the far right and the far left. Hyperconservative rural southerners and retired elderly folk, yearning for a return to the simplicity of earlier days, disliked "big government" and looked distrustfully at the young and restless "human tumbleweeds" who, without money and responsibility, flooded into the state. The ultra-conservative John Birch Society maintained its headquarters in California. Despite California's progressive past, nonpartisanship increasingly gave way to right-of-center sentiment. Reagan, and Nixon before him, projected the image of being moderates, accusing their opponents of extremism. By 1968 a new party, the Peace and Freedom advocates, arose to oppose the Vietnam War, but it stood little chance of success. The championing of civil rights also was about to be drowned out by an ultra-right tidal wave that would become national in scope.

Selected Readings

On postwar politics see John D. Weaver, *Warren: The Man, the Court, the Era* (1967); Leo Katcher, *Earl Warren: A Political Biography* (1967); Richard M. Nixon, *Six Crises* (1962); Earl Mazo, *Richard Nixon: A Political and Personal Portrait* (1959); William Costello, *The Facts About Nixon* (1960); Horace Jeremiah (Jerry) Voorhis, *Confessions of a Congressman* (1947) and Ingrid Scobie, *Center Stage: Helen Gahagan Douglas, A Life* (1992).

Biographical accounts include Lester Velie, "The Secret Boss of California," *Collier's* (August 13, 1949), 11–13, 71–73, and (August 20, 1949), 12–13, 60, 62–63; Arthur H. Samish and Bob Thomas, *The Secret Boss of California* (1971); James Mills, *A Disorderly House: The Brown-Unruh Years in Sacramento* (1987); Robert Dallek, *Ronald Reagan* (1984); John M. Allswang, "Tom Bradley of Los Angeles," *Southern California Quarterly* 74 (Spring 1992), 55–105; Lou Cannon, *Reagan* (1982) and his *Ronnie and Jesse: A Political Odyssey* (1969) as well as Roger Rapoport, *California Dreaming . . . Pat and Jerry Brown* (1982).

Electioneering practices are detailed in Robert Q. Wilson, *The Amateur Democrat: Club Politics in Three Cities* (1962); Francis M. Carney, "Auxiliary Party Organizations in California," *Western Political Quarterly* 11 (June 1958), 391–92; Currin V. Shields, "A Note on Party Organization," *Western Political Quarterly* 7 (December 1954), 683 ff.; and Robert J. Pitchell, "The Influence of Professional Campaign Management Firms in . . . California," *Western Political Quarterly* 11 (June 1958), 286 ff.; and "The Electoral System and Voting Behavior: The Case of California's Crossfiling," *Western Political Quarterly* 12 (June, 1959).

Regarding postwar urbanization see Norman M. Klein and Martin J. Schiesl, eds., *Twentieth Century Los Angeles: Power Promotion and Social Conflict* (1990) and Schiesl, "Airplanes to Aerospace: Defense Spending and Economic Growth in the Los Angeles Region, 1945–60," in Roger Lotchin, ed., *The Martial Metropolis . . .* (1984), 135–49; Roger Lotchin, "The City and the Sword Through . . . the Cold War," in Raymond Mohl, ed., *Essays on Sunbelt Cities* (1990); Mel Scott, *The San Francisco Bay Area: A Metropolis in Perspective* (1965); Edward Eichler and Marshall Kaplan, *The Community Builders* (1967); Richard Street, "Rural California, A Bibliographic Essay," *Southern California Quarterly* 70 (Fall, 1988), 299–328 and David Brodsly, *Los Angeles Freeway: An Appreciative Essay* (1981).

The Beleaguered Sixties

////// CHAPTER 35

Socially, as well as politically, the era of the 1960s saw severe unrest suddenly burst upon California and the nation. Students, dissatisfied with "The Establishment," joined older rebels in seeking to turn social conventions upside down.

Angry youths took a cool look at modern life and decided it was beyond hope of improvement. Militant advocates of the "Radical Left" set a shrill tone in attacking parents as well as the dominant government, business interests, and the universities. Campus revolts, centered in Berkeley, reflected estrangement between conflicting age groups.

The state's material wealth seemed to mask uneasiness beneath the surface. Especially disconcerting to middle-aged taxpayers were a growing number of "street people" who belonged to an underground culture. This era also featured the dawning of open homosexuality (or "Gay Liberation"). Some rebels strummed steel-stringed guitars or defiantly shook rattles in a drugged state. Youths who let their hair grow unusually long, and who crowded health food stores while wearing sandals or no shoes, resembled the former Beatniks. This new generation of dissidents were dubbed Hippies.

In the ghettoes of San Francisco, Oakland, or Venice West, alienated youths, thus, expressed their resentment against the war in Vietnam, which was absorbing millions of the nation's dollars for armaments— and taking the lives of thousands of young Americans, many of them from disadvantaged families and minority groups who could not, contrary to many privileged persons, evade the draft. This at a time when, young people saw, poverty was troweled over and largely ignored by the existing leadership of society. Young peoples' disgust over automation, the suppression of individuality, and seemingly hypocritical middle-class morals, increased estrangement between many different social groups.

In the 1960s, hundreds of transient idealists descended upon Berkeley and San Francisco's Haight-Ashbury district. Some of the discontented Hippie generation sought salvation in an alternative lifestyle that also featured the use of "psychedelic" drugs. Parents could not understand how children who had often enjoyed superior advantages could leave middle-class homes and, "turn on, tune in, and drop out." The coming-out of debutantes in California-designed Galanos dresses hardly impressed the legion of experimenters with marijuana and other more potent drugs.

The fact that California had half the swimming pools in the United States was a statistic not celebrated by California's new rebels. Instead, wide-eyed fans of folksingers Bob Dylan and Joan Baez were magnetized by the lyrics of discontent. Rebels, young and old, also expressed themselves in an "underground press." The Los Angeles *Free Press* was sold at curbside along the fancy Sunset Strip. In the Bay Area the Berkeley *Barb* and San Francisco *Oracle* also featured anti-establishment articles.

When vague Hippie ideals were not accepted by the majority, scores of dissidents founded rural communes, some taking up Zen meditation. Via communal living they emphasized new forms of "free love" and the sharing of food and property. Ironically, these new critics, who paid no taxes, were creating their own conformity, for the Hippie movement did not seem to diminish avarice. In fact, it embodied characteristics of the world against which it rebelled. The new rebels were hardly freed from illegitimacy, murder, and suicide. Indeed, the use of powerful drugs such as LSD sometimes resulted in "bad trips" or permanent tragedy.

A loud "Free Speech Movement" at Berkeley kept the University of California in turmoil. Its agitators insisted upon a greater voice in university administration and curriculum design. Following sit-ins during the fall of 1964, blatant public use of obscenity on campus led to demands that police move onto the Berkeley campus to restore order. That year the normally pacifist Governor Pat Brown ordered state police to break up a student sit-in at Berkeley. More than 700 youths, not all of them students, were dragged out of Sproul Hall, the administrative center, and jailed. Although Brown had been jeered at as "a tower of jello," he was actually a determined and consistent politician.

Ronald Reagan too, even before he became governor, spoke of the need to "clean up" campus extremism. He was joined at San Francisco State College by its forceful president, semanticist S. I. Hayakawa, who

Senator Sam I. Hayakawa, 1977.

physically confronted rebellious students. Hayakawa was seen as unusually brave; he thereby earned such public acclaim that he later won election to the U.S. Senate.

Undaunted, University of California undergraduates in the 1960s repeatedly questioned the wisdom of conservative, business-oriented university regents appointed by the governor for lengthy terms. Students at Berkeley militantly argued for decentralization of the university, and eventually the administration did take steps to reorganize its disparate campuses. At San Diego (UCSD) and Santa Cruz (UCSC) administrators approved the formation of small undergraduate colleges similar to those at Oxford. These represented a student ideal, partly because of the possibility of closer contact with favorite faculty members. These newer campuses also held out the prospect of greater curricular experimentation.

Despite such new academic innovation, under Governor Reagan's administration, public distrust of academia would increase. In 1967 the regents of the University of California actually dismissed its president, Clark Kerr. Conservative members of that board considered him too wishy-washy toward student militants. Repeated confrontations by demonstrators on public campuses convinced the public that "left-wing" professors and administrators were spineless allies of student activists.

The 1960s has been described as a period which saw "the ungluing of America." At a time when expanding educational budgets competed with accelerating welfare and health care costs, disgusted voters began to favor bond issues for greater public order and more police protection rather than for rebellious students and teachers. Confused taxpayers came to feel that state-operated campuses should teach students only those skills essential for employment and not become seats of public criticism, or sponsor distasteful dramatic and artistic productions. At Berkeley, a city in which the university dominates the community, its older residents showed scant understanding of its radical youths. The "generation gap" was a reality.

Although campus rebels lost much of their clout by the 1970s, not so California's oldsters. Known by a new euphemism, "senior citizens," not all of the state's huge population of elderly folk had the means to enter the growing number of "retirement communities." In fact, indigent old folks became a heavy charge on the state's increasingly crowded welfare rolls. Most communities welcomed the elderly—as long as they had the means to support themselves. Santa Barbara, once called the home of America's rich unburied dead, was also called, like San Clemente, "the cemetery of the living."

California also faced the continuing problem of what to do about its migratory laborers. Their plight was described by journalist Edward R. Murrow as a "harvest of shame." These workers hoed and thinned sugar beets, cut spinach, fed livestock, and pruned vineyards. Uncertain market conditions and an oversupply of workers could quickly depress their wages or suddenly leave them unemployed. Traditionally nonunionized, any bad freeze or drought also drastically reduced the income of hand laborers. They still lived in substandard housing, were not fed adequately,

Cesar Chavez. Cathy Murphy, staff photographer; courtesy United Farm Workers of America.

and their children seldom completed a grade-school education. In short, their job benefits were virtually nonexistent.

During the 1960s all migrant workers came into increasing competition with Mexican laborers. The debased condition of cherry pickers and almond harvesters had not improved markedly, in part due to the competition of thousands of "scabs" brought in temporarily from Mexico under the federal *braceros* program.

Further flooding the labor pool were *alambristas,* or "wetbacks," who crossed the international border "under the wire." In 1964 such clandestine immigration increased. That year Public Law 78, which had made migration from Mexico legally possible, expired. Henceforth potential laborers were shepherded across the border by "coyotes," or unscrupulous middlemen who marketed entire Mexican labor crews to American employers. If some illegals were caught as they attempted to cross the border, the coyotes, who charged the would-be employees exploitive fees, simply fled, leaving the confused and hapless people to fend for themselves. U.S. border authorities then swooped in to arrest them.

Unemployed migrants still wandered from farm to farm, following the harvests as birds follow the sun. In these groups men, women, and children still slept nightly in abandoned barns or warehouses. Some hovels in which they lived had dirt floors, or tin roofs with no ceilings. Cheesecloth or flour sacks hung over window openings in a sad attempt to keep out insects. Flies swarmed amid primitive sheds where sleeping areas were patched together from scraps of lumber, flattened oil cans, old signboards, or tar paper. With no indoor plumbing or cooking facilities, migrants cooked their meals outside over primitive open fire pits and frequently had no choice but to relieve themselves nearby.

In 1965, at Delano, scab grape harvesters imported by growers to break a strike ran into hostile picketers who fired marbles at them with slingshots. A fragile United Farm Workers Union, led by a new crusader, Cesar Chavez, then proclaimed a statewide boycott of stores that sold fresh grapes, or beverages derived from them, that had been picked by scab labor. Chavez was a quietly magnetic figure who had spent his youth in the labor camps of the Imperial Valley. He and his bedraggled strikers marched 300 miles to Sacramento (in the manner of Coxey's Army in 1893) to protest working conditions. In 1966, pickers employed by the powerful Di Giorgio Fruit Corporation voted in favor of Chavez's union. In 1968 the idealistic Chavez completed a personal twenty-five-day hunger fast while intensifying his continuing grape boycott.

By the summer of 1970 the big grape strike approached its fifth year. Many believed that the growers would never give in. But in June of that

Campaign flyer from RFK's 1968
presidential primary. Courtesy
of John Gaines.

year, Chavez won a minimum wage for his pickers of $1.70 per hour, a then unheard-of rate of pay for farmhands. Growers, however, maintained that Chavez ran his union in a chaotic fashion. One grower complained, "It isn't easy dealing with a man who thinks he's a saint, but who doesn't mind going back on his word."

Chavez, regularly speaking out against agribusinesses, labor contractors, and "body merchants," next turned to challenging the lettuce producers, moving his battle to the Salinas Valley. On December 4, 1970, he was jailed without bail for refusing to obey a legal injunction temporarily restraining his strikes. This court action drew further national attention to Chavez's lettuce boycott and he was released. But trouble in the fields was hardly over.

In the 1960s "Viva la Huelga," "Viva la Causa," and "Viva Chavez" became rallying phrases for students, labor reformers, and churchmen who joined Chavez's ranks. Some of these white-collar supporters were derisively labeled "limousine liberals." Shy and sad in appearance, Chavez had become the mobilizer of a once-despised heritage. His checkered shirt and blue jeans suggested a sincere wish to remain close to his people. He came from their ranks and knew what it was to do "stoop work," picking grapes or harvesting lettuce all day long. Like India's Mohandas Gandhi, he refused to allow violence to enter into his struggles on behalf of the farm workers.

Chavez repeatedly encountered opposition from the rival Teamsters Union, who also tried to organize migrant farm workers. Chavez was convinced that the Teamsters were working with major growers to break up his organization. Farmhands, caught in the middle of a jurisdictional dispute, often did not quite understand the ongoing labor conflict. They remained grateful to Chavez for having improved not only their wages but also for bringing such amenities as ice water and portable toilets into the stifling fields. Chavez charged that collusion with growers involved illegal payoffs to Teamster officials. It took years before he patched up a working agreement with that rival union, which allowed him to continue his crusade with lessened competition from the Teamsters.

In 1963 Chavez and his fellow Latinos were shocked by the assassination of President John Kennedy. A fellow Catholic, he had been nominated for the presidency at Los Angeles, hub of California's Mexican-American population where "Viva Kennedy" clubs operated during the 1960 presidential campaign. Less than five years after President Kennedy's death, Latino grief was to be repeated. In June 1968, JFK's brother, Robert Kennedy, was assassinated at Los Angeles following a stunning presidential primary victory in which Mexican Americans had strongly participated.

In the 1970s, while the discrimination directed against Latinos did not seem so overt as that which African Americans encountered, a large percentage of California's Mexican Americans remained unskilled laborers with low incomes. Some referred to themselves as *desgraciados,* or "born without grace." Years of employment as stoop laborers in the fields had cast *braceros* in an inferior role. Some Mexican-American children were forced to drop out of school by the time they reached the eighth grade in order to help their families earn money in the fields.

Slowly, however, California's Mexican-American community began to produce new leaders whose organizational aspirations were greater than those of Cesar Chavez. Numerous urbanized Latinos now began to call themselves "Chicanos," which became a politically charged term. Such folk remained far removed from the marches of Chavez's farm workers. Urban leaders belonged to such organizations as the Mexican-American Political Association and Latino Legislative Council.

During 1968, following demonstrations by Hispanic students and teachers in seven Los Angeles high schools, the city's pressured school board promised to implement new racial reforms. Among these was the appointment of minority school principals, as well as alleviation of restrictions on hairstyles and clothing, more bilingual instruction, and a modernized industrial training program for minority-group students who would not go on to college.

Accused of sparking the school walkouts were members of a group called the "Brown Berets," whose goal stood in contrast to the "Green Berets" of the U.S. Army in Vietnam. Their leaders sought to unite *"La Raza"* (the race) in California's barrios. Wearing clothing that resembled the revolutionary garb of Fidel Castro and his Cuban followers, these critics carried signs that read *"Viva la Revolucion!"* More and more young Chicanos were coming out of the colleges and universities. They were anxious to replace members of the older generation whom they labeled Tio Tacos or "Uncle Tacos," a parallel for the slur "Uncle Tom."

By the 1960s, the inequities that faced California's African-American population also cried out for reform. So said the oldest black newspaper in the state, *The California Eagle*. Black communities continued to grow in nascent ghettoes peopled by poorly paid custodians, waiters, railroad porters, handymen, and gardeners.

Increasing numbers of blacks from the southern states moved into Oakland, Compton, and Inglewood. But California hardly proved a haven from prejudice, and they were still resisted in the then "lily-white" communities of Glendale and San Marino. As early as 1924, blacks in California had founded their own resort community, Val Verde, near Santa Clarita in the Tehachapi foothills. Blacks also started lodges, businesses, and churches. At Los Angeles William Seymour, a black preacher, headed up the Pentecostal Holy Rollers, influencing Aimee Semple McPherson and other evangelists.

Only slowly had African Americans entered the professions, sports, and politics. Dr. Ralph Bunche, a graduate of UCLA, went from a State Department career to become undersecretary of the United Nations. Jackie Robinson began his baseball career at Pasadena Junior College. As a professional player he eventually "broke the sports color line."

To help overcome discrimination against blacks, the Rumford Fair Housing Act, passed by the legislature in 1963, broadened prohibitions against discrimination in the sale or rental of private dwellings. But the next year the voters adopted Proposition 14, which nullified the state's open-housing provisions. This proposition, however, was itself invalidated in court, and the Rumford Act remained in force.

But the sting of Proposition 14 had been felt. This setback for blacks occurred on the eve of the Watts riots in southeast Los Angeles. Although its streets were lined with palm trees, it was a crowded ghetto neighborhood. The August 1965 Watts uprisings epitomized the malaise of disenchanted blacks. Hundreds of frustrated rioters, shouting the anti-white epithets "Burn, Baby, Burn" and "Get Whitey," looted stores, set buildings afire, and shot at firemen and police. Governor Brown ordered National Guard troops out to help local police restore order. During the riots, which lasted for six days, 35 persons died and 600 others were injured. Some 4,000 persons were arrested within a square-mile burned-over area. Marauders invaded furniture stores, stealing television sets, freezers, and other electronic appliances.

The 1965 Watts outbursts underscored the deterioration of African-American family life as well as envy of white prerogatives and resentment against city police and local courts. Though the riots resulted in great damage to the very place in which many blacks lived, they did generate some moves toward reform, including a new cultural center and hospital at Watts. Yet there was a continuing failure to delve deeply into the roots of interracial misunderstanding. The McCone Commission, appointed by Governor Pat Brown after the outbreak, found that Watts needed much better transportation and recreational facilities. White businesspeople also tried to widen employment opportunities in order to aid rootless young blacks.

During the turbulent 1960s, California had, thus, made some progress in redressing racial inequalities. It revamped run-down neighborhoods and poured money into welfare programs. But "Black Power" advocates pushed for more antipoverty measures and progressive school programs such as "Head Start" and "Upward Bound" to aid disadvantaged youths.

California, which seemed to serve as an early warning system for the rest of America, still had to cope with the problems brought about by its seemingly endless growth. A brutalized society and a polluted environment became real possibilities as the age of the computer was about to dawn.

Selected Readings

Concerning educational ferment in the 1960s see Clark Kerr, *The Uses of a University* (1963); Gerard J. De Groot, "Ronald Reagan and Student Unrest in California, 1966–1970," *Pacific Historical Review* 65 (February 1996), 107–29; W. J. Rorabaugh, *Berkeley at War, The 1960s* (1989) See also Arthur G. Coons, *Crises in California Education* (1968); Seymour M. Lipset and Sheldon S. Wolin, eds., *The Berkeley Student Revolt: Facts and Interpretations* (1965); also "LSD Before Leary" by Steven J. Novak in *Isis,* (March 1997), 87–110.

For politics of the 1960s see Jackson K. Putnam, *Modern California Politics* (1996) and his "The Pattern of Modern California Politics," *Pacific Historical Review* 61 (February 1992), 23–52; Eugene C. Lee, ed., *The California Governmental Process: Problems and Issues* (1966); Thomas M. Storke, *I Write for Freedom* (1963); Charles M. Price, ed., *Consensus and Cleavage: Issues in California Politics* (1968); Leonard Pitt, ed., *California Controversies: Major Issues in the History of the State* (2d. ed. 1987).

Regarding blacks in this period see James de Abajian, compiler, *Blacks and Their Contributions to the American West: A Bibliography* (1974); Kenneth Goode, *California's Black Pioneers* (1973); James A. Fisher, "Political Development of the Black Community in California," *California Historical Quarterly* 50 (September 1971), 256–66; Thurman A. Odell, "The Negro in California Before 1890," *Pacific Historian* 19 (Winter 1975), 321–45; Albert S. Broussard, *Black San Francisco: the Struggle for Racial Equality in the West, 1900–1954* (1993); Douglas Daniels, *Pioneer Urbanites: A Social and Cultural History of Black San Francisco* (1980); Lawrence B. De Graaf, "The City of Black Angels: The Emergence of the Los Angeles Ghetto, 1890–1930," *Pacific Historical Review* 39 (August 1970), 323–52 also De Graaf, "Recognition, Racism, and Reflections on the Writing of Black History," *Pacific Historical Review* 44 (February 1975), 22–51; E. Berkeley Tompkins, "Black Ahab: William T. Shorey, Whaling Master," *California Historical Quarterly* 51 (Spring 1972), 75–84 and F. Ray Marshall, *The Negro and Organized Labor* (1965).

On the Watts riots, basic is *Violence in the City: An End or a Beginning* [the McCone Commission Report] (1965). Also see Gerald Horne, *Fire This Time: The Watts Uprisings and the 1960s* (1995); Raphael Sonenshein, *Politics in Black and White: Race and Power in Los Angeles* (1993); Spencer Crump, *Black Riot in Los Angeles: The Story of the Watts Tragedy* (1966); Nathan Cohen, *The Los Angeles Riots: A Socio-Psychological Study* (1970); Paul Bullock, ed., *Watts: The Aftermath* (1970); Joseph Boskin and Victor Pilson. "The Los Angeles Riot of 1965: A Medical Profile of an Urban Crisis," *Pacific Historical Review* 29 (August 1970), 353–65 and Mark Baldessare, ed., *The Los Angeles Riots: Lessons for the Urban Future* (1994).

On immigrants throughout this period see George E. Frakes and Curtis Solberg, eds., *Minorities in California History* (1971) and Moses Rischin, "Immigration, Migration, and Minorities in California: A Reassessment," *Pacific Historical Review* 41 (February 1972), 71–90; George J. Sánchez, *Becoming Mexican American . . .* (1993); N. Ray and Gladys Gilmore, "The Bracero in California," *Pacific Historical Review* 32 (August 1963), 265–82; Mark Reisler, "Always the Laborer: Anglo Perceptions of the Mexican Immigrant," *Pacific Historical Review* 45 (May 1976), 231–54; Fernando Penalosa, "The Changing Mexican-American in Southern California," *Sociology and Social Research* 51 (July 1967), 405–17; Richard Griswold del Castillo and Richard D. Garcia, *Cesar Chavez: A Triumph of Spirit* (1995); Gilbert G. González, *Labor and Community: Mexican Worker Villages in a Southern California County* (1994); John Gregory Dunne, *Delano: The Anatomy of the Great California Grapeworkers Strike* (1967); Ernesto Galarza, *Merchants of Labor: The Mexican Bracero Story* (1964); and Galarza, *Barrio Boy* (1971); as well as Truman E. Moore, *The Slaves We Rent* (1965).

Environmental
Realities

As hundreds of thousands of new residents continued to push into California, its environmental challenges grew especially urgent. These
included overcrowded schools, hospitals, a freeway system in constant
need of expansion, and severe water shortages. The state's major cities
were also plagued by a baffling problem, which came to be called smog.

Smog is an uncomfortable combination of smoke and fog. This haze
not only irritates one's eyes but reduces visibility, affects crop yields, and
discourages tourism. As early as 1947, Los Angeles organized a County
Air Pollution Control District. One of the first such regulatory agencies
in the entire country, the APCD spent millions of dollars trying to reduce the emission of noxious automobile and factory fumes. Ten years
later the city finally took the small step of banning backyard incinera-
tors. Until a state law allowed the APCD to override local jurisdiction,
its ordinances could not be applied to sixty-three suburban municipalities surrounding Los Angeles. Eventually the APCD strictly controlled
industries that produced sulphurous petrochemicals.

Los Angeles is located in a saucer-like basin that suffers from the
lowest wind velocity of any major city of the United States. If the air
could escape the surrounding rim of mountains, where the atmosphere
grows cooler with altitude, the smog would not be so troublesome. But
bright sunshine on hot, sunny days causes photochemical regrouping of
exhaust gas molecules. The airborne emissions that billow out of industrial smokestacks form a dense layer of smog that hangs over the area
for long periods.

Hydrocarbons from auto exhausts and vapor leaks from gas tanks also
contribute to smog. When in 1956 air pollution reached a prescribed

295

Los Angeles sprawl, 1954. Courtesy of William A. Garnett. © 1954 by William A. Garnett.

unacceptable level, the APCD forced local industries to burn only natural gas. Alternative fuels for autos, buses and trucks, such as ethanol, were also devised as a partial solution to ending air pollution. Auto companies also began a lengthy and not yet commercially successful attempt to market personal vehicles fueled by natural gas or powered by batteries. The problem persists and there is no doubt that California's air pollution contributes to mortality rates from emphysema and other upper respiratory diseases such as lung cancer, asthma, and allergies.

Although smog once seemed less of a problem in the north, San Francisco in 1955 also organized an Air Pollution Control District. This agency oversaw nine counties in the Bay Area and began by banning open rubbish fires. Municipal dumps, which deposited layers of filthy air over the bay on windless days, were forced to cover-and-fill city refuse. Legislative action to control auto exhausts was painfully slow, although this was clearly the main cause of airborne particulate matter. Commuting habits changed only gradually, reducing auto exhaust emissions somewhat via the use of car pooling, which, however, was shunned by car-loving Californians. But California's city-dwellers continued to complain about smog, which is at its worst during the critical months from May to October.

Another pressing problem concerned how to insure a constant water supply. Neither the Owens Valley Aqueduct nor the Boulder Canyon Project could permanently provide water for sun-parched southern California. Overpumping of underground aquifers became a serious danger. Near Long Beach seawater invaded these freshwater basins while in Suisun Bay and along the Sacramento–San Joaquin Delta, selenium and other toxic contaminants polluted underground water reservoirs. Salt build-up has also resulted from excessive reuse of water, as has occurred in the Santa Ana River Basin.

Yet the demand for water was unceasing. Today's average family of four uses approximately one acre-foot of water (or 325,851 gallons) per year, enough to cover nearly an entire football field with a foot of water. But only a small percentage of California's water is actually used by residential customers. Agriculture and industry consume most of it.

A new approach to water resources resulted in the planning of the Feather River Project. In order to harness that important tributary of the Sacramento, eight hundred miles of canals and tunnels had to be built. The largest structure of this new water network was the 730-foot-high Oroville Dam, part of a great "natural stairway" that provided for fish and game protection as well as flood control.

Debate over whether state or federal funds should be used—added to political sectionalism between northern and southern California—slowed

Flood control activity combined with conservation. Courtesy of the Los Angeles Department of Water Resources.

down the Feather River Project. Even after construction had begun on Oroville Dam, the legislature remained locked in discord over whether to complete it and whether to build a structure projected to accompany it—the San Luis Dam, 310 feet high, in Merced County. An adamant stand by southern legislators against appropriating money for water that could be recaptured by northern "counties of origin" contributed to a ten-year stalemate. The north required flood control as urgently as the industrializing but parched south needed water. The state legislature also had to weigh protection of the towns of Yuba City, Butte, and Marysville from floods against the need for life-giving water in southern California.

Some critics feared the enrichment of huge "corporation farmers" whose thousands of productive acres would be nourished by water paid for by others. Another stumbling block to adoption of the Feather River Project was its great cost. Largely, however, the issue was the north's basic interests as opposed to the south's.

Governor Pat Brown had succeeded in breaking the north-south deadlock by persuading representatives of competing counties that it was in their best interest to stop squabbling over water. This insured the trans-

The Forty-Four Counties of Northern California

0   50   100   150
miles

fer of water to points as far south as San Diego County. Protection of northern rights in the "counties of origin" was also part of Brown's compromise, which created the world's biggest water-transport system. This intricate complex of dams and canals also conserves water by sending it to areas where shortages are endemic. Over a north-south artery, water from the southern San Joaquin Valley is lifted over the Tehachapi mountains via tunnels and feeder lines into southern California.

A disappointing alternative to the state's costly water transport problem has been desalination. In 1967 the federal government provided funds to help build the largest desalination plant in the country near San Diego, but it has not proved economical to convert seawater into freshwater.

By the 1970s Californians experienced second thoughts about yet another water conservation program. This was a forty-three-mile peripheral canal to divert water around the Sacramento–San Joaquin Delta. Ecologists have properly maintained that diversion of too much water

The Fourteen Counties of Southern California

0   50   100   150
miles

Mono

Inyo

Tulare

Kings

San Luis Obispo

Kern

Santa Barbara

Ventura   Los Angeles

San Bernardino

Orange

Riverside

San Diego   Imperial

out of the Delta's sloughs and marshes could destroy its lush but help-less waterfowl and fish life. Yet, California was no longer able to count on its annual overpumping from the Colorado River (Boulder Canyon) beyond the 4.4 million acre-feet to which it is entitled.

Meanwhile, onshore and offshore water pollution continued apace. Dangerous bacteria and viruses still spill out of storm drains, depositing layers of muck into the Pacific Ocean. Also the disgorging, or bilging, by ships of oil and black grease sludge has produced millions of tons of slimy underwater pollutant discharges that scuba divers call "black may-onnaise." Oil tankers too discharge a sticky tar which fouls the beaches.

As pesticide-laden water has run off agricultural fields and entered the maritime food chain, one encounters mutant frogs, as well as con-taminated shellfish, and deformed pelicans, sea lions, and dolphins. Toxic wastes have been linked to deformities and abortion rates among cattle and sheep as well. Animals and humans too are endangered by con-taminated wells. Persons who eat ocean mollusks as well as other Cali-

Tunnel through Tehachapi Range bringing northern water into arid Southern California. Courtesy of the Deparment of Water Resources.

fornia seafood are regularly warned that they do so at their own risk of ingesting bacterial contamination.

The state tourist industry loses considerable money each year because of these pollution fears. Beachgoers are warned away from unsafe swimming or fishing zones located near storm drains. Some beaches are occasionally closed to swimmers. Conservationists also issue warnings concerning chemicals that do not break down in the soil and are eventually drained into wildlife refuges and the water table.

Some pure-water remedies have made possible California's agricultural success. Among these is massive water redemption, even from sewage. As 95 percent of its crops are grown on irrigated land, the state remains first nationally in the production of almost 40 crops. An estimated 25 percent of America's table food comes from its great Central Valley. No other region comes near the quantity of its production of fruits and vegetables. California continues to produce more than 275 crops—from cut flowers to kelp.

Large corporate ranchers have extended their operations into shipping and processing. Today's cattle ranchers breed, feed, ship, and sell their own livestock; some grow the alfalfa and sorghum used in cattle-fattening pens. Rancher-farmers operate motor pools and buy costly harvesters, tractors, and automatic potato pickers—a far cry from horse-drawn plows, haystacks, and milk wagons.

Modern corporate farming has largely replaced small family farms incapable of competing successfully. Among the state's mechanized agribusinesses is the Kern County Land Company, whose holdings were once gargantuan. Such firms are frequently absorbed by even larger companies. One of these entities, the Irvine Ranch Company, which controlled much of Orange County, became a major subdivider with land as far away as Imperial County. The Newhall Land and Farming Company has also converted large areas of farmland into real estate subdivisions at Valencia, a new town created by that company. In the San Joaquin Valley, the Di Giorgio and Sawyer fruit and vegetable farms generate millions of dollars of income annually. The Maggio Company in the Imperial Valley is the largest grower of carrots in the United States. The Brock Ranches near El Centro, and the Antle Ranches, growers of lettuce and carrots in the Imperial Valley and Arizona, are perhaps the leading producers of vegetables in the nation.

But California's agricultural land remains threatened. Each year 20,000 acres of prime farm land are gobbled up by industrial plants, space-consuming highways, and housing tracts. From Bakersfield to Reading, suburbs are sprouting on land that once produced more milk, tomatoes, cantaloupes, peaches, apricots, figs, and almonds than any other part of the world. Urban sprawl, whether it takes place in Calaveras, Kern, or Orange county, is no longer a local issue. Less than 10 percent of the state is still farmland. Even in California's prized Central Valley over 12 percent of the most fertile land has been paved over.

In addition to destroying a farming paradise, California has been losing other than agricultural markets to foreign competitors who pay lower wages. The state, once second only to Texas in oil production, has become a net importer of petroleum products. As oil wells produced less and less, a battle arose with the federal government over vast oil deposits that extend outward from the shoreline. Long Beach, after World War II, leased its offshore reserves to independent oil operators in defiance of both state and federal claims. Only after a lengthy dispute was a three-way agreement reached between the federal government, the state, and California coastal municipalities.

Federal versus state tension over offshore oil drilling has grown particularly angry along the Santa Barbara Channel because of repeated oil spills that destroy wildlife and putrefy beaches. Billions of barrels of oil are locked beneath the sea as far north as Morro Bay. The federal government continues to pressure the state for exploitation of this treasure, but environmentalists vigorously oppose further exploration for tideland oil.

Another natural phenomenon, one for which California is world renowned, continues to concern federal, state, and local authorities—earthquakes. Along the San Andreas Fault, which crosses the San Francisco area, serious tremors occurred in 1906, 1933, 1971, and 1989. The latter, the Loma Prieta quake, caused the collapse of an entire freeway in Oakland and crumpled stretches of the double-decker bay bridges. In addition to the loss of fifty-seven lives, and millions of dollars worth of damage to property, the 1989 quake interrupted the cross-bay World Series between the San Francisco Giants and Oakland A's. As a broadcast of the game was disrupted and television screens across the nation temporarily went blank, thousands of frightened fans in Candlestick Park were evacuated from the stadium, which had sustained some physical damage.

Other serious tremors jolted the Los Angeles basin in 1991 and 1994. The 1994 San Fernando Valley (or Northridge) quake killed sixty-one people, snarled rail and air transportation, and caused severe power and water outages. Another of California's natural phenomena, albeit one aggravated by man-made erosion, are landslides. Some hillside zones have been likened to the slithering of a deck of playing cards. Each year, at poorly chosen building sites, nature proves itself more powerful than man's feeble plaster and wood constructions.

As the population has grown, a widening stain of confusion marred California's shift from an agricultural to a postindustrial way of life. This explosive growth finally demolished whatever frontier ruralities remained.

San Fernando Valley earthquake damage—January 17, 1994. Courtesy of the Los Angeles Times.

The missions and ranchos of the Spanish period had long ago made way for film and television studios, oil derricks, aircraft factories, airports, steel mills, and seemingly countless subdivisions. In many areas rising land costs have made it uneconomical to build single-family dwellings. Urban dwellers increasingly orient their lives around high-rise "industrial parks."

Dynamite and bulldozers have gouged the landscape with deep scars. The National Park Service has estimated that there were once more than 2 million acres of redwoods between Monterey Bay and southern Oregon. Now only a fraction of that virgin forest remains. As buzzing chain saws continue to log whole groves of ancient trees, new cities seemed to have oozed out over the countryside. Suburbias, cluttered with billboards, mar the landscape. In a single generation smog has altered the unique Mediterranean climate of southern California.

Not all urbanization, however, has led to spoliation. In 1965 the legislature created a Conservation and Development Commission to stop communities alongside San Francisco Bay from filling in seaside lagoons and inlets in order to create more land for development. Also, the U.S. National Resources Conservation Service began to pay out millions of dollars to ranchers and farmers who promised to convert thousands of acres of their wetlands for migratory-bird refuges. The Sierra Club and "Calpers," the nation's largest pension fund, have also voted their considerable stock holdings against attempts to cut down stands of old-growth redwoods. Although population has spilled over into the wine-growing Napa and Livermore valleys, some agricultural reserves have been saved by citizens pressuring the state—just as seashore areas also have been preserved. Another unusual development has been the orderly opening up of the former Irvine Ranch in Orange County. This area, six times the size of Manhattan, once extended twenty-two miles inland from the coast. After 1960 a master plan was drawn up for its future use, including a new campus of the University of California.

Instances of protecting California's man-made landmarks include restoration of San Francisco's Palace of Fine Arts, the last remnant of the 1915 Panama Pacific International Exhibition. Its 160-foot-high rotunda was the tour de force of architect Bernard Maybeck. Nearby, the Ghirardelli Chocolate Factory also has been restored as a place to wine, dine, and shop. Conversion of an adjacent antique cannery near Fisherman's Wharf and of the city's cable-car barn combines preservation of historic sites with today's functional needs. Although threats to such green belts as San Francisco's Golden Gate Park and Los Angeles's Elysian Park have been unceasing, the U.S. Army recently surrendered the San Francisco Presidio to National Park Service supervision.

Mt. Shasta, a towering volcanic peak of the Cascade Range, reflected in a mill pond. Courtesy of the Union Pacific Railroad.

Yet, greedy developers continue to sell cheaply constructed tract homes, which too quickly fall into disrepair, sometimes lapsing into the hands of homeless migrants. These slum nests become magnets for gang activity; all of them undermine community pride. California's failure to provide enough public parks and playgrounds has hardly been made up for by the commercialism of expensive theme parks. These and such other synthetic recreation centers as Knotts Berry Farm and Six Flags Magic Mountain, were first begun within California. Some have become worldwide tourist attractions.

These for-profit amusement centers now form part of an artificial landscape that is a poor substitute for the lost greenery of a countryside increasingly paved over by freeways. Each freeway consumes twenty-eight acres of land per mile of construction. An interchange uses up to eighty acres. At Los Angeles, two-thirds of its center is occupied by streets, freeways, parking facilities, and garages. Not only do freeways take valuable property off the public tax rolls, they also disrupt existing neighborhoods, often dividing racial groups and occupational classes. While they do connect outlying areas, freeways also have fragmented formerly stable environments. Only a few communities, among them San Francisco and South Pasadena, have actually stopped their construction.

Indignant environmentalists, including animal rights groups and the Sierra Club, continue to press for the regulation of development. But these no-growth advocates have been frustrated by the construction industry, which claims to protect the rights of home buyers. Indeed, a number of developers, and manufacturers too, have left the state because of its perceived pro-environment, antibusiness climate.

But the growth continues. As the whine of rubber tires on concrete has become more intense, such suburbs as Daly City, Pacifica, and an unwieldy conglomerate called City of Commerce resemble industrial moonscapes. California's "supercities" now stretch inland and northward from San Diego, beyond Los Angeles, toward Santa Barbara and San Luis Obispo. In northern California a second sprawling complex has created a contiguous metropolis around San Francisco Bay. Such growth is unabated, and it continues to be equated with "progress." Even today, efforts to save Mono Lake or to retard construction around Lake Tahoe and to preserve the remaining unfenced coastline have all faced stiff public opposition.

Selected Readings

On water development see Norris Hundley, *The Great Thirst* (1991); William Kahrl, *Water and Power* (1982); John Walton, *Western Times and Water Wars ... Rebellion in California* (1992); Mary Montgomery and Marion Clawson, *History of Legislation and Policy Formation of the Central Valley Project* (1946); Vincent Ostrom, *Water and Politics* (1953); Erwin Cooper, *Aqueduct Empire* (1968).

See also Arthur McEvoy, *The Fisherman's Problem: Ecology and Law in California Fisheries* (1986); Michael Black, "Tragic Remedies: A Century of Failed Fishery Policy on California's Sacramento River," *Pacific Historical Review* 64 (February 1995), 37–70; Andrew Rolle, "Turbulent Waters: Navigation and California's Southern Central Valley," *California History* 75 (Summer 1996), 129–37, and *The California Water Atlas* (Sacramento, 1979).

Regarding the Los Angeles environs see Norman Klein, *Los Angeles and the Memory of Many Hopes* (1990); David Rieff, *Los Angeles: Capital of the Third World* (1991); David Clark, *Los Angeles, A City Apart* (1981); Stephen Longstreet, *All Star Cast: An Anecdotal History of Los Angeles* (1977); Christopher Rand, *Los Angeles, The Ultimate City* (1967); Alison Lurie, *The Nowhere City* (1966); Robert M. Fogelson, *The Fragmented Metropolis* (1967); John L. Chapman, *Incredible Los Angeles* (1967).

Other sources include Rob Kling, Spencer Olin, and Mark Poster, eds., *Postsuburban California: The Transformation of Orange County since World War II* (1991); Clark Davis, "From Oasis to Metropolis, Southern California and the Changing Context of American Leisure," *Pacific Historical Review* 61 (August 1992), 357–86; Raymond F. Dasmann, *The Destruction of California* (1965) and his *California's Changing Environment* (1981); William Bronson, *How to Kill a Golden State* (1968); Richard Lillard, *Eden in Jeopardy, Man's Prodigal Meddling With His Environment: The Southern California Experience* (1966); Ronald F. Lockman, *Guarding the Forests of Southern California* (1981); Robert Kelley, *Battling the Inland Sea . . . Public Policy and the Sacramento Valley* (1989) and Harold Gilliam, *Between the Devil and the Deep Blue Bay: The Struggle to Save San Francisco Bay* (1969).

Regarding offshore oil see Ernest R. Bartley, *The Tidelands Oil Controversy* (1953); Robert B. Krueger, "State Tidelands Leasing in California," *U.C.L.A. Law Review* 5 (May 1958), 427–89 and Robert Easton, *Black Tide: The Santa Barbara Oil Spill and its Consequences* (1972).

Seeking New Solutions

//////// CHAPTER 37

Toward the end of the 1960s, the new era of conservatism continued. But the gubernatorial election of 1966–1967 was held in an atmosphere of alarm over an increased crime rate, high property taxes, and civil disturbances—including riots in the black sections of its largest city and student disturbances at the state university in Berkeley. Racial tensions lurked in the background as Governor Edmund (Pat) Brown sought a third term against the popular film actor Ronald Reagan.

Reagan, formerly the conservative president of Hollywood's Screen Actors Guild, proudly stressed his political inexperience. Yet he made effective use of campaign funds provided by conservative business backers. A veteran of more than fifty motion pictures, during the campaign Reagan projected relaxed self-possession before television cameras. In 1967, by convincing the electorate that he was a moderate who had grown weary of massive social welfare programs, Reagan defeated Governor Pat Brown by nearly a million votes.

Reagan's campaign promises included tax relief, which voters now had come to expect. In order not to raise taxes, he hoped to make government more frugal. The new governor proposed state budget slashes of 10 percent, which caused an immediate storm of protest. In 1968 Reagan even faced a movement to recall him. He had barely assumed the governorship when his proposed university budget cuts placed him at odds with the state's professoriate. Yet Reagan's "anti-intellectualism" was partly applauded by the public. He also hoped to impose higher tuition fees upon California's public universities and, as we have noted, sought to control radicals on their campuses.

*Ronald Reagan, governor
of California, 1967–1974.
Courtesy of
Michael Evans,
The White House.*

When Reagan next proposed to trim public assistance agencies and to close some mental health clinics, he faced another uproar. Whenever such protests mounted, he held back temporarily from announced courses of action. One of his biggest economy targets was the cutting of medical funds for the elderly, the indigent, and welfare recipients. Reagan thereby hoped "to squeeze fraud and abuse out of California's welfare system." His opponents labeled these cuts heartless measures.

Some of the governor's proposals seemed petty. Toll collectors on bridges were forced to surrender their state-issued revolvers, which were then sold. Travel by state employees was drastically curtailed as was use of teletype and telephone services and even the purchase of equipment and supplies. The governor's office suspended the publication of road maps, brochures, and a park and recreation magazine. Reagan announced that some $50,000 was saved in typewriter ribbons alone and $2 million in the state's phone bill during the first few months of his governorship. Governor Reagan also sold his state-owned airplane.

But, like other governors, Reagan ran up against ingrained governmental programs. Early in 1968 there was a deficit of $210 million in the state's medical program, known as "Medi-Cal." The governor also proposed stronger penalties for rape, armed robbery, and theft. A fearful public encouraged the legislature to pass a stronger gun-control law. Passage of the measure was helped along after a Black Panther group (though armed with unloaded weapons) scared legislators witless by bursting into chambers while the law was being debated. Reagan, however, met fierce opposition concerning repeal of the open-housing law or passage of tighter obscenity laws, or the establishment of county welfare fraud units.

Reagan filled his administration with businessmen who served on task forces and commissions without pay while urging the loosening of state controls over business. Conversely, labor unions hated Reagan. When farm labor grew short during the 1968 harvest season, the governor sent convicts to help pick crops. He also ordered use during harvest seasons of employable welfare recipients. Labor leaders called such moves a subsidy to growers.

In the eight years Reagan served as governor he achieved only limited control over governmental growth. His wish to stem the growth of government was repeatedly defeated by a Democratic legislature that was hostile to him. Governmental inertia made it difficult to overhaul a lumbering bureaucracy in Sacramento. The legislators saw to it that the welfare rolls actually increased under Reagan.

Reagan's attempts to coax state employees into voluntarily working on holidays showed how distant he was from entrenched civil servants. The number of such employees was about the same when he left office as when he became governor. By 1974, Reagan's last year as governor, his annual budget had reached over $10 billion, more than double the amount spent when he first took office. This spending was fueled by three separate tax increases, and reflected the same rate of growth overseen by Reagan's alleged "spendthrift" predecessor, Pat Brown.

California's next governor (1975–1983) was Pat Brown's son, Edmund G. (Jerry) Brown, Jr. Pat Brown had governed during an era of unquestioned explosive growth. His son exhibited a self-imposed retrenchment

Edmund G. "Jerry" Brown, Jr.
former Democratic Governor
of California, 1975–1983.

when faced with the proliferation of state projects. Jerry Brown repeatedly reminded audiences that there was a limit to what government could undertake, even criticizing the "spending philosophy" of old New Dealers like his father. Although an advocate of civil rights, racial integration, and ecology, Jerry Brown also proved to be a fiscal conservative.

Jerry Brown, only thirty-seven years old when he became governor, stated that he had absolutely no national political aspirations. In 1975 he refused to attend the National Governors Conference. Brown claimed to be more concerned with California's problems: unemployment; crime; medical insurance; the plight of farm workers; and fighting the highway and auto lobbies, which wanted to build more freeways.

By 1976 Jerry Brown, however, entered the national presidential primaries as a "favorite son" candidate. His style blended austerity and idealism. Although he did not gain the Democratic presidential nomination (which went to Jimmy Carter), Brown, for a time at least, seemed to offer voters an alternative to President Gerald Ford's post-Watergate administration.

An English journal called Brown the "Little Prince of United States politics." Heavily influenced by E. F. Schumacher's economics text, *Small is Beautiful,* Brown seemed to promise his "baby boom generation" respite from post-Vietnam disillusionment with big government, business, and unions. His refusal to live in a new governor's mansion or to use an executive airplane or official limousine struck voters favorably.

Even in Orange County, the largely Protestant and conservative home of Richard Nixon and "the world's first drive-in church," Brown, an unmarried ex-Jesuit ascetic who dabbled in Zen meditation, remained quite popular. But, as with Governor Reagan, the public expected magical solutions to difficult problems. During 1975 a malpractice crisis inundated the medical community. This concerned the soaring rates that physicians had to pay for malpractice insurance. Hundreds of physicians throughout the state temporarily ceased practicing medicine. The governor's response was no more than a reassurance that his administration would continue to "monitor" the rise of insurance premiums.

The governor's boyish charm made him appear to be an old-fashioned Populist as well as a monk committed to sacrifice. "We're going to have to work harder," he stated in a 1976 speech to the California Democratic Council. One assemblyman chided the young governor's inaction: "I've heard that goddamned sanctimonious speech too many times. He lectures . . . people who know a lot more about public policy than he does."

Brown, however, did act upon some of his convictions. A new state Office of Appropriate Technology advocated environmentally designed buildings and supported wind power, solar heating, home organic farming, and bioconversion (use of human waste to produce energy). He also appointed unprecedented numbers of women, minority members, and consumer advocates to commissions and court offices. These included a controversial chief justice, Rose Bird. Brown was continually criticized because of his refusal to make firmer ideological commitments. The governor's admonition that "we are entering an era of limits," was not sufficiently persuasive to his fellow politicos.

Brown did find a soul mate in Cesar Chavez, the union farm organizer. In 1975 Brown sponsored the path-breaking Agricultural Labor Relations Act, which strengthened the bargaining power of Chavez's United Farm Workers. After that, however, Brown was accused of seeking to push Chavez into a leadership position for which he was scarcely suited; Chicanos looked in vain to Chavez as an organizer of their urban *barrios*.

Hundreds of thousands of Chicanos and other new residents continued to arrive each year. By 1976, Los Angeles County reached a population of 7 million persons, becoming the most populous county in the United States. San Diego had become the state's second largest city, whereas San Francisco dropped to third place. An American love affair with the Sun Belt cities of the Southwest accounted for some of California's modern growth. But it was also due to a tremendous increase of foreign-born immigrants, legal and illegal.

Jerry Brown's governorship also witnessed continuing tolerance for California's many homosexuals, as many gay people "came out of the closet." In San Francisco, by the 1970s, one-sixth of its population were acknowledged homosexuals. In 1978 a tragedy occurred there, involving Mayor George Moscone and a member of the Board of Supervisors, Harvey Milk, an avowed homosexual. Both men were shot to death in San Francisco's city hall by a disgruntled former official; in the shadows there lurked a still unexplained homosexual conflict.

Yet another change in the population pattern occurred in the Brown years. Upwardly-mobile aspirants to power and material affluence called "Yuppies," or Young Urban Professionals, took the place of the Hippies of the sixties. Some were, ironically, former Hippies who increasingly influenced journalism, law, medicine, and banking.

Although all classes of persons professed to an interest in urban renewal and the further development of mass transit, most potential commuters remained uninformed about the benefits of fixed light-rail systems operating elsewhere throughout the world. Plans for a high-speed "bullet train," that would have linked San Diego to Los Angeles, were scrapped in 1984. Time, money, and the patience of its Japanese developers simply ran out.

Young Brown realized that California's costly and ambitious freeway program also had to be modified or curtailed. Inflation and wavering tax collections had cut down on the number of such state projects that could be funded. Even urban transit enthusiasts were depressed by sky-rocketing construction estimates. To help combat air pollution, however, Californians erected tough new emission standards that succeeded in reducing exhaust emissions from a typical new car by a startling 90 percent. State-administered auto inspections henceforth cracked down on those who owned and operated polluting "old jalopies."

All such innovations depended upon adequate funding. California was once thought to be recession-proof. But an energy crisis of the mid-1970s, followed by cuts in government contracts, illustrated how much the state had become dependent upon outside aid. Home to a massive public-sector work force, California was hit hard by the reduction of federal defense spending after American withdrawal from Vietnam. The number of aerospace jobs declined from a high of 616,000 to fewer than 400,000. Partly as a result of such unemployment, the state treasury went from a surplus of $2.9 billion in 1979 to a deficit of $541 million by 1983. Brown refused to spend a treasury surplus on sometimes necessary improvements such as the repair of roads and educational needs.

The young governor's actions reflected voter dissatisfaction with the uneven tax system which touched off a taxpayer revolt. In 1978, Howard Jarvis, a harsh critic of government taxation, came up with a property-tax reduction initiative (Proposition 13) that passed by a landslide. It stabilized assessments on real estate for years to come. That measure encouraged tax rebellions in states throughout the nation.

It became especially difficult to pass school bond issues at a time when education grew to be the largest single item in the state budget. Expansion of the state college and university system had placed increasing fiscal burdens on the taxpayers, even as the job market for college graduates began to shrink.

Remedial instruction and runaway welfare expenditures also became more costly during Jerry Brown's last years as governor. His Republican successors, George Deukmejian and Pete Wilson, also would encounter a clamor for increased government services. California was said to be living beyond its means. Between 1987 and 1991, tax revenues grew at a 4 percent annual rate while public spending soared by 6 percent a year. In the five years prior to 1987, the opposite had occurred. Finally, toward the end of Wilson's second term as governor, the state began a slow economic recovery and tax revenues again increased. This allowed the governor to dispense state funds more freely, which made him seem more humane.

But, no matter who was governor, funding of the state's many social responsibilities required continued economic and political innovations. As we shall see, a continuing avalanche of newly arrived immigrants further complicated California's fiscal picture.

Selected Readings

Recent California politics and society are in Jackson K. Putnam, *Modern California Politics* (1990) and his *Old Age Politics in California, From Richardson to Reagan* (1970); Michael P. Rogin and John L. Shover, *Political Change in California* (1970); Royce D. Delmatier, Clarence F. McIntosh, and Earl G. Waters, eds., *The Rumble of California Politics, 1848–1970* (1970) and Raymond A. Mohl, ed., *Searching for the Sunbelt* (1990), 124–48.

Regarding the two Governor Browns and Reagan see John C. Bollens and G. Robert Williams, *Jerry Brown in a Plain Brown Wrapper* (1978); J. D. Lorenz, *Jerry Brown: The Man on the White Horse* (1978); Robert Peck, *Jerry Brown: The Philosopher Prince* (1978); Roger Rapoport, *California Dreaming: The Political Odyssey of Pat and Jerry Brown* (1982) and Orville Schell, *Brown* (1978); Gladwin Hill, *Dancing Bear: The Inside Look at California Politics* (1968); Bill Boyarsky, *The Rise of Ronald Reagan* (1968); Joseph Lewis, *What Makes Reagan Run? A Political Profile* (1968). Edmund G. Brown, Sr. wrote two books: *Reagan and Reality: The Two Californias* (1970), and (with Bill Brown) *Ronald Reagan, The Political Chameleon* (1976); see also Lou Cannon, *Ronnie and Jesse: A Political Odyssey* (1972); Gary Hamilton and Nicole Biggart, *Governor Reagan, Governor Brown* (1984); Gerard de Groot, "Ronald Reagan and Student Unrest in California" *Pacific Historical Review* 65 (February 1996), 107–29.

Regarding labor and racial strife see Francisco Balderrama, *In Defense of La Raza* (1982); Roger Daniels and Spencer C. Olin, eds., *Racism in California: A Reader in the History of Oppression* (1972); George D. Horowitz, *La Causa: The California Grape Strike* (1970); Ralph de Toledano, *Little Cesar* (1962); Ernesto Galarza, *Barrio Boy* (1971), as well as Galarza, *Spiders in the House and Workers in the Field* (1970); Leo Gobler, Joan W. Moore, and Ralph Guzman, *The Mexican-American People* (1970); Joan London and Henry Anderson, *So Shall Ye Reap* (1970).

Books about Cesar Chavez include: Richard Griswold del Castillo and Richard García, *Cesar Chavez: A Triumph of the Spirit* (1995); Ronald B. Taylor, *Chavez and the Farm Workers* (1975); Jacques Levy, *Cesar Chavez: Autobiography of La Causa* (1976); Peter Matthiessen, *Sal Si Puedes* (1969); James Terzian and Kathryn Cramer, *Mighty Hard Road: The Story of Cesar Chavez* (1970); Mark Day, *Forty Acres* (1970) as well as Linda and Theo Majka, *Farm Workers, Agribusiness, and the State* (1982). Daniel E. Cletus, *Bitter Harvest: A History of California Farmworkers* (1981).

For modern agriculture see Lawrence J. Jelinek, *Harvest Empire: A History of California Agriculture* (1979); Donald J. Pisani, *From the Family Farm to Agribusiness* (1984); Ellen Liebman, *California Farmland* (1983).

For more on Chicanos see David Gutiérrez, *Walls and Mirrors: Mexican Americans... and the Politics of Ethnicity* (1995). Now dated is Carey McWilliams, *Brothers under the Skin* (1951) and his *North from Mexico* (1949); Matt S. Meier and Feliciano Rivers, *The Chicanos* (1972); Raul Morin, *Among the Valiant* (1963); Julian Samora, ed., *La Raza: Forgotten Americans* (1969); Charles Wollenberg, ed., *Ethnic Conflict in California History* (1970); Gilbert Cruz and Jane Talbot, *Chicano Bibliography, 1960–1972* (1974); Gilberto Lopez y Rivas, *The Chicanos* (1974); Albert Camarillo, *Chicanos in California* (1985); Ricardo Romo, *East Los Angeles: History of a Barrio* (1984); Rodolfo Gonzalez, *I Am Joaquin* (1973); Edmund Villaseñor, *Macho* (1973); Herschel T. Manuel, *Spanish-Speaking Children of the Southwest* (1958) and Wayne Moquin, ed., *A Documentary History of the Mexican Americans* (1971).

Ethnicity Updated

///////// **CHAPTER 38**

Only a few decades ago California's population was referred to as "Anglo." This term, still often substituted for "whites," is a misnomer. As the number of Caucasians has diminished, the state has become the gateway of a vast Latin American and Asian immigration.

Uncertain conditions in Mexico, and better job opportunities up north, were among the reasons why Latinos continued to cross the border in large numbers. During World War II, California's labor shortages grew so severe that foreign migrants readily found employment. After the war their numbers increased exponentially. Today, Los Angeles contains the largest concentration of persons of Mexican origin outside of Mexico City itself.

One could almost say that the "third world" begins at the San Diego–Tijuana border, a virtual sieve for undocumented aliens. Latinos are too routinely labeled dysfunctional. A recent study, however, indicates that most documented immigrants are adaptable as well as upwardly mobile. A good many of their households have rather quickly achieved middle-class status. These people can hardly be called "marginalized." Hard-working permanent residents of Mexican descent are also increasingly electing representatives to public office. In 1996 the state legislature selected its first Latino Speaker by acclamation. He is two-term assemblyman Cruz Bustamante, the son of a Dinuba barber.

California has received by far the largest number of undocumented aliens than any other state. It has also become a center for the use of fraudulent documents that are necessary to obtain work legally. The 1986 Immigration Reform and Control Act was an admission that border

High rises in Los Angeles, Spring, 1976. Photograph by V. R. Plukas.

controls had not worked; this federal law granted amnesty to large numbers of undocumented aliens. Millions of illegals have posed a major financial strain upon the state's welfare, education, and health systems.

By the late 1980s, California Asians and Latinos were in the forefront to change a 1965 immigration law that favored Europeans with immediate relatives in the United States. Eventually the balance shifted to newer immigrants seeking to bring in family members from Asia and Latin America. In 1996 the opening up of the doors to more immigrants led to a public backlash in the form of the passage of Propositions 187 and 209. Irritated voters sought to limit government aid to undocumented immigrants. Proposition 209, a state constitutional amendment, was designed to end either "preferential treatment or discrimination based upon race, sex, color, or ethnicity": it sought to end years of affirmative action programs. After it was approved by California's voters, Governor Wilson ordered its implementation. But legal challenges by the ACLU and other civil rights advocates were immediate and protracted.

Agitation increased to bar illegals from receiving state-funded health care and schooling benefits. Bilingual education also has come under attack as more immigrants, illegal and legal, continue to inundate the state. Among them are Salvadorans, Costa Ricans, Nicaraguans, Cubans, Guatemalans, and Ecuadorians as well as Mexican nationals.

Border controls increasingly have been tightened by the Immigration and Naturalization Service (INS). As one travels northward along the coast from San Diego, a certain sight are INS checkpoints. Automobiles and trucks that immigration officers suspect of smuggling in illegal aliens are hailed to the roadside and examined. Offenders caught in this manner are sometimes searched, handcuffed, and sent back below the Mexican border for breaking federal immigration statutes. Occasionally violence occurs between border patrol officers and such illegals.

Competing with all these newcomers are California's African Americans. Although the state's black population grew rapidly, full realization of black Californians' civil rights remains a protracted struggle. In time, however, some blacks assumed leadership positions. Both Los Angeles and San Francisco would elect black politicians, Tom Bradley and Willie Brown, as their mayors. Many blacks, however, remained disenchanted. Restrictive housing covenants, the growth of crime, and high unemployment among innercity youths, all hurt the African-American communities of California.

In the 1990s, Latino demographics were eroding the electoral power of black voters. As the job market grew tighter, discord began to surface in Compton between blacks and Latinos. In south-central Los Angeles, also, black residents resented Asian merchants in their neighborhood who refused to hire blacks and who gave nothing back to the black community, spending their profits elsewhere. As such Asians bought up corner grocery stores and coffee shops, the polarization of the two groups increased. Several convenience stores owned by Korean merchants were firebombed after blacks accused of shoplifting were shot by angry storeowners. Black breadwinners also regularly complained of losing jobs

Willie Brown, Mayor of San Francisco.
Photo by Dennis DeSilva ©. Courtesy
of the Mayor's office.

to Latino *illegales*. Feelings of victimization occasionally got out of control as black gang members clashed with Latino rivals.

In April 1992 more serious violence broke out near Watts for the second time in twenty-seven years. This followed the acquittal of two Los Angeles police officers accused of beating Rodney King, a black motorist who resisted arrest after he had been stopped by the police. Though a third party provided the prosecution a videotape that clearly showed the officers hitting and kicking a prostrate King, in the first trial there was no conviction of the officers. Quickly after the verdict was announced, blacks in south-central Los Angeles took to the streets in rage. The riots, which were heavily televised, featured the uncontrollable turmoil. This time violators of all races used the King verdict as an excuse to steal merchandise and to beat up white motorists trapped in their vehicles. Arsonists once again set fire to business establishments, some of which were Asian-owned. Some proprietors, whose buildings had been looted and burned to the ground for the second time, refused to reopen their doors, leaving black neighborhoods with even fewer services. Among the thousands of persons arrested during and after the melee were Latinos, whites, blacks, as well as discontented Asians.

After the fall of Saigon in 1975, some 50,000 Vietnamese refugees had suddenly become California residents. Today's Westminster, known as "Little Saigon," contains the largest concentration of Vietnamese in North America. Thousands of Laotians and Cambodians also ended up in Los Angeles and Orange counties.

A substantial number of Filipinos settled in Daly City, while Beverly Hills became one of the wealthiest and most powerful Jewish-American communities in the nation. By 1997 the number of Glendale's Armenian residents rose to 30 percent of its population, and Iranian merchants began successful businesses in Beverly Hills. One "ethnoburb," Monterey Park, has a largely Latino and Asian population; South Gate is the only community on the United States mainland with an Asian majority. Asians and Latinos alike have begun to replace black majorities in Watts and south-central Los Angeles.

During these huge population shifts, Caucasians virtually disappeared from such suburbs as Baldwin Park, Rosemead, and El Monte. Enhanced real estate values, rather than "white flight" alone, led Caucasians to cash out their equity in older homes. Whites moved into less expensive retirement havens at La Verne, Claremont, San Dimas, Walnut, and Diamond Bar. Across southern California restaurant menus, traffic signs, and even graffiti have all come to feature Latino and Asian tastes.

Fragmentation and rivalries have, however, grown among Asians themselves. Vietnamese, Laotians, and Thais accuse affluent Chinese from

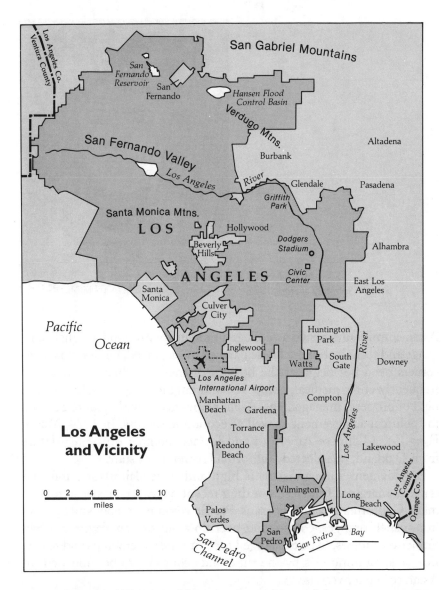

Los Angeles and Vicinity

Hong Kong and Taiwan of "moving in at the top," for they possess better homes and automobiles than other Asians. In addition to affluence, class origins, linguistic skill, and educational status play a part in whether one is employable as a manager or headed toward poverty in a new land. A virtual "Koreatown" quickly emerged along Olympic and Vermont boulevards in Los Angeles. It became the largest Korean settlement outside Seoul.

Most Californians view Asians as industrious and respectful of family values. Fewer Asian teenagers drop out of high school than whites. Some

March Fong Eu,
Secretary of State, 1977.

Asian immigrants arrive as college graduates with good English-language and technical skills. These partly Americanized, high-status newcomers need not begin at the bottom of the job ladder. Instead they frequently enter medical, computer, and engineering specialties or the field of property management. Asian names also have begun to be cited for political achievement as well as economic success. In 1974, March Fong Eu, a Chinese American and former member of the legislature from Oakland, was elected California's secretary of state.

Employment among Asians is high and their claims for public aid remains marginal. One result of their recent migration has been to help make California a center of trans-Pacific commerce. Foodstuffs, scrap iron, paper, oranges, cotton, and beef flow out of San Pedro and San Francisco harbors, to be exchanged for computer microchips and television sets. Automobiles by the thousands continue to be unloaded off Asian container vessels.

There is no one dominant culture in today's California, but many subcultures. The myth that foreigners would inevitably be integrated into one pattern of life has given way to the reality of "ethnic pluralism." As a result, tribalism in California could result in a Balkanized society. Individual ethnic groups can, indeed, impede unity by insisting upon clinging to native folkways that are sometimes antagonistic toward other groups.

Demographers tell us that by the year 2030, persons of Latino and Asian descent will constitute the state's majority population. As for its

Native Americans, they either live in towns and cities or remain dispersed on some one hundred small reservations. California is now home to more foreign-born residents than any other region in the United States. Half of these have arrived in the last ten years. Newly naturalized citizens will assume a larger role as registered voters. No longer underrepresented politically, California's minorities are creating a mosaic of diverse nationalities and races. These newcomers will need to find ways of sharing power in order to live together in what has become perhaps America's most fluid and multicultural society.

Selected Readings

A general introduction is Elliott Barkan, "Immigration Through the Port of Los Angeles," and Charles Wollenberg, "Immigration Through the Port of San Francisco," in M. M. Stolarik, ed., *Forgotten Doors* (1988), 143–60, 161–91. Additional Chicano references include Francisco E. Balderrama and Raymond Rodríguez, *Decade of Betrayal: Mexican Repatriation in the 1930s* (1995); Juan Gómez-Quiñones, *Mexican American Labor, 1790–1900* (1995) and his *Chicano Politics: Reality and Promise, 1940–1990* (1992); David G. Gutiérrez, *Walls and Mirrors: Mexican Immigrants . . . and the Politics of Ethnicity* (1995); Ricardo Romo, *East Los Angeles: History of a Barrio* (1983); Marguerite Marin, *Social Protest in an Urban Barrio . . . 1966–74* (1991); Rodolfo Acuña, *Community Under Siege: A Chronicle of Chicanos East of the Los Angeles River* (1984); Edward J. Escobar, "The Dialectics of Repression: The Los Angeles Police Department and the Chicano Movement," *Journal of American History* 79 (March 1993), 1483–1514; Mario Barrera, *Race and Class in the Southwest* (1979); Alfredo Mirande, *The Chicano Experience* (1985); Zena Pearlstone, *Ethnic L. A.* (1990); Antonio Ríos-Bustamente and Pedro Castillo, *An Illustrated History of Mexican Los Angeles, 1781–1985* (1986); Gilbert Gonzalez, *Labor and Community, Mexican Citrus Worker Villages . . .* (1994) and George J. Sanchez, *Becoming Mexican American . . .* (1993).

Regarding blacks see Delores McBroome, *Parallel Communities: African Americans in California's East Bay, 1850–63* (1993); Gordon Wheeler, *Black California . . .* (1993); E. Frederick Anderson, *The Development of . . . the Black Community of Los Angeles* (1980); Mark Baldessare, *The Los Angeles Riots* (1994); Rudolph Lapp, *Afro-Americans in California* (1980); W. Sherman Savage, *Blacks in the West* (1976); Byron Skinner, *Black Origins in the Inland Empire* (1983); Douglas Daniels, *Pioneer Urbanites: A Social and Cultural History of Black San Francisco* (1980); Nathan Cohen, ed., *The Los Angeles Riots: A Socio-Psychological Study* (1971); Fred Viehe "Black Gold Suburbs . . . of Los Angeles, 1890–1930," *Journal of Urban History* 8 (November 1981), 3–26 and Michael Goldstein, "The Political Careers of Fred Roberts and Tom Bradley," *Western Journal of Black Studies* 5 (Summer 1981), 139–46.

Native Americans appear in Robert F. Heizer and Alan F. Almquist, *The Other Californians: Prejudice and Discrimination Under Spain, Mexico, and the United States* (1971); Joan Weibel-Orlando, *Indian Country; L. A.* (1991) and Diana Bahr, *From Mission to Metropolis: Cupeño Indian Women in Los Angeles* (1993).

For Asians consult Sucheng Chan, *Asian Californians* (1991); Ronald Takaki, *Strangers From a Different Shore* (1989); David Yoo, "Enlightened Identities: Buddhism and Japanese Americans of California, 1924–41," *Western Historical Quarterly* 27 (Autumn 1996), 281–302; Thomas Chinn, *Bridging the Pacific: San Francisco Chinatown* (1989); Benson Tong, *Unsubmissive Women: Chinese Prostitutes in Nineteenth Century California* (1994); Judy Yung, *Unbound Feet: A Social History of Chinese Women in San Francisco* (1995); Julia Costello, *Rice Bowls in the Delta* (1988); Timothy Fong, *The First Urban Chinatown, Monterey Park* (1994); Karl Yoneda, *Ganbatte: Sixty-Year Struggle of a Kibei Worker* (1983); Pyong Gap Min, *Caught in the Middle: Korean Communities in New York and Los Angeles* (1996); Ivan Light and Edna Bonacich, *Immigrant Entrepreneurs: Koreans in Los Angeles, 1965–1982* (1988); E. Y. Yu, and E. H. Phillips, *Koreans in Los Angeles* (1982); Gary Peters, "Migration . . . Among the Vietnamese in Southern California," *Sociology and Social Research* 72 (October, 1987), 33–38; Craig Scharlin and Lillian Villanueva, . . . *Filipino Immigrants and the Farmworkers Movement* (1992); Michael Showalter, "The Watsonville Anti-Filipino Riot of 1930," *Southern California Quarterly* 71 (Winter 1989), 341–48.

Facing the
Future

//////// CHAPTER 39

"The Golden State" was surely an apt motto for early Californians to adopt. The land's physical beauty and appealing climate were praised long before modern chambers of commerce were organized. The infectious boosterism of hide-and-tallow traders, sailors, and gold hunters reflected a vision of a new and romantic utopia.

Today's visitors, by the millions, still come under the state's persuasive spell—despite crowding, crime, smog, earthquakes, and repeated floods and fires which have tarnished its image. Californians continue to take special pride in their state. Just as the Sierra Club guards the backcountry, San Franciscans revel in their cable cars and palatial hotels as romantic symbols of the past. Their stately city's power has, however, been challenged by the growth of Los Angeles to the south. "L.A." is frequently described as a new global crossroads. No longer a nirvana of waving palm trees and citrus groves, it has become a sprawling and internationally important megalopolis, as have Oakland, San Diego, and San Jose.

California's city dwellers, however, have grown increasingly concerned about their deteriorating neighborhoods as well as soaring crime rates. By the 1970s a series of lurid events began to plague the state. These included the mass murders, committed in 1971, by cult leader Charles Manson and his groupies. Four years later, Los Angeles police and the Federal Bureau of Investigation were baffled by the sensational kidnapping of Patricia Hearst, heiress of the Hearst newspaper dynasty. She had strangely sided with her captors, even helping them to stage a holdup. Police swat teams finally cornered her and the bizarre group who called themselves the Symbionese Liberation Army. A bloody shootout

San Francisco. Courtesy of William A. Garnett, © 1954 by William A. Garnett.

followed. Other psychopathic criminals included the Zodiac Killer, the Zebra Murderer, and a veritable butcher known as the Hillside Strangler. Public anguish mounted as police authorities sought to apprehend such persons.

Perhaps the most brutal offenses to mar the state's image featured a Reverend Jim Jones. His 1978 flight from San Francisco to Guyana led to a mass murder-suicide there of more than nine-hundred of his followers. Only a few weeks later there occurred the duel killing of San Francisco Mayor George Moscone and city councilman Harvey Milk.

In 1982 the eight stormy years of the second Brown's political era came to a close. Californians again turned to a Republican governor, George Deukmejian, in part because they identified him with "law and order" issues. As attorney general, this son of Armenian parents had authored the state's death penalty law and its "Use a Gun, Go to Prison" law. In 1978 Deukmejian's initial proposal was supplanted by the tougher Briggs initiative. A strong new conservatism swept over California and the nation. Reelected in 1986, Deukmejian was, however, able to make only limited inroads on the crime problem at the state level despite a

Governor George Deukmejian signs a bill into law. Courtesy of State of California, Department of Transportation.

massive prison-building program and a four-fold increase in incarcerations. Extreme partisanship in the legislature marred Deukmejian's last years as governor; without its effective backing, his programs were stymied.

But no one seemed able to stop California's increasing homicide rate. Local newspapers and television reporters claimed that the average urbanite stood a greater chance of dying by knife or gun than in an auto accident. Many urban murders have come to be gang-related. Replete with dress codes, nicknames, hand signals, and a frightening array of weapons, young hoodlums form a veritable counterculture. Rivalries among competing gangs result in repeated fatal "drive-by" shootings and self-destructive street warfare in which innocent bystanders are also slain. Some homicides occur over drug-dealing disputes. Unemployment and the breakdown of the family are also frequently linked to the growth of city crime, as disoriented youngsters turn to gang membership for support. Rapes, aggravated assaults, robberies, and burglaries committed by people of all ages also have reached epidemic proportions. All are heavily reported by the increasingly pervasive media.

Legislators have repeatedly claimed that they want to make California a zero-tolerance zone for criminals by instituting Draconian measures. One of these, passed in 1994, was a "Three Strikes Law." This legislation mandates 25-year-to-life sentences for anyone convicted of three felony crimes, including the possession of drugs. Californians continued to demand such stricter sentencing.

Crime and environmental concerns have regrettably tended to crowd out the historical past. A big part of that overshadowed record involves great progress in science and technology. Since the astronomical discoveries of Edwin Hubble in the 1930s, the state has become a world-class scientific center. Hubble developed a theory of the expanding universe, "The Big Bang," at the Mount Wilson Observatory above Pasadena. Much later, another generation of California technicians would place the first astronauts on the moon. Today, a formidable number of scholars labor in space-age "think tanks."

As late as 1985, California retained over $10 billion in federal contracts. Thereafter, national defense expenditures were drastically curtailed. Heavy down-sizing of government spending occurred after 1991, when Republican Governor "Pete" Wilson, the former mayor of San Diego and a U.S. senator, assumed office. He, like previous governors, faced a budget tied up in welfare entitlements and other mandated spending. An example was the expensive state mental health system, which is forced to deal with serious cases that private caregivers refuse to treat.

In 1994 Wilson won a smashing reelection victory over Kathleen Brown, the daughter of Pat Brown and sister of Jerry Brown. Like Jerry

Governor Pete Wilson.

Brown, Wilson, could not resist the lure of presidential ambition. In 1995, despite a promise not to run for national office while governor, Wilson jumped into the presidential primary race. But his candidacy generated little grassroots support, especially in midwestern and eastern states where he was relatively unknown. An annoying throat irritation also impaired his chance of gaining the Republican nomination over Kansas Senator Robert Dole, who (running with his California-born vice presidential candidate Jack Kemp) ultimately failed to unseat the incumbent Democrat, President William Clinton.

Governor Wilson, despite his initial promise, neglected state business during the 1996 campaign year. This cost him the support even of confirmed Republican voters. When his campaigning for the Republican presidential nomination ended, the governor returned home, finally focussing upon state matters. Wilson advocated steep cuts in welfare grants to children, the aged, and the blind. The governor also vigorously opposed affirmative action for minority university applicants. And he became a fierce foe of illegal immigration. Education, another big part of the state budget, required constant attention. California had moved from national leadership to become one of the lowest-ranked states in per capita expenditure on education. In recent years the performance scores of California students had also plummeted. An extreme symbol of general educational decline is the increasing involvement of rootless youngsters with guns and criminal gangs.

All these pressing needs created continuing controversy between a liberal state legislature and California's conservative governors. This at a time when the state's complex society has required increasingly wise planning and when public distrust of politicians has grown in intensity. In 1996 Wilson's raising of taxes came under especially heavy attack. An anti-tax movement was gathering steam. That year the voters adopted Proposition 218, supplanting the Jarvis-Gann "taxpayer's revolt" of 1978. Proposition 13 had severely limited property taxes. Proposition 218 went even further, making some municipal fees illegal and also requiring a popular vote before local governments could raise new taxes. As a result, some city and county services, even rudimentary ones such as garbage collection, faced serious curtailment. Currently counties receive more than 50 percent of their revenues from the state and national governments. Each county is heavily dependent upon taxation beyond its control while demands upon government are unceasing.

California possesses the sixth-largest economy in the world. Its annual output of goods and services has reached $1 trillion. It has emerged as a virtual nation-state, a global economic center. Today it is North America's chief outlet for trade with high-growth countries that, like it, border the Pacific Rim. One-third of the state's economy is tied to trade with Asia. In 1994 the port of Los Angeles became the largest financial entry-point in the United States, quadrupling its customs collections over the last twenty years.

Surfer, photographed from a jetty at Newport Beach, executes a turn. Photo by Ker; courtesy of Surfer Magazine.

Economic and political influences too have begun to shift from the Atlantic to the Pacific coast. California's increasing national importance has affected its population growth. During the 1980s the state reached 29.8 million inhabitants, an increase of 6.2 million persons. This growth occurred during a period of unprecedented high employment, which more recently has tapered off. Nevertheless, by 1997 California, approaching 32 million, remained the nation's most populous state. Each year more than 400,000 of its school children attend the fourth grade alone. In excess of 10 percent of the nation lives in California, more than the entire population of Canada. Orange County in southern California has more residents than does the state of Montana. Southern California alone is expected to continue gaining 300,000 new residents per year. Projected state population should reach 39.6 million by the year 2020.

Almost 1,500 persons are now added to California's population each day. Yet this figure is considerably below the growth rate in prior boom years. Recently arrived residents reversed what was only a temporary trend, begun in 1991, that saw the state lose residents for the first time in its history. The curtailment of government defense contracts led to the dumping of numerous high-tech specialists onto the job market. Not all such unemployed workers could be successfully retrained. Today, many jobs are of the low-wage and low-skill variety, causing economic distress in some communities.

No longer can California claim to be a "Garden of the World" in which magical things happen automatically. But neither is it a paradise lost. Its harshest critics have also witnessed the appearance of a bicoastal society linked to the wider world of art, music, theater, and gastronomy. Californians are also undeniably plagued by increased crime, overcrowding, and illegal immigration. These are among the new realities faced by its residents. What happens in California is closely watched throughout the world. Via television, film, and the print media, manufacturers, designers, politicians, and high school and college students follow the state's cutting-edge trends.

Innovative merchandising concepts are also repeatedly launched in California. In an age of "global information services," dozens of multimedia and computer firms have sprung up in the "Silicon Valley." New software and other high-tech firms continue to be formed each year. Although the state itself provides a gigantic market for computers and peripherals, rising international demand has made San Jose the top national metropolitan area in export sales of these products.

Another technology center has emerged along Orange County's "Tech Coast." This region extends for fifty miles in all directions, encompassing parts of San Bernardino, Riverside, Los Angeles, and San Diego counties. It now has 20 percent more high-tech companies than the Silicon Valley. A booming computer, electronics, and biomedical economy in 1996 turned out $85 billion in goods and services.

Particularly rapid expansion has also occurred in the manufacturing of biotechnology, film and television production, as well as apparel wear. By 1997, California's start-up businesses were attracting more than 25 percent of the nation's venture capital. Of its 500 fastest growing companies, 82 are located within the state (Texas is a distant second, with 39).

California is on the verge of exporting as much to the rest of the world as to the other markets within the nation. Although it remains the nation's top agricultural state, California's frontier rurality has mostly given way to a post-suburban lifestyle. However, the symbolic sports cars, supermarket chains, and poolside barbecues can hardly knit so complex a society firmly together.

Facing so many new challenges, Californians have come to realize that bigness alone cannot assure a great culture—such as characterized fifth-century Greece, Republican Rome, or Europe's Renaissance cities. Unless the diverse backgrounds of its many newcomers can be harmonized, the state could strangle on its own growth. The influx of these immigrants has made California's polyglot society even more experimental and unfinished.

Yet, most Californians do not share either dire or apocalyptic predictions of their future. For many residents, the so-called "California Dream" has been a success. Such fortunate folk have come to believe that there is no place on earth where they would rather live.

Selected Readings

Regarding recent culture see George H. Knoles, ed., *Essays and Assays: California History Reconsidered* (1973); Lawrence Clark Powell, *The Creative Literature of the Golden State* (1971); William Storrs Lee, ed., *California, A Literary Chronicle* (1968); Leslie Freudenheim, *Building With Nature: Roots of the San Francisco Bay Tradition* (1974); Mellier Scott, *Partnership in the Arts: Public and Private Support of Cultural Activities in the San Francisco Bay Area* (1963) and Arthur Bloomfield, *The San Francisco Opera, 1923–1961* (1961).

Architectural and city studies include Harold Kirker, "California Architecture and its Relation to Contemporary Trends in Europe and America," *California Historical Quarterly* 51 (Winter 1972), 289–305; Richard De Leon, *Left Coast City: Progressive Politics in San Francisco, 1975–91* (1992);

George A. Pettit, *Berkeley: The Town and Gown of It* (1973); Gloria Lothrop, *Pomona, A Centennial History* (1988); Augusta Fink, *Palos Verde Peninsula: Time and the Terraced Land* (1987).

Regarding Los Angeles, see Reyner Banham, *Los Angeles, The Architecture of Four Ecologies* (1971); Leonard and Dale Pitt, eds., *Los Angeles A to Z* (1997); Michael Dear, ed., *Atlas of Southern California* (1996) and Dear (with H. Eric Schockman and Greg Hise), *Rethinking Los Angeles* (1996); Andrew Rolle, *Los Angeles: From Pueblo to City of the Future*, 2d ed. (1995); Allen J. Scott and Edward W. Soja, *The City: Los Angeles and Urban Theory* (1996).

Political details about California are in Jackson K. Putnam, "The Pattern of Modern California Politics," *Pacific Historical Review* 61 (February 1992), 23–52; Charles G. Bell and Charles M. Price, *California Government Today* (1988); Richard B. Harvey, *Dynamics of California Government and Politics* (1995) and Dan Walters, *The New California: Facing the 21st Century* (1992).

Social and cultural matters appear in Norman M. Klein and Martin J. Schiesl, eds., *20th Century Los Angeles . . .* (1990); Robert Kling, Spencer Olin, and Mark Poster, eds., *Postsuburban California . . .* (1991); Peter Theroux, *Translating L.A.* (1994); Pamela Hallan-Gibson, *The Golden Promise: An Illustrated History of Orange County* (1986); Marshall Berges, *The Life and Times of the Los Angeles Times* (1984); Robert Gottlieb and Irene Wolt, *Thinking Big: The Story of the Los Angeles Times* (1977); William Wilson, *The Los Angeles Times Book of California Museums* (1984); Jonathan Eisen and David Fine, *Unknown California* (1985) as well as U.S. Department of Housing and Urban Development, *State of the Nation's Cities* (April 1996).

Appendix

The Governors of California

SPANISH REGIME, 1767–1821

(Dates of service for each governor are from assumption to surrender of office.)

Gaspar de Portolá
November 30, 1767, to July 9, 1770
> From May 21, 1769, Portolá was *comandante-militar* for Alta California. From July 9, 1770, to May 25, 1774, the position of comandante was filled by Pedro Fages; and from May 25, 1774, to February 1777, by Fernando Rivera y Moncada.

Matías de Armona
June 12, 1769, to November 9, 1770

Felipe de Barri
March ?, 1770, to March 4, 1775
> Governor of *Las Californias,* residing at Loreto.

Felipe de Neve
March 4, 1775, to July 12, 1782
> In February 1777, Neve took up residence at Monterey. Rivera y Moncada went south to assume the lieutenant governorship at Loreto. The acting lieutenant-governor, pending Rivera's arrival, was Joaquín Cañete.

Pedro Fages
July 12, 1782, to April 16, 1791
> On July 18, 1781, Rivera y Moncada was killed on the Colorado River, and Joaquín Cañete served as lieutenant-governor until November 1783, when he was succeeded by José Joaquín de Arrillaga.

José Antonio Roméu
April 16, 1791, to April 9, 1792

335

José Joaquín de Arrillaga
April 9, 1792, to May 14, 1794

During this period, Arrillaga was lieutenant-governor and comandante of Lower California, and governor of *Las Californias ad interim.*

Diego de Borica
May 14, 1794, to March 8, 1800

José Joaquín de Arrillaga
March 8, 1800, to July 24, 1814

Until March 11, 1802, when he died, Pedro de Alberni was *comandante-militar* for Alta California. The decree making Alta California a separate province bore the date August 29, 1804, and it reached Arrillaga November 16.

José Darío Argüello
July 24, 1814, to August 30, 1815

Governor *ad interim.*

Pablo Vicente de Solá
August 30, 1815, to November 10, 1822

Held over from Spanish regime to November 1822.

MEXICAN REGIME, 1821–1847

Luís Antonio Argüello
November 10, 1822, to November ?, 1825

Until April 2, 1823, Argüello's authority derived from the Spanish Regency. After that date it derived from Iturbide as Agustin I. After November 17 it derived from the *Congreso Constituyente* (National Congress). In March 1823, Iturbide named Naval Captain Bonifacio de Tosta governor of Alta California. In 1824 José Miñón was appointed governor of Alta California but declined the office.

José María de Echeandía
November ?, 1825, to January 31, 1831

Antonia García was appointed as Echeandía's successor, but the appointment was revoked.

Manuel Victoria
January 31, 1831, to December 6, 1831

José María de Echeandía
December 6, 1831, to January 14, 1833

De facto *jefe político* and *jefe militar* in the district south of, but not including, Santa Barbara.

Pío Pico
January 27 to February 16, 1832
Jefe político by appointment of the *Diputación* for only twenty days.

Agustín Vicente Zamorano
February 1, 1832, to January 14, 1833
De facto *jefe militar* only in the district north of and including Santa Barbara.

José Figueroa
January 14, 1833, to September 29, 1835
Early in 1833 Figueroa asked to be relieved of office. On July 16, 1833, José María Hijar was appointed *jefe político,* but the appointment was revoked by Mexico's President Santa Anna on July 25. On July 18, 1834, Figueroa withdrew his request to be relieved.

José Castro
September 29, 1835, to January 2, 1836
From October 8, 1835, to January 1, 1836, the position of *jefe militar* was held by Nicolás Gutiérrez.

Nicolás Gutiérrez
January 2 to May 3, 1836

Mariano Chico
May 3 to August 1, 1836

Nicolás Gutiérrez
August 1 to November 5, 1836

José Castro
November 5 to December 7, 1836
Castro was *jefe militar* until November 29, when he was succeeded by Mariano Guadalupe Vallejo. He then became acting governor.

Juan Bautista Alvarado
December 7, 1836, to December 31, 1842
Until August 7, 1839, Alvarado was governor *ad interim.* On June 6, 1837, Carlos Carillo was appointed governor, and on December 6 he assumed office at Los Angeles, but was arrested and deposed by Alvarado on May 20, 1838.

Manuel Micheltorena
December 31, 1842, to February 22, 1845

Pío Pico
February 22, 1845, to August 10, 1846
By the departmental junta Pío Pico was declared governor *ad interim* on February 15, 1845. José Castro served as *jefe militar* for the same period.

José María Flores
October 31, 1846, to January 11, 1847

Andrés Pico
January 11 to January 13, 1847

AMERICAN GOVERNORS UNDER MILITARY RULE
(Dates given are beginning of term.)

Commodore John D. Sloat
July 7, 1846

Commodore Robert F. Stockton
July 29, 1846

Captain John C. Frémont
January 19, 1847

General Stephen W. Kearny
March 1, 1847

Colonel Richard B. Mason
May 31, 1847

General Persifor F. Smith
February 28, 1849

General Bennett Riley
April 12, 1849

GOVERNORS OF THE STATE OF CALIFORNIA
(Dates given are date of inauguration.)

Peter H. Burnett
Ind. Dem. Dec. 20, 1849

John McDougal
Ind. Dem. Jan. 9, 1851

John Bigler
Dem. Jan. 8, 1852

John Neely Johnson
Amer. Jan. 9, 1856

John B. Weller
Dem. Jan. 8, 1858

Milton S. Latham
Lecomp. Dem. Jan. 9, 1860

John G. Downey
Lecomp. Dem. Jan. 14, 1860

Leland Stanford
Rep. Jan. 10, 1862

Frederick F. Low
Union Dec. 10, 1863

Henry H. Haight
Dem. Dec. 5, 1867

Newton Booth
Rep. Dec. 8, 1871

Romualdo Pacheco
Rep. Feb. 27, 1875

William Irwin
Dem. Dec. 9, 1875

George C. Perkins
Rep. Jan. 8, 1880

George Stoneman
Dem. Jan. 10, 1883

Washington Bartlett
Dem. Jan. 8, 1887

Robert W. Waterman
Rep. Sept. 13, 1887

Henry H. Markham
Rep. Jan. 8, 1891

James H. Budd
Dem. Jan. 11, 1895

Henry T. Gage
Rep. Jan. 4, 1899

George C. Pardee
Rep. Jan. 7, 1903

James N. Gillett
Rep. Jan. 9, 1907

Hiram W. Johnson
Prog. Rep. Jan. 3, 1911

William D. Stephens
Rep. Mar. 15, 1917

Friend W. Richardson
Rep. Jan. 8, 1923

Clement C. Young
Rep. Jan. 4, 1927

James Rolph, Jr.
Rep. Jan. 6, 1931

Frank F. Merriam
Rep. Jan. 7, 1935

Culbert L. Olson
Dem. Jan. 2, 1939

Earl F. Warren
Rep. Jan. 4, 1943

Goodwin F. Knight
Rep. Oct. 5, 1953

Edmund G. Brown
Dem. Jan. 5, 1959

Ronald Reagan
Rep. Jan. 5, 1967

Edmund G. Brown, Jr.
Dem. Jan. 5, 1975

George Deukmejian
Rep. Jan. 5, 1983

Pete Wilson
Rep. Jan. 5, 1991

Index of
Authors Cited

Index

California: A History, Fifth Edition
Developmental Editor and Copy Editor: Andrew J. Davidson
Proofreader: Claudia Siler
Production Editor and Text Designer: Lucy Herz
Indexer: Frances Squires Rolle
Printer: McNaughton & Gunn, Inc.

OREGON

Crescent
City

Klamath River

Alturas

Redding

Eureka

Red
Bluff

Chico

Sacramento

Yuba
City

Sacramento

Santa Rosa

Napa

Vallejo

Stockton

Modesto

Richmond

Berkeley

Oakland

Alameda

Hayward

San

San Francisco

San Mateo

Palo
Alto

Santa Clara

San Jose

Joaquin

Fresno

Santa Cruz

Salinas

Monterey

San
Obis

Santa Maria

Pacific

Ocean

CALIFORNIA

0   50   100   150

miles